LOCAL TV

THE PEABODY SERIES IN MEDIA HISTORY

SERIES EDITORS

Jeffrey P. Jones, *University of Georgia*
Ethan Thompson, *Texas A&M University, Corpus Christi*

LOCAL TV

HISTORIES, COMMUNITIES, AND AESTHETICS

EDITED BY **LAUREN HEROLD
AND
ANNIE LAURIE SULLIVAN**

THE UNIVERSITY OF GEORGIA PRESS | ATHENS

© 2025 by the University of Georgia Press
Athens, Georgia 30602
www.ugapress.org
All rights reserved
Set in by 10.75/13.5 Garamond Premier Pro Regular
by Rebecca A. Norton

Most University of Georgia Press titles are
available from popular e-book vendors.

Printed digitally

EU Authorized Representative
Easy Access System Europe—Mustamäe tee 50, 10621
Tallinn, Estonia, gpsr.requests@easproject.com

Library of Congress Cataloging-in-Publication Data

Names: Herold, Lauren, 1990– editor | Sullivan, Annie Laurie, 1986– editor
Title: Local TV : histories, communities, and aesthetics /
    edited by Lauren Herold and Annie Laurie Sullivan.
Description: Athens : The University of Georgia Press, [2025] |
    Series: The Peabody series in media history |
    Includes bibliographical references and index.
Identifiers: LCCN 2025017286 | ISBN 9780820374727 hardback |
    ISBN 9780820374758 paperback | ISBN 9780820374765 epub |
    ISBN 9780820374772 pdf
Subjects: LCSH: Public-access television—United States—History |
    Local mass media—United States—History | Public television—
    United States—History | Television stations—United States—History
Classification: LCC HE8700.72.U6 L626 2025 |
    DDC 384.55093—dc23/eng/20250814
LC record available at https://lccn.loc.gov/2025017286

CONTENTS

List of Illustrations vii

Acknowledgments ix

Introduction: Local Television Studies, Past and Present 1
ANNIE LAURIE SULLIVAN AND LAUREN HEROLD

PART I. DEVELOPING AND DISTRIBUTING LOCAL TELEVISION

Chapter 1. Placing Local Media:
The Chicago School of Television, Revisited 29
SHAWN VANCOUR

Chapter 2. Local and National, Public and Private: WOI-TV and Early Educational Television in the United States 54
DYFRIG JONES

Chapter 3. "Vocal Voyeurs": Local Television Meets National Syndication in Norman Lear's *The Baxters* 72
TAYLOR COLE MILLER

Chapter 4. Video as Local Television: "Becoming Cable" at the Long Beach Museum of Art 94
ANA HOWE BUKOWSKI

Chapter 5. "To Call It a Zoo Would Be Unkind to Animals": How Cable Television Came to Miami 112
DANIEL MARCUS

PART II. AESTHETICS AND GENRES OF LOCAL TELEVISION PROGRAMS

Chapter 6. Broadcasting Faith in Detroit:
Local Televangelism, Black Gospel Traditions, and the Commerce of Community Worship 133
ANNIE LAURIE SULLIVAN

Chapter 7. Learning the *Basic Issues of Man*: Midcentury Humanism, Social Science, and Educational Television 152
JONATHAN MACDONALD

Chapter 8. WSB-TV, Atlanta:
Broadcasting the New Old South   172
CAROLINE N. BAYNE

Chapter 9. Busting Beethoven:
Nam June Paik's Electronic Operas at WGBH   191
EVELYN KREUTZER

Chapter 10. Creative Beyond Their Years:
The Unique Alchemy of *Beyond Our Control*   211
CHRISTINE BECKER

PART III. AMPLIFYING COMMUNITY VOICES THROUGH LOCAL TELEVISION

Chapter 11. Placemaking and Community Access Media
in Vermont: Histories, Archives, and Activism   231
HELEN MORGAN PARMETT

Chapter 12. Minority Media for the Majority:
The Survival Strategies of the Milwaukee
Gay/Lesbian Cable Network (1986–1994)   250
DAPHNE GERSHON

Chapter 13. The First Wave of Latina/o TV:
Early Chicana/o and Puerto Rican Programming   268
MARY BELTRÁN

Chapter 14. Chicago Renaissance Redux: Black Cultural
Production and the Social Practice Art of Television   285
AYMAR JEAN CHRISTIAN

Chapter 15. Telling Our Stories: A Reflection on Realizing
the Promise of Public Access TV in Philadelphia   303
ANTOINE HAYWOOD

Epilogue: Moving Local Television
Forward in the Digital Era   321
LORI KIDO LOPEZ

List of Contributors   337

Index   341

ILLUSTRATIONS

1.1. Ransom Sherman poses with John the moose head   37

1.2. Scenes from *Garroway at Large* in the 1950s   38

1.3. Scenes of *Garroway at Large*   44

1.4. Saxophonist Johnny Hodges on *Garroway at Large*   45

3.1. Norman Lear hosting the Los Angeles audience of *The Baxters*   73

3.2. Advertisement for *The Baxters*   82

3.3. Steve Edwards hosting the Los Angeles audience of *The Baxters*   84

3.4. Screengrabs from episodes of *The Baxters*   87

7.1. Socially determined "types" in the confines of their boxes   165

8.1. WSB-TV staff in front of White Columns studio   185

E.1. News anchor Yau Muas hosting the 3HMONGTV news brief   327

E.2. Mohamed Ahmed interviewing local rideshare advocacy representatives   332

ACKNOWLEDGMENTS

The idea for this edited collection first emerged at the 2021 Society of Cinema and Media Studies conference, after a panel on community television cochaired by Lauren Herold and Daphne Gershon that included Annie Laurie Sullivan and Christopher Ali. The generative discussion after the panel connected us with a range of scholars working in the small but vibrant subfield of local television studies. Soon after, Ethan Thompson reached out to us to discuss editing a book on this subject for the Peabody Series in Media History. We sincerely thank series editors Ethan Thompson and Jeffrey Jones for their ongoing support, guidance, and mentorship with this multiyear project. Thanks as well to the staff at the University of Georgia Press for their hard work and support with the editorial process.

Thank you to the scholars who contributed their research to this book: Caroline Bayne, Christine Becker, Mary Beltrán, Ana Howe Bukowski, Aymar Jean Christian, Daphne Gershon, Antoine Haywood, Dyfrig Jones, Evelyn Kreutzer, Lori Kido Lopez, Jonathan MacDonald, Daniel Marcus, Taylor Cole Miller, Helen Morgan Parmett, and Shawn VanCour. We are grateful for your important contributions and commitment to this understudied area of media history.

We would like to give a special acknowledgment to the people who read early drafts of different chapters of this book and offered invaluable guidance toward our editing process. This includes the members of Lauren's writing group (Rebecca Ballard, Katharine Mershon, Nicole Morse, Rebecca Oh, and Allison Page) as well as Hannah Spaulding and Reem Hilu. We would also like to thank Beth Corzo-Duchardt, our colleague and friend, who expertly created the book's thorough index.

Finally, we are profoundly grateful to the producers, preservationists, and archivists of local television, the stewards of this community history. Our efforts would not be possible without them.

ACKNOWLEDGMENTS FROM LAUREN

I would first like to express gratitude for my wonderful coeditor, Annie Sullivan. Annie is not only a brilliant scholar and an eloquent writer but also a diplomatic thinker, a discerning editor, and a caring friend. Her deep knowledge of television history and local media enriched each aspect of this project. I appreciate the many hours we spent together, often via Zoom, working hard to put this project together; I especially appreciate that she traveled to visit me in Columbus, Ohio, so we could prepare a draft of our manuscript together in person. I feel lucky to have worked with a collaborator with whom I shared both a cohesive vision and a set of political commitments.

I would also like to thank my writing group (members listed above), and particularly Nicole Morse, for all of their encouragement as well as their wisdom about the writing, editing, and publishing process. Finally, special thanks to my friends and family members, especially to my sisters Steph and Bella, for their emotional support and unconditional love.

ACKNOWLEDGMENTS FROM ANNIE

I would like to extend my heartfelt thanks to my coeditor, Lauren. Her hard work and intellectual prowess were instrumental in starting our conversation about local television and bringing this project to fruition. Lauren's exceptional ability to keep us organized and on track was invaluable, especially when I needed that extra push. Beyond her extraordinary editorial and writing skills, her thoughtfulness and unwavering support created a truly positive atmosphere for collaboration where we were able to hone our shared vision of this book. Working alongside her has been a joy, and I am grateful for her partnership every step of the way.

I also want to thank all my friends and family who have offered support to me over the years as I pursue my scholarship. There are too many people to list here individually. However, I offer a special thank-you to my colleagues at Oakland University, my scholarly friends and community from graduate school, my sister Maggie, and my "pleasure to have in class" crew who've been there for me through it all. Your support and encouragement are immeasurable. I thank Avery for always taking care of me when I don't have time to take care of myself. You are the best bud a girl could ask for. Above all, I thank my parents for raising me with unwavering love and in a household that always kept the TV on. I wouldn't care about any of this without you.

LOCAL TV

ANNIE LAURIE SULLIVAN AND LAUREN HEROLD

INTRODUCTION

LOCAL TELEVISION STUDIES, PAST AND PRESENT

Local TV: Histories, Communities, and Aesthetics explores a diverse variety of local television genres, production and distribution practices, and activism to center local television production as integral to both television history and American culture. Essays in the collection showcase a breadth of approaches to the study of local television and offer instructive theories of televisual localism across the United States. Our contributors build upon trailblazing, though still scant, studies of local television stations, programs, and personalities. This anthology documents social and industrial histories too often obfuscated in discussions of telecommunications that might help us productively consider ways citizens use local media to navigate both the challenges and the possibilities facing American communities. In so doing, we expand television history to include case studies that have seldom received scholarly attention yet provide alternatives to dominant understandings of television itself.

Local television is undertheorized in scholarship on media history and culture. The local television industry (or industries) is too often perceived as a secondary circuit of distribution, less significant than national commercial or educational networks. Discussions of the aesthetics of local television programs are rare, as is attention to the ideological or informational rhetoric of local productions. The scholarly and popular appeals of local television are generally circumscribed to specific regions of interest, with presumed viewers in signal reach of a nearby or "local" station. Yet local stations have played critical roles in the development of television industry standards, the administration of television policy, and programming practices. Today, local stations continue to produce and distribute large portions of the televisual content screened nationally. At the same time, communities have always participated in the production of television to create media relevant to their localized needs, interests, and concerns. We hope that the expansive discussion of local television introduced in the pages that follow will catalyze further debate in the field of media studies and bring more marginalized histories of "the local" to the forefront of television scholarship.

DEFINING THE "LOCAL" IN LOCAL TELEVISION

Throughout this book, we use the term "local television" to discuss a variety of production and distribution practices designed to speak to the perceived needs and interests of communities in a shared geographic area. Chapters in this volume explore the diversity of content produced by and for local audiences and the production standards adopted by different communities over time. The variety of this content can impede scholarly discussions of local television as a cohesive form of media. Rather than strictly codifying what local television is and does, this collection presents it as a multidimensional paradigm that prompts us to consider a range of aesthetic practices, modes of address, programming decisions, and industrial models that have emerged in different localities across U.S. history. Moving forward, we identify some of the overlapping, and at times contradictory, critical attributes of local television that guide current scholarly inquiry and to generate future research directions for media scholars.

First and foremost, every contributor to this collection is attentive to the politics of place and considers how local television relates to municipal histories. While local stations may air programs that respond to national and global issues, reproduce dominant ideologies of American society, or model show formats on major network programs, they still do so with local viewers or service markets in mind. In *Media Localism*, Christopher Ali (2017) marks a distinction between "place based" programming, which refers to shows produced and presented within a local community, and "content based" programming, which refers to segments or shows produced elsewhere but deemed relevant to a community (e.g., a syndicated series or information segments incorporated into news broadcasts). In either case, local stations mediate the flow of content to viewers and make programming decisions based on their understanding of their respective community's politics, tastes, and customs. Consequently, some local programs lack broad appeal and may appear idiosyncratic when analyzed outside of a local context; other programs seem remarkably similar to fare produced in many cities, towns, or regions across the United States. This makes it difficult to detangle the local from the national or global, the affiliate station from the network, or one local market from another. Chapters in this anthology focus primarily on "place-based" content and the cultural or industrial contexts that shape local television practices. Yet scholars like Shawn VanCour, Taylor Cole Miller, and Mary Beltrán call attention to ways local television may simultaneously reflect the socioeconomic conditions of a historical moment and point of origin, while still crafting an address that extends beyond one locale. As Ali puts it, "Concepts such as 'community' and 'place' are contingent upon individual subjectivities, experiences, histories, politics, cultures, and discourses" of residents who access or produce local TV content, which accounts for a range of divergences among stations and across the study of local television histories in different spaces (2017, 33).

While station practices and content may vary from place to place, local television often forges an intimate relationship with residents. Local stations, and the personalities that appear on local programs, address viewers with greater familiarity than typical national network fare. On-air talent may use speech patterns or terms that will resonate with nearby residents, present news stories on regional issues, and announce cultural events happening in the area. Viewers may tune into local television to watch hometown sporting events, learn about weather forecasts, listen to governmental proceedings, or watch a religious service that they would normally attend in person. As such, residents often discuss their local program histories with tinges of nostalgia: a fondness for the newscasters who greeted them on air every morning, the hosts of children's shows they watched growing up, the quirky presenters who introduced old movies or classic TV episodes syndicated for local broadcasts, and local celebrities who were given a platform to shine. It's perhaps unsurprising that while scholarly monographs on local television are rare, there are many popular books and articles in newspapers written by citizens that document their respective station histories and celebrate television figures who gained notoriety through the local airwaves. Arcadia Books has released numerous local television histories of cities like Honolulu, Cincinnati, Philadelphia, Louisville, and New Orleans. Local TV professionals and enthusiasts have likewise published their own ethnographic reflections of local TV cultures, like Gordon Castelnero's *TV Land Detroit* (2006) or Tom Feran and Richard D. Heldenfels's *Cleveland TV Memories* (1999). Framed as "sentimental journeys" or "heartwarming romps" that revisit the beloved characters and shows that resonated with community viewers, such books demonstrate the collective, place-bound identities formulated through local programming.

Accordingly, foregrounding "the local" in both popular and critical television scholarship can help us better examine the material conditions of media production and the ways television intersects with quotidian experiences. Precarity is a recurring theme in scholarly discussions of local television production. Many, if not most, local television producers operate with shoestring budgets, outdated technology, underequipped studio spaces, limited viewership, small crews filling multiple roles, and ongoing threats of cancellation. Often, community-oriented programming relies on external funds and fundraising processes to bring content to air. Some philanthropic organizations may sponsor programs; meanwhile, community groups and religious organizations are often forced to buy air slots or donate time. Contributors to this anthology reveal that many programs were produced, funded, and sustained by community members, who dedicated a great deal of time, energy, and their own financial resources to bring meaningful and informative content to other members of their shared community. Local programs are borne through the visions and personal investments of local producers, citizens, and station managers and are made meaningful by their engagement with the communities they serve. These production conditions have undoubtedly led to the popular perception of local television's amateur aesthetics and yokel flare. Yet they also invite us to adopt a "history from below" approach to media studies and consider how television shapes the quotidian experiences of individuals and social groups. Scholars of local television invite us to consider what microhistories of television stations and programs—those typically known only by a small community of viewers and producers—tell us about broader trends in media aesthetics, labor, politics, and culture.

Our broad understanding of local television includes affiliate stations of the national broadcast networks (ABC, NBC, CBS, FOX), local affiliates of the national Public Broadcasting Service (PBS), public access cable television stations, as well as independently owned and operated stations that customize content for cities and towns within signal reach. However, in addition to broadcasting UHF and VHF, closed circuit television systems and multichannel video programming distributors that use cable wires or satellites to reach TV sets still rely upon local production facilities and local maintenance to reach an intended audience. For instance, Class A or full-power stations and cable systems have primarily emerged in major urban centers with substantial market reach and have devoted their resources to developing content to attract advertisers and thereby cover commercial operating budgets. Meanwhile, "TV translators" have been built to reproduce and thereby extend the signal reach of Class A stations or offer additional "low-signal" programming to smaller geographic areas, either sections of dense urban areas with a substantially increased demand for television content or remote, rural regions with fewer direct television services available (Hilliard and Keith 1999). Low-power television has consequently been essential to the development of television in a range of places, from small college towns to Indigenous reservations.

Residents in major urban centers have historically had more access to television stations and a greater diversity of programming than viewers in rural or remote areas. However, since the advent of television, communities have also debated the implementation of television into their local communities and adapted technologies to suit their spatial and ideological needs. For instance, as Frank H. Tyro has discussed, the low-power Salish Kootenai College station SKC-TV, located on the Flathead Indian Reservation in northwestern Montana, was the only station serving the Indigenous community in the late 1980s and 1990s. Even as new technologies expanded viewing options, SKC-TV was the only station offering programming to benefit residents; it aired local sports, Salish and Kootenai language classes, early childhood development classes, rural news and farming tips, a wild-game cooking show, and music programs (Tyro 2001). As such, studying local television also calls attention to the specific technological affordances, urban planning parameters, economic practices, and social needs of a city or region as well as the widespread cultural, geographic, and political inequalities of mainstream television systems.

While comparative studies help us see commonalities and divergences across programming, local television research can also reveal the divisive politics within cities, as the "majority of the nation's television stations [are] located in urban centers with large populations that are frequently divided along some combination of ethnic, racial, class, or religious allegiances" (Godfried 2002, 118). For instance, Christopher Anderson and Michael Curtin's (1997, 291) study of early Chicago television notes that while "the principle of localism presumes that a modern city can be imagined, in Raymond Williams's term, as a 'knowable community,' one with a recognizable identity... regulators found it virtually impossible to construct a coherent identity for Chicago; they struggled to understand the internal social conflicts that divided the city and to recognize the external forces, like network television, that had become deeply embedded in the experience of local identity." Two contributors to this anthology likewise focus on local Chicago TV history and reinforce Anderson and Curtin's arguments. For instance, while Shawn VanCour focuses on ways local 1950s television producers aimed to establish Chicago as an epicenter of commercial programming for an imagined national audience, Aymar Jean Christian offers a history of Chicago TV that centers how Black, Indigenous, and people of color (BIPOC) producers have long crafted programs to highlight community-engaged culture and politics.

Many of the shows we have categorized as "local" television may also fit another descriptor. Scholars could aptly replace "local" with words like "community," "regional," "non-network," "educational," "alternative," "independent," and "grassroots" in many discussions of the form. In countries or territories with nationalized television systems, the term "regional television" is used more frequently than "local television" to distinguish the geographically, linguistically, or politically distinctive networks for television exhibition. For example, BBC Scotland is a regional satellite network within the U.K. broadcasting system (Scriven and Lecomte 1999), and in India Kannada-language stations broadcast to the state of Karnataka (Desai 2021). Television aesthetics, production models, and program formats have been shaped by both politics of locality and exposure to global flows of media content at different historical junctures. It is challenging to parse the overlay of local, regional, national, and global influences in twentieth-century media practices. Yet, in an American context, the term "local" is more often used as a modifier for television content directed toward a "designated market area" or service area determined by license policies of the Federal Communications Commission (FCC), which oversees the regulation of local radio, broadcast, and cable content. As such, we have selected chapters that examine the interplay of media technologies and cultural forces in specific U.S. geographic localities.

We prefer "local television" for several additional reasons. First, the television programs analyzed in this anthology are a function of existing broadcast and cable systems. Their production and distribution methods may differ from national commercial programming, but as institutional facets of broadcast and cable systems that rely on cooperation from executives and operators, these programs are not as "alternative," "independent," or "guerrilla" as those concepts might suggest. Similarly, much of the work we discuss has been produced by local communities underrepresented and underserved by broadcast and commercial programming, many of whom are interested in creating resistant television series that reject stereotypes and instead promote community formation and solidarity. However, this is not the case for all local television programming, which is created by producers from across the political spectrum as well as those uninterested in spreading awareness of a particular political agenda. Using the terms "community" and "grassroots" television to describe all the shows examined in our collection would simplify the political and cultural differences between the television series and stations discussed. We instead use the term "local television" to preserve the differences between nationally broadcast programming and programming distributed within a specific geographic or market region, without erasing the ways these series are tied to corporate television structures and without imbuing these programs with political meanings or motivations.

That said, many of the approaches to local television in this anthology indeed overlap with discussions of community media activism. Kevin Howley uses the term "community media" in reference to "grassroots or locally oriented media access initiatives predicated on a profound sense of dissatisfaction with mainstream media form and content, dedicated to the principles of free expression and participatory democracy, and committed to enhancing community relations and promoting community solidarity" (2009, 2). The control, ownership, and content production of local television are built into structures of ideological power and privilege. While a great deal of local television programming may seem innocuous to the casual viewer, media scholars have long emphasized the ways television shapes public discourse and affirms social values for viewing publics. This raises questions about who has access to, and control over, local television programming and consequently which perspectives are available to broadcast communities. As television companies continue to prioritize corporatized hegemonic interests and profit margins over public welfare and as news items increasingly circulate on media platforms with little regulatory interference or fact-checking, it is crucial to turn a critical eye to the ways local television negotiates dominant ideologies. As such, many of the chapters in the collection, particularly in part III, consider the use of television by marginalized groups, whose perspectives are too often sidelined or distorted in mainstream fare. While acknowledging the ways local television infrastructure is embedded in local economies and business models, we also see local programming as platforms for local community formation, cultural expression, civic engagement, and political action.

THE DEVELOPMENT OF LOCAL TELEVISION: AN ABRIDGED HISTORY

The chapters in this collection span the full range of the history of local television, from its early days in the 1940s to its contemporary iterations online and in community media centers. Because all of our contributors offer a partial examination of this history via their particular case study, here we offer an overview of significant moments and policies in broadcast and cable history to provide larger cultural and political context for the development of local television across the United States.

Variations in population, urban design, social norms, and technological affordances of different geographic areas led to the uneven implementation and evolution of television across spaces throughout the twentieth and twenty-first centuries. Nevertheless, television stations share technological origins and similar histories of regulatory governance. The development of local television has likewise been imbricated in long-standing debates about the utility of mass media technology to the American public sphere: Will broadcasting enrich American minds or corrupt them? Is broadcasting a tool for education, entertainment, or ideological indoctrination? Should broadcasting be a commercial enterprise or a free public service? Who should oversee the development and dissemination of media, and in whose interest will the media serve? Is it better to create a centralized national mode of address or to enable a multiplicity of voices to speak to and for local communities? These philosophical quandaries—which still preoccupy scholars, media makers, regulators, and activists—contoured the implementation of radio technologies in American cities and towns in the early to mid-twentieth century and the subsequent expansion of radio policies and practices into television.

The roots of television's industrial and political regulation are deeply intertwined with the history of radio. The Radio Act of 1927 privileged an interpretation of radio as a national, commercial enterprise. The act fortified congressional control of the airwaves, while allowing the newly formed Federal Radio Commission to grant licenses to networks that agreed to serve in the "public interest, convenience, and necessity." However, the act did not stipulate any additional information as to what constitutes public interest and how communications technologies would serve the needs of the growing American populace. This act was reformed by the Federal Communications Act of 1934, which created the FCC, replacing the Radio Commission to oversee the regulation of the nation's expanding telecommunications technologies into television and increasing demands for local station broadcast licenses. This legislation further solidified the dominant commercial model for broadcasting in which national networks (e.g., NBC, ABC, CBS, DuMont) supplied radio and television content to local station "affiliates" at nominal costs. Local affiliate stations would profit from advertisements and produce some content locally to fill gaps in the national broadcast schedule. While independent low-power stations and nonprofit educational broadcast systems existed in the first half of the twentieth century, especially in college and university towns, the majority of local stations worked to "promote and publicize the main business of the parent company" (Hilmes 2013, 48).

Government oversight of television programming sparked cultural debates about the role of television as a commercial enterprise versus a public utility. FCC oversight of early broadcasting was lax, and the commercial power of the major networks continued to expand through World War II. Consequently, public demands for broadcasters to reprioritize public interests, education, and community service intensified. As Allison Perlman puts it, "Free speech advocates feared that concentration of ownership within centralized national networks threatened the marketplace of ideas and hindered the circulation of diverse perspectives" (2016, 17). In 1946, the FCC responded to ongoing debates about the unchecked power of commercial media by issuing the "Public Service Responsibilities of Broadcasters," a report that outlined four requirements for broadcast licensees: "they must sustain experimental programs deemed unsponsorable; promote local live programs; devote programs to the discussion of local public issues; and eliminate 'excessive advertising'" (Pickard 2011, 182). The report even responded to complaints of stereotype and caricature on commercial programs by suggesting that stations "provide programs for significant minority tastes and interests" (Federal Communications Commission 1946, 12). This was a groundbreaking, progressive shift that revalued broadcasting as a public service that was answerable to local community partners.

In the 1940s and 1950s, television became a mass medium central to American cultural life. The growing interest in television in cities and towns across the country put a great deal of pressure on the FCC to expand frequencies and licenses. Concerns about expansion of both UHF and VHF broadcasts, demands for educational allocations, complaints of frequency interference, and the emergence of color television led the FCC to freeze the local station license application process until policies could be sorted; this lasted from 1948 to 1952. The freeze was a boon to existing local stations and national networks, which continued to develop content without competition. Its thaw saw the increase of UHF and VHF licenses on a city-by-city basis, introducing local television to regions in the American South, West, and Pacific Northwest (Boddy 1993). Television sets would continue to find a central place in more American homes through the 1950s. Yet smaller stations still struggled to compete in established television markets, and communities in remote, rural areas often had limited, if any, stations in signal reach. In the decades that followed, communities underserved by existing television stations would adapt technologies to expand their viewing options and, at times, develop their own community content to offset dominant local station trends and better serve their own perceived viewing needs.

TV stations throughout the country worked to offset national programming by creating locally oriented news coverage, sporting events, religious programming, and public affairs shows. The interpretation of regulatory guidelines to require local public interest content further empowered television reformers to push for increased funding for educational and public affairs programming that would better enrich community life. Although broadcasting histories typically emphasize the early programming innovations of national networks, the development of television has always been filtered through local stations. According to Mark Williams (1997, 221), in early television history "every network and non-network television station was necessarily a local station. Local stations negotiated the role TV would play in their communities, coordinating the new medium to local rhythms, interests, sentiments, and ideologies." Entertaining and educational programs for children as well as content oriented toward homemakers—cooking shows, chat shows, soap operas—were often developed by local stations as they filled air slots outside of the "prime-time" blocks reserved for national network fare. As Lynn Spigel (2019, 6) has argued, examining such local programming allows historians to "discern accents not registered in prime-time network fare" and complicate "well-rehearsed theories and histories of television's aesthetics, revealing outliers—those programs or moments in programs that seem not to fit into our memories or histories of what TV was at a particular time."

Programming innovations at the local level have been highly influential to the development of television genres and formats. As chapters in this collection demonstrate, local television stations, especially in the early years of the medium, experimented with television style and content delivery. For local stations in major markets—typically those near urban centers—popular series could be syndicated for distribution to other stations or have their formats replicated. In television's initial decades, the networks made a substantial portion of their profits by broadcasting content produced by local affiliates or syndicating local programs to the affiliate market (Lafferty 1997). Many prominent television personalities began in local television before shifting to national networks with broader audience reach. The same holds true for television formats and styles. For instance, Susan Murray (2019) has shown that medical programming and surgical telecasts were first broadcast on local airwaves as an extension of closed-circuit medical educational programs. Local dance programs hosted by popular deejays were a common mainstay of station schedules in the after-school hours (Hutchison 2012). Craig Allen (1997) has also demonstrated that the fast-paced "action news" and "eyewitness news" formats developed by WABC-TV were quickly adopted by other New York stations and soon national news programs. Indeed, local news has been a significant site of programming innovation, as news and public information is the most prominent type of local production. According to Charles L. Ponce de Leon (2015, 7), "News programs were among the first kinds of broadcasts that aired in the waning years of war, and virtually everyone in the industry expected them to be part of the program mix as the networks increased programming to fill the broadcast day." News broadcasts were a clear way for local stations to fulfill the "public service" requirement for licensure. Local anchors could address how national topics impacted community members while also offering customized information and announcements of special interests to viewers. As such, local news accounts for around 40 percent of local station revenues (B. Anderson 2004; Horwitz 2005) and remains the most frequently watched form of local public service programming (Ponce de Leon 2015).

In the 1950s and 1960s, local television news programs frequently served as forums for the discussion of current events and debates about contemporary political and social movements. Local television news and public or cultural affairs programming have typically received more scholarly attention than other types of local programming. In the 1950s, as stations customized their news and informational content toward the perceived public interests of viewers in signal reach, they faced increasing contestation from activists and public reformers who did not believe all viewers were given equitable consideration. The FCC's "Fairness Doctrine" of 1949 prescribed that local stations provide balanced coverage of controversial issues and political debates. However, as Annie Sullivan (2022, 321) has argued elsewhere, local television stations have historically been "owned and managed almost exclusively by white men, [who] imagined their 'publics' as an upwardly mobile white middle class and offered local educational, informational, and entertainment content with that demographic in mind—without much consideration of the actual population demographics and the needs of diverse viewers." Or as Lynn Spigel (2019, 6) puts it, "Cultural affairs programs produced by local stations demonstrate how different parts of the country deal with—or fail to deal with—issues of importance into their local communities and or the nation and world." Taylor Cole Miller's chapter in this collection on Normal Leer's syndicated series *The Baxters* reveals how live audiences respond to controversial content in different U.S. cities. Meanwhile, Aniko Bodroghkozy (2012) has documented ways pro-segregationist southern stations blacked out national programs that highlighted civil rights protests and pro-integrationist perspectives.

While nonwhite voices were largely excluded from broadcasting, local television stations became a battleground in the Black liberation struggle. Sasha Torres's *Black, White, and In Color* (2003) discusses how media-savvy local activists strategically staged nonviolent protests to forge empathy among television audiences if caught on the evening news and boycotted stations that scripted pro-segregationist news coverage or aired racist film and TV programs. The civil rights struggle over local television content on WLBT and WJTV in Jackson, Mississippi, is perhaps the most infamous example of citizens challenging stations' discriminatory protocols: Steven Classen's *Watching Jim Crow* (2004) traces efforts to integrate local television and the stations' resistance to broadcasting any local or national coverage that promoted integrationist efforts. While an exceptional case study, it shows how studying local television offers invaluable insights into how sociopolitical issues are negotiated by diverse American communities.

The civil rights battles over local television programming overlapped with ongoing efforts to reimagine television as an educational and/or noncommercial medium. According to the Carnegie Commission on Educational Television (1967), "To be truly local, a station must arise out of a sense of need within a community, must have roots in the community, and must be under community control." The commission hoped public affairs and educational programs on local noncommercial stations would serve as a forum for community discourse, especially for groups that have historically been marginalized in dominant television. Although the commission's vision for local public television was never fully realized, it served as a catalyst and model for the Public Broadcasting Act of 1967, which required strict adherence to fairness and objectivity in the presentation of news content, noting "public telecommunications services constitute valuable local community resources for utilizing electronic media to address national concerns and solve local problems through community programs and out-reach programs." More significantly, the act set up the Corporation for Public Broadcasting (CPB) and established parameters for the allocations of national funds to local educational television stations. This enabled local stations in every state to produce or acquire programming that emphasized community services, public safety, education, and cultural enrichment. In 1969, the CPB formed the Public Broadcasting System (PBS), a private nonprofit company that would comprise 171 noncommercial licensees and 347 member stations around the country. Local public television was conceived as distinctive from commercial television in terms of both content and funding. Financing would rely on grants, charitable contributions, and donations that would shield programmers from the sway of corporate interests and advertisers.

In the 1960s, the Black liberation struggle along with the national endorsement of public television catalyzed a new wave of local content produced by and for local marginalized communities. The "Kerner Report," the result of a commission tasked with investigating the recent racial uprisings across U.S. cities, argued that a lack of adequate media representation and balanced news reporting of African American life was among the underlying causes of civil rebellion. Not only was there little representation of nonwhite people on television, but on the rare occasions they did appear they were represented as white anchors and writers saw them, not as they saw themselves. Of course, BIPOC residents had long fought for inclusive community programming. However, their demands went largely unanswered until the late 1960s. As scholars like Devorah Heitner (2013), Alice Tait (2003), Herman Gray (2019), and Gayle Wald

(2015) have documented, Black public affairs programs emerged at this historical moment to offset the inadequate, and often racist, coverage of Black politics and culture found on mainstream television. Mary Beltrán, in this collection and in her groundbreaking book *Latino TV* (2022), has also demonstrated how philanthropic interests in educational and community television gave rise to television programs produced by and for Latinx communities, often broadcast in Spanish. While many of the Black and Latinx public affairs programs that emerged in the late 1960s were short-lived, they demonstrate a dominant trend in local television in which local community activists have used local airwaves to address the needs and interests of marginalized residents. Other scholars like Hamid Naficy (1993), Heather Hendershot (1998), Kathryn Montgomery (1991), and Chon Noriega (2000) have shown how BIPOC, exilic and immigrant communities, LGBTQIA+ groups, and other marginalized subjects forge or maintain community ties through educational niche programming, often on noncommercial stations. These programs also migrated from local nonprofit stations to public access channels as cable infrastructure was implemented in cities in the 1970s and 1980s.

The invention of cable television, first known as community antenna television (CATV), signaled a new era of television history: it added a number of channels to the television dial, greatly expanding local and national programming. Originally intended to improve reception of broadcasting to rural areas in the 1940s and 1950s, the cable industry experienced rapid growth in the 1970s as established media companies speculated on cable's potential as a lucrative new medium for commercial television programming (Banet-Weiser, Chris, and Freitas 2007, 18–19). The launch of new cable channels and the inauguration of satellite television distribution generated excitement about the possibility for "pay TV" to cater television programming to niche markets of paying subscribers across the country.

In 1972, the FCC issued an order requiring cable television systems in the country's top one hundred markets to offer access channels for public use, creating new opportunities for residents to create television content for their local communities. As a new category of television programming, public access channels would ideally shift power away from the cable operator and toward the general public. The FCC mandated that cable companies make available airtime and rent equipment and studio space to individuals and community groups to use for their own programming. The impetus for public access was similar to the ethos of public broadcasting, which sought to create noncommercial and educational television programming in the service of the public interest; indeed, the Public Broadcasting Act in 1967 created "the philosophical and legal foundation" for public access television five years later (Linder 1999, 1). The 1972 FCC order created four types of access channels—noncommercial public, educational, and government (PEG)—and leased access channels run on a commercial basis. Airtime on PEG channels was offered to the public on a first-come, first-served basis, whereas producers had to purchase airtime for leased access programming and, in exchange, could run advertisements during their shows.

Public access was a key part of the "blue skies" discourse about cable television in the 1970s and 1980s. The term "blue skies" "came to suggest the unlimited, cloudless horizon of possibilities embodied in the emerging technology" (Parsons 2008, 7). According to Thomas Streeter, the enthusiasm for cable, expressed by a cross section of social groups including activists, cable operators, policymakers, television executives, and economists, centered around its potential to solve a number of social, political, and economic problems (1997, 228). Progressive policymakers as well as community media activists imagined that cable television could interrupt the traditional "one-way" nature of broadcast programming by offering a way for individuals to interact with and create their own television. Public access channels provided this opportunity: these channels were imagined as an "electronic soapbox" (Linder 1999) or televisual town square that could cultivate a democratized form of local and mass communication (Parsons 2008, 374). Community activists hoped public access could fulfill "the dream of localism," or the desire for televisual media to serve underrepresented communities (Howell 2017, 4). Media activist and scholar DeeDee Halleck, founder of the nonprofit video collective Paper Tiger Television, stressed, "The opportunity that public access provides for wide dissemination of progressive issue-oriented media is an emancipatory moment yet to be realized" (2002, 123). The optimistic promise that cable could serve the public interest lasted well into the 1990s.

A number of regulatory decisions have impacted the structure and impact of public access programming since the 1970s. The Cable Communications Policy Act of 1984 "contained strong language in support of PEG access channels" but, unlike the 1972 FCC order, did not require cable operators to establish these channels themselves (Freedman 2017, 172). Instead, the 1984 Cable Act and subsequent regulations "allow franchisers, usually municipalities, to require public access of the cable operator as part of the franchise agreement" (Linder 1999, 31). State and local governments may opt out of providing cable access programming because there is no federal mandate for it. According to one study, public access stations have experienced a sharp decline in funding and "more than 100 communities have lost their PEG access stations since 2005" (Chen et al. 2013, 266). As Streeter suggests, "The cable fable is a story of repeated utopian high hopes followed by repeated disappointments" (1997, 238). While discourse and scholarship about public access television have argued that it has the potential to create a public sphere that produces democratic forms of communication, recent scholars have interrogated these qualities as inherent to the form (Ali 2014, 71). Legal regulation, the threat of censorship, and financial precarity have curtailed the ability of public access programming to achieve democratic ideals. The "blue skies" rhetoric about cable faded as the cable industry became increasingly marked by business competition, deregulation, and corporate conglomeration. Public access programming still exists, yet it rarely inspires the kind of utopian rhetoric expressed in its early years. Despite this decline, according to the Alliance for Community Media (n.d.), hundreds of community television stations across the country are still currently in operation.

The 1990s marked a turning point for local television policy, as new legislation cleared the way for the market competition, deregulation, and corporate conglomeration mentioned above. In particular, the 1996 Telecommunications Act significantly overhauled the Federal Communications Act of 1934. The 1996 Telecommunications Act permitted open competition among telecommunications companies offering multiple services (satellite, cable, broadcast, telephone, and the internet), which led to greater media consolidation via company mergers and acquisitions (Banet-Weiser, Chris, and Freitas 2007). Coupled with the rescinding of the Financial Interest and Syndication Rules in 1993 and the Prime Time Access Rule in 1996, legislation enforced by the FCC that limited the power of television networks to control programming and airtime, 1990s telecommunications laws ushered in an era of deregulation in the American media landscape (Parsons 2008). These regulatory changes decreased the power of small-scale and local productions, which have had to compete with corporate conglomerates more interested in the bottom line than in public and community concerns.

The chapters in this collection primarily explore histories of local television that occurred within the period detailed above, the 1940s to

1990s. In the epilogue, "Moving Local Television Forward in the Digital Era," Lori Kido Lopez gestures to the ways that contemporary local television continues to evolve in our digital era, particularly as marginalized producers utilize digital media to create their own programming and platforms. Similarly, chapters by Aymar Jean Christian and Antoine Haywood connect historical and contemporary histories of local television to explore continuities in these forms and to argue for their continued cultural significance. Over the past thirty years, the television industry has increasingly favored financial gains and corporate consolidation over the preservation of local television infrastructure; however, as chapters in this collection demonstrate, local television has remarkable longevity despite myriad changes in television technology, policy, and regulation over the decades. Engaging deeply with these histories, the chapters in this collection demonstrate how local television production and distribution respond to these shifts, at times creating new genres of programming in the process.

A NOTE ON ARCHIVES AND RECEPTION

One unifying characteristic of local television scholarship is the uneven documentation of the topic within media histories. Television is a largely ephemeral medium, and archivism for local television stations and independent producers tends to be even more unpredictable than well-funded national network fare. Stations often lack the resources to comprehensively archive their documents and preserve their history. With the invention of magnetic videotape, stations with precarious funding often recorded over their own materials to save on costs, inadvertently contributing to their own historical erasure as a means to create content for the future. Indeed, the lack of access to audiovisual recordings of shows and the absence of stable archives is a familiar, albeit tragic refrain through this monograph. Some local producers meticulously saved and archived their own content, which they personally share with scholars. Producers who valued their content on a national scale would send tapes to the Peabody Institute or other relevant institutional archives for preservation. The availability of formal or informal archival access strongly informs what content receives close attention and what conclusions scholars can draw from it. That said, scholars who study local television have employed varied creative methods to fill in historical gaps and make sense of archival lacunae. Such methods include but are not limited to autoethnographies, oral histories, and discourse analyses of archival fragments and newspaper articles.

While many stories of local television production have yet to be recovered and documented, it is even harder to study and make sense of local television reception. Television ratings measurements have historically ignored local programs. Consequently, it is difficult to estimate the audience sizes of most local programming. As Pamela Wilson (1997, 326) has aptly put it, "One particular challenge in this endeavor is a historiographical problem which has plagued those of us interested in historical reception studies of television, that is, how to locate and conceptualize the historical television audience. This process is messy and incomplete, since we are forced to rely on fragmentary evidence and to make use of every resource at our disposal." Histories of trauma, loss, and lack of resources have hit marginalized communities particularly hard, rendering nonhegemonic histories within local history even more prone to archival erasure. Scholarship on commercial television often implicitly assumes that large audience size determines the social significance of TV, which occasionally and implicitly dismisses the ways programs with comparatively smaller audiences create meaning for those particular audiences. This collection helps demonstrate the social, political, and historical significance of local programming with smaller and indeterminate audience sizes. Still, we hope this anthology not only contributes to a growing body of scholarship on local television production and distribution but encourages more research on local television preservation and reception. This will provide residents and scholars not only more nuanced accounts of television's role in American culture but also clearer understandings of quotidian engagement with the medium.

CHAPTER BREAKDOWN AND ORGANIZATION

This collection showcases a range of methods to explore and authorize televisual historiography and brings those histories to life. For the purposes of the Peabody Series, we have prioritized essays that emphasize historical analyses of local television in distinctive regions across the United States. Rather than a comprehensive historical or geographic survey, which, given the sheer number of local television productions, would be impossible, the collection is organized into three sections that assess the possibilities and limitations of television's mission to serve local publics in comparative ways.

Part I, "Developing and Distributing Local Television," includes essays that situate efforts to establish and produce local media in relation to the institutional policies of sponsoring agencies, national industry trends, and the shifting conditions of municipal infrastructure. Shawn VanCour's "Placing Local Media: The Chicago School of Television, Revisited" explores the legacy of 1940s and 1950s experiments in television production in Chicago, a set of programs dubbed "the Chicago School," via theorist Henri Lefebvre's theories of space and place. VanCour analyzes the production practices, aesthetics, and debates surrounding the Chicago School to show how the series influenced national television production practices and can shape scholarly understandings of local media history more broadly. Next, Dyfrig Jones's "Local and National, Public and Private: WOI-TV and Early Educational Television in the United States" examines the early history of WOI-TV in Iowa, the first U.S. station operated by an educational institution. Drawing upon archival research, Jones demonstrates how WOI-TV blended together public and private, commercial and educational, and local and national content and as such can help scholars understand how educational television emerged in the 1950s as an enduring mode of programming. "'Vocal Voyeurs': Local Television Meets National Syndication in Norman Lear's *The Baxters*," Taylor Cole Miller's contribution to the collection, expands scholarly understandings of syndication through analysis of Norman Lear's short-lived *The Baxters*, which combined short narrative vignettes about hot-button issues with taped, town-hall-style talk shows produced by local stations. Drawing upon media policy, production, reviews, and textual analysis, Miller assesses *The Baxters* as an important case study in the critical yet undertheorized relationship between syndication and local television. Ana Howe Bukowski's "Video as Local Television: 'Becoming Cable' at the Long Beach Museum of Art" examines experiments in the development of televisual infrastructure and cable networks at the Long Beach Museum of Art in the 1970s. Rather than exploring televisual content and aesthetics, Bukowski highlights the dynamic but infrequently explored connections between art institutions and telecommunications systems to forward a theoretical and methodological focus on the role of material infrastructure in the development of cable. The final chapter in this section, Daniel Marcus's "'To Call It a Zoo Would Be Unkind to Animals': How Cable Television Came to Miami," offers a complex and detailed analysis of the deals brokered between cable operators, political elites, and lobbyists that led to the creation of the Miami cable system in the 1980s. Building upon political coverage of cable contract bids as well as his own personal experiences, Marcus argues that microhistories of cable systems allow scholars to trace the growth of media companies that remain powerful today.

Part II, "Aesthetics and Genres of Local Television Programs," includes chapters that explore the innovative genres, aesthetic experimentation, and content of specific local productions. To begin, Annie Laurie Sullivan's "Broadcasting Faith in Detroit: Local Televangelism, Black Gospel Traditions, and the Commerce of Community Worship" discusses the racial politics, economics, and aesthetics of Black religious programming in Detroit. She argues these shows model Black community engagement, celebrate Black gospel performance, and proffer political and spiritual lessons to shepherd Detroit's majority-Black population through the tumults of urban crises. In contrast, Jonathan MacDonald's "Learning the *Basic Issues of Man*: Midcentury Humanism, Social Science, and Educational Television" investigates how the twelve-part television series *Basic Issues of Man* (1962), created by the University of Georgia, attempted to educate viewers about the liberal humanistic values necessary for "good" citizenship while disavowing the racial histories and tensions of its Atlanta campus in the midst of the civil rights movement. Via archival and textual analysis of the series' episodes, MacDonald argues that *Basic Issues of Man* demonstrates how locally produced television can at times silence community concerns as readily as amplify them. In a similar vein, Caroline Bayne's "WSB-TV, Atlanta: Broadcasting the New Old South" presents a set of interdependent histories: that of WSB-TV, the first television station to go on the air in the southern United States, it's long-running locally produced daytime program *Today in Georgia*, and a cultural geography of Atlanta, told largely through the city's growth into a televisual center of the South. Using the history of WSB-TV as a lens, Bayne explores the tension between Atlanta's growth as a site of industry, culture, and technology and its persistent investment in the memorialization of its racist and antebellum past. Next, Evelyn Kreutzer's "Busting Beethoven: Nam June Paik's Electronic Operas at WGBH" explores performance and video artist Nam June Paik's experimental video programming on Boston's public TV station WGBH. Closely analyzing the aesthetics of Paik's anthology series, Kreutzer demonstrates how his programs attempted to turn individual viewers of his programs into a virtual community of participants, envisioning television as a medium of intimacy and immediacy, all while challenging and subverting standards of "highbrow" and "lowbrow" art on TV. Finally, Christine Becker's "Creative Beyond Their Years: The Unique Alchemy of *Beyond Our Control*" follows the development of *Beyond Our Control*, a long-running sketch comedy series created by teenagers in South Bend, Indiana. Via interviews with *Beyond Our Control*'s now-adult participants, Becker explores how the show's production history and use of parody establish youth television production as an alternative form of media literacy, professional development, and cultural training ground.

Part III, "Amplifying Community Voices through Local Television," highlights a range of practices adopted by communities typically underrepresented on legacy television as a form of counterhegemonic civic engagement and political or cultural dissent. Helen Morgan Parmett, in "Placemaking and Community Access Media in Vermont: Histories, Archives, and Activism," explores the history of community access television in Vermont via analysis of Bernie Sanders's series *Bernie Speaks with the Community*. Using archival research and interviews, Parmett articulates how community access media are intimately bound up with the production of place and locality and how their contemporary digitization can contribute to a nostalgic imagination of rural Vermont in particular. "Minority Media for the Majority: The Survival Strategies of the Milwaukee Gay/Lesbian Cable Network (1986–1994)," Daphne Gershon's chapter, recounts the operations of the groundbreaking Milwaukee Gay/Lesbian Cable Network (MGLCN), one of the few organizations to produce numerous specials as well as three regular series about LGBTQ issues in the 1980s and 1990s. Drawing on archival research and textual analysis of series produced by the network, Gershon argues that while MGLCN attempted to create content by and for its local gay community, its operations and programming were largely defined by its objective of garnering support from straight midwesterners, a strategy that both contributed to and confined MGLCN's revolutionary potential. Mary Beltrán, in "The First Wave of Latina/o TV: Early Chicana/o and Puerto Rican Programming," considers how four local English-language and bilingual public affairs programs in the sixties and seventies aimed to serve, document the lives of, and inspire the Latina/o residents of their local communities. Beltrán argues that these series created televisual forums for Latina/o Americans, illustrating the rich possibilities of television programming with a focus on the interests and needs of local and national Latina/o communities as well as the untapped potential of putting television production and programming decisions in the hands of Latina/o creative professionals. Aymar Jean Christian's "Chicago Renaissance Redux: Black Cultural Production and the Social Practice Art of Television" highlights the history and contemporary legacy of what he calls "social practice television" in Chicago, television practices that engage and center community participation in production and distribution. Centering innovative art and media created by Black, Brown, queer, and working-class people over the twentieth and twenty-first centuries, Christian explores social practice television as a solidarity project as well as a necessary means of surviving and thriving for marginalized artists and producers. Finally, in "Telling Our Stories: A Reflection on Realizing the Promise of Public Access TV in Philadelphia," Antoine Haywood shares his own autoethnographic memories and accounts of working at and volunteering with Philadelphia Community Access Media (PhillyCAM). Recounting the history of PhillyCAM alongside excerpts from his oral history project that amplifies the voices of BIPOC local media producers, Haywood's contribution emphasizes that local and community television centers remain central to providing diverse and marginalized communities the space to create their own media.

While most of this anthology looks backward, we recognize that local television continues to play a vital role in mediating community life. Even as channels of telecommunications expand, local programs provide critical news and information to residents daily and trusted local personalities facilitate ongoing cultural exchange and political debates for dedicated audiences. As the second Trump administration demands federal funding cuts to NPR and PBS and more broadly targets journalism, news media, and the freedom of speech, local public television and radio stations across the country are in peril. These attacks risk depriving much of the American public, especially communities underserved by the broadcast networks, the news, culture, and educational programming they rely on. In the wake of this moment, this anthology speaks to the historical and contemporary importance of local television in American culture and ignites further discussion of its political, aesthetic, cultural, and institutional possibilities.

REFERENCES

Ali, Christopher. 2014. "The Last PEG or Community Media 2.0? Negotiating Place and Placelessness at PhillyCAM." *Media, Culture & Society* 36 (1): 69–86.

———. 2017. *Media Localism: The Policies of Place*. University of Illinois Press.

Allen, Craig. 1997. "Tackling the TV Titans in Their Own Backyard: WABC-TV, New York City." In *Television in America: Local Station History from Across the Nation*, edited by Michael D. Murray and Donald G. Godfrey, 3–18. Iowa State University Press.

Alliance for Community Media. n.d. "Community Media Directory." Accessed July 17, 2020. https://www.allcommunitymedia.org/ACM/About/Community_Media_Directory/ACM/Directory/Community_Media_Directory.aspx?hkey=8936f226-f206-43fd-b24e-2b4b337e1afo.

Anderson, Bonnie. 2004. *News Flash: Journalism, Infotainment and the Bottom-Line Business of Broadcast News*. Wiley.

Anderson, Christopher, and Michael Curtin. 1997. "Mapping the Ethereal City: Chicago Television, the FCC, and the Politics of Place." *Quarterly Review of Film and Video* 16 (3–4): 289–305.

Banet-Weiser, Sarah, Cynthia Chris, and Anthony Freitas, eds. 2007. *Cable Visions: Television Beyond Broadcasting*. New York University Press.

Beltrán, Mary. 2022. *Latino TV: A History*. New York University Press.

Boddy, William. 1993. *Fifties Television: The Industry and Its Critics*. University of Illinois Press.

Bodroghkozy, Aniko. 2012. *Equal Time: Television and the Civil Rights Movement*. University of Illinois Press.

Carnegie Commission on Educational Television. 1967. "Public Television, a Program for Action: The Report and Recommendations of the Carnegie Commission on Educational Television." Carnegie Corporation.

Castelnero, Gordon. 2006. *TV Land Detroit*. University of Michigan Press.

Chen, Wenhong, Marcus Funk, Joseph D. Straubhaar, and Jeremiah Spence. 2013. "Still Relevant? An Audience Analysis of Public and Government Access Channels." *Journal of Broadcasting & Electronic Media* 57 (3): 263–81.

Classen, Steven D. 2004. *Watching Jim Crow: The Struggles over Mississippi TV, 1955–1969*. Duke University Press.

Desai, Mira K. 2021. *Regional Language Television in India: Profiles and Perspectives*. Taylor & Francis.

Federal Communications Commission. 1946. "Public Service Responsibility of Broadcast Licensees." Federal Communications Commission.

Feran, Tom, and Richard D. Heldenfels. 1999. *Cleveland TV Memories*. Gray & Company.

Freedman, Eric. 2017. "From Excess to Access: Televising the Subculture." In *Spectatorship: Shifting Theories of Gender, Sexuality, and Media*, edited by Roxanne Samer and William Whittington, 163–76. University of Texas Press.

Godfried, Nathan. 2002. "Identity, Power, and Local Television: African Americans, Organized Labor and UHF-TV in Chicago, 1962–1968." *Historical Journal of Film, Radio and Television* 22 (2): 117–34. https://doi.org/10.1080/01439680220133756.

Gray, Herman. 2019. "Reading Peabody: Transparency, Opacity, and the Black Subjection of Twentieth-Century American Television." In Thompson, Jones, and Hatlen, *Television History, the Peabody Archives, and Cultural Memory*, 79–95.

Halleck, DeeDee. 2002. "Paper Tiger Television: Smashing the Myths of the Information Industry Every Week on Public Access Cable." In *Hand-Held Visions: The Impossible Possibilities of Community Media*, 114–23. Fordham University Press.

Heitner, Devorah. 2013. *Black Power TV*. Duke University Press.

Hendershot, Heather. 1998. *Saturday Morning Censors: Television Regulation Before the V-Chip*. Duke University Press.

Hilliard, Robert L., and Michael C. Keith. 1999. *The Hidden Screen: Low-Power Television in America*. M. E. Sharpe.

Hilmes, Michele. 2013. *Only Connect: A Cultural History of Broadcasting in the United States*. Cengage.

Horwitz, Robert B. 2005. "US Media Policy Then and Now." In *Converging Media, Diverging Politics: A Political Economy of News Media in the United States and Canada*, edited by Mike Gasher, David Skinner, and James R. Compton, 24–43. Lexington Books.

Howell, Charlotte E. 2017. "Symbolic Capital and the Production Discourse of *The American Music Show*: A Microhistory of Atlanta Cable Access." *Cinema Journal* 57 (1): 1–24.

Howley, Kevin. 2009. *Understanding Community Media*. SAGE.

Hutchison, Phillip J. 2012. "Magic Windows and the Serious Life: Rituals and Community in Early American Local Television." *Journal of Broadcasting & Electronic Media* 56 (1): 21–37.

Lafferty, William. 1997. "'A New Era in TV Programming' Becomes 'Business as Usual': Videotape Technology, Local Stations, and Network Power, 1957–1961." *Quarterly Review of Film and Video* 16 (3–4): 405–19. https://doi.org/10.1080/10509209709361473.

Linder, Laura. 1999. *Public Access Television: America's Electronic Soapbox*. Praeger.

Montgomery, Kathryn C. 1991. *Target, Prime Time: Advocacy Groups and the Struggle over Entertainment Television*. EBSCO.

Murray, Susan. 2019. "'Medical School of the World': Education and Public Service through Postwar Medical Television." In Thompson, Jones, and Hatlen, *Television History, the Peabody Archives, and Cultural Memory*, 192–205.

Naficy, Hamid. 1993. *The Making of Exile Cultures: Iranian Television in Los Angeles*. University of Minnesota Press.

Noriega, Chon A. 2000. *Shot in America: Television, the State, and the Rise of Chicano Cinema*. University of Minnesota Press.

Parsons, Patrick R. 2008. *Blue Skies: A History of Cable Television*. Temple University Press.

Perlman, Allison. 2016. *Public Interests: Media Advocacy and Struggles over U.S. Television*. Rutgers University Press.

Pickard, Victor. 2011. "The Battle over the FCC Blue Book: Determining the Role of Broadcast Media in a Democratic Society." *Media, Culture & Society* 30 (2): 171–91.

Ponce de Leon, Charles L. 2015. *That's the Way It Is: A History of Television News in America*. University of Chicago Press.

Scriven, Michael, and Monia Lecomte. 1999. *Television Broadcasting in Contemporary France and Britain*. Berghahn Books.

Spigel, Lynn. 2019. "Introduction: The Peabody Awards Collection, the Archive, and Local TV History." In *Television History, the Peabody Archive, and Cultural Memory*, edited by Ethan Thompson, Jeffrey P. Jones, and Lucas Hatlen, 1–16. University of Georgia Press.

Streeter, Thomas. 1997. "Blue Skies and Strange Bedfellows: The Discourse of Cable Television." In *The Revolution Wasn't Televised: Sixties Television and Social Conflict*, edited by Lynn Spigel and Michael Curtin, 221–42. Routledge.

Sullivan, Annie. 2022. "Who Controls the Media: The Racial Politics of Local Television: Negotiating Public Interests and the Black Freedom Struggle." In *The Routledge Companion to Media and the City*, edited by Erica Stein, Germaine R. Halegoua, and Brendan Kredell, 317–28. Taylor & Francis.

Tait, Alice. 2003. "Ethic Voices: Ethnocentric Public Affairs Television Programming." In *Television: Critical Concepts in Media and Cultural Studies*, edited by Toby Miller, 32–38. Taylor & Francis.

Thompson, Ethan, Jeffrey P. Jones, and Lucas Hatlen, eds. 2019. *Television History, the Peabody Archive, and Cultural Memory*. University of Georgia Press.

Torres, Sasha. 1998. *Living Color: Race and Television in the United States*. Duke University Press.

———. 2003. *Black, White, and In Color: Television and Black Civil Rights*. Princeton University Press.

Tyro, Frank H. 2001. "Localism and Low-Power Public Television on the Flathead Indian Reservation." *Wicazo Sa Review* 16 (2): 19–28.

Wald, Gayle. 2015. *It's Been Beautiful: Soul! and Black Power Television*. Duke University Press.

Williams, Mark. 1997. "Issue Introduction: U.S. Regional and Non-network Television History." *Quarterly Review of Film and Video* 16 (3–4): 221–28.

Wilson, Pamela. 1997. "All Eyes on Montana: Television Audiences, Social Activism, and Native American Cultural Politics in the 1950s." *Quarterly Review of Film and Video* 16 (3–4): 325–56.

PART I

DEVELOPING AND DISTRIBUTING LOCAL TELEVISION

CHAPTER 1

SHAWN VANCOUR

PLACING LOCAL MEDIA

THE CHICAGO SCHOOL OF TELEVISION, REVISITED

For its September 1950 television review section, *Time* (1950a, 73–74) featured a two-page spread on NBC's "Chicago School," highlighting Sunday-night comedy-musical variety show *Garroway at Large* and its host, local broadcasting personality Dave Garroway. Carried live from WNBQ-Chicago over NBC's East Coast network, Garroway's was among a growing number of shows created in what *Time* called the "Chicago style." Lacking "big budgets, elaborate equipment and big-name talent" of New York or Hollywood, they were marked by an "informality and inventiveness... born of necessity," with producers "specializ[ing] in what they call 'simplified realism' and 'ad-lib drama'" using "the four walls of every set" and "never switch[ing] from one camera to another without a good reason." As early as 1949, trade coverage argued shows like Garroway's would help Chicago "reassert itself as one of the nation's key production centers" (*Variety* 1949, 28), and by 1950 Chicago originations ranged from musical variety to children's shows and a parody of women's talk shows by Ransom Sherman—another veteran Chicago performer whose "low-geared whimsy and relaxed emceeing" was likened to Garroway's (Dave 1950, 26) and won him a spread in *Life* magazine (1950, 112). By fall 1951, the city produced twenty-two network programs in an achievement of which local critics argued "Chicago can be proud" (Mabley 1951). But success was short-lived, with declining productions by 1955 (Sternberg 1997, 246) marking the beginning of the end for the Chicago School and critics by 1958 offering final dirges for "Chicago's local TV corpse" (Shayon 1958, 32).

A forgotten chapter in the annals of television history, the Chicago School experiment offers an instructive tale for analyzing the nature and functions of localism in U.S. television. Actively developing experimental systems in the 1920s and 1930s, Chicago broadcasters also held some of the nation's first commercial television licenses in the 1940s, including WBKB in 1946—a CBS station by 1953 (*Variety* 1953, 25)—plus NBC's WNBQ, ABC's WENR, and independent WGN in 1949 (Sternberg 1973, 104). Throughout the 1930s and 1940s, Chicago had supplied top-rated network radio programs, with the "Chicago School" label invoking this legacy though itself a product of the television era. Garroway and Sherman, in particular, were synonymous with the Chicago School— to the extent that when NBC canceled them, *Time* (1950b) declared "School's Out" for Chicago television, and Chicago's Television Council excoriated the network for leaving the school "practically dead" in their wake (*Broadcasting-Telecasting* 1951a, 75). Renewed investment by ABC spurred a brief recovery in 1953 (*Hollywood Reporter* 1953, 1), but by the late 1950s "Chicago originations were something of the past" (Sternberg 1997, 246). Federal Communications Commission investigations of licensee failures to meet their local community obligations raised brief hopes of a Chicago School revival in 1962 but ultimately affirmed the status quo, and "instead of clarifying the ambiguities surrounding the principle of localism," merely demonstrated the challenges of defining television "as a local phenomenon" rooted in a particular "community" or "place" (Anderson and Curtin 1997, 301–2).

Revisiting the Chicago School experiments of the late 1940s and 1950s, this essay explores them as both instructive examples of and challenges to ideas of media localism. Signifying a place, style, and branded product, the Chicago School bore the marks of its origins but was also designed for travel, operating not in opposition to national television but as part of bids to establish Chicago as a key production center in emerging network markets. Results were mixed: while performers like Sherman failed to secure reliable national audiences, Garroway went on to even greater success, bringing his style to New York as host of NBC's *Today* show and prestige documentary series *Wide, Wide World*, before stepping down in 1961. Chicago ultimately lost the battle to dominate network production, and the Chicago School did not endure as a distinctive brand. As a style, however, it was not a casualty of network television so much as strategically absorbed into national programming created at sites beyond Chicago itself.

To explore these complex intersections and divergences between the "local" as a place, style, and product designed for larger network circulation, I use Marxist theorist Henri Lefebvre's influential *The Production of Space* (1991), focusing on the "spatial triad" that forms the crux of his theory. I begin with a brief overview of three key problematics in defining local media. I then review key tenets of Lefebvre's own theory, applying these to more detailed analysis of production practices, stylistic tendencies, and cultural debates surrounding the Chicago School, with a focus on programs by Sherman and Garroway. Through analysis of trade and popular press coverage, critical reviews, extant recordings, and archival production records, I show how Chicago productions both navigated and contributed to changing spatial practices, representational spaces, and spaces of representation in postwar U.S. television, then conclude by assessing the utility of Lefebvre's theory for understanding the Chicago School's "place" in television history and local media history at large.

THE CHICAGO SCHOOL, TAKE 1: DEFINING "LOCAL" TELEVISION

Concerns over the "demise of localism" (Hilliard and Keith 2005) with the lifting of federal caps on station ownership in the late 1990s prompted an initial wave of scholarly interest in local television (Williams 1997; Godfrey and Murray 1997). While more recent scholarship has affirmed this work as a necessary corrective to persistent "national bias" in received histories (Spigel 2019), defining the "local" presents persistent challenges, yielding less a coherent definition than three enduring problematics—the first focused on tensions between locally originated versus locally oriented content, the second on place-based versus interest-based conceptions of communities served by local television, and the third on local television's uneasy relationship with mainstream, national media to which it is often counterposed. Elaborating these points, I argue that Chicago School productions were locally originated but not necessarily locally oriented, affirmed but exceeded place-based identities in their intended audience appeals, and offered not radical alternatives to so much as alternative forms of mainstream network fare. Defying any easy conception of the "local," these programs illustrate persistent challenges in studying local television history.

As policy scholars remind us, all stations are licensed to operate in specific localities, making localism a "bedrock concept" (Kirkpatrick

2006) of communications policy, but "local origination" does not necessarily entail "local expression" through content focused on community needs and interests (Napoli 2001, 212). Federal regulatory guidelines during the 1940s and 1950s affirmed the importance of both "local live programs" produced at locally owned facilities and "public service programs" tailored to local needs, but simultaneously facilitated the development of national network infrastructures (Pickard 2011). Chicago School productions were locally produced with content that often engaged in local boosterism but also sought to establish the city's prominence as what Curtin (2014, 544) calls a "media capital," in the sense of both a "geographic center" for network television production and a site for "accumulation of resources, talent, and reputation." Surviving kinescopes of both Sherman's and Garroway's shows affirm their network status through opening "NBC Television presents" and NBC end slates but in closing credits also played up their Chicago origins, often to comic effect. Sherman's final summer 1950 broadcast (*RSS* 1950b) concluded with him shrugging at the camera, asking, "Why do people refuse to believe it, it comes from Chicago?," while the closing shot for a January 14, 1951, *Garroway at Large* broadcast (*GAL* 1951a) featured guest star Faye Emerson remarking, "Well, they sure do things differently here on the show that comes from Chicago!"[1] Such tactics positioned the shows' Chicago origins as a source of programming distinction, while still centering them as network programs for broader national consumption.

Whether framed in terms of point of origination or content orientation, definitions of localism traditionally favor "spatial" conceptions of community, while neglecting "social" conceptions based on shared affiliations (Napoli 2001, 220). But as Christopher Ali notes, though audiences are "place-based" by nature, they are rarely "place-bound" in their identities and interests (2017, 45)—a proposition confirmed by the FCC's 1962 investigations of Chicago television, which concluded that local interests were defined less by viewers' shared identity as Chicagoans than by their broader racial, class, and political affiliations (Anderson and Curtin 1997). However, to say Chicago School productions were "from" Chicago but not strictly "for" Chicagoans would still leave uninterrogated "Chicago" itself as a sign of community produced in and through these programs. Recognizing that "place" is "not [an] intrinsically coherent," stable concept but rather "open . . . internally multiple," and subject to constant reinvention (Massey 2005, 141), I embrace the concept of critical regionalism propounded by cultural geographers and media scholars who cast the local as at least, in part, a product of discourses mobilized in and around cultural texts (Powell 2007; Ali 2017). Naming "the show that comes from Chicago" in this sense does not merely designate a preexisting point of geographical origin but actively constructs a place-based identity, affirming "Chicago" as a site of cultural production while also producing it as a culturally branded product for circulation in the national marketplace.

Chicago School productions also trouble the "alternative" status commonly ascribed to local media. This label often connotes an "explicitly oppositional quality" (Lievrouw 2011, 18–19), with scholars of local media citing their role in defending "local cultural identities and sociopolitical autonomy" (Howley 2005, 40) and promoting the "social and political 'empowerment'" of underrepresented groups (Jankowski 2003, 7). Others, however, argue alternative media as not inherently oppositional but nonetheless having different missions and goals, funding sources and organizational models, content and production practices, and audiences and distribution ranges than mainstream media (Lewis 1993, 12). Chicago originations like Garroway's and Sherman's were created by industry professionals at network owned and operated stations that sought to move their local successes to a national stage. Lacking what Mills (qtd. in Shayon 1950) described as the "money-built," "zim-zam-zowie" appeal of East Coast shows backed by Madison Avenue dollars or access to LA acting talent, Chicago productions were embraced by critics as a third way "between New York and Hollywood" (Shayon 1950), with a stripped-down aesthetic centered on hosts who roamed freely over skeletal studio sets to expose backstage machinery and break the "fourth wall," creating a "feeling of immediacy" and "sense of a show that was happening now" (Sternberg 1997, 244). Their performance styles accentuated this feeling through direct, informal modes of address that communication scholars Donald Horton and Richard Wohl likened to "chatting with a friend over a highball late in the evening" and cited as exemplary of the new forms of "parasocial interaction" (1956) engendered by television. Chicago productions might in this sense meet Spigel's (2019, 6) conception of local television as often employing "highly conventionalized forms of presentation and representation" but speaking with distinctive local "accents." Yet there was also little necessary connection between the Chicago style and its namesake, with WNBQ manager Jules Herbuveaux (1953, 34) himself conceding it was "just a name for something that started here but could be done anywhere."

Being local in origin but not necessarily in orientation, Chicago School productions catered to audiences that were place based but never strictly place bound in their viewing interests. Converting their economically driven production strategies into signs of aesthetic distinction, producers celebrated their Chicago origins as a branding strategy and point of cultural pride but positioned their shows not as radical alternatives to so much as alternative forms of network programming. Understanding the spatial politics of the network spaces through which these programs circulated, the production logics behind them, and the styles and meanings associated with them, the next section takes another look at Chicago School programming through the lens of Lefebvre's spatial theories.

THE CHICAGO SCHOOL, TAKE 2: A LEFEBVRIAN APPROACH

While Lefebvre's work is seldom mentioned in traditional media histories, several recent studies have suggested its value for understanding both production (Ali 2017, 203; Fuchs 2019) and reception practices (Spigel 2022, 42). Applying Lefebvre to the Chicago School, I focus specifically on his "spatial triad," which includes (1) a society's dominant mode of "spatial practice" (organized by larger socioeconomic forces to create a "perceived space" for prestructured public and private uses), (2) "representations of space" (the abstract, "conceived space" of society's planners that reveals often unseen logics behind its spatial practice), and (3) "spaces of representation" (the "lived space" of everyday experience, expressed through cultural works and other meaning-making activities that can either reinforce or contradict dominant spatial practice) (Lefebvre 1991, 38–39).[2] Addressing his triad's relevance for communication studies, Lefebvre (369) proposes analyzing spatial practices entailed by the physical configurations, or "form," of a given communication system (belonging to the "realm of the *perceived*"), their supporting structural logics (how that "structure is *conceived*" by its controlling institutions), and functional meanings of the communications generated within and around them (which are "carried out, effectively or not," through "the *directly experienced* in a space of representation"). Casting my three problematics for defining local media in these terms, local television's relationship to national broadcasting may be studied through the *forms* of their communication systems (locally originated and/or oriented content), their *conceived* goals (the communities and services at which they aim), and the *programming styles* and *mean-*

ings they afford (whether dominant or oppositional). Elaborating each in turn, I show how Lefebvre's triad can help illuminate Chicago School interventions into historical production practices, industrial logics, and cultural meanings of an emerging postwar U.S. television system.

SPATIAL PRACTICE

Lefebvre (1991, 38) defines spatial practice under modern capitalism as the "routes and networks that link up the places set aside for work, 'private' life and leisure," which social agents navigate through "daily routines" with a learned "spatial competence and performance."[3] The foundational assumption of local television as a distinctive form of communication is that its routes and networks differ substantially from national broadcasting, being often smaller in scale and more closely tied to its point of origin in its content and viewership. While local television sometimes uses citizen producers or formats with active viewer participation, its sociospatial architecture entails the same, one-to-many transmission and separation of production and reception sites as other mass media—a constitutive gap whose bridging demands mastery of effective habits and competencies at both ends of the communication chain. Chicago School productions emphasized their local origination but sought to compete at a national level and reflexively invoked the network architectures of which they were a part, while also explicitly acknowledging spatial practices of both their audiences and production staff in efforts to bridge the gaps in television's inherently distanciated modes of communication.

National broadcasting offers an enduring fiction of a homogeneous programming space and unified national address, but television production and reception always occur in specific locales with their own inherent logics of place. As Lefebvre (1991, 347) notes, while capitalism produces an "abstract space" that can be manipulated to facilitate global flows of capital, communication, commodities, and labor, it also fragments and variegates space through distributed networks whose different nodes and centers have their own spatial territories; "radiating out from centres, each space, each spatial interval, is a vector of constraints and a bearer of norms and 'values,'" which can sometimes reinforce but other times contradict each other (356). Upon completion of a coaxial connection between WNBQ and New York in January 1949, Chicago programs were transmitted live to NBC's East Coast affiliates and recorded off-screen onto kinescope films for distribution to stations beyond its wired network.[4]

Experienced at different times in different places, Garroway and Sherman's shows also held uneven regional appeal. Sherman's show was cut by NBC early in 1951 due to poor ratings but maintained sufficient midwestern appeal to continue at WBKB-Chicago (Dave 1951), with network executives noting a similar "drop in national ratings" for Garroway's second season, despite his continued "popularity in Chicago," due to declining East Coast viewership (McFadyen 1951). This unevenness in regional ratings also indexed larger power struggles between NBC's New York and Chicago branches over control of national markets. Highlighting these tensions in closing "snappers" after the end credits, Garroway would quip, "'This is Chicago, the short end of the coaxial cable,'" then "pick up a cable, and disappear in a puff of smoke" (Gillenson 1954, 124–25), or announce that "[this] telecast is coming to you by coaxial cable—" as he sliced a wire in half, the image went black, then returned to show him "putting the ends together again as you heard the words, '—from Chicago'" (Wolters 1949, N8). Offering viewers phatic affirmation of the fact of connection, such gags also dramatized gaps and tensions within NBC's evolving network infrastructure, asserting local differences within the routes and connections of an otherwise abstract network space.

Producing stable network spaces demanded inculcating regular audience viewing habits that could be integrated into routines of daily life. In his initial theory of space, Lefebvre (1991, 205) proposed the concept of a "'rhythm analysis'" that he later developed into a "theory of moments" whose regularized form, content, and meaning are achieved through systematic repetition that makes each moment distinctive but also habitual (2014, 634–52). Television viewing, he argued, possessed these characteristics, with the viewer "sitting in his armchair . . . witness[ing] the universe . . . at the same time, day in and day out" (370). The routine qualities of this domestic viewing, he cautioned, left audiences vulnerable to manipulation by "highly skillful" but insincere screen personalities whose "art of presenting the everyday" reduced it to empty signs through "personalized (but superficial) anecdotes, trivial incidents" and everyday "language . . . values, and symbols" that were "worn down" and stripped of meaning (370). While reception spaces for postwar U.S. television ranged from taverns (McCarthy 2001, 29–62) to public theaters (Hilmes 1990, 120–23), Chicago productions actively catered to domestic viewing contexts using techniques well established by Lefebvre's time. Sherman began each show seated in a parlor chair, thanking his audience "for coming over this afternoon" and sharing a personal anecdote, then previewing what-

Fig. 1.1. Ransom Sherman poses with John the moose head from the set of his show in a publicity still for a December 1950 issue of *TV Times*. While Sherman's program was short-lived, it was celebrated by critics and heavily promoted in period magazines. Author's collection.

ever (assuredly disastrous) "home improvement" features he had in store (Cassidy 2005, 32), while also referencing events from earlier broadcasts that week—thus affirming his show's status as serial daytime viewing for domestic audiences (figure 1.1). Garroway similarly opened with greetings like, "Good evening, good to see you at home... if you weren't home... we wouldn't be together on Sunday nights, which we love pretty much" (*GAL* 1951a), then offering what Mills (1950b) described as "warm homilies... about the world we live in and its occasional travail[s] as well as its gaiety," delivered in a "totally sincere," unaffected manner. Lefebvre's concerns about potential abuses of these techniques aside, their deployment in Chicago productions helped cultivate regular viewing habits and restore a sense of direct connection to television's otherwise distanciated mass communications.

While on-screen performance practices were vital for producing effective spatial connections for television communication, so too were activities of off-screen workers who pursued their own routinized practices in broadcasting studios and connected spaces. This normally off-screen work was placed on prominent display in Sherman's and Garroway's shows, which employed an "operational aesthetic" (Harris 1973) that

Fig. 1.2. Both Sherman's and Garroway's shows reveled in an operational aesthetic that laid bare their own production mechanisms. A 1950 Christmas broadcast of *Garroway at Large* (top) told the tale of a senior stagehand, shown walking past a closet of exposed set pieces to adjust a piano in front of the in-frame camera, while a 1951 broadcast (bottom) made the boom mic a featured character and showcased the work of microphone operator Walt McKechnie. Author's collection.

took listeners behind the scenes to see how their illusions were created. Both hosts regularly engaged in on-screen banter with their respective bandleaders Art Van Demme and Joseph Gallicio, with Sherman centering an entire bit in one broadcast (*RSS* 1950a) on repairing his bassist's instrument (broken by Sherman, it was revealed) so his band could do its usual background accompaniment. Garroway also regularly interacted with crew members, and in a 1950 Christmas Eve broadcast from WNBQ's Merchandise Mart studios (*GAL* 1950) brought staff writer Charlie Andrews on-screen to acknowledge his labor and introduce an ode he had written to the production crew. Dedicated to "the guys who make the show possible—the electricians, ... stagehands ... dolly pushers ... set designers, costume people, makeup people ... the people ... you never see but who make what you see look good," the segment brought these off-screen workers into the frame and ended with the camera dollying past exposed set pieces down a row of assembled crew members (figure 1.2a). Another broadcast two weeks later (*GAL* 1951a) featured the boom microphone as on-screen character, whom Garroway greeted as it dipped into frame, saying, "Why don't you just stay down... and let the folks see how you work," then plied with questions as operator Walt McKechnie, introduced by Garroway and visible in the background, adjusted its height and angle to simulate shakes yes and no (figure 1.2b). Creating a sense of authentic connection for program viewers, these strategies brought normally off-screen spaces into the television picture, placing its production apparatus on direct public display.

Spaces beyond the walls of the studio were highlighted to similar effect, most notably in Sherman's broadcasts from Chicago's Studebaker Theater. Leased by WNBQ, the theater was connected to the station by coax and from there to the rest of NBC's network. In addition to musical numbers, fashion tips, and home improvement segments, Sherman featured a weekly "film review" during which he threw to control room operators to run a prepared clip (*RSS* 1950a, 1950b), invariably the same stock footage of a horse-drawn carriage bearing no connection to the previewed content. Sherman continued on seemingly unaware of the mix-up—no doubt puzzling newcomers but rewarding regular viewers who were in on the joke, as well as his production crew, who could be heard laughing off-camera. Like Garroway's gag of severing his station's coax connection only to magically reappear moments later, these contrived technological failures underscored a tenuousness of connection that Paddy Scannell (2014) argues is part of television's essential architecture and allure—offering a sense of "being in the moment" that opened onto a distinctly televisual sublime, in Kant's (1989, 115) sense of "look[ing] out into . . . the abyss" to triumph in the survival of one's own destruction. Bringing viewers to the edge and back again from within the safety of their own homes, these staged collapses of communication invited critical reflection on tensions and liabilities of an emergent network space, while affirming television's capacity to endure such disruptions and connect its spatially dispersed audiences in a shared cultural experience.

REPRESENTATIONS OF SPACE

Dominant spatial practices are reinforced in Lefebvre's (1991) theory through hegemonic representations of space, which he sees as the province of "scientists, planners, urbanists, technocratic subdividers and . . . a certain type of artist with a scientific bent," who work across state and civil institutions to ensure the needs of society's prevailing mode of production are successfully met (38–39). Representations of space, he elaborates, are abstract conceptions revealed through architectural drawings or other planning documents that provide blueprints for construction of real-life spaces, as well as verbally through "discourses on space" that are fixed through professional training and produce dominant "spatial codes" (16) such as the "code of linear perspective" that emerged during the Renaissance and impacted everything from urban planning to painting and modern architecture (41). Applying Lefebvre's theory to popular entertainment, theater scholar Ceri Watkins (2005, 212–13) notes that the conceived space of a performance is often documented in "the script ... the composer's score ... 'notes' from the director [or] producer," and other production records, using standardized "symbol systems and codifications." Surviving records for Garroway's and Sherman's shows enable close analysis of production logics structuring their own staging and shooting, which despite their alternative status largely conformed to industry norms. Nonetheless, these shows also broke with convention in several noteworthy ways, which were celebrated by period critics and flaunted by the programs themselves in overt parodies of standard television formats.

While Chicago School promoters championed its programs as more improvised and pared down in style than their flashier, over-rehearsed New York and Hollywood competitors, extant production records suggest production processes were largely consistent with other programs. Newspaper critic John Crosby (1950b, B13), seldom a fan of New York production trends, applauded Sherman for "methods of putting a show together [that] flabbergast everybody else in the business" since "there isn't any script," with dialogue largely improvised and staging worked out in rehearsals of just twelve minutes for each half-hour program. Producer Ted Mills (qtd. in Sternberg 1997, 244) cast this "scriptlessness" as "the distinguishing characteristic" of the Chicago School, insisting they "didn't believe in the conventional form of first you get a script, then you get actors to rehearse it and then you go," while Herbuveaux (qtd. in *Time* 1950a, 74) explained this improvised character as part of a larger economical style whose stripped-down scenery, limited camera changes, and sparing use of special effects stemmed from lack of staff and equipment. Launched on a "sustaining" basis, Sherman failed to attract national sponsors (*Variety* 1950) and may have enjoyed more leeway; but, as a single-sponsor show bankrolled by linoleum maker Congoleum-Nairn, Garroway's underwent the same planning and rehearsals as other network productions. Scripts for commercials were submitted by New York advertising agency McCann-Erickson for sponsor approval over a month in advance and included precise dialogue for Garroway's product pitches and lists of needed props and set pieces (Nairn 1951), with remaining planning starting three weeks before scheduled airdates (Mills 1951; Stasheff and Bretz 1951, 313). While Herbuveaux cited his shows' minimalist style and lack of resources, 1950 print promotions touted *Garroway at Large* as a three-camera production shot in WNBQ's fully decked, "ultra-modern" studios with "elaborate" special effects (*Broadcasting* 1950c, 60), and scripts provided by Mills himself for a 1951 production book (Stasheff and Bretz 1951, acknowledgments) showed the program now using a state-of-the-art, four-camera setup (318–39). On-screen dialogue highlighted these multicamera capabilities, which were mentioned twice in the 1950 Christmas show alone as director Bill Hobin, then Garroway, instructed staff to switch to Camera 4 while the image changed on cue. Final scripts had mere synopses of dialogue in places, leaving Garroway substantial latitude in delivery (312–13), but also featured semiregular fully scripted sketches from which he was even shown reading on-camera (*GAL* 1950).[5] Scripts also included standard notation of camera changes and music cues, with Mills demanding close rehearsal. "It's imperative . . . you . . . go over the entire script . . . shot-by-shot" (Mills 1950a), he warned, giving staff at least one week to work out each show's staging and effects, then a full day for final camera rehearsals (Stasheff and Bretz 1951, 212–14).

Codes of representation for on-screen space in Chicago programs similarly both respected and refuted hegemonic industry norms. While deviating from mainstream programming in terms of *what* they shot by including normally invisible areas of the studio floor and backstage regions, *how* they shot these spaces followed established conventions of "invisible editing," creating a seamless diegetic space with adequate lighting and close miking for intelligible dialogue, wherever in the studio their program hosts might roam. But different programs also have their own, genre-specific codes of representation, from which Sherman and Garroway strategically distanced themselves through active parody. One of Sherman's broadcasts (*RSS* 1950a) featured a "Do It Yourself" session with shelves bearing the unsightly products of past weeks' lessons, which he boasted, "you, too, can make at home," using "the American know-how" extolled in "the magazines that you read," then launched a new lesson on picket fences replete with tips like "never let your fingers get under the hammer if you can help it—because it spoils any manicure," drawing off-screen chuckles from his female cast members. A satirical sketch from a 1951 Garroway broadcast titled "Television Tube" (*GAL* 1951b) took prime-time programming as its target, featuring cast member Cliff Norton channel surfing in a segment designed to "show you what the television eye sees when the average viewers turns on his set." First tuning in a comedy variety host with bad jokes and blander guest (billed as the world's "greatest bird imitator"), Norton changes to an episode of "Dick Glory, Private Eye," whose violent gunplay makes him cringe but is mercifully interrupted by an ad for Oooomslaught Quick Frozen Pre-Dunked Doughnuts ("enjoy soggy doughnuts any time of the day or night!"), which sends him to his own fridge for a beer. Returning to find a romance film playing, he leans in for the climactic kiss but is startled by a cut to a commercial for Floops Beer, spilling his own then storming out in disgust. Such commentary on prevailing genre conventions produced signs of distinction for Chicago School programs, though suggests the representational codes they parodied were not just the province of expert planners but also recognized and shared with a knowing public who was in on the joke. Codes of spatial representation, in other words, are not always abstract, hidden, or hegemonic but may themselves be subjects of explicit commentary in works that deploy and critique them. Assessing the efficacy of those interventions, however, requires consideration of the final point in Lefebvre's triad.

SPACES OF REPRESENTATION

Determining whether styles and meanings of Chicago School programming were experienced by audiences as recognizably different and valued alternatives to standard network fare demands closer study of the spaces of representation cultivated in and by these productions. For Lefebvre (1991, 39), a space of representation is "space as directly *lived* through its associated images and symbols, and hence the space of 'inhabitants' and 'users'" (39). "Products of spaces of representation" range from individual "memories [and] dreams" of everyday laypeople to "symbolic works" of "artists . . . writers and philosophers" (41–42) who interpret the world around them through representational styles that can be "unique [or] sometimes shape larger aesthetic movements" (1981, 53). While subscribing in this sense to expressionist theories that see artworks as expressing artists' own experience of the world, Lefebvre is ultimately concerned with how these works resonate with their intended viewership and their capacity, "by putting up resistance, [to inaugurate] the project of a different space (either in the space of a counter-culture, or a counter-space in the sense of an initially utopian alternative to actually existing real space)" (1991, 349). "That the lived, conceived and perceived realms should be interconnected ... is a logical necessity," he elaborates, but "whether they constitute a coherent whole is another matter" and a key question for materialist histories of art and popular culture (40). While the Chicago style held recognizably distinct and salient attributes for period audiences that distinguished it from other programming, at a functional level it failed to radically alter dominant production practices or disrupt control of power within the emerging network system. At the same time, its aesthetic innovations did not simply disappear but were rather subsumed by the same New York- and Hollywood-based programs they initially sought to supplant.

Proponents of the Chicago style typically highlighted as a distinguishing feature its producers' ability to play to the distinctly visual nature of their medium. Mills explained that at the core of WNBQ's philosophy was that "TV is a new field ... for creative work" (qtd. in *Broadcasting* 1950c, 50), insisting on the need to free it from "rigid patterns of radio thinking" by cultivating distinctly telegenic modes of screen presentation (Mills 1956). As Crosby (1950a, B11) noted in reviews of Sherman's show, his screen persona was familiar to audiences of the *Club Matinee* program he had hosted for CBS radio, and he was "borrowing liberally from his old radio show"; but his wildly poor demonstrations—from baffling charts and graphs to false animal identifications and frequent fashion disasters—achieved their full impact only on television. "It would have been a shame to have wasted those wonderfully crazy stunts on a nonvisual medium," Crosby concluded, adding that "Sherman has to be seen to be fully appreciated." *Chicago Tribune* columnist Larry Wolters (1949, N8) showed a similar fascination with Garroway's on-screen antics, as a performer who "with big horn rim glasses and deadpan look, wanders a bit aimlessly but always amiably thru the sketches, the music and the gags." Stressing the program's visual qualities, he concluded, "It is no easy matter to set down in words just what the Garroway show is like," as "you have to see it to savor it."

Production planning for Garroway's program focused mainly on elaborate camera changes, lighting, and special effects for its weekly musical productions, which offered more dynamic and stylized counterpoints

Fig. 1.3. Segments of *Garroway at Large* where Garroway spoke to audiences between performances had a relatively stripped-down visual style, but musical numbers were more stylized, with experimental cinematography and special effects. The first-season rendering of Richard Rodgers's *Slaughter on Tenth Avenue* (1949–50) featured creative framings of performers shot through a percussion triangle as well as shots of dancers superimposed on a piano keyboard to give the effect of them sliding down the keys as the pianist executed a run. Author's collection.

to his surrounding dialogue. A prominent example was the first-season broadcast of composer Richard Rodgers's jazz ballet *Slaughter on Tenth Avenue* (*GAL* 1949–50).[6] Billed as a production "for Dancers, Cameras, and Orchestra," it opened with dollies in and pans across the orchestra, then cut to a close-up of a gong strike with superimposed shot of two dancers spinning against a black background. More pans across the orchestra followed, then close-ups of the pianist's fingers sliding across the keyboard, shots of different instruments making their entrances, graphic matches between the bouncing tympani mallets and dancers bobbing up and down, shots through harp strings, and dancers weaving through lit columns that receded in forced perspective against an otherwise darkened stage (figures 1.3a, 1.3b, 1.3c). Mobilizing discourses of visual distinction in his introduction, Garroway proclaimed that "television is very different than anything else—it's different than the movies, different than the radio, quite different than the stage . . . a thing all in itself" and applauded his director, Hobin, for "[showing us] how to use it." Garroway's personal penchant for jazz (Garroway n.d.) inspired other noteworthy experiments, such as a summer 1951 broadcast (*GAL* 1951c) featuring Duke Ellington saxophonist Johnny Hodges that included split-screen shots of him playing wild riffs on the left as waveforms captured off an oscilloscope raced

Fig. 1.4. A summer 1951 broadcast of *Garroway at Large* featured performances by Duke Ellington saxophonist Johnny Hodges, using a split-screen effect with Hodges playing on one side and close-ups of the corresponding oscilloscope waveforms on the other. Author's collection.

up the right (figures 1.4a, 1.4b). Similar incorporations of oscilloscope imagery were featured a decade later on Ernie Kovacs's celebrated ABC program, for which Kovacs cited Garroway as a key influence (Spigel 2008, 196–97), while NBC and CBS soon embraced experimental cinematography and "skeletal sets" similar to Slaughter's alongside other elements of "modern design" across their prime-time programming (47–57). Functionally speaking, these shows may have innovated but failed to revolutionize, their stylistic experiments proving largely compatible with an emerging network system that absorbed them into its broader production palette. Nonetheless, they cultivated a distinctive space of representation by promoting an experimental, countercultural ethos that set them apart from other productions in the eyes of their audiences and critics.

While NBC canceled both shows within months of each other in spring 1951, the performers' fates proved markedly different. Sherman's anarchic parody was cloistered away in an undesirable daytime slot where defenders complained it "never even had a chance" to attract appreciative audiences or sponsors (*Broadcasting-Telecasting* 1951a, 75). An ardent supporter, Crosby (1952, 13) continued advocating for Sherman through 1952, arguing that congressional attention to smoking and drinking on television might be better directed toward circumstances surrounding "removal of Ransom Sherman, a genuinely witty man, from the air"; however, his calls fell on deaf ears, with Sherman returning to local broadcasting (Dave 1951, 43) but never regaining his former national reach. In a 1953 column, Chicago broadcaster Studs Terkel (1953, 34) explained that Garroway, like his own short-lived *Stud's Place* on ABC, fared better than Sherman in winning successful sponsors but fell victim to the same "Manhattan monkey-monks" and "Eastern panjandrums," who preferred tried-and-true formulas over programming with more "imagination"—"it appears," he opined, "the cards are stacked against Chicago by the Big Dealers on the sunny side of the Hudson."[7] But if Garroway's program was gone, his NBC contract had not expired (Wolters 1951), with network president Sylvester "Pat" Weaver selecting him to host their New York–based *Today* show launched in January 1952 and concurrent *Dial Dave Garroway* radio program. Garroway would additionally host NBC's prestige international news program, *Wide, Wide World* (1955–58)—billed as "giv[ing] people a chance to go out of their homes to almost every part of our wide world" through live feeds from North American affiliates and throughout the world (National Broadcasting Company ca. 1956)—becoming the face of an entire network who appeared on everything from *Wide, Wide World* soundtrack album covers (Broekman 1955) to a *Mad* magazine parody (Davis 1955). If Sherman's anarchic comedy was managed through a strategy of containment that deflected it back to the local level, Garroway's post-*Garroway* success thus suggests a separate strategy of incorporation, with proclamations of the "death" of the Chicago School overlooking the extent to which his style was successfully absorbed by other network programs issuing from production centers outside of Chicago itself.

TARRYING WITH THE LOCAL: LESSONS OF THE CHICAGO SCHOOL

Subverting the network system was never the goal of Chicago producers, who instead sought to position themselves at the heart of emerging network markets by filling schedules with alternative content supplied by their "third coast" production centers. Approaches to media localism that cast the local in strict opposition to the national or global will prove inherently ill-equipped to capture the nuances of these relationships and types of production strategies, content, and forms of audience engagement they entailed. Conceptions of localism promoting it as fundamentally place based must also distinguish between television's relatively finite points of production and its more diverse sites of reception and audience identities, while allowing for definitions of alternative media content that do not cast it in inherently oppositional terms. Chicago School programs were locally produced but intended for broader national audiences, with the Chicago style serving as much as a national brand as any locally bound style geared toward viewers in a particular geographical place.

Lefebvre's theory of space offers a useful lens for apprehending the complex, shifting relationships between local and national production, content, and viewership that confront television histories at all levels. Locating a "style" within Lefebvre's spatial triad presents challenges for traditional television studies approaches, in that his system purposefully integrates analysis of production and consumption, while consideration of the "text" itself similarly traverses all three moments. The event of television communication and its attendant forms of spatial practice implicate both producers and viewers, who serve as coparticipants and through their respective production routines and viewing habits repeatedly enact its defining sets of sociospatial connections. While Chicago School producers positioned their shows as alternatives to New York and Hollywood, performers like Sherman and Garroway encouraged the same regularized viewing practices favored for other network programs, while bridging gaps between sender and receiver through direct, intimate modes of address and by inviting audiences backstage to be part of the action. At a structural level, spatial practice in Lefebvre's theory relies on shared codes of representation that originate within expert systems and tend to reflect dominant economic interests but whose efficacy I have argued also require public acceptance and validation. The types of diegetic spaces displayed in programs like Sherman's and Garroway's differed from other shows by reflexively foregrounding off-screen technologies and labor, showing higher degrees of improvisation, and parodying standard genre conventions. Nonetheless, their production methods remained largely consistent and compatible with other network programming.

In treating artistic schools and movements, Lefebvre focuses especially on spaces of representation, which as spaces of shared experience demand consideration of stylistic attributes with salient meanings for their intended viewing communities. Tracing these meanings requires close analysis not just of audience response but also of the programs themselves, while additionally recognizing discursive interventions by producers seeking to preemptively prime or shape viewer interpretations. To emphasize the Chicago School's efforts to exploit television's unique aesthetic capabilities through innovations in visual style is to accept what was in fact a strategic industrial positioning of these programs by cultural producers operating with tacit complicity of period viewers. Objectively speaking, these qualities are not empirically absent from Chicago School programs, but their purported uniqueness as distinguishing properties of the "Chicago style" says as much about the cultural meanings accorded them as any truth of the programs themselves. Lefebvre's concept of a space of representation invites a more unified theory of style that considers both its industrial positioning and its collective cultural meanings, combining elements of production studies, formalist analysis, and cultural studies approaches alike.

Equally important when considering spaces of representation in Lefebvre's theory are their potential to either reinforce or disrupt other moments in his triad. Assessing the impact of the Chicago School, I have argued, requires moving beyond the "death-of" narrative proffered by period commentators to evaluate the terms on which success of such "local" production initiatives is measured on a national stage. For historians who position the local in a struggle against the national, it may seem forever subject to encroachment, assault, and disappearance. Lessons of the Chicago School, by contrast, encourage consideration of what modes of appearance for the local are opened by the national, and how local productions might not just serve as alternatives to but can actively transform the larger totality in which they take place. The story of the Chicago School did not end with Sherman or Garroway; but the persistence of the Chicago style and its incorporation into mainstream television demands rethinking the terms of its success or failure, as well as the potential for any style to radically alter standing production systems without concomitant structural changes.

NOTES

1. Starting as a summer replacement series for *Kukla, Fran and Ollie* in July–August 1950 (*Broadcasting* 1950a, 1950b), Sherman's show then continued from October to December (Don 1950), at least into January (*Variety* 1951). Two undated episodes are preserved in undated kinescope copies, with rough dates assigned based on in-episode references.
2. While I largely respect translations by Nicholson-Smith (Lefebvre 1991), for Lefebvre's third category, *espaces de representation*, I embrace the more literal translation proposed by Shields (1999, 162n5, 165) and pursue several additional direct translations from the original French (Lefebvre 1981).
3. Lefebvre uses *l'espace perçu*, playing on its double meaning of space as actively "perceived" but also given or "received." As Lefebvre's interpreters have noted, dominant uses of space in his theory are continually (re)enacted by social agents but also prescribed and routinized through prior social conventions (Kinkaid 2020).
4. Live transcontinental broadcasts did not begin until after the fall of 1951 (*Broadcasting-Telecasting* 1951b), with East Coast programs still often time-delayed for later West Coast viewing.

5. While these sketches required extra payment beyond writers' normal salaries, Mills petitioned NBC for funds to include them as frequently as possible (Mills 1951).
6. Separate from a second-season appearance by Rodgers himself (*New York Herald Tribune* 1950), this broadcast is identified in internal correspondence as airing sometime prior to May 29, 1950 (Mills 1950b).
7. Terkel's show (WENR, 1949–50) featured him as a Chicago diner owner conversing with local characters.

REFERENCES

ARCHIVAL COLLECTIONS

Dave Garroway Papers, American Heritage Center, University of Wyoming, Laramie (DGP-AHC).

Herbert Sussan Papers, American Heritage Center, University of Wyoming, Laramie (HSP-AHC).

Lee Lawrence Papers, Special Collections in Mass Media and Culture, Hornbake Library, University of Maryland, College Park (LLP-UMD).

National Broadcasting Company Records, Wisconsin Historical Society, Madison (NBC-WHS).

President's Office Records, Indiana University Archives, Wells Library, Bloomington (PR-IUA).

Ransom Sherman Papers, American Heritage Center, University of Wyoming, Laramie (RSP-AHC).

Rich Samuels, "The Best of 'Garroway at Large,'" http://www.richsamuels.com/nbcmm/garroway/bestofgal.html (GAL-BIC).

Television Collection, Museum of Broadcast Communications, Chicago (TC-MBC).

SOURCES

Ali, Christopher. 2017. *Media Localism: The Policies of Place*. University of Illinois Press.

Anderson, Christopher, and Michael Curtin. 1997. "Mapping the Ethereal City: Chicago Television, the FCC, and the Politics of Place." *Quarterly Review of Film and Video* 16 (3–4): 289–305.

Billboard. 1950. "Brief and Important." October 7, 6.

Broadcasting. 1950a. "Network Shows, August 1950." August 7, insert facing 54–55.

———. 1950b. "Network Shows, July 1950." July 3, 58–59.

———. 1950c. "Telefile: Creative Programming Highlights WNBQ (TV) Success." January 9, 50–51, 60–61.

Broadcasting-Telecasting. 1951a. "Chicago TV Loss: Davis Blames Networks." December 3, 75.

———. 1951b. "Coast-to-Coast TV: Truman Inaugurates." September 10, 26, 30.

Broekman, David, and His Orchestra. 1955. *Music from Wide, Wide World*. LP, RCA-Victor.

Cassidy, Marsha F. 2005. *What Women Watched: Daytime Television in the 1950s*. University of Texas Press.
Crosby, John. 1950a. "How Can Sherman Be Funny So Often?" *Washington Post*, August 22, B11.
———. 1950b. "Sherman Still Has Faith in People." *Washington Post*, October 11, B13.
———. 1952. "The Smoke Blowers and the Lip Smackers." *New York Herald Tribune*, September 29, 13.
Curtin, Michael. 2014. "Global Media Capital and Local Media Policy." In *Handbook of Political Economy of Communications*, edited by Janet Wasko, Graham Murdock, and Helena Sousa, 541–57. Wiley-Blackwell.
Dave. 1950. "The Ransom Sherman Show." *Variety*, July 12, 26.
———. 1951. "Ransom Sherman Show." *Variety*, October 24, 43.
Davis, Jack. 1955. "The Dave Garronaway Show." *Mad*, November, 6–11.
Don. 1950. "Ransom Sherman Show." *Variety*, October 18, 29.
Fuchs, Christian. 2019. "Henri Lefebvre's Theory of the Production of Space and the Critical Theory of Communication." *Critical Theory* 29:129–50.
Garroway at Large (GAL). 1949–50. 16mm NBC kinescope film transfer from WNBQ (Chicago), first season broadcast (airdate unknown). Partial copy at GAL-BIC, "The Best of 'Garroway at Large': Part I."
———. 1950. 16mm NBC kinescope film transfer from WNBQ (Chicago), originally aired December 24 (aka "The Christmas Show"). Full copy at Television Collection, Museum of Broadcast Communications, Chicago (TC-MBC).
———. 1951a. 16mm NBC kinescope film transfer from WNBQ (Chicago), originally aired January 14. Full copy at TC-MBC.
———. 1951b. Script for April 8 broadcast. DGP-AHC, box 2, Programs and Appearances—Misc, ca. 1951–76 folder.
———. 1951c. 16mm NBC kinescope film transfer from WNBQ (Chicago), originally aired June 10. Partial copy at GAL-BIC, "The Best of 'Garroway at Large': Part IV."
Garroway, Dave. n.d. Undated autobiography, transcribed by Lee Lawrence, LLP-UMD, series 5.5, folders 1–3.
Gillenson, Lewis W. 1954. "Garroway Today." *Cosmopolitan*, September, 120–25.
Godfrey, Donald G., and Michael D. Murray. 1997. "Introduction: Origins of Innovation." In *Television in America: Local Station History from Across the Nation*, edited by Godfrey and Murray, xiii–xxvii. Iowa State University.
Harris, Neil. 1973. *Humbug: The Art of P. T. Barnum*. University of Chicago Press.
Herbuveaux, Jules. 1953. "Chi TV Parlays a Myth into B.O. Inventiveness." *Variety*, May 27, 34.
Hilliard, Robert L., and Michael C. Keith. 2005. *The Quieted Voice: The Rise and Demise of Localism in American Radio*. Southern Illinois University.
Hilmes, Michele. 1990. *Hollywood and Broadcasting: From Radio to Cable*. University of Illinois Press.

Hollywood Reporter. 1953. "ABC Spurs Chi Radio-TV Rebirth." June 5, 1, 4.

Horton, Donald, and R. Richard Wohl. 1956. "Mass Communication and Parasocial Interaction: Observations on Intimacy at a Distance." *Psychiatry*, August 1, 215–25.

Howley, Kevin. 2005. *Community Media: People, Places, and Communication Technologies.* Cambridge University Press.

Jankowski, Nicholas. 2003. "Community Media Research: A Quest for Theoretically-Grounded Models." *Journal of the European Institute for Communication and Culture* 10 (1): 5–14.

Kant, Immanuel. 1989. *The Critique of Judgement.* Translated by James Creed Meredith. Oxford University Press.

Kinkaid, Eden. 2020. "Re-encountering Lefebvre: Toward a Critical Phenomenology of Social Space." *Society and Space* 38 (1): 167–86.

Kirkpatrick, Bill. 2006. "Localism in American Media Policy, 1920–1934: Reconsidering a 'Bedrock Concept.'" *Radio Journal* 4 (1–3): 87–110.

Lefebvre, Henri. 1981. *La production de l'espace.* 2nd ed. Anthropos.

———. 1991. *The Production of Space.* Translated by Donald Nicholson-Smith. Blackwell.

———. 2014. *Critique of Everyday Life.* One-volume ed. Translated by John Moore and Gregory Elliott. Verso.

Lewis, Peter, ed. 1993. *Alternative Media: Linking Global and Local.* UNESCO.

Lievrouw, Leah A. 2011. *Alternative and Activist New Media: Digital Media and Society Series.* Polity.

Life. 1950. "Mr. No Fixit: Ransom Sherman Is a TV Apostle of Self-Satisfied Incompetence." August 20, 112, 115.

Mabley, Jack. 1951. "City Feeds TV Chains 22 Shows." *Chicago Daily News*, September 17. DGP, box 1, Newspaper Clippings, 1951 folder.

Massey, Doreen. 2005. *For Space.* SAGE.

McCarthy, Anna. 2001. *Ambient Television.* Duke University Press.

McFadyen, Robert W. 1951. Letter to Ted Mills, January 11. NBC-WHS, box 119, folder 88.

Mills, Ted. 1950a. Letter to Bill Hobin, January 25. DGP-AHC, box 1, Misc. Inter-Office Memos, 1949–51 folder.

———. 1950b. Letter to Dave Garroway, May 29. DGP-AHC, box 1, Misc. Inter-Office Memos, 1949–51 folder.

———. 1951. Letter to Sylvester L. Weaver, January 9. DGP-AHC, box 1, Misc. Inter-Office Memos, 1949–51 folder.

———. 1956. "Television Comes of Age." Speech delivered at Annual Indiana University Radio and Television Banquet, May 1. PR-IUA, box 458, Radio and Television 1955–56 folder.

Nairn Inlaid Linoleum. 1951. Commercial script and spec sheet for April 8 *Garroway at Large* broadcast. DGP-AHC, box 2, Programs and Appearances—Misc. ca. 1951–76 folder.

Napoli, Philip M. 2001. *Foundations of Communications Policy: Principles and Process in the Regulation of Electronic Media*. Hampton.

National Broadcasting Company. ca. 1956. *Wide, Wide World* promotional booklet. HSP-AHC, box 2, loose materials.

New York Herald Tribune. 1950. "Today's Television Notes." November 12, D8.

Pickard, Victor. 2011. "The Battle over the FCC Blue Book: Determining the Role of Broadcast Media in a Democratic Society, 1945–8." *Media, Culture & Society* 33 (2): 171–91.

Powell, Douglas Reichert. 2007. *Critical Regionalism: Connecting Politics and Culture in the American Landscape*. University of North Carolina Press.

Ransom Sherman Show (RSS). 1950a. RSP, box 1, 16mm NBC kinescope film, WNBQ (Chicago) broadcast ca. July.

———. 1950b. RSP, box 1, 16mm NBC kinescope film, WNBQ (Chicago) broadcast ca. August–September.

Scannell, Paddy. 2014. *Television and the Meaning of Live*. Polity.

Shayon, Robert Lewis. 1950. "Toynbee, TV, and Chicago." *Christian Science Monitor*, June 3. Reprinted in Robert Lewis Shayon, *Open to Criticism* (Beacon, 1971), 97–104.

———. 1958. "Chicago's Local TV Corpse." *Saturday Review*, October 11, 32.

Shields, Rob. 1999. *Lefebvre, Love and Struggle: Spatial Dialectics*. Routledge.

Spigel, Lynn. 2008. *TV by Design: Modern Art and the Rise of Network Television*. University of Chicago.

———. 2019. "Introduction: The Peabody Awards Collection, the Archive, and Local TV History." In *Television History, the Peabody Archive, and Cultural Memory*, edited by Ethan Thompson, Jeffrey P. Jones, and Lucas Hatlen, 1–16. University of Georgia Press.

———. 2022. *TV Snapshots: An Archive of Everyday Life*. Duke University Press.

Stasheff, Edward, and Rudy Bretz. 1951. *The Television Program: Its Writing, Direction and Production*. A. A Wyn.

Sternberg, Joel. 1973. "A Descriptive History and Critical Analysis of the Chicago School of Television: Chicago Network Programming in the Chicago Style from 1948 to 1954." Ph.D. diss., Northwestern University.

———. 1997. "Chicago Television: A History." *Quarterly Review of Film and Video* 16 (3–4): 229–52.

Terkel, Studs. 1953. "Chi's TV Imagination vs. Radio City Panjandrums." *Variety*, May 27, 34.

Time. 1950a. "The Chicago School." September 11, 73–74.

———. 1950b. "School's Out." September 10. DGB, box 1, Newspaper Clippings, 1951 folder.

Variety. 1949. "Chi's Bid for TV Eminence." December 28, 23, 28.

———. 1950. "NBC Eyes Expansion of Comm'l Daytime Segments." December 27, 22.

———. 1951. "Tele-Chatter." January 10, 34.

———. 1953. "CBS Happy to Let Atlass Call Own Shots on Newly-Acquired WBBM-TV." February 25, 25.

Watkins, Ceri. 2005. "Representations of Space, Spatial Practices and Spaces of Representation: An Application of Lefebvre's Spatial Triad." *Culture and Organization* 11 (3): 209–20.

Williams, Mark. 1997. "U.S. Regional and Non-network Television History." *Quarterly Review of Film and Video* 16 (3–4): 221–28.

Wolters, Larry. 1949. "Garroway Has What It Takes for Television." *Chicago Daily Tribune*, October 9, N8.

———. 1951. "It's Wayne King on Video Again Each Thursday—Garroway, Alas, Has No Such Good Luck." *Chicago Tribune*, August 28, 1951. DGP-AHC, box 1, Newspaper Clippings, 1951 folder.

CHAPTER 2

DYFRIG JONES

LOCAL AND NATIONAL, PUBLIC AND PRIVATE

WOI-TV AND EARLY EDUCATIONAL TELEVISION IN THE UNITED STATES

This chapter examines the early history of WOI-TV, the first television station in the United States to be operated by an educational institution. Owned by Iowa State College (ISC), WOI-TV represented an approach to television entirely distinct from the rest of the nation, blending together public and private, commercial and educational, local and national. Inaugurated on February 21, 1950, WOI-TV boasted of being "1st in Educational Broadcasting," but what it offered its viewers during its early years was a mixture of education and entertainment, reflecting its status as a public institution operating in a commercial world. From 1950 until 1955 WOI-TV carried programs from each of the four national networks, ABC, CBS, DuMont, and NBC. This commercial offering was used to attract audiences but was interspersed with educational and sustaining programs produced by the station and squarely aimed at a local audience. Advertising was tightly regulated and commercial income reinvested in the production and broadcast of sustaining programs. The goal was to develop a television station that brought the best of American television to Ames, but also to build an audience for high-quality educational broadcasts that reflected the needs and the experiences of the local community.

This was a model that emerged from a unique set of circumstances in Ames, Iowa, but which—at the turn of the 1940s, at least—had the potential to be adopted in other parts of the United States. Indeed, this was the vision of its director, Richard Hull, who saw his hybrid of commercial and educational television as a model for other stations, particularly those outside major urban centers. As president of the National Association of Educational Broadcasters (NAEB), Hull sought to persuade other educational broadcasters of the merits of his hybrid model but was ultimately unsuccessful. WOI-TV's first broadcasts had taken place during the "Television Freeze" of 1948 to 1952, and the regulatory restrictions that existed during this period had initially protected the station from commercial competition. When the Federal Communications Commission (FCC) began issuing new television broadcast licenses in 1952, the new regulatory landscape was not able to accommodate WOI-TV's innovative ownership model and program policy. By the mid-1950s the pressure from its competitors had become too great, and there was little to distinguish the station's output from most commercial television. While WOI-TV remained in ISC's ownership until it was controversially sold in 1994, Hull's vision of a hybrid broadcasting model did not survive his departure from the station in 1956.

This chapter, drawing upon material held in the U.S. National Archives, the National Public Broadcasting Archives at the University of Maryland, and the Iowa State University Archives, explores the conditions that led to the establishment of WOI-TV and how the early history of this station can help us understand the ways in which local technological and regulatory factors shaped television—and particularly educational television (ETV)—as a national medium.

IOWA STATE COLLEGE: FIRST IN EDUCATIONAL BROADCASTING

While the establishment of WOI-TV represented a bold new experiment for ISC, it was not entirely without precedent. The college had played a prominent role in the development of educational radio throughout the 1930s and 1940s and had been an important member of NAEB. The college began to explore the possibilities of television as an educational medium as early as 1941 (Harl 2001, 1) and applied to the FCC for permission to build a television and FM radio transmitter in 1945. Permission was granted, and ISC soon found itself in the unique position of being an educational establishment in receipt of a commercial television license. This, as Richard Hull explained to college president Charles Friley on March 1, 1948 (WOI-TV Original Planning 1946–48), was a matter of necessity, as the FCC did not—in the 1940s at least—reserve television licenses for educational broadcasting.

In establishing WOI-TV, ISC understood that it was taking on an enormous challenge. Not least was the cost associated with establishing and running a television station, something that had proved a major stumbling block during the early years of educational radio. Powell (1962, 29) notes that several educational institutions had secured radio licenses during the late 1920s but were forced to sell them to commercial enterprises as they couldn't justify the investment necessary to get the station up and running.

Ensuring that the new venture was financially viable was far from ISC's only concern. Television advocates at Iowa State were conscious of the fact that they were the standard-bearers for a new medium, within both the university and the local community. WOI-TV would be the only television station broadcasting to central Iowa, including Des Moines, an area populated by some six hundred thousand people. In December 1949, a few months before WOI-TV began broadcasting, the ISC Standing Committee on Information and Public Relations wrote to President Friley to emphasize the significance of the venture that they were shortly due to embark upon. In contrast to the college's radio station, which offered purely educational fare, the commercially licensed WOI-TV would need to be "all things to all people" (Reports, Committee on Radio, FM and Television 1948).

As Lowe and Savage (2020 11) note, the principle of universalism—of "all things to all people"—had served as "a foundational principle for legitimating broadcasting as a public trust" since the 1930s. In practice, however, educational and noncommercial programing had often been pushed to the margins of the schedule, with both broadcasters and regulators relying upon pluralism to deliver a universal service. Technological and geographic constraints meant that central Iowa could not accommodate multiple television broadcasters, and ISC was therefore forced to grapple with the challenge of single-channel universalism. The college knew that it needed to both provide a range of programs that would attract an audience and sustain a reasonable number of broadcast hours per week. It also knew that their local station lacked the resources to achieve this by itself.

The committee's proposed solution was that WOI-TV enter into negotiations with ABC, CBS, DuMont, and NBC to discuss the possibility of network affiliation on a "semicommercial" basis. The college would retain "direct and continuous control of the television facility" at all times and would not accept advertisements from any businesses based in Iowa, nor would it accept advertisements for alcoholic drinks from any national sellers. The station would not enter into an exclusive arrangement with any single network and would only deal directly with their national headquarters, not local affiliates. WOI-TV would retain full control over the schedule, retaining "complete rights of program control and ability to cancel, discard, or censor network programs at will for good and sufficient reason." Such an agreement, it was estimated, would bring in around $200,000 a year in revenue. The money would be invested in an ISC TV Foundation Fund, which would be used to complete the construction of the station and to purchase additional equipment (Reports, Committee on Radio, FM and Television 1948).

This was, as the committee itself conceded, a novel solution. The semicommercial nature of the proposal was "contrary to the policy followed by choice in the case of WOI and by law in the case of WOI-FM" (Reports, Committee on Radio, FM and Television 1948). When the original AM radio station had been established in 1922, it had been awarded a commercial license, but the college had chosen to operate it on a noncommercial basis. When Iowa State applied for an FM license in 1945, the FCC had taken the decision to allocate a portion of the FM spectrum for educational radio, with the stipulation that educational licenses could be awarded only on a noncommercial basis. The television license awarded to WOI-TV—like its original AM radio license—had been given on a commercial basis, allowing Iowa State considerable autonomy when shaping its relationship with the networks. Yet ISC was aware that the regulatory environment was in a state of flux. The FCC had ceased issuing new TV broadcast licenses in 1948 as part of the so-called Television Freeze, but WOI-TV understood this freeze would eventually end. Their proposal recognized that the existence of a semicommercial broadcaster would be tolerated for the time being, and the Standing Committee instructed TV-radio director Richard Hull to negotiate two-year contracts with the networks, anticipating that the regulatory landscape would look very different by 1952.

The committee was also aware that their proposal had implications far beyond Iowa. Since the late 1920s there had been a debate raging about the relationship between educational and commercial broadcasting. During the 1930s and 1940s, the National Advisory Council on Radio in Education (NACRE) had argued for what Leach (1983) has termed "the Doctrine of Cooperation," where educators would work together with the commercial networks to broadcast sustaining programs. While NACRE had received the backing of both the Carnegie Corporation and—nominally at least—NBC, their attempts to attract mass audiences had failed, and educational programming had been increasingly marginalized by the networks. The model proposed by Iowa State, however, offered an opportunity to turn the old cooperative relationship on its head. By retaining control over the schedule, and by having a monopoly over the local television market, WOI-TV could ensure that educational programs were given due prominence in the schedule. The Iowa State Standing Committee were keenly aware that their local proposal had national significance: "The eyes of the commercial and educational broadcasting world are already fixed on this experiment. In a very real sense the success or failure of educational television in the United States rests on the success or failure of the Iowa State College television project" (Reports, Committee on Radio, FM and Television 1948). While the program offering that WOI-TV developed during the years 1950 to 1955 was primarily designed to foster and develop a loyal local audience, it was also designed to guard against criticism from outside central Iowa. Richard Hull, in particular, would push for original local programming that was benchmarked against national standards, aware that the judgments of the nation would reflect not only on what WOI-TV was doing but on public perceptions of noncommercial television in general.

WOI-TV GOES TO AIR

Following years of preparation, WOI-TV finally began airing a regular television service on February 21, 1950. For most of the first year of broadcasting, the station possessed only rudimentary studio equipment with means of connecting to any of the national networks. On its first day the station's output consisted of "three educational films from the college's film library and three kinescopes of network programs" (Caristi 1997, 203). This continued for the first six months of the station's existence, but by the fall of 1950 it had joined the national broadcast network constructed by Bell Telephone and in November was broadcasting live local programs (Harl 2001, 23).

The prominence of network programs, however, was a cause of concern to some at ISC. At a meeting of the college's Program and Policy Committee held on October 25, 1950, members of the committee warned that WOI-TV could not "afford to leave itself open to criticism that ISC is operating a purely commercial station" and that it was a matter of urgency that "the educational aspects of the station be put into operation as soon as possible" (Television Policy and Program Committee 1950–52). WOI's director Richard Hull, however, felt that the station should not rush to produce educational programs until they could be guaranteed of their quality, arguing that "professional standards of performance should be maintained at all times." On October 24, 1950, he wrote to President Friley and the other members of the TV Policy Committee to argue that "setting up an adequate and honest graduate and undergraduate program in TV at Iowa State College seems to me to be one of our most pressing problems." The creation of such a program would allow the college to recruit properly qualified teaching personnel to "maintain high broadcast standards and at the same time . . . offer maximum student participation at the proper level" (Television Policy and Program Committee 1950–52). This emphasis on quality was entirely typical of Hull, whose influence on the development of WOI-TV during these early years cannot be overstated. Throughout his time at the station, he would argue, time and again, that the future of ETV relied on its ability to compete with the commercial networks; unless the programs produced by ETV were of the same standard as those being broadcast by its competitors, Hull did not see a future for the medium.

Hull had first worked at WOI while an undergraduate student at ISC and had developed a deep and lasting passion for radio, but also an understanding that "educators' unwillingness to work with or learn from commercial broadcasters had led to stunted development by university stations" (Shepperd 2023, 48). When ISC originally applied for its television license, Hull was determined to ensure that ETV did not repeat the mistakes of educational radio. While schools, universities, and colleges were predominantly responsible for producing and broadcasting ETV, Hull was absolutely clear that the audience for ETV programs should not be confined to schoolchildren and college students. One of the central purposes of ETV should be to provide those who were not enrolled in formal education with programs that would enlighten and enrich their lives, drawing upon the resources of schools and universities to do so.

One major problem, in Hull's opinion, was that the proponents of educational broadcasting were deeply skeptical, and often snobby, about television. In Hull's view they saw it as a medium permanently and fatally sullied by its commercial associations. Writing almost a decade later—looking back, this time, at his early experiences with ETV—he complained that "educators often fail to distinguish among the purpose, content and technique in the programs they see and hear. If they dislike the commercial program's purpose, content or standards, they may also reject its techniques" ("Educational Television in the United States" 1957).

By 1950, Hull was firmly in the driving seat at WOI-TV, and his ideas were shaping the development of the new station. At a meeting of the ISC Program and Policy Committee on October 9, 1950, he was appointed "Supreme Director of Communication . . . responsible only to the president." The job title was amended to the more modest Director of Communication Facilities at the committee's meeting on October 25, but the responsibilities and powers of the post remained the same. He would possess "the authority and control of finance to integrate and implement all activities" involving the college's broadcasting facilities (Television Policy and Program Committee 1950–52).

By the 1950s, Hull's influence was growing on a national as well as a local level. He was increasingly aware that the long-term success of WOI-TV relied on its ability to forge partnerships with organizations outside Iowa. The decision to affiliate with the networks was, in part, a commercial one designed to support the station financially. But it was also a strategic decision, designed to allow Iowa State to benefit from the commercial broadcasters' expertise. Louis Lewis, WOI-TV's chief engineer, was invited to visit network television stations in Chicago in January 1951 and wrote detailed reports on CBS and NBC's technical standards, for use at ISC (Television Policy and Program Committee 1950–52). This was key, in Hull's mind, to developing the kind of quality ETV programming that was so important to his vision.

It was also an audience-building strategy, one that owed much to ideas of Levering Tyson and NACRE a decade and a half earlier. Hull realized that the "Cooperation Doctrine" had failed on the radio because the networks controlled the schedule. Educational programs were refused peak time broadcast slots and struggled to attract an audience as a result (Leach 1983). At WOI-TV, it was the educators who controlled the schedule and could use this to ensure that educational programs were given due prominence. Caristi (1997, 204) describes the way that WOI-TV adopted a policy of "sandwiching" local programs between two popular network shows, to try and build an audience for the educational content. But as CBS warned advertisers in 1950, the television viewer was a fickle beast: "Man is dangerous. He's got to like what he sees or he'll turn you off" (1950). During its early years, WOI-TV held a local monopoly on the airwaves, so the risk of losing viewers in the break between network shows was relatively low. But Hull was aware that their monopoly was a temporary one, and once it was over each individual program would have to compete for viewers on its own merits.

One of Hull's great insights was that ETV contained two separate, often competing, tendencies. On the one hand, television could be used as a "point-to-point communications device for the systematic instruction of captive audiences within the framework of formal education," a usage that Hull termed "Classroom ETV." But the medium also offered an opportunity to do something more than simply operate as an electronic extension of the school or college classroom. Television could also provide "intellectual and cultural entertainment, information, spiritual stimulation, clarification and perspective"; this second, broader, concept he labeled "Broadcast ETV." One of Hull's enduring frustrations was that many within the field of educational broadcasting failed to grasp the distinction between the two. If broadcast ETV was to reach the "free-choice audiences" then it needed to "translate approved educational values into good television programs designed for acceptance by the viewing audience in *their terms, not to please the educational expert in his terms*" ("Educational Television in the United States" 1957). As a memo dated January 7, 1952, noted, WOI-TV's own programs needed to "tell a story visually, a la the new, modern film techniques" if they were to succeed (Correspondence and Memorandum 1952). Control of the television schedule mattered, but it wasn't a panacea. Once WOI-TV lost its monopoly, each program that featured in its peak-time schedule would need to compete for its audience. Sandwiching educational programs between commercial network offerings helped to introduce the audience to these programs, but little more. Broadcast ETV needed to learn the skills and techniques of commercial television and commit itself to producing educational programs that borrowed some of the style and tone of entertainment.

Providing such a service would prove costly. This had been anticipated by ISC when deciding to move ahead with their license application in 1948. A Special Report by the ISC Committee on Radio, FM, and Television dated December 16, 1948, had laid out the financial challenges clearly: "embarking on television means operating in terms of costs and scope which [ISC] has not previously encountered in sound broadcasting." The committee was clear, however, that the value of the television license—in both financial and educational terms—clearly justified the costs. It proposed three potential means of producing income to fund the operation of the station: "limited commercial operation," a television training school that would attract higher tuition fees, and "grant-in-aid from the Federal government and from manufacturers" (Special Report by ISC Committee on Radio and Television 1948).

When grant-in-aid was eventually secured, however, it didn't come from the government or the manufacturers but instead from the Ford Foundation. Philanthropic foundations had a long history of supporting educational radio, and in 1950 the Ford Foundation had been endowed with some 90 percent of the Ford Motor Company nonvoting stock (Lashner 1977). Overnight, it became the largest philanthropic foundation in the world. A number of those involved in deciding how to spend this money—most notably Robert Hutchins and C. Scott Fletcher—had an interest in educational broadcasting and were keen to offer their support.

In an interview for the Public Television's Roots Oral History Project, Fletcher recounts how Richard Hull sought financial support from the Ford Foundation's Fund for Adult Education (FAE) before the fund had officially been launched. Hull had approached Robert Hutchins to inquire about foundation support, and Hutchins had directed him to Fletcher. Fletcher took an immediate liking to Hull and persuaded the Ford Foundation to approve a $15,000 grant in February 1951. This was followed by a further $90,000 grant awarded by the FAE at its first official meeting in April of the same year. It was an important victory for ETV, but Hull did not approach Fletcher and the FAE on behalf of WOI-TV in this first instance; instead, he was acting in his capacity as president of NAEB, and the grant would be used to fund the creation of the Joint Committee on Educational Television (JCET), a new national lobbying group (C. Scott Fletcher Papers) that was formed to try and secure a fair proportion of television frequencies for educational purposes.

Hull had previously considered the possibility of direct foundation support for WOI-TV but was not convinced that there was a realistic prospect of success. Initial discussions between Hull and John Marshall of the Rockefeller Foundation had taken place in early 1949 (Rockefeller Foundation Correspondence Reports 1949–50), but Marshall wrote to Hull on February 15, 1949, to decline his request for financial support.

Following his success in persuading the Ford Foundation to support the JCET, Hull presumably decided that they were more amenable to his cause than the Rockefeller Foundation. In June 1951, ISC was awarded $260,000 "for the purpose of experimentation and program development in educational television," $80,000 of which should be spent on equipment, the other $180,000 on program development and research.

This money allowed WOI-TV to build a new studio, buy a kinescope and a rapid developer, considerably upgrading the production facilities at the station. It also allowed the college to appoint new staff, including Dr. Burton Paulu from the University of Minnesota. Paulu was both an accomplished station manager and a media scholar, and Hull held him in the highest regard. More importantly, perhaps, the grant allowed WOI-TV to build direct links with the Ford Foundation. During this period the Ford Foundation played a key role in the long-term development of ETV. Their vision was to "make possible the broadest use of television in the public service" by building "non-profit networks, primarily under the control of educators." Funding WOI-TV provided the Ford Foundation with an opportunity to "experiment with the one educationally controlled television station now in existence, to enable them to demonstrate what such a station might accomplish with more effective programming" (Television and Radio Workshop 1951).

During the first year of Ford Foundation support, WOI-TV considered its main success to be in community discussion program development. Its flagship program was *The Whole Town's Talking*, a current affairs series that sought to televise the democratic process. WOI-TV would organize a town hall meeting to discuss a local political issue, inviting both ordinary citizens and experts. The citizens would be asked their views in advance of the broadcast and then be given an opportunity both to listen to the experts' views, but also to quiz them. At the end of the broadcast, they were asked to express their views again, by means of an electronic voting machine, to see if they had been persuaded by the debate.

It was an ambitious endeavor, and one that was creatively innovative and technically accomplished. The experts were presented using filmed sequences that were seamlessly inserted into the live broadcast. Following the first "dry-run," the producers decided to adopt a style that eschewed any pretense of there being an invisible camera observing a town hall meeting. Instead, the crew and equipment were visible to the audience; as Mayo Simon wrote in a 1952 report to the FAE, "What we see is not a small-town meeting, but television covering a small-town meeting . . . the open acknowledgment of the cameras allows us to take advantage of television's greatest asset—dramatic 'on-the-spot' coverage. The presence of cameras and technical equipment creates the impression that news is taking place, that history is being recorded, that the viewer is truly 'on-the-spot.'" Simon's report to the FAE reflected the genuine enthusiasm within WOI-TV, and a feeling that the station was demonstrating that an ETV station could produce innovative programming, if properly funded. While the first season of *The Whole Town's Talking* had focused exclusively on educational redistricting, Simon promised that future programs would "take up other Iowa Community problems which have considerable national significance" such as "juvenile delinquency, gambling and law enforcement, re-apportionment, housing" (NAEB Records 1958).

The issue, however, was that the FAE seemed unconvinced of the potential "national significance" of *The Whole Town's Talking*. As well produced and formally innovative as it may have been, it remained very clearly a local program aimed squarely at the residents of Iowa. The experimental format could be replicated elsewhere, but to do so would come at a significant further cost to the FAE. What it was seeking was kinescope recordings that could be shared with other ETV stations, at low cost, rather than experimental formats that would have to be made and remade in each locale.

In awarding WOI-TV a second grant for 1952–53, the FAE made it perfectly clear to WOI-TV that the second tranche of money was "for the purpose of producing programs suitable for educational television network distribution. These programs should be designed to have the longest possible life, that is, the greatest potentiality for various residual uses. This requirement will, quite naturally, exclude the production of programs which are only of local Iowa interest" (Report of Progress 1952). This entreaty was likely the result of the FAE's substantial investment in the creation, in November 1952, of the Educational Television and Radio Center (ETRC). The ETRC's aim was to centrally organize the work of exchanging the highest-quality ETV programs between member stations, replicating the network system that had been so central to the success of commercial broadcasting. But this investment from the FAE required programs that had national appeal. Having succeeded, in their own view, to produce a television series that was a "sparkplug" for democratic action (NAEB Records 1958), WOI-TV was now effectively being told that it was too local, too parochial to be of use to the FAE.

In responding to the FAE, WOI-TV admitted that "quite frankly, we have experienced considerable difficulty getting 'on target'" in addressing "the problem of design for universality of appeal to a heterogeneous audience." Not only did Hull and his colleagues bristle at the FAE's prohibition against local programming, but they also complained that television was "the medium of immediacy and reality," yet they were being asked to produce programs designed to sit on the shelf at ETRC, "which will have no immediate use, but must have the quality of immediacy indefinitely in the future" (Report of Progress 1952).

Having, in their own view, created a genuinely pioneering program with their 1951–52 grant, WOI-TV was forced to turn to "predictable 'best-sellers' of high quality" in 1952–53. *From the Mind of Man* was a series discussing the so-called great books that would doubtless have pleased Robert Hutchins at the Ford Foundation. *Counterpart* brought ordinary Americans face-to-face with their foreign counterparts, while *Art for Man's Sake* looked at art as a "reflection of [man's] attitudes and beliefs, his values, his aspirations." The final series was the only one that bore particular local relevance to WOI-TV's audience, *One-Fifth of a Nation*, a series of documentaries that looked at the economics of American agriculture, drawing upon the academic expertise found at ISC (Report of Progress 1952). These were considered high-quality programs, produced by WOI-TV for viewers of ETV across the United States. It was content that was aimed at satisfying the demands of the Ford Foundation's FAE while also enriching the programming being offered to local viewers, which it undoubtedly did. Its weakness, however, was that—unlike *The Whole Town's Talking*—it provided little direct commentary upon, or insight into, life in central Iowa.

LIFE AFTER THE FREEZE

Hull realized that the WOI-TV model was borne from specific local circumstances and that their semicommercial status existed only because they had applied for a broadcast license before the Television Freeze of 1948, in a geographic area where no one else was broadcasting. Yet he also believed that it would have been possible to replicate their model in other local markets, had the regulatory environment been amenable. As it became clear that the Television Freeze was coming to an end, he used his platform within the JCET to argue that the WOI-TV model should be afforded some protection in federal regulation.

His was a lone voice, however, and was unable to persuade any of his fellow JCET members to support license allocation on a nonprofit basis. The FCC published its *Third Notice of Proposed Rule Making* on March 21, 1951, in which it proposed to reserve a portion of the television broadcast spectrum for noncommercial educational use. By this point the FCC and the educators had reached a compromise, thanks in part to an alliance that had been formed between members of the JCET and Frieda Hennock, the newest member of the commission.[1]

Hennock had persuaded her fellow commissioners that the precedent set by the FCC's FM radio allocations in 1945 should be the basis for television licensing post-1952. In 1945 the commission had reserved channels for educational broadcasting on a strictly noncommercial basis. As Wayne Coy, FCC chair, explained to William Benton in a letter dated July 24, 1951, the precedent that was set in the 1945 allocation decision made it perfectly clear "that educational institutions could not keep their non-commercial status if they began to take money for the programs broadcast over their television stations." Coy went on to explain that if an educational establishment wanted to raise commercial income to support their television station, then they should drop their request for a reserved educational license and apply instead for a commercial license.

Had the FCC agreed to reserve broadcast spectrum for ETV on a nonprofit basis it would—in theory—have created conditions amenable to the spread of the WOI-TV model. Educational broadcasters in other states would have been given the opportunity to secure television broadcast licenses with the knowledge that they could exploit the value of those licenses commercially, as long as the commercial income was reinvested into producing ETV. The compromise reached between the JCET and the FCC at the conclusion of the Television Freeze ruled out this possibility, the strict prohibition against raising commercial revenues to fund ETV meaning that ETV stations would be forced to rely on either state funding or the largesse of philanthropic foundations.

The license allocations suggested by the FCC in the *Third Notice* did not have a direct impact on WOI-TV, already broadcasting under their commercial license. But in establishing the principle that television should be divided into two clearly demarcated spheres—commercial and noncommercial—the Iowa station became increasingly isolated. On April 13, 1951, Hull wrote to President Friley warning that the station would now become "to a degree a target" for the FCC (Freeze Hearings, Filings and Statements 1951). Almost immediately after the publication of the *Third Notice* proposals, the station's commercial rivals began to petition the FCC to "hang the educational star" on WOI-TV, as Robert Mulhall put it in a letter dated May 10, 1951 (Freeze Hearings, Filings and Statements 1951). What he meant was that these rivals were arguing that WOI-TV should relinquish their commercial license and take up the newly created educational license for central Iowa. When the final license allocations were published, as part of the FCC's *Sixth Report and Order*, on April 14, 1952, the pressure on WOI-TV did not abate.

Although the station managed to fend off these initial regulatory threats and kept hold of their commercial license, the end of the Television Freeze meant the end of their monopoly position. Two new commercial television stations were licensed for central Iowa in 1955, and as a result WOI-TV lost CBS affiliation to one of its new rivals, KRNT-TV, while NBC would partner with the other, WHO-TV. In commercial terms, this meant that the station's income was reduced "by approximately one half" according to an all-staff memo sent by C. R. Elder, ISC director of information services, on November 4, 1955. The station sought to maintain the same programming and operational objectives; it would continue to be an "educational public service" station that aimed to service "thousands and tens of thousands, not hundreds" of viewers. The loss of income meant, however, that the station would from 1955 onward have "fewer 'fancy trimmings,' less elaborate sets, and fewer attempts at special effects" (Advertising Policies 1951–52).

While the loss of CBS and NBC was damaging, WOI-TV continued to receive income from broadcasting programs provided by DuMont and Weed Television as well as their production-for-pay relationships with both the Ford Foundation–funded ETRC and ABC-TV. The station's main source of income after 1955 was through its affiliation with the ABC network. While Elder had remained publicly optimistic that WOI-TV could continue to provide largely the same service, Hull was privately more pessimistic. "In essence we financially rise or fall with the rise or fall of the American Broadcasting Company," he wrote to ISC's new president, James Hilton, on May 3, 1955, "Should our 'forced gamble' be unsuccessful, then our next and only recourse is complete state support" (Policies 1952–55).

A few months later, on August 29, Hull wrote to all WOI staff informing them that he would be taking a leave of absence to undertake an FAE-funded "nationwide appraisal of educational television" (Policies 1952–55). While this was originally due to be a temporary arrangement, on June 18, 1956, C. R. Elder informed the station's staff that Hull would be leaving permanently, to take up a position at Ohio State University.

The years that followed Hull's departure were not easy ones for the station. In 1952 the Bureau of Internal Revenue had challenged the tax-exempt status of WOI-TV, arguing that it was a commercial business that was generating unrelated income for ISC and therefore subject to tax. ISC argued that the station was an integral part of its educational offering, but struggled to convince the federal government of this fact. The case would not ultimately be resolved until 1974, when the U.S. Court of Claims ruled in favor of the Internal Revenue Service. In making its decision, the Court was forced to pass judgment on WOI-TV's claim that it was categorically distinct from other commercial broadcasters. On this question the Court's verdict was damning: "The maximization of revenues was the primary, not to mention overwhelming, goal in the conduct of the business. . . . Local programming, although a fine effort and of great value to audiences, did not differ substantially either in quantity or subject matter from that of stations whose admitted goal was profit maximization" (*Iowa State University v. United States* 357). In the Court's view, therefore, WOI-TV had by the early 1960s become almost indistinguishable from any other commercial television station. Hull's original vision of a hybrid public-private broadcaster, it seems, had been entirely lost.

ISC continued to value the station and resisted attempts to sell it throughout the 1960s and 1970s. By the 1990s, however, as Robert Mullhall had warned, WOI-TV was forced to give in to commercial television, and the station was eventually sold to Capital Communications Company in 1994. This was despite the vociferous objections of many local citizens, some of whom brought a lawsuit against the Board of Regents to try to prevent the sale.

WOI-TV's long decline and eventual sale should not, however, overshadow the significance of what the station achieved during its earliest years. Goodman and Hayes (2022, 2) have argued that understanding the late development of American public broadcasting is a "central problem of US broadcasting history." In addressing this problem, they note the importance of examining the "path[s] not taken," of looking at those bold experiments that may have led American broadcasting in a different direction to the one that it took. WOI-TV during the 1940s and 1950s was among the boldest of those experiments. Driven by the vision of Richard Hull, ISC developed and implemented a model of educational broadcasting that was—too briefly—successful by any measure. It was financially viable, produced public service programs of the highest quality, reflected the character of its local area, and both attracted and maintained a substantial audience across its whole schedule. The fact that this model did not survive beyond the mid-1950s can be explained, in part, by a shift in the priorities of the advocates of ETV and the Ford Foundation's desire to build a noncommercial "Fourth Network" to rival commercial television. It can also be explained by a new regulatory environment after 1952, which facilitated the development of the existing commercial television networks. Facing intense pressure from its purely commercial competitors and lacking sufficient support from its erstwhile allies and benefactors, WOI-TV would eventually lose that which had made it distinctive—but not before demonstrating to the viewers of central Iowa that an alternative model of television was possible.

NOTES

The author wishes to thank Denise Gripp for her assistance in researching this chapter.
1. For an extended discussion of the debate between Hennock and Hull, see Jones (2022).

REFERENCES

Advertising Policies, University of Iowa and Drake Policies. 1951–52. 4, box 21, folder 8. WOI Radio and Television Records, RS 5/6, Special Collections and University Archives, Iowa State University, Ames.

Balas, Glenda R. 2003. *Recovering a Public Vision for Public Television*. Rowman & Littlefield.

Board of Regents—Notes, Correspondence, Legal Documents. 1944–71. 3, box 11, folder 2–4. WOI Radio and Television Records, RS 5/6, Special Collections and University Archives, Iowa State University, Ames.

Caristi, Dom. 1997. "First in Education: WOI-TV, Ames, Iowa." In *Television in America: Local Station History from Across the Nation*, edited by Michael D. Murray and Donald G. Godfrey. Iowa State University Press.

CBS. "Man Is Dangerous," advertisement. Television, vol. 7, no. 2, February 1950.

Correspondence and Memorandum, 1952, 8, box 47, folder 4–5. WOI Radio and Television Records, RS 5/6, Special Collections and University Archives, Iowa State University, Ames.

C. Scott Fletcher Papers, series 1, box 2. National Public Broadcasting Archives, Special Collections, University of Maryland Libraries, College Park.

"Educational Television in the United States" by Richard Hull. 1957. 8, box 49, folder 14. WOI Radio and Television Records, RS 5/6, Special Collections and University Archives, Iowa State University, Ames.

Freeze Hearings, Filings and Statements. 1951. 4, box 21, folder 6. WOI Radio and Television Records, RS 5/6, Special Collections and University Archives, Iowa State University, Ames.

General Correspondence. 1947–56. 89-6, box 131, —92-6f, June 1, 1950–November 30, 1952. Mail and Files Branch, RG 173 Federal Communications Commission, Office of the Executive Director, National Archives at College Park, Md.

Goodman, David, and Joy Elizabeth Hayes. 2022. *New Deal Radio: The Educational Radio Project*. Rutgers University Press.

Harl, Neil E. 2001. *Arrogance and Power: The Saga of WOI-TV*. Heuss.

Harper, William A. 1956. "The Educational Television and Radio Center." *Quarterly of Film Radio and Television* 11 (2): 197–203.

Iowa State University v. United States, 500 F.2d 508 (Ct. Cl. 1974).

Jaramillo, Deborah L. 2018. *The Television Code: Regulating the Screen to Save the Industry*. University of Texas Press.

JCET History and Development. National Educational Television records, series 5A, box 156. Wisconsin Historical Society, Division of Library, Archives, and Museum Collections, Madison.

Jones, Dyfrig. 2022. "'Go the Way of Radio?' American Public Broadcasting, Media Reform, and the Federal Communications Commission's Hearings on Educational Television, 1950–51." In *Media, Power and Public Opinion: Essays on Communication and Politics in a Historical Perspective*, edited by D. M. Bruni, 183–203. Peter Lang.

Lashner, Marilyn A. 1977. "The Role of Foundations in Public Broadcasting, II: The Ford Foundation." *Journal of Broadcasting & Electronic Media* 21 (2): 235–54.

Leach, Eugene E. 1983. "Tuning Out Education: The Cooperation Doctrine in Radio, 1922–38." *Current*, August.

Levin, Harvey J. 2013. *The Invisible Resource: Use and Regulation of the Radio Spectrum*. RFF Press.

Litman, Barry Russell. 1979. *The Vertical Structure of the Television Broadcasting Industry*. Michigan State University.

Lowe, Gregory Ferrell, and Philip Savage. 2020. "Universalism in Public Service Media: Paradoxes, Challenges, and Development." In *Universalism in Public Service Media*, edited by Philip Savage, Mercedes Medina, and Gregory Ferrell Lowe. Nordicom, University of Gothenburg.

NAEB Records 1958, box 56, folder 1. National Association of Educational Broadcasters Records, 1925–77, Wisconsin Historical Society, Division of Library, Archives, and Museum Collections, Madison.

Policies. 1952–55. 8, box 47, folder 9. WOI Radio and Television Records, RS 5/6, Special Collections and University Archives, Iowa State University, Ames.

Powell, John Walker. 1962. *Channels of Learning: The Story of Educational Television*. PublicAffairs.

Public Television's Roots Oral History Project, box/folder 2/9, U.S. Mss 193AF. Wisconsin Historical Society, Division of Library, Archives, and Museum Collections, Madison.

Report of Progress. 1952. 8, box 47, folder 3. WOI Radio and Television Records, RS 5/6, Special Collections and University Archives, Iowa State University, Ames.

Reports, Committee on Radio, FM, and Television. 1948. 8, box 44, folder 5. WOI Radio and Television Records, RS 5/6, Special Collections and University Archives, Iowa State University, Ames.

Rockefeller Foundation Correspondence Reports. 1949–50. 1, box 1, folder 2. Robert Mulhall papers, RS 5/6/14, Special Collections and University Archives, Iowa State University, Ames.

Shepperd, Josh. 2023. *Shadow of the New Deal: The Victory of Public Broadcasting.* University of Illinois Press.

Slotten, Hugh. 2009. *Radio's Hidden Voice: The Origins of Public Broadcasting in the United States.* University of Illinois Press.

Special Report by ISC Committee on Radio and Television. 1948. RS 5/6/1, box 1, folder 10. WOI Radio and Television Records, RS 5/6, Special Collections and University Archives, Iowa State University, Ames.

Summary of Special Report by Iowa State College Committee on Radio, Television, and FM. 1948. 8, box 44, folder 3. WOI Radio and Television Records, RS 5/6, Special Collections and University Archives, Iowa State University, Ames.

Television Administrative Records. 1941–2000. WOI Radio and Television Records, RS 5/6, Special Collections and University Archives, Iowa State University, Ames.

Television and Radio Workshop. 1951. Office Files of Robert M Hutchins (FA 703). Series 1: Correspondence, box 9 (SK 46635), Ford Foundation Records, Rockefeller Archive Center, Sleepy Hollow, N.Y.

Television Policy and Program Committee. 1950–52. WOI Radio and Television Records, RS 5/6, Special Collections and University Archives, Iowa State University, Ames.

WOI-TV Original Planning. 1946–48. 4, box 20, folder 2; Iowa State University, WOI Radio and Television Records, RS 5/6, Special Collections and University Archives, Iowa State University, Ames.

CHAPTER 3

TAYLOR COLE MILLER

"VOCAL VOYEURS"

LOCAL TELEVISION MEETS NATIONAL SYNDICATION IN NORMAN LEAR'S *THE BAXTERS*

"Did you think it was rape?" asks Norman Lear, framed by two large television sets behind him and a small crowd of viewers watching from folding chairs on carpeted risers. "Do you feel she should have submitted?" Under discussion is a scene depicting spousal sexual assault in the first of two pilots of Lear's experimental show *The Baxters*, but this discussion, featuring an audience of everyday Angelenos talking *about* the episode, is still *a part of* the episode in the inventive if short-lived syndicated series. In 1979, Norman Lear married national syndication with local production in a thirty-minute program called *The Baxters*, itself a reboot of local Boston station WCVB-TV's eponymous show, not quite a sitcom, not quite a drama but both and neither in feel. Each episode featured two halves: first, a Lear-produced eleven-minute vignette without resolution of the fictional Baxter family experiencing an issue "dripping with relevancy," as *Variety* described it, such as gay teachers, socialized medicine, mainstreaming in schools, incest, and the death penalty; and second, a taped, town-hall-style talk show segment produced by the local station syndicating *The Baxters* featuring members of the station's local community debating the issues and resolutions of each situation (Demp 1979, 121).

Billed as an interactive opportunity, *The Baxters*' tagline was "more than entertainment . . . the right to respond," promising the viewers whom the *Daily News* called "vocal voyeurs" the first real opportunity to talk back to their televisions and be heard (Gardella 1979, 346). The AP reported that Lear, "television's resident innovator," wanted to blend what he called "the comedy and the tears in the reality of our lives" in a situa-

Fig. 3.1. Norman Lear hosting the Los Angeles audience in the first pilot of his show *The Baxters*.

tion skit constituting 49 percent of each episode with the other 51 percent left to the local station to produce (Boyer 1979, 7). These programming percentages and use of local hosts were precisely designed to qualify each episode of *The Baxters* for the station's local public affairs requirements then set for each station by the Federal Communications Commission (FCC). The *Washington Post* called this the show's sweetheart deal for broadcasters: Lending the popularity of Lear's name to a local show that also counted for a station's community-programming commitment "is like having your cake, eating it too and then learning that it has fattened nothing but your wallet. It could only happen in a business like the television business" (Shales 1979).

In this chapter, my objective in elaborating the history and development of *The Baxters* is to explore the deeply complex and mutually constituting relationship between local broadcasting and national television syndication. Although nuanced discussions of syndication are rare in overviews of the television industry, when syndication does appear we mostly describe it as a national phenomenon. In histories describing local television, syndication (often considered TV's lowest form of programming) is usually portrayed as a bit of a boogeyman or a crutch for a struggling industry. Examples might describe the use of syndicated shows (syndies) as local stations cheating a system of regulations meant to enhance local production and/or as syndicators taking advantage of local stations too poor to create their own shows. While neither of these representations is entirely false, I argue that the tendency to dismiss syndication in such a way does obscure the vital and often robust partnerships local stations develop with national syndicators and studios. In network television, a whole corporate machinery divides creators and affiliates who have little control over prime-time network streams. In syndication, however, local stations make numerous decisions impacting creators, like scheduling (hence the catchphrase "check your local listings"). Because individual stations have been their primary exhibitors, syndicators of national shows often consult local stakeholders to continuously finesse their productions to better serve audiences. So while syndication connotes a mainstream national presence, it is also always inherently local.

Demonstrating the ephemerality of both local and syndicated television, the publicly unavailable episodes I screened for this chapter were personally provided to me by Norman Lear. And yet even he does not own a complete collection of all *The Baxters*' episodes with local segments intact. Those, like so many other local programs, were thrown away, taped over, or caged in obsolete media left rotting on shelves in backrooms or storage closets of stations across the nation, waiting to be considered important enough to archive. Through a historical framework on media policy, production, and text, I explore *The Baxters* as an important case study in the long and critical relationship between syndication and local television. Because each episode includes both national and local production work—with immediate reactions from members of numerous communities—*The Baxters* remains a unique historical artifact of regional attitudes toward major cultural issues and a peek into the important work of local programming throughout television's past. Indeed, advertising for the show promised the best of Lear's social comedy that also "provokes and reveals the convictions, emotions, and prejudices of the people in your community" so viewers could better understand big cultural issues as well as the on-the-ground politics and beliefs of those in their regions.

Although today it is remembered, if at all, as a failure, *The Baxters* highlighted possibilities for nontraditional programming that could be quite different for efforts to promote localism. Even though it ultimately "failed" (that is, was canceled after just a season), the trade publication *Broadcasting* still described it years later as an icon of the do-it-yourself movement in local programming (1980a, 36). But *The Baxters* should prompt us to reconsider what "failure" even signifies in television, by which I mean thinking beyond the industry's bottom line. The skills local stations gained creating and filming their own discussion segments for *The Baxters* taught them technical and aesthetic sophistication in production. And the influence of working with Lear modeled how local programs could be tailored for national syndication. This notoriety of local programming through syndication has helped local shows become drivers of social change with consequent effects for television production throughout the 1980s. But yes, *The Baxters* was canceled after a single season.

In television, syndication is the last refuge of failure. There are numerous examples of canceled network shows saved from the brink of extinction by syndication in local TV markets including shows from the rural purge (*Lassie, Hee Haw, The Lawrence Welk Show*), network shows with poor ratings (*Mama's Family, It's a Living, Charles in Charge, Punky Brewster, Baywatch* but also talk shows like Mike Douglas's and Merv Griffin's), shows networks never picked up (*Mary Hartman, Mary Hartman; Small Wonder; Throb*), and others like *Mister Ed*, originally network rejects but picked up after successful syndicated seasons. In return, syndication created great opportunities for local productions to go national, including series like *The Phil Donahue Show, The Oprah Winfrey Show, Crusader Rabbit, Life with Elizabeth* (which gave Betty White a national audience), and, as I discuss here, WCVB-TV's *The Baxters*.

Through a focus on *The Baxters*, this chapter provides an important and sustained discussion of the critical, symbiotic relationships developed between the two primary cornerstones of American television: local broadcasting and television syndication. Along with *PM Magazine*, Lear's *The Baxters* remains one of very few shows to be a local and national coproduction, making it both anomalous but an exemplary case study of the sometimes deep connections cultivated between local TV and syndication more generally.[1] Discussing what they called a new kind of participatory television, creators of WCVB-TV's *The Baxters* Hubert Jessup and Bruce Marsan said that "while much television provides entertainment and tells stories, very little television offers viewers an opportunity to talk about it. We wanted to give viewers a right to respond" (*Broadcast Management/Engineering* 1979, 31). Before delving into a discussion of the text, I start by defining syndication and establishing a timeline of the policies and regulations that ultimately set the stage for a show like *The*

Baxters, including how the FCC first quantified the "public interest" aspect of television.

REGULATORY AND HISTORICAL CONTEXT

Syndication

While defining what it means and everything it encompasses is complicated, for its purposes here syndication is the licensing of content by its owners to multiple, mostly unconnected exhibitors (e.g., independent stations, station groups, networks, cable channels, or even streamers) and usually by a contracted third party called a syndicator. The content may be new, airing for the first time in syndication (first-run syndication), may have previously run in another exhibition context (second-run syndication or reruns), or some combination of the two (see Miller 2021). The exhibitor pays for the content in one of three ways: straight cash (exhibitor pays for a show directly), barter/trade (show is provided to the exhibitor for free in exchange for owners keeping more advertising profits), and cash plus trade (a mixture of both). In traditional television broadcasting, the types of deals made by a syndicator between owners and exhibitors are geographically based (in designated market areas or DMAs) even if owned by national station groups.

Over the years, many local stations could not afford enough original programming to fill their full schedules, so they turned to syndicators. That is why first-run syndication experienced waves with peaks at moments stations most desperately needed content. Some historical examples include the collapse of the DuMont Television Network in 1955, the spawning of independent stations following a 1964 law requiring UHF dials on TV sets, the mid-1960s color boom, and, most relevant here, the complex implementation of FCC regulations aimed at bolstering localism throughout the 1970s.

The successes of traditional syndication, meanwhile, also rely upon local television as shows cannot responsibly enter syndication without a strong network of local stations. Exhibitors can then air syndies whenever they choose (daytime, prime time, late night, etc.), but without the stability of a nationally scheduled airtime with genres audiences are trained to expect at particular times, producers have to create shows flexible enough to appeal to a variety of different kinds of audiences. Also, without the built-in marketing arms, infrastructure, and production budgets of a major network, syndies rely on local programmers to cultivate audiences for them. But when the relationship between a program and its exhibitor is strongest, there is significant opportunity for profit without the network's bloated profit participants.

Syndicators handle contracts for owners, selling and negotiating licenses, and these negotiations occur at an annual hotel-based conference for the National Association of Television Programming Executives (NATPE) where local station managers and buyers convene to option syndicated content. Buying the exclusive rights to a show can be quite competitive. Many outlets reported that *The Baxters* was the darling of the 1979 NATPE conference: it was "the clear-cut winner of this year's NATPE hallway conversation piece championship" (Knight 1979, 32) and caused "more hospitality-suite action ... than any other new show in the marketplace," immediately landing sales at thirty-two stations (*Variety* 1979a). In his opening remarks as NATPE keynote speaker that year, then-FCC chairman Charles D. Ferris praised *The Baxters* as a new kind of television to emulate elsewhere on the dial, innovative for combining "comedy, social issues, and local audience reaction" in a unique format (*Broadcasting* 1979a, 47).

As sold, *The Baxters* was a joint venture between Lear's T.A.T. Communications and its production partner Boston Broadcasters, Inc. (BBI). T.A.T. served as both owner and syndicator, having developed its own syndication arm through sales of Lear's lucrative catalog of off-network sitcoms and first-run scripted syndicated hits earlier in the decade including *Mary Hartman* and *Fernwood 2 Nite*. As part of a push to create more localism in television, the FCC quantified the public interest standard for licensees, clearing a path for the national plus local formula later utilized to make *The Baxters* qualify as local public affairs television, which, I will describe, gave Lear a unique programming opportunity.

The Public Interest, FCC Regulations, and 1970s Television

Early American broadcasting regulations stressed that local license holders had a public interest requirement. They needed to serve their communities in exchange for the right to profit from licensed airwaves. The notion of a public interest standard exists in the earliest communications regulations. The "licensing authority" of the Federal Radio Commission (FRC), the predecessor to today's FCC, itself established in the Communications Act of 1934, first loosely determined the public interest in the 1927 Radio Act. While both stressed the importance of serving the public interest, what even constituted the "public interest" remained undefined and perhaps strategically so.

The FCC's broad powers and its role as arbitrator of the public interest have been upheld numerous times by courts, including 1943's *NBC v. United States*, which "declared that the public interest standard is the touchstone of FCC authority" ("Charting the Digital Broadcasting Future" 1998, 22), where competition and localism joined diversity as a triad of public interest principles guiding the commission in mapping policies. Subsequent deliberations eventuated the FCC's Blue Book rules in 1946 ("Public Service Responsibility of Broadcast Licensees"), creating four basic components to assess stations' public interest performance for license renewals: live local programs, public affairs programming, limits on excessive advertising, and "sustaining" or noncommercial programs.

While the Blue Book ultimately had no legal force, in response to the national and political discourse spawning its creation, the private National Association of Broadcasters (NAB) strengthened its own Television Code for network censors in 1948. In the late 1950s, quiz show scandals prompted the FCC to clarify further the public interest standard with nineteen days of hearings featuring testimony from more than ninety witnesses. The FCC's 1960 "Programming Policy Statement" identified fourteen public interest elements: among them, opportunities for local self-expression, public affairs programs, service to minority groups, and the development and use of local talent ("Charting the Digital Broadcasting Future" 1998, 23). These rules prevailed for the next two decades but were not quantified until 1976. I will circle back to these public interest rules and their implications for *The Baxters* in the next section. First, it is important to contextualize what made Lear such a powerful Hollywood figure with connections to local stations through syndication.

Leading to Lear

A variety of industrial and cultural circumstances collided in the seventies, precipitating the rise of independent studios like Lear's Tandem / T.A.T. Communications and Mary Tyler Moore and Grant Tinker's MTM Enterprises. FCC-commissioned studies vindicated concerns about a bottleneck market created by the dominance of the big three (NBC,

CBS, and ABC), leading to a commission culture focused on diversifying televisual content by creating more robust local production. To achieve its goals for more localism in television, the FCC created the Financial Interest and Syndication Rules (Fin-Syn), which effectively split networks from their film libraries (and syndication divisions) and necessitated networks to find new program suppliers. And the Prime Time Access Rule (PTAR) limited the amount of programming stations could air that their networks owned, switching off their network feeds and punching holes in their schedules syndicators were happy to help them fill. During this time, new independent UHF stations also popped up, similarly hungry for cheap content.

A trusted hitmaker, Lear became television's preeminent program supplier: by 1974, five of the top ten network shows were his (*All in the Family*, *Sanford and Son*, *The Jeffersons*, *Good Times*, and *Maude*) with one hundred million Americans watching weekly. Despite these successes, all three networks rejected Lear's pitch for *Mary Hartman*, calling it "too weird" and deeming a satirical soap opera "impossible" for American audiences (Mock 2013, 119). Meanwhile, after losing out on much of the back-end profits from reruns of *All in the Family*, Lear established a syndication arm for T.A.T. to control the aftermarket distribution of his later shows, in so doing building a network of close relationships with local affiliate and independent stations across the country. Frustrated by the networks' rejection of *Mary Hartman* layered atop his famous battles with network censors, Lear decided to circumvent the networks altogether, taking *Mary Hartman* directly to first-run syndication. There, he enjoyed more creative freedom and the show became a huge boon for the mostly independent stations carrying it that began calling themselves the *Mary Hartman* Network (Miller 2017, 163).

Later that year in its "Amendments to Delegations of Authority" to staff, the FCC quantified public interest standards for licensees based on a composite week including at least 5 percent local programming, 5 percent informational programming (which could mean news and/or public affairs), and 10 percent total nonentertainment programming.[2] Stations meeting these expectations would streamline license renewal, avoiding referral to the full commission. By incentivizing local public affairs programming, the FCC once again handed Lear a creative business opportunity: produce an entertaining Lear original that also technically fulfilled new licensee guidelines.

THE BAXTERS: ON INDUSTRY AND CONTENT

A WCVB-TV Production

In May 1978, Lear visited Boston to receive an award from the local chapter of the Academy of Television Arts and Sciences. While there, an executive at BBI showed him a sample of WCVB-TV's production of *The Baxters* that impressed him and his partners. Boston's version reportedly had an "inauspicious beginning as a segment of WCVB's Sunday morning religious program" (*New Heaven, New Earth*) before moving to its own half-hour spot six months later in 1977 (*Broadcast Management/Engineering* 1979, 31). Creators Hubert Jessup and Bruce Marsan admitted they did not know what they were doing when they created the format: "We knew we wanted to create a program in which matters of personal decision-making could be presented in a public-affairs format, but none of us had ever done a sitcom before" (*Broadcast Management/Engineering* 1979, 31). On the condition it would not cost more than a syndie, WCVB gave the green light. "Jessup has mingled sitcom, soap opera, and symposium in a social-issues show that raises and discusses problems without achieving a point of view about them," the *Boston Globe* reported after screening an episode about teenagers with sexually transmitted illnesses. "The acted segments are slickly stereotypic and well-played. The discussion approaches sex as crime and punishment" (Henry 1977, 19). Because *The Baxters* was locally produced, featured local talent, discussed issues of community importance, and even offered opportunities for local self-expression, its innovative breakdown of genre checked off several new public interest guidelines, making its unique format and issues-heavy content appealing for Lear.

In 1978, T.A.T. and BBI announced *The Baxters* as a joint venture in first-run syndication. Lear penned the original pilot, played for "extremely enthusiastic audiences" at NATPE. "Somehow it seems that the format fitted Lear's ideas about television like a glove," *Broadcast Management/Engineering* wrote, "permitting him to present highly controversial and often delicate subjects. Any viewer who is offended then has a chance to have his or her viewpoint echoed during the audience discussion" (1979, 36). With the show bought by nearly fifty stations, *The Baxters* and BBI set up four regional, two-day workshops (in Boston, Jacksonville, Fort Wayne, and Los Angeles) to train exhibiting stations on how to create locally produced segments (*Variety* 1979b, 45). Because each station could opt to produce their own talk segments or syndicate another market's, it is unclear how many different local segments were produced for *The Baxters*.

These trainings reportedly covered everything from "what kinds of audiences to invite to the discussion and how the moderator might be chosen to what the local studio set should look like and how many cameras to commission for the taping" (*Variety* 1979b, 45). Lear's pilot dealing with spousal sexual assault or rape is among the heaviest of topics the show explores in the twenty-four episodes produced. "I thought we'd start with a very difficult subject, just to prove it could be handled in 11 minutes . . . on the theory you can't get wetter than wet," Lear explained (Shales 1979). As one of *The Baxters*' local hosts explained, "This was the show's pilot episode and it's a very, very strong show, and it's the show that made WRAL decide to pick it up" (Herrin 1979, 15).

"The Right to Respond"
(Note: This section describes a fictional sexual assault.)

Starring Rue McClanahan and Larry Keith, Lear's first pilot, titled "The Right to Respond," dramatized the topic of spousal sexual assault. "A man returns from a sales convention, emotionally down because of poor sales year [*sic*]," a local review from the screening explains. "He tries to forget his troubles through drinking and sex. His wife, in turn, seeks more open communication. . . . The dramatization ends leaving the audience with the inkling that the husband raped his wife. The local audience is left to discuss marital rape" (Hoffman 1979, A-8). For this pilot, three different formats for local segments were taped (in LA, Boston, and Fort Wayne, Ind.) to demonstrate different ways local stations could approach their part of the production (McLean 1979, 27). Fort Wayne utilized three couples and a sex therapist discussing the scene in a living room atmosphere with a mental health clinic on call (McLean 1979, 27). Boston and LA, however, featured a large studio audience with Lear himself hosting the LA taping. In the pilot, just as Nancy Baxter fights off her husband Fred, the camera cuts to large television sets with the studio audience sitting before them, who, Lear says, have just watched a "tough scene" (Boyer 1979, 7). Jessup, meanwhile, hosted the Boston session with a similar audience setup.

The publicity campaign for *The Baxters* was "The Right to Respond." Targeting station managers, the ads describe *The Baxters* as "the first situation comedy where the viewers in your market can actually participate. Each week, our Baxter family presents a provocative issue which your

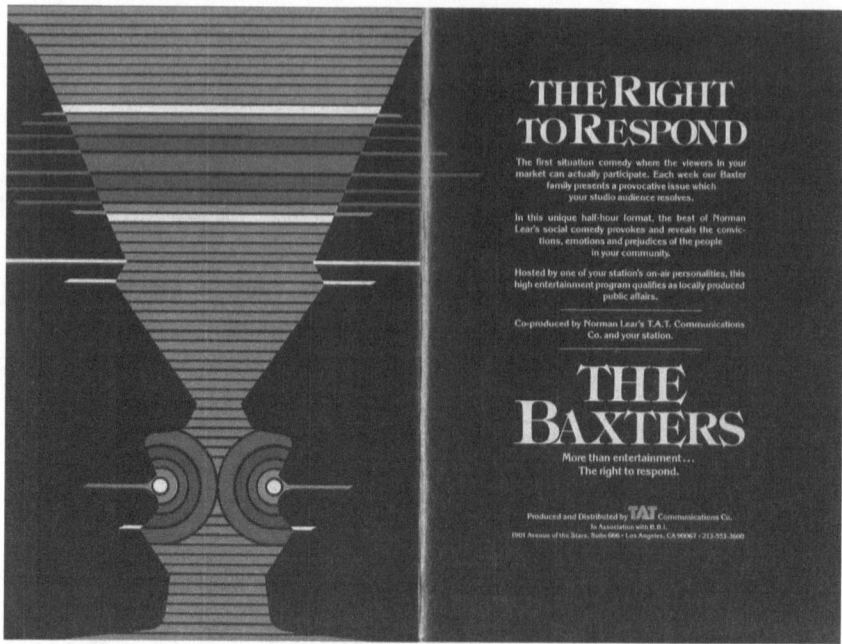

Fig. 3.2. Trade press advertising campaign for *The Baxters*, as appeared in *Broadcasting*, February 26, 1979, 20–21.

studio audience resolves" (*Broadcasting* 1979b, 21). Ads also insist on the program's ability to cultivate localism, fulfilling new FCC regulations. As production began, McClanahan dropped out for contractual reasons and Lear cast Anita Gillette as Nancy, fresh off another of Lear's syndicated experiments, *All That Glitters*. McClanahan does later appear in an episode about socialized medicine.

Like many syndies, *The Baxters* is not available for purchase. While I could not locate McClanahan's pilot and rely instead on reportage, Lear provided me with Gillette's pilot as well as several other episodes, many of which include discussion segments aired on KTLA in Los Angeles. KTLA's presentation begins with a content warning recommending the program for "mature audiences." The theme song for *The Baxters*—a whimsical jazzy instrumental heavy on harmonica and piano—plays, followed by the first commercial break. There are four commercial breaks in this episode, most of which underscore the localism of this airing. Commercials include local ads (the LA Master Chorale and Sinfonia Orchestra, the local chapter of the Juvenile Diabetes Foundation, the

Norton Simon Museum in Pasadena, the California Army National Guard, and a carpet and flooring store called Carpeteria), ads for KTLA's other syndies (*Donahue* and "feature-length" rerun versions of *The Love Boat*, *Little House on the Prairie*, and two ads for *Happy Days*), and one minute of national ads reserved by T.A.T. (Dry Idea roll-on deodorant and Toni Lightwaves, a self-timing home perm).

Gillette's pilot recycles McClanahan's original: Fred and Nancy return one evening from an insurance sales convention where he learned many of his peers had million-dollar years while he struggled. Fred is drunk but exuberant, gathering up the youngest daughter Rachel in a hug while Nancy jokes about his behavior with eldest daughter Naomi (son Jonah is at a friend's sleepover). "He's had so many martinis, at 30,000 feet I thought he was higher than the plane," Nancy says. "Didn't it go well, mom?" Naomi replies. "Well, he hasn't said anything, but I'm afraid not," she answers.

The Baxters climb the stairs for bed, Fred leaning on Nancy who shows her affection while he sings, "Oh, I'm in love with you!" Cutting to the main bedroom, Nancy is now asleep in her nightgown with a television on and her robe draped over the chest. Fred stumbles into the room with a drink in his hand, switches off the set, crawls into bed, and startles Nancy awake kissing her. "Hello Fred," she says, smiling, "goodnight, Fred," she finishes, rolling over to go back to sleep. For the next several minutes, Fred becomes increasingly aggressive in attempting to seduce Nancy. Switching on the light, she says she would agree to *be* with him, "but honey, do you think we could have a little talk first?" Nancy attempts numerous times to discuss Fred's convention, but he continually dismisses the conversation, groping at her instead. The back-and-forth continues to swell until she stands up and ties on her robe, while he follows continuously untying it. He begins unbuttoning his shirt as she pleads with him to listen to her.

> **NANCY**: We go away for the first time in years, and I am really looking forward to it. And what happens? I go to bed every night in a beautiful big king-size bed, and I fall asleep watching television alone. Then about two or three AM, you come reeling in the door, drunk as a skunk, jump out of your pants, wake me up out of a dead sound sleep, and expect me to rip off my nightie and yell "Thank God you're home, Freddy! Take me, I'm yours!"

Fig. 3.3. Steve Edwards hosting the Los Angeles audience of *The Baxters*.

FRED: Yeah!

NANCY: No! No, that's not how it works, honey. Just think how that must make me feel. It's just slam, bam, thank you ma'am....

FRED: What about me, huh? What about my feelings, don't they matter?

Becoming increasingly agitated at Nancy's attempt to talk, Fred grabs her and pushes her to the bed, saying, "I love you, I want you, now get undressed" and "You see what you do? You make me hurt you," while she struggles against him. "Don't force me," she screams. "Don't make me force you," he yells back, kissing her on the mouth to quiet her. After a dip to black, the camera cuts to the screen of a large studio television set replaying this scene on mute. On the forced kiss, the camera slowly zooms out, revealing a studio audience facing a white male TV host. "When is sex in marriage rape? I'm Steve Edwards; we'll be talking about that when we come back in just a moment. Stay tuned," he announces as *The Baxters* theme music plays out to the second commercial break.

The LA audience segment, hosted by a local talk show personality, is in two segments that have been edited for time. Edwards is a roving host with a long microphone he uses to interview audience members of diverse ages and races. The first words spoken in the pilot segment are by a middle-aged man: "[He] was a drunk moron. And she was trying to be an intelligent woman. They shouldn't have been together." As Edwards weaves back and forth among participants, we learn this audience is divided on whether or not this scene even qualifies as rape because Nancy and Fred are married. "I think she picked a very inopportune moment. I'm sorry, I'm married, I've been married for many years, and my gut reaction is that . . . if she does not choose to be intimate with him at that point, for valid reasons, you don't talk to a man when he's drunk," an older woman says. "So therefore, you know, she set up that situation. I felt more sympathetic for him than her." Several men and women in the crowd agree, alluding to Nancy's words that she did want to "make love" or *be* with Fred (but only after they had a conversation) as implied consent. A younger woman says she didn't believe it was rape because "she kept saying 'I want to, but . . . I want to, but . . . but I want to talk first.' But she shouldn't have tried to talk then about it if she wanted her husband then." The older woman agrees with her, "I'm quarreling with the term 'rape' in a marital relationship. I can see a husband can assault a wife, but. . . ."

Several other audience members are incredulous at these statements. "Under no circumstances does anyone have a right to use physical force on another person. And especially in a relationship that should be intimate," a different, younger woman says. "I don't care if it's a woman trying to force a man, a man trying to force a woman, a homosexual relationship, force should not be involved!" Several married couples are also in the audience. One man suggests that his wife, who sits uncomfortably between him and Edwards reaching with the microphone, says whenever his wife rejects him, he thinks more foreplay might entice her, but when she says no, he goes to sleep rejected. "One of his problems is he gives up too soon," the woman responds as the audience bursts into laughter. Even through the seriousness of the content, jokes are not uncommon in any of the discussion segments.

Edwards then asks if any of the audience members have personal experience, leading to the most poignant share. A soft-spoken young woman sitting in the back says her husband abused her many times, often in the bedroom. "My husband said that it's a woman's role, and because of the fact that it's a woman's role, she takes as she takes, and no more."

Edwards asks if she was still with her husband, and she smiles and says she is not, as a woman sitting in front of her begins applauding her. "No, I'm in a woman's home now," she says before describing the scene through her perspective.

> The woman doesn't say ["listen to me"] for the simple fact that she's afraid of hurting her husband's feelings. And she will stay quiet and hope that some way there will be a chance to make an opening to let him know that things are not going rightly. That they're not communicating... when she waits these long periods of time after a while, she begins to realize there's not gonna be that opening. And she finally does try to make that opening and when she does it's like a total blow up.... At first, I thought I could handle it and slowly get things going. But as years passed on and hints were made... I did love my husband very, very much, and I do to this day, but I know now it will never work. And I know that it had to end.

Her story is difficult, and Edwards's follow-ups are blunt and invasive, but bravely sharing her experience does seem to move many in the studio audience and by extension viewers at home. Edwards finishes the segment by asking another young woman if she would forgive Fred if he apologized the next morning. "No, I wouldn't forgive him," she says. "Because 'I'm sorry' means 'I'm gonna do it again.'"

Meanwhile, the audience for WRAL-TV in Raleigh, North Carolina, led by local Episcopal pastor Bill Coolidge, reportedly was similarly divided. Instead of roving through the crowd, Coolidge remains seated on a raised platform stool as a hanging boom mic finds audience participants. This audience was told the subject would be "spouse rape" ahead of taping, and the group included marriage counselors, therapists, and a rape crisis center volunteer along with local married couples (Herrin 1979, 15).

"There was a lot of heavy throat-clearing as the lights came up in the studio. 'Okay,' Coolidge said. 'Now what did you think was going on?'" (Herrin 1979, 15). Women are more direct in this audience: "I believe in meeting force with force. I would have ... got the frying pan," one woman said. "If she submitted that night, it would be harder to convince him tomorrow that he was wrong. You know society believes a woman says no when she really means yes," another added. One woman commented on the show itself. "I'm wondering if anybody else here resents this as a form of public programming," she said. "I don't think its [sic] a good kind of show. It's explicit, a waste of time, and it bothers me."

Fig. 3.4. Screengrabs from episodes of *The Baxters* assembled and labeled as appeared in a *Daily News* review of the show by Kay Gardella, October 7, 1979, 24.

Another woman leapt to the show's defense. "I'm shocked that you said that; I felt we had a nice big balloon going along and you put a pin in it" (Herrin 1979, 15).

After instructing viewers to stay tuned through another commercial break, the second half of audience segments are very short with only a couple clarifying comments from the audience if any. In LA, Edwards merely ends by saying, "You have all been very, very open, and I appreciate what you have to say. Thank you for coming tonight on *The Baxters*, we will see you next week. Goodnight, everybody." Text appears over B-roll shots of the audience applauding. "The views expressed on 'The Baxters' are those of the participants and do not necessarily reflect those of Golden

West Broadcasters, KTLA, or its advertisers." Chicago, meanwhile, ended episodes with a title card instructing how at-home viewers could request tickets and join other community members in the audience.[3]

In total, I screened fifteen other episodes. Their topics included nuclear energy, gay teachers, the right to die, teenage bullying, gender roles, guns, the death penalty, infidelity, organized religion, socialized medicine, school dropouts, mainstreaming and/or disability integration, incest, and energy conservation. Besides the lack of a studio audience, *The Baxters* has the look and feel of a Norman Lear sitcom both aesthetically and in its racy content, a calling card of Lear's famous envelope pushing in television. The *Washington Post* suggested that although Lear "earned a reputation as the king of controversy in television, some viewers may still get an unexpected jolt from the intimacy and candor of 'The Baxters' [which shows off] Lear's genius for intermingling social comment and entertainment," similar to but different from his other shows because "there's really more social questioning than social commenting. Easy answers are not beamed in just prior to fade-out" (Herrin 1979, 15).

Despite their signature Lear treatment, however, story ideas reportedly came from participating stations on the theory that local stations were more attuned to audiences and "real America" than Hollywood producers (Shales 1979). As Jessup explained, Lear was "most excited and intrigued by the idea of local participation, in all parts of the nation, which may be the true way to sample and judge the public pulse, to see and hear what people think in that big 'out there' country" (McLean 1979, 29). This aspect may have interested him most because of his political activism; he established the progressive advocacy group People for the American Way shortly after *The Baxters* ended.

The *syndicatedness* of a television show like *The Baxters* on a local station matters because it enabled subversive content through radical departures in the historical, industrial, and discursive contexts of normal national network programming, which was still adhering to a weakened Television Code (see Miller 2017). And unlike Lear's experience battling network censors, in this sweetheart syndie deal, "no stations have made even a peep of complaint, either, about the explicit content of some of the programs; partly because the public-service angle acts as a protective shield" (Shales 1979) and the local aspect of the shows allowed stations to contextualize Lear's content with trusted local figures and experts further meeting FCC guidelines for localism. Ultimately, I think that *Variety*'s summary of T.A.T. VP Gary Liberthal's pitch may be the best existing description of *The Baxters*' general appeal:

> a combination of familiar Lear values, a flattering opportunity to have a local station share an essential coproduction status with a leading Hollywood supplier, a vehicle that provides access to private citizens to participate in TV at the local station level, a "surefire" way to press for acclaim and community service brownie points and a sense of having a piece of access product that rather definitely reminds viewers of what most of them had hoped access programming would be when the FCC first decreased the access requirements. The fact that it can be logged as public service fare is just frosting on the cake. (Knight 1979, 52)

Even with all these benefits in tow, *The Baxters* was not the "surefire" success anyone had hoped. Although the program was similarly priced to other prime access shows, the local production component ballooned budgets, the ratings were fair to bad (with a 14 share in Miami [Reddicliffe 1980, 4B] but dire enough in Fort Worth to be replaced by *The Muppets* [Coffee 1979, 7C]), and although critics lauded the concept's innovation, reviews were tepid. Of New York's airing on WPIX, *Variety* wrote, "For a show that's billed as a social comedy, 'The Baxters' came off as stilted and didactic, with the characters serving as mouthpieces for points of view rather than as flesh-and-blood people arguing the way real families might," adding that the studio discussion "was understandably sluggish. Too many people were invited, and it was difficult for any interchange to take place because the seats were arranged in rows facing the moderator" (Demp 1979, 121). "A good idea, yes, but a good show? Not quite," the *Miami Herald* wrote. "*Baxters*' comedy segments always seemed too glib and goofy—feeble video foreplay—and the coffee klatch that followed often seemed little more than bad talk radio" (Reddicliffe 1980, 28).

Zeal for *The Baxters* as an innovative form of television as well as local coverage of episodes and their topics quickly faded away. But it remained a symbol of the collaborative possibilities between local television and national syndicators. Camera operators, producers, set designers, and executives at local stations trained by T.A.T. and BBI for *The Baxters* utilized those skills to create their own productions for syndication throughout the 1980s, and the legacy of that industrial talent provides at least the possibility of reconsidering *The Baxters* as a "failure."

CONCLUSION: SYNDICATION AND LOCAL TELEVISION

The excitement reported for Norman Lear's *The Baxters* at NATPE in 1979 is understandable—it seemed like everyone would be a winner. It offered local television programmers the opportunity to enhance the profiles of their stations through a close partnership with a powerful Hollywood producer while satisfying the FCC's push for more television localism. Curiously, although the show was partially nationally produced, stations lauded *The Baxters* for helping them to become *more* local and responsible to the public interest in their communities. WKRC-TV program director Mel Smith, for example, said he picked it up "because we were looking for a local involvement program . . . because we want to be the most local station in Cincinnati," boasting "we already have the best and most popular network" (Hoffman 1979, A-8).

In the summer of 1980, *Broadcasting* credited *The Baxters* as the icon of a small but growing trend in the DIY television movement. The trade reported Minneapolis, Seattle, Boston, Washington, and Raleigh stations breaking with their networks to create their own prime-time programming and nicknaming themselves the Eighth Decade Consortium. "The difference in the syndication world of the 1980s is that local stations are increasingly evident in the national programming business," it argued. "The kingdoms of Hollywood and New York continue supreme, but new programming principalities are emerging elsewhere . . . forerunners have shown it can be done, and local stations, with big dreams, couldn't be more confident" (*Broadcasting* 1980a, 36). After *The Baxters*' pickup, WCVB-TV's health specials and series became a regular part of the national syndication scene, and its practice with a sitcom format encouraged experimentation, green-lighting the sitcom *Park Street Under* and dramatization legal show *Miller's Court* hosted by law professor Arthur R. Miller (*Broadcasting* 1980a, 36–38).

Beyond mere ambition, with new and cheaper videotape technologies making such work plausible, local stations experimented with original programming because it could also be cheaper than rerun commitments. While *Park Street Under* cost WCVB-TV ten to twelve thousand dollars per episode, for instance, reruns of *Laverne & Shirley* at the time were selling for thirty thousand (*Broadcasting* 1980a, 38). "The price of off-network fare is causing many stations to consider going into the production business," *Broadcasting* wrote. "And once the show is produced, the logical progression is to put that product in the national [syndication] market to recoup costs and make money" (*Broadcasting* 1980a, 38). In explaining the origination of the local channel's sitcom, WCVB-TV president Bob Bennett said, "We had no right in God's green earth to try [making a sitcom], but we had one season with *The Baxters*, working with Norman Lear, and our guys had been out there, and they saw how he shot it with four cameras and ran it simultaneously and it all got put together in the editing room" (*Broadcasting* 1983, 140). Far from being just a "get out of jail free card" for local stations with scheduling gaps, syndication helped to create vital, symbiotic relationships between local stations and national studios, and *The Baxters*, even as a "failed show," is an excellent case study of this rarely discussed but common partnership.

After T.A.T. pulled out of the production, *The Baxters* taped a second season, moving to Toronto and recast with Canadian actors, but it too lasted only one season. Besides fair to bad ratings, numerous other factors contributed to the demise of *The Baxters*, including Lear's own struggles maintaining ratings for iconoclastic shows while the country swung rightward politically and televisual tastes became more conservative.

With the Reagan administration came a new FCC culture increasingly dedicated to deregulating the policies put in place the decade before. Fearing the demise of PTAR after an FCC staff report calling it a regulatory failure, the Station Representatives Association (SRA) said that the rule had accomplished what it set out to—and more. The SRA argued PTAR's elimination would disservice viewers, stations, independent program suppliers, and local and regional advertisers as the seven to eight o'clock prime-time hour would be "recaptured by the networks"; the SRA continued, "PTAR has fostered the development of an independent syndication industry, has restrained total network domination of prime viewing time and, most important, has assisted local licensees in exercising their own judgment in choosing programs, local and syndicated, which best responds to the needs, interests, and tastes of their communities" (*Broadcasting* 1980b, 34). From its use here, "failure" is clearly often a useful political or industrial discourse rather than a helpful evaluative metric.

Even while Norman Lear's *The Baxters* "failed" after only one season on the air, it stands as an exemplar of an experimental moment in both television history and telecommunications policy, illustrating how producers on all levels of the television business ladder responded to a cultural push for a more robust and progressive local TV culture. While I have screened several of the sitcom portions of the show, I can't help but wonder how many talk show segments paired with them still exist out there somewhere in pockets, filing cabinets, and backrooms at local stations across the country waiting to give vocal voyeurs the right to respond and be heard once again.

NOTES

1. There is also a history of children's cartoons developed for national syndication sometimes inserted as segments in local kids' shows, including *Q. T. Hush*, *Colonel Bleep*, and *Bucky and Pepito*.
2. The FCC repealed these guidelines in 1984 ("Charting the Digital Broadcasting Future" 1998, 35–36).
3. The Museum of Classic Chicago Television uploaded to YouTube (in two parts) one episode of *The Baxters* from a WFLD-TV taping.

REFERENCES

Boyer, Peter. 1979. "Fall Fireworks Provided by a Little Number." *Beatrice Daily Sun*, June 19.

Broadcasting. 1979a. "Prods from Ferris: Forget Self-Pity, Work for Solutions, Accept New Delivery Systems." March 19.

———. 1979b. "The Right to Respond." February 26.

———. 1980a. "Do-It-Yourself Movement: Stations into Syndication." June 30.

———. 1980b. "Praising PTAR." September 8.

———. 1983. "The 'Can-Do' Style of Robert Bennett." April 11.

Broadcast Management/Engineering. 1979. "The Baxters: National Programming with a Local Twist." June.

"Charting the Digital Broadcasting Future: Final Report of the Advisory Committee on Public Interest Obligations of Digital Television Broadcasters." 1998. Secretariat, National Telecommunications and Information Administration, U.S. Department of Commerce.

Coffee, Jerry. 1979. "Muppets Moving Back to Monday on Channel 5." *Fort Worth Star Telegram*, October 30.

Demp. 1979. "Reviews of Syndie TV Shows." *Variety*, October 10.

Gardella, Kay. 1979. "Talk Back to the Tube." *Daily News*, October 7, 1979.

Henry, William A. 1977. "A Dimwitted Start for ABC Cop Show." *Boston Globe*, March 5.

Herrin, Angelina. 1979. "Lights, Camera, Talk: A New Kind of TV Show." *News and Observer*, October 13.

Hoffman, Steve. 1979. "Local Involvement Built in Lear Series." *Cincinnati Enquirer*, April 24.

Knight, Bob. 1979. "Bally High for 'The Baxters' at NATPE." *Variety*, March 14.

McLean, Robert A. 1979. "Viewers Join 'The Baxters.'" *Boston Globe*, March 22.

Miller, Taylor Cole. 2017. "Syndicated Queerness: Television Talk Shows, Rerun Syndication, and the Serials of Norman Lear." Ph.D. diss., University of Wisconsin–Madison.

———. 2021. "Re*witched*: Retextuality and the Queering of *Bewitched*." *Camera Obscura: Feminism, Culture, and Media Studies* 36 (3): 1–31.

Mock, Erin Lee. 2013. "'The Soap Opera Is a Hell of an Exciting Form': Norman Lear's *Mary Hartman, Mary Hartman* and the 1970s Viewer." *Camera Obscura* 28 (2): 109–48.

Reddicliffe, Steven. 1980. "'Baxters' May Be Back, But It Won't Be Lear's." *Miami Herald*, June 7.

Shales, Tom. 1979. "The Baxters Come to Bat in the Bunker Tradition." *Washington Post*, September 15. www.washingtonpost.com.

Variety. 1979a. "'Baxters' Sold to 32 Outlets." March 21.

———. 1979b. "'Baxters' Gets TAT Go-Ahead: How-To Seminars Set by BBI." June 13.

CHAPTER 4

ANA HOWE BUKOWSKI

VIDEO AS LOCAL TELEVISION

"BECOMING CABLE" AT THE
LONG BEACH MUSEUM OF ART

In 1975, the Long Beach Museum of Art (LBMA) organized their first-ever *Southland Video Anthology* exhibition. A staggering logistical feat, the group show screened more than thirty hours of video artwork by a notable cast of sixty-five artists working in Southern California, including John Baldessari, Allan Kaprow, Shigeko Kubota, Suzanne Lacy, Paul McCarthy, Ilene Segalove, Susan Mogul, and Bruce Nauman. Arriving eight years after Sony's 1967 release of the Portapak camera, the first lightweight and portable tape recording system widely available on the commercial market, *Southland Video Anthology* broadly documents the extensive and frenetic artistic experimentation with video in the Los Angeles County area beginning in the late 1960s. LA County grew over this decade into a national center for video art, rescaling the region's primary associations with the commercial film and television industries. Registering an abundant moment of regional media production, the show is emblematic of some of the most active years in what has been termed "California Video."[1]

The show's titular emphasis on video, however, represents something of a misnomer. As curator David Ross claims in the *Anthology*'s catalogue, it is rather television that constitutes the formal emphasis of the show. In his catalogue essay, Ross outlines a vision of the communicative role that television will play in shaping the future of arts institutions. He argues that works on videotape explicitly tailored to the viewing context and "semiotic structure" of broadcast television complicate traditional "sculptural" methods of gallery display (Ross 1975, 3). Responding to this problem, Ross outlines an ethical imperative toward structural transformation, noting that as a "communication oriented institution with a responsibility to ideas . . . and the demands of an increasingly sophisticated public," the museum "stands susceptible to change as a result of the undertaking signaled by this anthology exhibition" (3). In this frame, Ross's envisioned outcome is a museum that functions more like an electronic distribution network in service of ideas: "The further the museum moves towards functional invisibility, the further the museum moves towards a responsible and effective posture" (3). A televisual manifesto veiled as an exhibition text, his entry is worth quoting at length:

> Televisions don't just seem out of place in art museums; for the most part, they are. It becomes obvious that the museum's role vis-à-vis television and art is not the keeper of the television set (as a replacement for the object displaced by the work on tape), but rather as a conduit for the work to reach the home. This raises the more general idea that museums could and should expand the way they intercede between the work of art and the audience. Central to this is the notion of museums *becoming cable or broadcasting systems* in a fashion analogous to the way in which museums use physical gallery space to hang traditional art works. (Ross 1975, 3–4, emphasis added)

Ross's description of the museum as a communicative "conduit" and appeal to cable television as a structure interceding between art and audience represents not only a drive toward production—for video artists to make television—but a desire to see the LBMA radically shift its institutional posture by *becoming* a televisual system. While this totalized vision would never come to be realized, it did nevertheless shape activities at the museum in the years following the 1975 *Anthology*.

I examine these early stages of televisual interest at the LBMA in this chapter. This period is marked by the introduction of the museum's video program in 1974, the activities that arose around the opening of their Artists Post-Production Studio (APPS) in 1976, and the conceptual and logistical developments that contributed to their first airing of artists' works on regional cable networks as early as 1977. Through a discursive and production-oriented study of its extant oral histories, exhibition materials, and the LBMA's administrative archives housed at the Getty Research Institute (GRI), I probe how the goal of "becoming cable" and imaginaries of access, expansion, and public engagement contoured museum planning and programming at this time. To this end, I am interested in how the museum's intention to become a "distinct part of the telecommunications system" represented a specifically materialist politics articulated to museum audiences, public funding bodies, and local government (Ross 1975, 4). The value of this work derives from its examination of a robust yet underexplored field of regional media production and the ways in which the sociomaterial form of local television infrastructure can be thought alongside networks of artistic administration, production, and exchange. While the LBMA did go on to produce cable access content that was distributed locally and nationally, I equally foreground the museum's video exhibition and postproduction activities in this study. This more expansive examination of the museum as a site for community media production, distribution, and exchange contributes to the field a recognition of the broader practices that might be included under the rubric of public access television. The majority of scholarship on local TV programming has centered on formal and textual analysis of on-the-air series (Hawkins 2015; Wald 2015; Stiffler 2018; Herold 2020). While these scholars offer significant insights into televisual content, my study forwards a theoretical and methodological focus on the role of infrastructure and material networks in the development of programming, understanding cable access as a mode of connection, an administrative posture, a method of production, and a form of desire. Despite the series of technological, policy, and administrative roadblocks that prevented the LBMA's network from coming to be, their initial video distribution projects and postproduction facilities that materialized from this vision may nevertheless be studied as expanded forms of television.

Here I attend to how local cable was historically implemented in relation to the work of artists and arts institutions. My approach positions the museum as a vital node in the development of public telecommunications infrastructure and the expansion of local media geographies. This perspective is in step with that of John Durham Peters, who identifies a "deep infrastructural ethic" within media theory committed to "mak[ing] environments visible" (Peters 2015, 35, 38). Public infrastructure is often conceived as a material system of occlusion, designed to remain unseen and unintelligible to regular users; I thus embrace Peters's "infrastructural ethic" as both method and analytic. Examining the LBMA's historically active role in the media networking of LA County, I equally explore how the museum's production resources make seen their coordination with technological systems and local politics. Such an approach argues for the study of cable access as a specific *aesthetic* phenomenon, which I argue was born in part from the coterminous encounter of contemporary art institutions and public media infrastructure. Within this microhistory, video production emerges as a dynamic lens onto the ongoing, and occasionally fraught, relationship between museum spaces and telecommunications systems. Alongside television studies that foreground how grassroots efforts and subcultural communities have contributed to dominant cable histories, here I develop a more complex civic profile of arts institutions and the significant role they played in the development of regional telecommunications infrastructure in Southern California over the early to mid-1970s.

Media histories of LA County have documented the rich overlap between artistic practice, cultural scenes, and their shifting geographic orientations. This chapter favors an opportunity to think of cable access as a sociospatial infrastructure linking and organizing arts institutions, artists' networks, and media subcultures across the region over the 1970s. As I argue here, Ross's interest in "becoming cable" points to an emerging sphere of artistic and infrastructural activity at the museum. While a station was never established at the LBMA, its provision of postproduction facilities brought many artists through Long Beach over the decade, remapping social geographies of both regional and international arts communities. My inquiry builds upon the GRI's landmark 2008 exhibition *California Video*, a retrospective cataloging the LBMA's video programs from the 1970s through the 1990s (Phillips 2008). Vast and sprawling, *California Video* offers by its own admission a necessarily incomplete historical portrait of a major regional artistic movement, inviting further meditations on the LBMA's influence and vitality within broader U.S. video histories. Significant as an art world account, my research pushes this storytelling further by asking what technological and social systems are witnessed if we consider the LBMA as a distinct infrastructural node within the local television landscape of 1970s LA County, a region commonly understood in terms of its networked dispersion. I consequently approach the cultural topography initiated in Ross's incipient desire to *be* cable television in terms akin to C. Ondine Chavoya and David Evans Frantz's discussion of queer artistic networks in their exhibition *Axis Mundo: Queer Networks in Chicano L.A.*: "promiscuous and capacious" in their reach, comprising a spread of "affinities, connections, affiliated aesthetic and conceptual practices, and political alignments" (Chavoya and Frantz 2018, 25). To this point, I argue that television studies might nuance and enliven its historical storytelling by attending to the formal contributions of artists and arts institutions who desired to make something of telecommunications infrastructure. With these sorts of relations in mind, I look to the LBMA's desire to become a "distinct part of the telecommunications system" to highlight the interaction between regional media infrastructure and cultural network building, gesturing toward connections that radiate along and across like a coaxial cable map.

ARTISTS' TELEVISION AND THE PUBLIC SECTOR

The ratification of cable television as part of the U.S. telecommunications landscape in 1972 was the result of a rare entwinement of public and commercial media infrastructures: initial FCC policy required system operators to reserve access channels and studio space for community use. Even as television's emergence was tethered to the expansion of the private, for-profit telecommunications sector, these affordances attracted interest from artists and arts institutions looking to experiment with television and establish their own channels outside of the networked mainstream. These policy changes established a framework for video's, and eventually television's, arrival at the LBMA in the first half of the 1970s, which I lay out in this section. This said, the multiple origins of artists' television predate 1972, and video's emergence in Southern California was the product of the confluence of multiple institutional, administrative, and aesthetic factors. Guided by an infrastructural ethic, these speak in particular to the shifting conceptualizations of public media and the art museum in the 1970s, the latter of which was being rethought as a broader civic node and a technological gateway into the social, political, and televisual networking of LA County. As I discuss in this section, LBMA's status as a municipally run institution is essential to this story of video and cable's entwinements with the museum. To this day LBMA remains a public art center owned by the City of Long Beach and operated by the Long Beach Museum of Art Foundation. Located thirty miles south of Los Angeles, Long Beach and the museum maintain a status distinct from LA's as a global art and entertainment capital.

The early 1970s were the peak years of what Hall and Fifer (1990) term the "video revolution." By the early part of the decade, video was relatively widespread across California and especially popular with the experimental artist communities of San Francisco and the Southland. The format's presence and use additionally grew via the development of video programs at Southern California's "critical mass of art schools"

(Jones 2017, 269) such as CalArts, UC Irvine, UCLA, and UC San Diego. Video represented a new material vanguard for artistic production and distribution, and the portability and easy transferability of tape offered extensive possibilities for experimentation in documentation, editing, and distribution. The late 1960s and early 1970s equally saw the establishment of independent production and development centers for artistic work in public television. Funded in large part by grants from the Rockefeller Foundation, these included the National Center for Experiments in Television (NCET) in San Francisco, WGBH Boston's New Television Workshop, and the Television Laboratory at WNET/Thirteen New York. Moreover, projects to decentralize the power of commercial television had been pursued by the likes of the video collective Raindance Corporation, publishers of the DIY technology journal *Radical Software* and progenitors of the "Guerrilla Television" movement of the early 1970s (Joselit 2007; Boyle 1997). Experimenters were driven by aspirations to decentralize broadcast television as a mass conditioning agent of society and set their sights on launching a parallel, independent system that could function as a source of utopian enlightenment and a free structure of information exchange. As LBMA video curator Kathy Rae Huffman describes, "When artists referred to their video artwork as television, they meant that it was an experimental alternative to the mainstream, not a commercial program" (2008, 279).

Video was still an institutionally and culturally marginal medium when it first entered the LBMA. The museum's earliest video exhibitions were mounted in early 1974, including one of works by Jay D McCafferty curated by director J. E. Adlmann and another of videos made by eight- to thirteen-year-olds produced during a city-run television and film production workshop. Amid much art world excitement around the format, the museum would inaugurate its permanent video program later that year when Adlmann invited twenty-three-year-old Ross, then–video curator of the Everson Museum of Art in Syracuse, New York, to join the West Coast gallery. The timing of Ross's arrival at the LBMA was fortuitous, coinciding with a moment of proposed institutional expansion and redefinition. The City of Long Beach was then in talks with the museum to design a new "Arts Forum," with famed architect I. M. Pei touted as a possible candidate for design. Compelled by ideals of publicness and civic engagement—as well as a vision to enlarge Long Beach's cultural stature—the Arts Forum project benchmarked a critical opportunity to seriously consider the form of the "museum of the future" (Huffman et al. 2008, 258). For Ross, the envisioned affordances of a newly emergent *cable television* were primary within his proposed configuration for a new museum of art:

> It was very important at the time to try to understand the potential and the reality of [cable]. To figure out what it meant, in terms of changes in the larger social fabric, when artists had access to their audience in a totally different way. That's what brought me to Long Beach in the first place, the idea of building a museum with its own channel. It was originally Nam June Paik's idea—one that he planted in my little, very empty, fertile mind at that time. The idea was that the museum of the future has to be a television channel, among other things; that the museum needs to be a catalyst; it needs to be a participant in a structured community; it needed to push boundaries and be an active agent for change. In this case, the change that we were talking about was the ability for artists to eventually—as they fairly soon will be able to do—just sidestep that entire museum superstructure that comes between an artists and his or her audience, his or her viewer; the other individual, the other side of the equation. (Huffman et al. 2008, 258)

Broad political and financial corruption and the siphoning of all municipal funds toward the redevelopment of the Port of Los Angeles eventually led to the dramatic combustion of this project in 1977. However, as I discuss in this essay, cable television as telecommunications infrastructure and cultural imaginary significantly transformed video art and its production locally and regionally. In the affective and ethical posturing of Ross's desire for the museum to "be a television channel" (258), his words evoke a particular understanding of how cable access was already being imagined as an enriching of the built environment of the city. At the LBMA, Ross's desire to open an access station at the museum serves as a model for witnessing how cable was then understood as both a technological and a socioethical system appealing to a distinct program of community media engagement.

Curators and artists alike saw in cable access a promise of building more immediate relationships with audiences by "[sidestepping] that entire museum superstructure" (Huffman et al. 2008, 258). Under Ross and subsequent video curators such as Kathy Rae Huffman (1978–84), cable television quietly revolutionized the museum, its programs, and its space. Throughout this essay, I trace the impact of cable on the identity, architecture, and institutional affiliations of the LBMA. I note how the brief and often complex encounter between cable and video at the museum not only influenced its administrative and artistic practices but offered an imagined renegotiation of the relationships between artistic scenes, art institutions, television, and local audiences. This intervention in both art and television histories brings forth the vitality of their meeting and the role that cable television had in the aesthetics, production, distribution, and broader *possibilities* of art. Ross's image of the future museum centers cable television as a core civic infrastructure, one whose potentially direct address to local audiences was imagined as a possible agent of social change. Brian Larkin notes how existing infrastructures often interpenetrate and overlap, "generat[ing] [their] own mode of spatiality, linking ... into new economic and social networks" (2008, 240). To this point, I use the term "artists' television" in this essay to evoke the interpenetration of cable and video, describing the nexus of interconnecting technological, policy-based, and institutional pathways that underline their overlap—many of which were politicized by nature of their administrative entanglement with local bureaucracy, funding bodies, and corporate interests. Reading the LBMA as a vital site of overlap in the conceptual, aesthetic, and technological expansions of cable and video art in Southern California, we witness how cable television as a medium of distribution, method of production, and practice of engagement transformed video art and its possibilities for artists, curators, and publics alike.

ARTISTS' TELEVISION IS A PLACE

Outside of the first *Southland* show, archival traces of the initial years of televisual interest at the LBMA are limited. Stymied by political corruption and financial woes, the Arts Forum development never took off, caused by a rift in city management that ultimately caused museum director Jan Adlmann to resign in 1977. Ross would depart that same year for a curatorship at the Berkeley Art Museum. His short tenure in Long Beach, however, set a rich conceptual and administrative mandate for the museum. This period saw a major increase in video exhibitions and the creation of a significant televisual resource in the establishment of their APPS in 1976. Materials related to the APPS offer a glimpse into how an infrastructural ethic influenced the museum's public disposition in years to come. Via programming and the provision of production tools, the LBMA cemented itself as a center for video, attracting a network of regional and international artists in the process.

By 1976, the LBMA was producing upward of seven video exhibitions a year alongside its traditional arts programming, a focus unique in LA County. These included four additional iterations of the *Southland Video Anthology*. As I described earlier, the inaugural *Southland* exhibition was a frenetic survey humming with intense formal and tonal variety, featuring the work of sixty-five artists. The exhibition followed a rationale in the form of Ross's (1975, 4) question: "How can video art exist outside of the confines of the museum's sanctuary?" For Ross and several of the show's artists, the negotiated answer to this query was "television"; they deliberately used the technology, communicative structure, and semiotic content of this dominant media vernacular to richly contrasting ends. For example, videos by William Wegman see the artist taking a literal approach to television tropes, performing the role of the TV pitch man with an exaggerated drollness. Similarly, Martha Rosler's now-classic video *Semiotics of the Kitchen* (1975) sees her in the guise of a surrealist Julia Child, taking the viewer on a tour of her kitchen in a wry commentary on gendered space. Comparably, many of the show's works were formally dense and sensorially confronting. Chris Burden's video *Back to You* (1974) replays a performance in which he lay in a cramped elevator while plastic push pins were inserted into his forearm. During its documentation, Burden was visible only through a closed-circuit television monitor in an adjacent gallery space, a violent intensification of the engrossing horror and physical remove of commercial media. Additionally, Paul McCarthy's *Sauce* (1974) offers a more abject rejoinder to Rosler's domestic vision. McCarthy's video—a rare colorized entry in the show—records a performance of the same name in a "straight, commercial television style" (Ross 1975, 8) where the artist smears ketchup over his nude body, sliding and contorting across a tabletop. In both Burden and McCarthy's renderings, television becomes difficult to watch and even stomach, testing the expectations of audiences. With commercial television dominating the telecommunications landscape of America, Southern Californian artists used video as a means of formally and semiotically responding to the expressions of mainstream media.

Much tighter in scope than its sprawling inaugural show, the 1977 *Anthologies* were driven by issues of form and theme. The second *Southland*, for example, focused on the relationship between television and live performance art in LA and the following iteration presented a collaborative video portrait of ex-Hollywood wrestlers by Ilene Segalove and Lowell Darling. Made continually explicit by Ross in exhibition materials was the frame of cable television. Regardless of whether his interest in cable was actually shared by featured video artists, this organizing rationale was intentional and continually expressed what he saw as television's potential. Writing in the introduction to its fourth edition, Ross finds urgency in "the willingness of contemporary artists to maintain a more visible and responsible position in a community that had formerly been the domain of corporate control" (1977b, 93). Taking up this position, he argues the task of museums is to go beyond its "insular" structure and address a wider audience in the home, calling on cable television's ability "to make the issues of contemporary art available to a wider public" (93). As Ross writes in the preface to the third *Southland* edition, "Video, after all, is a tool not an attitude or a style," making an emphatic case for its aesthetic and functional advantages over standard exhibition models (1977a, 74). What I am most attentive to here is how Ross prefigures cable television as a powerful telecommunications medium and as an affective and intentionally *social* infrastructure. Occasionally, public media infrastructure becomes a site by which "people and cities imagine and understand their social and spatial relationships with each other," as Matthew Dewey (2021, 782) describes. In these terms, it is possible to witness how Ross's imagining of the LBMA as part of the telecommunications grid required seeing its capacities as a networked structure that could shape regional art scenes. He describes with conviction in the first *Southland* catalogue the LBMA's movement toward establishing a television station as a "responsible and effective posture" reflecting a "general idea that museums could and should expand the way they intercede between the work of art and the audience" (Ross 1975, 3). Even as these systems failed to arise at the museum, Ross's vision of expansion articulates a certain "infrastructural ethic" wherein the desired transmission of video art *as* television required an attunement to how artistic scenes might be structured and connected across space.

Ross's tenure at the LBMA was brief, spanning just under three years, unable to establish an access station at the museum as he concretely dreamed of doing. We can nevertheless trace a similar infrastructural ethic in the lasting project of his time in Long Beach: the opening of its APPS in 1976. Unlike in New York and Boston, Southern California then lacked an accessible, experimental postproduction facility and Portapaks remained prohibitively expensive. Ross (quoted in Huffman et al. 2008, 253) remarks how this lack of access to hardware directly affected the form and quality of videos being produced regionally: "[a] lot of artists were making very long and very boring videotapes, because nobody had any editing equipment." Through the Rockefeller Foundation, the LBMA secured a fifty-thousand-dollar grant to purchase cameras, a Convergence ECS-1 controller with a pair of three-quarter-inch decks as well as two reel-to-reel decks with manual editing capabilities (Huffman et al. 2008, 254). Run out of the museum's attic, which was painted white to resemble a traditional artist studio, the facility was initially staffed by technicians John Baker and Peter Kirby. Until the APPS was incorporated as the off-site "Video Annex" in 1979, artists were charged almost nothing for use of the space, which they could access at all hours, a complete rarity for a museum and any public facility of this scope.

News of the APPS spread nationally and internationally via Ross's extensive artistic relationships and regionally by word of mouth, and artists rapidly began using the studio.[2] At the time, the LBMA was receiving virtually no money or administrative oversight from the city and subsisting off of grants from the National Endowment from the Arts and the Rockefeller Foundation. Reflecting on his time as museum technical director from 1976 through 1977, Kirby (quoted in Huffman et al. 2008, 257, emphasis added) describes the feeling of this relative isolation from dominant institutional networks: "There was a great deal of energy and generosity emanating from the museum during this period. . . . That created an environment of trust and excitement, as well as a social scene. . . . It was good because you couldn't make any money, even though you had to have money to do it. I enjoyed that contradiction. *It seemed like an ideology almost.*" As the APPS energetically grew a scene of its own via the many sociotechnical encounters taking place at the studio, the museum was able to build up an unparalleled video collection, acquiring a copy of every production edited on site (a practice continued until the closing of the Video Annex in the late 1990s). Appealing to an ethic—or, as Kirby puts it, an ideology—of access to resources conjoined with possibilities for experimental freedom and even failure, the video infrastructure of the APPS was able to generate an artistic scene in production, one potentially invisible in contexts of circulation and exhibition. For these reasons, better understanding artists' television and its histories demands that we look behind what appears on the gallery monitor. While the APPS did not possess broadcasting capabilities, its accessible provision of video equipment and freewheeling organization reflect the "importance of socio-spatial elements in the organization of media projects like public access television" (Dewey 2021, 781). This was a place of practical encounter for video artists, accounting for a more expansive definition of "public access" outside of the functions of networked distribution.

The great thematic and aesthetic variety of the LBMA's *Southland* exhibitions and the rich social and technological affordances of the APPS capture a notion of cable access as an ideological and geographically situated *practice*. Some of the video works exhibited in the *Southland* shows and produced at the APPS did eventually make it to air, as I discuss in the following section. That these works originated in a standard exhibition context speaks to the entwined growth of art institutions and the wider implementation of cable in LA County. The arrival of the APPS functionally altered the social energy and institutional mandate of the LBMA, allowing us to locate the APPS as a material link in the televisual networking of Southern California.

ARTISTS' TELEVISION AS A SOCIAL INFRASTRUCTURE

The desire to "become cable" partially materialized with the APPS and was pushed further with the arrival of Kathy Rae Huffman, initially Ross's intern and eventually his successor as video curator. Huffman was administratively and logistically instrumental in developing the museum's first-ever foray into broadcasting: the literally titled program *Video Art*. A video compilation series aired on regional cable access from late 1976 through 1977, the program premiered around the time of the APPS's opening and featured works exhibited at the museum, primarily its *Southland* shows. As I discuss in this section, *Video Art* possessed its own curatorial mandate distinct from in-house programming, reflecting an understanding of public access as a social mode of "[interceding] between the work of art and the audience" (Ross 1975, 3). *Video Art*'s infrastructural ethic exemplifies how television became a social outlet for airing regional media subcultures to potentially wider publics, documenting the encounter of sometimes-dispersed Southern California art scenes.

According to a letter written by Huffman (Long Beach Museum of Art Video Archive, GRI) to Los Angeles's Theta Public Access on December 21, 1976, a curated selection of videotapes was to be broadcast on the service's Channel F through early February 1977. Aired in weekly installments repeated three times, the short series comprised a five-week showing schedule organized around single artists, beginning with Hildegarde Duane and proceeding to Terry Fox, Susan Mogul, John Sturgeon, and Bill Viola. Documentation of *Video Art* is not available, meaning it is unknown how these works were contextualized for audiences. Nor can we be sure how *Video Art* was framed within the flow of Theta's prime-time programming block. Huffman's letter, for its part, simply lists the run time of each installment, ranging from sixteen to thirty-five minutes, and the color quality of each work.

This said, conceptual inferences can be drawn from these selections. In the mid-1970s cable subscribers were small in number and television audiences had generally "lower" cultural associations than those of a specialized museum public. These boundaries are reflected in program selections. Unlike some of the longer, more explicitly challenging selections from the *Southland* shows, such as the confrontational, neo-grotesque work of Paul McCarthy, Huffman's choices extend a softer, sometimes humorous invitation toward viewership. Duane's piece *East Is Red*, which begins the series, documents a 1976 LBMA show on contemporary Chinese art, transporting the exhibition into home viewing space and setting a pedagogical tone. Conversely, Mogul's episode included an extended version of her video *Dressing Up* (1975) featured in the first *Southland* edition. Dry and witty, the tape begins with the artist seated naked and snacking on corn nuts while she models clothing, discussing her love of bargain hunting inherited from her mother. The piece is irreverent and emotionally disarming, emphasizing video's aesthetic intimacy. Fox, Sturgeon, and Viola's tapes are similarly engaging, rendering kinetic portraits of the body and slow, meditative menageries of household objects made unfamiliar through camera work, editing techniques, and vibrant usages of color and sound. As something of an "introductory course" in artists' television, *Video Art* plays with and against its typical content and temporal pacing of commercial broadcasting, while appealing to viewers via its familiar scenes and conversational tone.

Three more installments of *Video Art* were released over 1977. Compilations rather than single artist presentations, episodes predominantly spotlighted artists from the *Southland* shows, including Ilene Segalove, Lowell Darling, William Wegman, Nam June Paik, Eleanor Antin, and Lynda Benglis. Also included was *The David Ross Show*, a one-off segment documenting snippets of interviews with over thirty video artists Ross conducted during a raucous, live, twenty-four-hour broadcast aired at the Hilton Hotel during the College Art Association (CAA) meetings in LA in February 1977. Chosen to "cover the major areas of interest in the field of video art" and "clarifying the underlying intentions of the video artist and his approach to the medium of video" (Long Beach

Museum of Art Video Archive, box 101 folder 8), these selections work to assemble a visible network of faces and names associated with an emergent video scene in Southern California. Once again, video in the form of artists' television was being proposed as an inherently *social* infrastructure, linking regional sites of production, conversation, and exhibition.

The infrastructural connotations in this first outing of the LBMA "becoming cable" are similarly tracked in the distribution of *Video Art*. Following the airing of two series on Theta Cable's Channel F and Channel 3, scheduling documents note that additional installments were broadcast on Santa Barbara Cable and Long Beach Cable between May and August 1977. We know that in the linking of noncontiguous cable systems through a dispersed programming model, videotapes were transported to stations by Huffman herself, who relied on Southern California's extensive freeway network in the delivery of artists' television (Huffman et al. 2008). In this view, *Video Art*'s sociospatial structure reflects the flow and movement of people across space, forging new links across the telecommunications and automotive mapping of Southern California. Writing about Los Angeles, Kazys Varnelis (2008, 47) describes the city as a mesh of "hybridized ecologies" sustained by extensive infrastructures, or "life-support systems" that sustain communities. Varnelis notes that these systems are often made of "the unseen world of cables, wires, connections, codes, agreements, and capital" whose operation and form "determine the structure of urban areas." The distribution pathways of *Video Art* reflect the cable network expansion throughout Southern California over the 1970s, with stations increasingly desirous of content to put to air; moreover, there are infrastructural resonances to be found in the materiality of program correspondence. Visually, Huffman's programming letters are telling documents. Printed on City of Long Beach letterhead, like most correspondence of this era, her scheduling notes to station administrators also feature the museum's name, Adlmann's as director, the title and visual insignia of the doomed Arts Forum project still linked to Pei, and even a tagline: "LONG BEACH MUSEUM OF ART—a lively arts forum for the people of Long Beach—and the coast" (Long Beach Museum of Art Video Archive, box 101 folder 8). This paper trace suggests the power of cable broadcasting as a modality of institutional expansion and promotion within both local and more expansive regional contexts, potential evidence of attempts to raise the museum's profile while it was mired in delayed infrastructural development.

More than simple evidence of the museum's negotiated activities in expansion, *Video Art* also demonstrates how regional artistic scenes have been historically mapped and mediated via telecommunications infrastructure. Other than Viola, who was then based in New York and later moved to Long Beach in the 1980s with his partner Perov, nearly all of the featured artists lived and worked in the Southland. Discussions of New York's Downtown scenes of the seventies and eighties have discussed how cable programs such as Glenn O'Brien's *TV Party* (1978–82) and *Public Access Poetry* (1977–78) aired artistic communities for local audiences (Galvin 2013; Olin 2018). Writing on the former, for example, Ben Olin describes public access as a "relational network" made in performance, with poets "illustrat[ing] the social fabric of their local literary scene by improvising with . . . rudimentary studio equipment" (2018, 48). While we can assume *Video Art* lacked the interactive, conversational, and personality-driven dimensions of both these programs—save for Ross's interview segments—the show nevertheless draws attention to cable access as a platform for "visually 'screening'" artistic scenes to a greater viewing public. Within the context of LA County, the role of public access and artists' television has only recently been considered as a networked space for the development of dispersed aesthetic scenes. As with the APPS, a television-forward historiographic framework orients the video production studio and access station as sociogeographic nodes connected to the network of artist-run spaces established in the early 1970s (Chavoya and Frantz 2018, 31). Further study of programs such as *Video Art* offers a critical opportunity to consider how historical interface with public telecommunications infrastructure has significantly mediated the social feelings, geographic organization, and cultural and political exchanges cultivated across media subcultures in LA County.

Even as we cannot revisit *Video Art* as it originally appeared, its archival traces nevertheless gesture toward the function of artists' television as a social infrastructure linking the LBMA to various sites of artistic production, distribution, and circulation across LA County. Here we are left with a keen sense of the bifurcated role that the promise of "becoming cable" proposed for the LBMA's administration: on the one hand, a means of emboldening its public stature for legislators and civic funding bodies and, on another, a means of enriching institutional connections with artists and subcultural audiences. Tracking the packaged circulation of artists' television across LA County's various cable access stations moreover speaks to the infrastructural traces of *Video Art*. Serialization of contents, dispersed programming models, and a proliferation of partner stations render an image of the Southland region animated by an "invisible" network of cables and wires tethering artistic scenes and institutions.

CONCLUSION

This study of the initial years of televisual interest at the Long Beach Museum of Art contributes new insights into television histories and brings forth one story of cable's significant impact on the aesthetics, production, and broader possibilities of video art as a medium. Given the existing gaps in the institutional archive, this story is a necessarily speculative rendering of how mid-1970s Southern California video scenes were networked via local television infrastructure and resources. With the role of artists and museums largely excluded from cable television histories, this essay nevertheless argues that the complex proximities of the two had a significant influence on how art was produced, distributed, and understood as a tool of local engagement. In fact, witnessing the relationship between cable and video at the LBMA allows us to approach a renewed understanding of museum practices as an intended part of public life. Following the partial realization of Ross's desire to "become cable" with the APPS and video work brought to air in the mid- to late 1970s, the museum would go on to produce original programming for Long Beach Cablevision in the 1980s and establish "Open Channels," a broadcasting grant program for local artists. Reviewing this later trajectory, we can see how television has always already functioned as a geographically situated practice defined according to access to studio space, hardware, and vectors of institutional and local political power. Here, television remains at the vanguard of expanded artistic practice.

If read according to the method and analytic of the "infrastructural ethic," the growth of cable programs at the LBMA portrays how artists pushed the function and meaning of television as a telecommunications infrastructure and imaginary of engagement. The importance of these years, despite their brevity, cannot be overstated: a model of access for artists, the APPS offering the framework for the museum's eventual Video Annex, which would support some of the most critical productions in California video history. To this end, the museum's early television programs and resources connote how the desires of both artists and arts administrators to "become cable" shaped the development of local artistic scenes explicitly made in production. Such a vision of the museum as a technological gateway to broader publics, scenes, and regional telecommunications infrastructures demonstrates the influential model that public access television held as both technological framework and social infrastructure encompassing various sites of imagination, production, and distribution, and multiple built environments. Moreover, this model asks us to push our definition of what might be properly considered cable television, accounting for the various desires, production centers, relationships, exhibition formats, material and infrastructural systems, and aesthetics that collectively cohere public access as a practice. Ross's dream of establishing a television station at the museum was never properly realized. However, if we return to his "general idea that museums could and should expand the way they intercede between the work of art and the audience" (1975, 3), material traces of these infrastructural desires may be found everywhere across the museum's curatorial projects, facilities, scene-based networks, and eventual cable television programming. In the catalog of *California Video*, Phillips writes, "California's artists and their histories far exceed what has been documented here, and the true complexity of these accounts resides with the artists themselves—in their artworks, their archives, and their memories" (2008, 13). So too does this particular story remain incomplete, calling for additional accounts to give form to these networked histories of artistic communication.

NOTES

1. This is the title of both a 1980 anthology exhibition curated at the LBMA by Kathy Rae Huffman and a 2007 Getty Research Institute exhibition.
2. A June 6, 1977, letter from Ross to Howard Klein, director of arts at the Rockefeller Foundation, notes eighty-five artists working for over fourteen hundred hours at the APPS since its opening the year prior.

REFERENCES

Boyle, Deirdre. 1997. *Subject to Change: Guerrilla Television Revisited*. Oxford University Press.

Chavoya, C. Ondine, and David Evans Frantz. 2018. "Axis Mundo: Constellations and Connections." In *Axis Mundo: Queer Networks in Chicano L.A.*, edited by C. Ondine Chavoya and David Evans Frantz, 24–55. Prestel.

Dewey, Matthew. 2021. "Anyone Can Do YouTube, but Not Everyone Can Do Public Access: Urban Politics, Production Tools, and a Communications Infrastructure to Call Home." *Television & New Media* 22 (7): 779–98.

Galvin, Kristen. 2013. "TV Party: Downtown New York Scenes Live on Your TV Screen." *Journal of Popular Music Studies* 25 (3): 326–48.

Hall, Doug, and Sally Jo Fifer, eds. 1990. *Illuminating Video: An Essential Guide to Video Art*. Aperture.

Hawkins, Joan, ed. 2015. *Downtown Film and TV Culture 1975–2001*. Intellect.

Herold, Lauren. 2020. "Televisual Emotional Pedagogy: AIDS, Affect, and Activism on Vito Russo's Our Time." *Television & New Media* 21 (1): 25–40.

Huffman, Kathy Rae. 2008. "Art, TV, and the Long Beach Museum of Art: A Short History." In Phillips, *California Video*, 279–84.

Huffman, Kathy Rae, David A. Ross, Peter Kirby, Kira Perov, Joe Leonardi, and Carole Ann Klonarides. 2008. "Recollections: A Brief History of the Video Programs at the Long Beach Museum of Art." In Phillips, *California Video*, 252–68.

Jones, Kellie. 2017. *South of Pico: African American Artists in Los Angeles in the 1960s and 1970s*. Duke University Press.

Joselit, David. 2007. *Feedback: Television against Democracy*. MIT Press.

Larkin, Brian. 2008. *Signal and Noise: Media, Infrastructure, and Urban Culture in Nigeria*. Duke University Press.

Long Beach Museum of Art Video Archive. Special Collections, Getty Research Institute, Los Angeles.

Olin, Ben. 2018. "Reframing the New York School: Public Access Poetry and the Screening of Poetic Coterie." *Framework* 59 (1): 47–85.

Peters, John Durham. 2015. *The Marvelous Clouds: Toward a Philosophy of Elemental Media*. University of Chicago Press.

Phillips, Glenn, ed. 2008. *California Video: Artists and Histories*. Getty Research Institute.

Ross, David A. 1975. *Southland Video Anthology: June 8–September 7, 1975*. Long Beach Museum of Art.

———. 1977a. "Introduction to Part 3." In *Southland Video Anthology: [Exhibition], 1976–77*, edited by Long Beach Museum of Art, 74–75. Long Beach Museum of Art.

———. 1977b. "Introduction to Part 4." In *Southland Video Anthology: [Exhibition], 1976–77*, edited by Long Beach Museum of Art, 91–93. Long Beach Museum of Art.

Stiffler, Brad. 2018. "Punk Subculture and the Queer Critique of Community on 1980s Cable TV: The Case of New Wave Theatre." *Television & New Media* 19 (1): 42–58.

Varnelis, Kazys. 2008. *The Infrastructural City: Networked Ecologies in Los Angeles*. Actar.

Wald, Gayle. 2015. *It's Been Beautiful:* Soul! *and Black Power Television*. Duke University Press.

CHAPTER 5

DANIEL MARCUS

"TO CALL IT A ZOO WOULD BE UNKIND TO ANIMALS"

HOW CABLE TELEVISION CAME TO MIAMI

In 2022, Discovery Inc., owner of the Discovery informational cable channels, merged with WarnerMedia, heir to the Time Warner media empire and owner of CNN, HBO, Warner Bros. Entertainment, and other high-profile producers and outlets (Koblin 2022). The new leadership team began making significant changes at CNN and HBO soon after the merger became public. CNN announced that it would try to hold an ideological position between the left-leaning MSNBC news channel and the right-wing FOX News, which many media analysts interpreted as a move to the political right to appease Republicans and corporate interests who were critical of the network's negative reporting about the Trump administration. The network canceled the media watchdog show *Reliable Sources*, which had been hosted by Brian Stelter, one of CNN's biggest critics of FOX, and he left the network (Mullin 2022). (Stelter returned to CNN in 2024.) Other CNN voices grew muted in their criticism of the American right. HBO cut programming from its streaming service HBO Max, even as the merged company said it hoped for more streaming success for older Warner properties (Foreman 2022).

The merger was more of a friendly takeover than an equal partnership; Warner spun off from its parent company, AT&T, to land under the control of Discovery and its leader John Malone. Malone had emerged from the rise of cable television in the United States first to direct TCI (which eventually became the most successful cable system provider) in 1973, and then Discovery, which gave Malone the dominant position in the new company called Warner Bros. Discovery. Malone, long one of the major media moguls in the country, had now attained new heights of power, taking control of some of the most famous and influential content providers in the country.

In the current era of streaming platforms, social media empires, and promises of virtual reality universes, the cable television system as it developed in the last third of the twentieth century may seem nearly as antiquated as the Big Three television era and bunny-ear antennas. A content delivery system dependent on telephone poles and geographically determined by municipal boundaries of city, town, and suburb appears hopelessly out of date and irrelevant in an era of wireless and globalized media. Yet despite recurrent reports of cable's imminent demise in the face of cord-cutting, accession of content through computers, and the turning away from television by the younger generation, cable giants like Discovery remain, well, giants, and their financial resources over the past fifty years are still put to use in this era's wave of new megadeals. Malone started as a cable executive and is now determining the political tilt of a major news source in global media and the future direction of platforms, studios, and channels. How did cable television grow so large as to provide Malone with this level of power?

Answering this question is more difficult than it might seem. The basic facts of how quickly cable spread as households subscribed to its services in providing old and new television channels do not provide an understanding of how the industry came to be dominated by a few suppliers large enough to mingle with the AT&Ts and Warner Bros. of the world. The structure of the industry came into formation by a multitude of small, localized deals between municipal governments and cable companies, often without much notice by the public or understanding by other media outlets. These agreements lent themselves to a normalized system of influence peddling and insider deals that attempted to evade the scrutiny of those outside the corridors of local power. Only rarely did this system get exposed to the light of public attention. This article looks at one of these times in Miami, Florida, to illuminate how the machinations of previous decades put our media system on a course of oligopoly and political dominance by media moguls. Examining in detail the deals between cable operators, political elites, and lobbyists that led to creation of the Miami cable system, as well as the news coverage of these dealings in the early 1980s, allows us to trace the history of the growth of the media companies that remain powerful in the contemporary moment. Toward the end of the chapter, I discuss the difficulties in researching such cases. A number of challenges in the media historiography of local cable, most notably the lack of existent and accessible primary sources, have allowed the foundations of the post-broadcast era of American television to become obscured.

GOVERNMENT REGULATION OF THE CABLE INDUSTRY

Government efforts to regulate the cable television industry gained steam in the early 1970s. Cable technology seemed ready to enter a new period of growth after sporadic efforts to send television signals through wires to households in the preceding decades. The Federal Communications Commission (FCC) empowered local governments to negotiate terms of cable franchises in 1972, leading city planners to believe that fees paid by cable companies to wire their territory could create a financial windfall for local governments and usher in a new era of customized and interactive entertainment options. Dozens of companies rose to compete for the usually exclusive right to access public land to provide cable to cities. The FCC rules, which provided great negotiating leverage for local governments, were cut back by court order in 1978, encouraging the still-struggling industry to raise sufficient capital to cover the high initial costs of establishing service (*Midwest Video Corp. v. FCC*, 571 F.2d 1025).

The 1984 Cable Act reduced local control further without eliminating it. In 1996, far-reaching deregulatory reform by Congress ended significant oversight by local authorities, by which time the industry was well on its way to radical consolidation in addressing a massive customer base, creating huge profits for the handful of surviving companies. The cable provider TCI, for example, became the best stock performer in America over a two-decade period; one dollar of TCI stock in 1975 was worth $913 in 1989, enabling its purchase of AT&T in the late 1990s (Parsons 2008, 516; Robichaux 2002, ix).

In most accounts of media history, after a quick mention that cable franchises were organized on a local basis, focus moves to the FCC, Congress, and the courts to follow the twists and turns of federal laws and policies. The creation and strategies of national cable channels also feature prominently. Ronald Garay, Megan Mullen, and Robert Crandall and Harold Furchtgott-Roth have provided useful overviews of industry structure and regulation but do not attend to local dynamics in cable franchising (Garay 1988; Mullen 2008; Crandall and Furchtgott-Roth 1996). If local cable is treated at any depth at all, it is to discuss Qube, the failed interactive system in Columbus, Ohio, and other early efforts at fusing television with shopping, household management, and civic functions (Barnouw 1990; MacDonald 1990; Hilmes 2002).

The biggest regulation and shaping of cable service, however, happened piecemeal at the local level. Negotiations between municipalities and cable companies were certainly affected by policies emanating from Washington; when federal regulations were canceled, cities lost some leverage. The negotiations, however, were initially held within, and subject to the vagaries of, local political contexts and institutions.

Bill Kirkpatrick's study of the early struggles over the proper vision for Madison, Wisconsin's, system focuses on activist groups' strategies, which ultimately failed to create the community-centered resource they hoped for the city (2012). Vicki Mayer details a citizens' board input in the New Orleans system (2011). Patrick Parsons's heroically exhaustive study of cable offers the most informed history of local franchising across the country, but this discussion takes up fewer than twenty pages in a book of more than eight hundred (2008). Yuya Kiuchi provides the most detailed study of local franchise debates in his study of how African American communities tried to influence the awarding and final provisions of contracts in Boston and Detroit (2012).

Among media activists of the 1980s, there was a general understanding that the awarding of local cable franchises around the country was rife with improper dealings and influence peddling by cable companies and their lobbyists, but only in Parsons's *Blue Skies* is this sordid history reflected in the scholarly literature. Indeed, the major source that goes into detail about the mechanics of awarding local franchises was published in 1979 and has no discussion of deal-making between cable companies and local political elites (Hamburg 1979). Let us now turn to Miami to see how this occurred.

CABLE COMES TO MIAMI

In the Miami metropolitan area, most of the political power in the era of its explosive population growth in the 1960s and 1970s was held by the Dade County government (now Miami-Dade County) because most of the land and population lay in unincorporated areas with no city government. The biggest local government within the county was the actual City of Miami, which included downtown and adjoining neighborhoods, such as the famous Calle Ocho, the center of the Cuban community; Liberty City and Overtown, two largely low-income and Black neighborhoods that were sites of famous cases of police brutality and racially based civil unrest; and Coconut Grove, a neighborhood of wide variations in income and racial demographics that had served as Miami's center of sixties counterculture before largely returning to the bourgeois artiness of its previous decades.

By the late 1960s, the Miami metropolitan area was served by affiliates of the Big Three networks of ABC, CBS, and NBC, a PBS station, and one independent station that relied heavily on network reruns and films for its programming. The growing Cuban population in the 1970s inspired the introduction of a few syndicated series in Spanish on the latter station, a locally produced Spanish-language comedy on the PBS affiliate, and an all-Spanish UHF channel. Cable television operators tried to introduce a wired system into unincorporated Dade County in the late 1960s, offering the chance to see more films at home than was provided by existing channels. They were defeated by an alliance, previously thought to be strange or impossible, between broadcast television stations and movie theater owners. This coalition between competitors used "Keep TV Free" as its rallying cry against the new pay TV alternative. *Wait, start paying for something you could get now for free? That doesn't make any sense.* At least it did not to this author, as a child living in unincorporated South Dade who saw banners proclaiming the benefits of free TV and the dangers of pay cable displayed at the local Sunniland movie theater. Paying for TV seemed downright un-American, a violation of an inalienable right to watch *Gilligan's Island* and *The Ed Sullivan Show* at no cost to my allowance. My fellow citizens and the Dade County Commission agreed, and the county passed on getting cable.

More than a decade later, the public and government officials became increasingly open to the idea of cable. Franchises were parceled out in rather chaotic fashion around the county, but the City of Miami was still unwired, years after the introduction of HBO, WTBS, and other national channels available only through cable systems. With about 350,000 residents, the City of Miami was one of the last unclaimed population centers in Florida, so when the City Commission introduced the idea of bringing in cable in 1981, major industry players responded with interest. In keeping with standard practice, the commission hired a consultant to oversee the process and put out a notice for bids detailing what it was looking for in terms of channel lineups, speed of wiring, costs to consumers, and other issues. Five companies ended up filing applications and engaged in a process that had become known as "rent-a-citizen," in which local political movers and shakers were to be given a percentage of the local operation in exchange for lobbying the government on behalf of their new partners (Salant 1981).

The five applicants were, alphabetically, the following:

(1) Americable: The principal owner of Americable, Charles Hermanowski, lived in the county but not in the city and owned other systems out of state that had largely established a bad reputation for service. Americable had a poor record in hiring racial and ethnic minorities, had no minority investors, and offered no jobs or scholarship programs in its proposal, deal sweeteners that were common in the industry by that time. Americable offered ownership stakes to Dick Knight and Steve Ross, who ran a successful political public relations company involved in campaigns and lobbying in Miami. Ross was a friend and financial supporter of city mayor Maurice Ferre, who had a vote on the commission; Ross had also made donations to the campaigns of two out of the four seated commissioners. Knight and Ross each received 3 percent of the local operation, worth at least $750,000 each, and likely worth more than $3 million. Americable was willing to ultimately pay more than $6 million to these two local individuals—not to operate the franchise, as they had no experience or desire to do that but ostensibly to make public presentations to the commission on behalf of the company. Knight and Ross would also receive upfront money, an expenditure that a smaller cable operator may have found difficult to make to entice local citizens to its cause. Americable also hired a respected former member of the state legislature to lobby on its behalf and a second well-known public relations firm (Salant 1981; Gjebre and Moore 1981a). The company had the most extensive roster of A-list power brokers among the applicants.

(2) Cablesystems: Owned by a major system operator in Canada, Cablesystems had given 20 percent of its Miami ownership stake to locals—up to $20 million worth of equity—including to another veteran of the state legislature, a radio station, and the *Miami Times*, the leading Black newspaper in the area. Cablesystems also established noninvesting advisory relationships with other members of the Black and Cuban communities in the city and sketched out plans for local programming that reflected the area's racial and ethnic diversity (Salant 1981; Gjebre and Moore 1981b).

(3) Miami Telecommunications (MT): MT was a subsidiary created by TCI, which was already the biggest company in the American cable industry and run by its most notorious figure, John Malone. Malone's

aggressive attitude toward public authorities can be summed up by this snippet of an interview he gave:

> **INTERVIEWER**: There are those who have said, "Gee, John has a blind spot and the blind spot might have something to do with public policy, regulation, and public process."
> **MALONE**: I hate those guys! (Malone 2001)

TCI had already been involved in some of the most controversial conflicts with local franchising authorities around the country. TCI's chief local lobbyist was Richard Gerstein, a former high-profile state's attorney who had ties to Mayor Ferre and was also a city commissioner's personal lawyer (Salant 1981; Gjebre and Moore 1981c).

(4) Six Star Nielson Cablevision (SSN): SSN was a California company that developed no local ties but had developed a reputation for scandals in other jurisdictions. Three of its principal owners had been indicted for fraud and racketeering, for which they were later convicted, resulting in its bankruptcy (Salant 1981; Gjebre and Moore 1981d; Crook 1985).

(5) Vision Cable: A company from New York, Vision Cable had links to the Newhouse media empire and a mixed reputation for service. It gave 22 percent of the proposed franchise to locals, most notably to Athalie Range, a state legislator who was the most esteemed African American officeholder in the city (Salant 1981; Gjebre and Moore 1981e).

In their proposals, each company sketched out how many channels it would provide in a variety of plans from which customers could choose as well as the initial financial outlay required to subscribe and the monthly fees it would charge. Vision Cable offered the best terms, while Americable's proposal was clearly the worst in terms of customer charges, smallest payout to the city treasury, and other categories. As ranked by the consultant, TCI came in first, Vision Cable second, and Americable dead last in the five-company competition (Salant 1981; Salant and Zaldivar 1981; Zaldivar and Salant 1981). The commission voted to give the franchise to Americable.

The vote was not unanimous. Americable beat out TCI, three votes to two. (So yes, in this story, John Malone and the growing behemoth TCI start out as the wronged victims of the system. That's how crazy Miami politics can get.) The TCI lobbyist's legal client voted for TCI, as did Mayor Ferre, despite his links to Americable lobbyist Ross. The commissioners who supported Americable asserted that they did so because it was mainly owned by almost-local resident Hermanowski and they liked the idea of boosting local businesses. One of the commissioners who asserted this argument was Theodore Gibson, the sole Black commissioner, who was also a leading minister in the Black church community and former president of the local chapter of the NAACP. Gibson caught some heat from losing applicants and his erstwhile colleagues at the NAACP for siding with a white county resident with no Black partners over companies that had cultivated Black city dwellers as lobbyists and "investors" (Zaldivar and Salant 1981; Gjebre 1981a; WTVJ 1981a, 1981b).[1]

The *Miami Herald*, the most popular newspaper in South Florida, covered the franchising process from the beginning. After the commission vote, the *Herald* kicked its coverage into high gear. The *Herald* was not a rabble-rousing paper, but it imagined itself as the guardian of basic civic virtue. The *Herald* was part of the Knight-Ridder chain, one of the newspaper industry's more journalistically serious players that was continuing to commit resources to investigative reporting and covering complex issues. The rise of cable had become a big and familiar enough story nationally for *Herald* reporters on the municipal beat to pay attention to the process of awarding the city franchise and to understand the details of the proposals. The *Herald*'s coverage was augmented by stories in the *Miami News*, a smaller, afternoon paper that often presented a feistier attitude toward the Miami political power structure, and by reporting by the news operations of the local broadcast affiliates, who did not appear to be reluctant to make their competitors in the cable industry look bad (WTVJ 1981a, 1981b).

The *Herald* stories on the vote centered on the roles of Americable's Knight and Ross as powerful lobbyists in local government (Zaldivar 1981a). They did not explicitly say that the two would funnel some of the Americable cash they received directly to commissioners or in the more respectable route of campaign donations in the next electoral cycle, but the implication was clear. At the very least, access to an established network of political insiders seemed to be worth many millions of dollars to the competitors for the franchise. As a lead editorial in the *Herald* was headlined, "Influence Peddlers Win Miami's Cable-TV Show" (*Miami Herald* 1981). The voting debacle spurred the *Herald* to devote space to coverage of the cable industry nationally, highlighting other controversies (Gyllenhaal 1981).

The *Miami News* went further than just detailing conflicts in other municipalities; it featured an article that opened up the possibility of bypassing private companies altogether and having the city run the cable operation itself (Gjebre 1981b). The editor-in-chief of the paper recounted his personal difficulties in getting Americable to even hook up his house in a suburb it was supposed to serve—one year and counting since he had asked to start giving the company his money (Kleinberg 1981). In another story detailing the possibility of corruption in the granting of a franchise, the newspaper ran an illustration of a giant squid-like creature, labeled "Miami Cable TV," with tentacles labeled "Political Pull," tethered to the surface. The article featured lists of local investors tied to each cable company, with their pictures included. Suddenly, the murky structure of local political power was being exposed for readers to see (Moore and Gjebre 1981).

A recall drive was started against the commissioners who voted for Americable, and TCI successfully asked for an FBI investigation into the lobbying process (Zaldivar 1981b, 1981c; WTVJ 1981c, 1981d).[2] The recall leaders, who had ties to the losing applicants Cablesystems and Vision Cable, emphasized that they wanted a diverse campaign that would appeal to Anglo (non-Latino white), Black, and Cuban voters (perhaps because they were targeting the Anglo, Black, and Cuban commissioners who had comprised the winning Americable coalition). The recall drive failed and the FBI returned no indictments, but the commission did back off from its decision, saying retroactively that the vote had been only a tentative, rehearsal vote on the whole issue. They were able to avoid litigation from Americable for their just-for-kicks tease of a vote by pointing out that any deal was subject to negotiation of its finer points by the city manager, who now pledged to drive a hard bargain with Americable to improve the contract for city residents (Zaldivar 1981d, 1981e; Veciana-Suarez 1981a).

The main negotiating goals for the city became lower fees, more jobs provided by the system, and minority participation in ownership. The city's leverage was made stronger by revelations that Americable had failed to disclose a number of serious concerns in its application, including that it had defaulted on systems in New Jersey and that Hermanowski had been accused of offering kickbacks to officials in other jurisdictions. The city, however, refused to entertain TCI's offer to compete for customers with Americable, which would have created a nonexclusive competitive environment and might have at least strengthened the city's negotiating position. To please the commission,

Americable added Black and Cuban residents to its ownership structure, reduced proposed fees to customers by 30 percent, and added $25 million to city benefits provided by the company (Veciana-Suarez 1981b; Zaldivar 1981f; Gjebre 1981c; Gyllenhaal and Arnold 1981). Clearly, the commission majority, after the lobbying efforts fueled by the "rent-a-citizen" campaign, had agreed initially to a plan that not only lacked diverse local ownership but also overcharged customers and underpaid the city.

By the time the final vote was scheduled by the commission, Americable and its supporters had been subject to raucous criticism at public hearings, close monitoring by municipal reporters who also provided contextual stories about the rise of cable and deals made around the country, and persistent hectoring by the *Herald* and *News* editorial writers for their ethical and logical failures. At the crucial vote, commissioner Joe Carollo, who had always claimed his support for Americable was primarily an anti-TCI stance, hid in his office, which created a deadlock at two votes each in approving the deal; the pro-TCI faction continued to oppose the Americable proposal. Eight hours of delay and further arguing prompted the line by *Herald* columnist Charles Whited to describe the commission meeting that makes up this chapter's title—"To call it a zoo would be unkind to animals." The recalcitrant commissioner Carollo finally took his seat and delivered a rambling monologue. He suggested that the commission start over with the entire licensing process (Whited 1981).

Suddenly, the pro-Americable Theodore Gibson suggested a new course to break the deadlock—that Americable and TCI create an ad hoc joint venture to run the city system, without competition. The TCI faction jumped at the chance to salvage the company's participation at some level, added their votes to Gibson's, and a new company was born (Zaldivar 1981g; Gjebre 1981c). The two groups of rented citizens could be relatively happy with the result since even with half the shares of their original deal, the payoff for their participation remained so out of proportion to their efforts. TCI got partial rights to another territory, building on its growing domination of the field. Americable increased its presence in its own backyard. The alliance between major operators and local political elites squelched competitive pressures that could have threatened the growing cable oligopoly, while maintaining elite lobbyists' influence over local politics by huge infusions of cash into their accounts courtesy of the newly profitable industry.

LESSONS AND CONSEQUENCES

Miami's cable history offers a number of lessons about the development of the industry and the importance of local political institutions and processes in its consolidation. The first is that the news media can play an important watchdog role over the industry and its interactions with the government, if they are primed to pay attention to an issue and have the resources to educate themselves about new areas of technology and business practices. Cable had grown enough by 1981 to be considered a significant feature of daily life, with economic consequences for city governments and consumers. This watchdog function is more likely to be activated when political and economic elites are divided, providing incentives for them to share information with reporters in their struggle against each other. Further, media outlets without financial connections to the institutions under question are freer to pursue stories in the name of the public good. The chains that owned the *Herald* and the *News* had invested in the television industry, but their properties were broadcast stations, not cable systems. In 1981, broadcasters and cable operators still saw themselves as competitors and adversaries; in later decades, the two facets of television made peace with each other, removing some incentive for muckraking coverage of one by the other.

The second lesson is that local coverage counts, even in an industry with national scope. Most scholarly discussion of the cable industry has focused on the peregrinations of national policy, which can be covered by national media companies and documented by federal publications. The nitty-gritty of local bidding and negotiations, however, depends on media coverage of municipal matters to inform the public and establish an historical record. The internet has famously widened users' attention to global perspectives and concomitantly reduced attention to local matters. With the decline in local newspapers and consumer attention distracted away from other outlets for local reporting over the past few decades, industries that operate on a city-by-city basis no longer receive the level of scrutiny they may have once garnered (though there were many obstacles to such scrutiny even in the heyday of localized media).

Finally, the results of the controversy in Miami were mixed. Spurred by media and public outcry, the city did obtain significantly better terms for the franchise than the original Americable bid contained. Consumers would pay less, the city would make more, and the demographics of the ownership group became more diverse. The commission, however, demurred from having Americable and TCI compete against each other for customers, leaving the franchise in the hands of the joint holding company created by the two companies. This result presaged the future shape of the industry, in which joint ventures, mergers, and consolidation led to an increasingly small number of corporate behemoths controlling media industries, stifling competition, and jacking up prices for cable service once the federal government removed local municipalities' leverage in overseeing franchises. TCI bought out Americable's interest in their joint venture in 1987, leaving the industry giant with sole control of the franchise in Miami (*Miami Tele-Communications, Inc. v. City of Miami*, 743 F. Supp. 1573 [S.D. Fla. 1990]).

This conglomeration has been celebrated by TCI's John Malone, the prime mover and beneficiary in the narrowing of choices within the industry. As he told an interviewer, "We became very aggressive in consolidating the cable industry because I saw from the beginning that scale economics was going to determine who was going to survive and who wasn't. . . . [A] lot of our . . . larger acquisitions were done in partnerships with other cable operators. . . . The franchising wars were largely over, so cable operators weren't really competitive with each other. . . . It really allowed the industry to be cooperative with each other. . . . It made it . . . a much more fun industry to be in" (Malone 2001). This collusion among the biggest players in cable, eventually immersed in interlocking ownership structures, constituted a largely unregulated oligopoly. This lack of both competition and regulatory oversight was a deadly combination for consumers, which ultimately led to the spread of satellite television services bypassing cable and the game-changing rise of Netflix.

The insider politics of cable franchising favored a small number of operators who could gather the support of local elites—and their answer to scandal and exposure in Miami was simply to join together to please a slightly bigger circle of municipal players. This solution presaged the anticompetitive orientation of the industry as the 1980s progressed—and they had little need to please even local officials once the renewal of contracts became virtually automatic after Congress imposed restrictions against local regulation. TCI became the most profitable stock in America, building the empire that Malone could use to eventually purchase CNN, HBO, and Warner Bros., remaking political coverage and refashioning major players in the new era of streaming platforms.

THE DIFFICULTIES IN WRITING THE HISTORY OF CABLE

I'd like to turn away from the high jinks at Miami City Hall to consider some of the issues this episode brings up within media historiography. Why have we not seen more studies of local conflicts and agreements, given that these constituted the front lines of cable regulation during its period of great growth? First, the decentralized nature of these cases works against researching any particular case. The returns seem small and too narrow in scope compared to the work needed to research a topic not easily accessed on the Web, as is true for many local histories of pre-Web events. It is relatively easy to study a comprehensive history of FCC decisions or relevant court cases, though my hat is off to anyone who is willing to work through the legal and regulatory language encountered in such research. To write anything close to a comprehensive history of local agreements, however, would call for analyzing many separate incidents, spread across the country over two decades. This is beyond the resources of the small number of researchers even interested in communication industry issues that are now forty years old.

Second, the primary research sources need to have been created and remained accessible. Most cable agreements attracted scant attention in the press; few had the protracted and nakedly obvious problematics of the Miami case, which the *Herald* and *News* could then track and investigate before the final vote. A local media outlet would have to devote sufficient resources to produce worthwhile coverage—the *Herald* was a good regional paper that was a significant asset of a major publishing chain, and the *News* prided itself on being the serious-minded underdog in covering the Miami metropolitan area. Other cities might not be so lucky. Further, researchers need to know where to look for cases that have been covered sufficiently. I happened to be visiting family in Miami in 1987 when a second cable controversy in Dade County hit the papers, and my involvement in media activism in New York made me sufficiently sensitized to cable issues to keep that episode in mind. Only by exploring that second episode did I discover references to the even more dramatic controversy of 1981. Where does one start looking for the interesting and historically significant cases that remain unexplored? Can we count on coincidence?

Even when a story was covered initially, what remains of that work? The *Herald* has yet to be digitized back to 1981; I found the 1987 stories on the Web, but to investigate the 1981 coverage I had to go to the Library of Congress in Washington, D.C., and endure microfilm hell. And I had it relatively easy, living in Baltimore, a short train ride away. How many scholars would venture a trip to D.C. in the hope that vague mentions of a local occurrence six years after it happened would pan out as a research project? Would the project be of sufficient scope and importance to warrant a cross-country trip and associated expenses? I was lucky as well that the *Herald* stories were written by several reporters, from different editorial departments, so as to mitigate the potential for having to base my research on a single reporter's work.

The precepts of good research practice encourage seeking out more than one institutional source of information and opinion. Other local newspapers and magazines, local television reports, and private correspondence are traditional sources used by media historians. They can be difficult to access, however. The Vanderbilt Television News Archive in Nashville, Tennessee, is good for national news coverage by the broadcast networks, but not for any local-based research, and most television stations do not make access to their older telecasts easy or even feasible. The decline of the newspaper industry, especially the closing of second, afternoon papers in midsize and small cities, leaves the work of many of them inaccessible, though Newspapers.com holds the digitized archives for some smaller publications not archived in the Library of Congress. Miami happens to be relatively rich in these secondary resources. The *Miami News* went defunct in 1988 and was never collected by the Library of Congress. Its archives are held by a paper in Palm Beach but have finally become available on the Web, through Newspapers.com. The alternative and minority weekly newspapers of the time in Miami are not digitized at all.

Local television news shows picked up on the *Herald* stories and, happy to embarrass their cable upstart rivals, played up the controversy. WTVJ, the CBS affiliate, was owned in the 1980s by Wometco, a media and entertainment company controlled by the Wolfson family of Miami. The family, along with public institutions and former station personnel, created the Wolfson Archives, which collects media from Florida and is one of the most extensive collections of local television telecasts in the country. WTVJ's news archives are available online, unlike most local stations' work from previous decades. Talk radio played a large role within the Cuban community at the time, but early forays into this important medium of political discussion enjoy almost no documentation of its content, leaving us uncertain of any discussion of the cable issue on local stations.

As with any subject, national or local personal interviews might be possible, but many of the major players from 1981 are no longer living, and how many still around would want to talk about it honestly? The Cable Center was created by industry players as a research repository and has made accessible a series of interviews with important figures from across the country. The conversations are hardly muckraking, however, even if, as with Malone's interview cited above, they can sometimes be inadvertently revealing. The Cable Center has no interviews that directly pertain to the events in Miami.

New interviews with key figures cannot be pursued. City commissioner Theodore Gibson played a crucial role in resolving the dispute within the commission in 1981, but unfortunately died the following year. Americable's Charles Hermanowski fled the country while being investigated for corrupt practices elsewhere, returned after six years in hiding, and pleaded guilty to thirty-nine counts of tax evasion and fraud. He was sentenced to over eight years in prison and died in 2010 (*South Florida Business Journal* 2007). That fine gentleman John Malone is on record as disliking scholarly inquiry into his business practices.

As the franchising phase of the development of cable television recedes further into the past, it will likely become even more difficult to preserve and extend our knowledge of how the media environment fundamentally changed in the last third of the twentieth century. If media historians do not make these sorts of efforts, the local history on the front lines of regulation will continue to remain unwritten. A few case studies may have to stand in for a process that lasted two decades and involved many different companies, public officials, and private citizens. To turn away from such a project, however, is to perpetuate ignorance of a central factor in the creation of the contemporary mediascape. The case study of Miami in 1981 offers us a chance to revise our view of cable history and begin to understand the local dynamics that pervaded the industry in its prime decades of growth. The results of these processes live with us today through the continued use of cable by American households, the dominance of the cable competition survivors in the contemporary mediascape, and their influence on many of the biggest media issues confronting us today.

NOTES

1. The coverage of the issue by the CBS affiliate WTVJ-TV can be found at the Lynn and Louis Wolfson II Florida Moving Image Archives, in the WTVJ Newstape Cut Stories collection, https://www.mdc.edu/archives/wolfson-archives/ (Wolfson Archives). I put "investors" in quotes because none of the locals were asked to pony up any sizable capital in return for ownership stakes in any of the applicants, only their time and effort in supporting the bid.
2. Years later, TCI's representative in Miami claimed that he had told the FBI that Americable had offered $250,000 to $300,000 for each favorable vote from the commissioners, though he now admitted he had no hard evidence to back up the accusation (*Miami Herald* 1987). If this accusation was true, it demonstrated audacious corruption by Americable. If false, TCI was guilty of egregiously lying to the FBI. Take your pick.

REFERENCES

Barnouw, Erik. 1990. *Tube of Plenty: The Evolution of American Television*. 2nd ed. Oxford University Press.

Crandall, Robert W., and Harold Furchtgott-Roth. 1996. *Cable TV: Regulation or Competition?* Brookings Institution.

Crook, David. 1985. "L.A.'s Largest Cable TV Firm Files for Bankruptcy." *Los Angeles Times*, February 1.

Foreman, Alison. 2022. "All 81 Titles Unceremoniously Removed from HBO Max (So Far)." *IndieWire*, December 14. https://www.indiewire.com/gallery/removed-hbo-max-movies-shows-warner-bros-discovery-merger-list/12-days-of-christmas.html.

Garay, Ronald. 1988. *Cable Television: A Reference Guide to Information*. Greenwood.

Gjebre, Bill. 1981a. "Americable Will Plug into Miami." *Miami News*, July 15.

———. 1981b. "Other Cities Investigate Alternatives to Franchises." *Miami News*, July 4.

———. 1981c. "Ferre: A Super Offer on Cable TV." *Miami News*, September 4.

———. 1981d. "Two Cable TV Rivals to Begin Talks Tomorrow on Joint Venture in City." *Miami News*, September 11.

Gjebre, Bill, and Marilyn A. Moore. 1981a. "Americable Counting on Hometown Edge." *Miami News*, July 4.

———. 1981b. "Cablesystems Relies on Its Local Partners." *Miami News*, July 4.

———. 1981c. "TCI Got Best Reviews, and Local Clout to Match." *Miami News*, July 4.

———. 1981d. "Six Star Only One to Forego Local Investors." *Miami News*, July 4.

———. 1981e. "Vision Cable Lures Elite to Be Local Shareholders." *Miami News*, July 4.

Gyllenhaal, Anders. 1981. "Cable TV Wars Not Just in Miami Area." *Miami Herald*, August 1.

Gyllenhaal, Anders, and John Arnold. 1981. "Americable Manual Borrows from Denver Firm." *Miami Herald*, September 10.

Hamburg, Morton I. 1979. *All About Cable: Legal and Business Aspects of Cable and Pay Television*. Law Journal Seminars-Press.

Hilmes, Michele. 2002. *Only Connect: A Cultural History of Broadcasting in the United States*. Wadsworth.

Kirkpatrick, Bill. 2012. "Bringing Blue Skies Back to Earth: Citizen Policymaking in Negotiations for Cable Television, 1965–1975." *Television & New Media* 13 (4): 307–28.

Kiuchi, Yuya. 2012. *Struggles for Equal Voice: The History of African American Media Democracy*. State University of New York Press.

Kleinberg, Howard. 1981. "Getting Strung Out on Americable's Lines." *Miami News*, August 17.

Koblin, John. 2022. "In Hollywood, a New Giant Joins the Ranks." *New York Times*, April 9. https://www.nytimes.com/1987/05/14/nyregion/ex-franchise-chief-takes-the-5th-and-asks-immediate-citypension.html?searchResultPosition=21.

MacDonald, J. Fred. 1990. *One Nation Under Television: The Rise and Decline of Network TV*. Pantheon.

Malone, John. 2001. "John Malone." Interview by Trgyve Myhren, Cable Center Barco Library Hauser Oral History Project. https://www.cablecenter.org/the-barco-library/the-hauser-oral-history-project/m-o-listings/john-malone.

Mayer, Vicki. 2011. *Below the Line: Producers and Production Studies in the New Television Economy*. Duke University Press.

Miami Herald. 1981. "Influence Peddlers Win Miami's Cable-TV Show." July 17.

———. 1987. "Ex-Cable Chief Admits Making Allegations." June 22.

Moore, Marilyn A., and Bill Gjebre. 1981. "Cable Television: Influential Enlist in War for Miami Franchise." *Miami News*, July 4.

Mullen, Megan. 2008. *Television in the Multichannel Age*. Blackwell.

Mullin, Benjamin. 2022. "CNN Cancels Media Show; Host Departs." *New York Times*, August 19. https://www.nytimes.com/2022/08/18/business/media/cnn-brian-stelter-reliable-sources.html.

Parsons, Patrick R. 2008. *Blue Skies: A History of Cable Television*. Temple University Press.

Robichaux, Mark. 2002. *Cable Cowboy: John Malone and the Rise of the Modern Cable Business*. Wiley.

Salant, Jonathan D. 1981. "Leaders Star in Cable TV Battle." *Miami Herald*, June 3.

Salant, Jonathan D., and R. A. Zaldivar. 1981. "Miami May Change Rules on Cable TV." *Miami Herald*, July 14, 1981.

South Florida Business Journal. 2007. "Former Cable Fraudster Gets Time, Fine." March 6. https://bizjournals.com/southflorida/stories/2007/03/05/daily15.html.

Tate, Charles, ed. 1971. *Cable Television in the Cities: Community Control, Public Access, and Minority Ownership*. Urban Institute.
Veciana-Suarez, Ana. 1981a. "City: Cut the rates for Americable." *Miami News*, August 28.
———. 1981b. "Charles Hermanowski: Americable Boss Is a Gambler Who Often Wins Big." *Miami News*, August 18.
Whited, Charles. 1981. "Words Cannot Capture Scene of Cable Furor." *Miami Herald*, September 11.
WTVJ. 1981a. WTVJ Newstape Cut Stories Collection, WC 375, July 13, 1981. Lynn and Louis Wolfson II Florida Moving Image Archives (Wolfson Archives). https://www.mdc.edu/archives/wolfson-archives/.
———. 1981b. WC 376, July 14, 1981. Wolfson Archives.
———. 1981c. CT 383, September 9, 1981. Wolfson Archives.
———. 1981d. CT 397, September 22, 1981. Wolfson Archives.
Zaldivar, R. A. 1981a. "Dade Lobbyists Profit if Americable Gains Miami Cable License." *Miami Herald*, August 29, 1981.
———. 1981b. "Cable TV Losers Mounting Recall Drive, Ad Campaign." *Miami Herald*, July, 22, 1981.
———. 1981c. "Hearing Turns into Critique of Cable TV Award." *Miami Herald*, August 7, 1981.
———. 1981d. "City Wants Top Benefits in Cable Pact." *Miami Herald*, July 16, 1981.
———. 1981e. "Toughest Cable Fight May Lie Ahead as Miami and Americable Open Talks." *Miami Herald*, August 2, 1981.
———. 1981f. "Americable Slashes Fees to Gain OK." *Miami Herald*, September 4, 1981.
———. 1981g. "Partner Forced on Americable." *Miami Herald*, September 11, 1981.
Zaldivar, R. A., and Jonathan D. Salant. 1981. "Americable Wins TV rights." *Miami Herald*, July 15.

PART II

AESTHETICS AND GENRES OF LOCAL TELEVISION PROGRAMS

CHAPTER 6

ANNIE LAURIE SULLIVAN

BROADCASTING FAITH IN DETROIT

LOCAL TELEVANGELISM, BLACK GOSPEL TRADITIONS,
AND THE COMMERCE OF COMMUNITY WORSHIP

In 2021, Detroit's long-running Black public affairs program, *America's Black Journal*, featured a special series dedicated to the city's Black churches. In one episode, host Stephen Henderson asks local Black ministers how they have reimagined religious services for the COVID-19 era. Now, "everyone's a televangelist!" Rev. Charles Williams exclaims as they discuss a range of technologically mediated approaches to pandemic preaching. While the episode frames the ecumenical turn to digital platforms as a novel response to crisis conditions, Williams's use of the word "televangelist" gestures to a long history in which Black leaders have adapted audiovisual technologies to preach spiritual values to local parishioners while also increasing Black visibility in American life.

Of course, the history of religious broadcasting extends far beyond the Black church. Technology has long been adapted to disseminate a range of spiritual content and facilitate dialogues between religious leaders and dispersed congregants on local and global scales, across faiths and denominations. Media scholars have been attentive to the union of religion, television, and social governance around the world, from Muslim states to Hindi-language television in India, to the megachurch movement in Christian-majority countries like the United States, Ghana, Nigeria, Guatemala, and Brazil (Thomas and Lee 2012, 12). However, scholars have largely overlooked the smaller-scale religious programs ubiquitous on local channels. Most Sunday morning television rosters in the United States from the 1950s to the present have been dominated by Christian fare, though program formats and theological messages they expound vary across historical moments, places, and regions. Studying religious programs within the social context of place can help elucidate the dynamics between local television producers, religious leaders, and the shared communities both serve. Thus, I contend that examining staples of local television programming—in this case, religious broadcasts—can help us understand how media practices connect to the dynamics of quotidian life in a city or region.

I arrived at the topic of televangelism while researching the intersecting histories of local television and Black activism in my hometown of Detroit. I noticed that a sizable portion of original Black programs have been dually interested in promoting Black liberation and Christian values. Religious broadcasts may be staples of local media praxis, but Detroit has historically aired an array of Black-oriented gospel programs that would not be found in most other local markets. While this trend is remarkable, it is not necessarily surprising if considered in a local context. Black religious leaders have guided residents through decades of civil rights battles, strategically using media platforms to amplify their messages to the majority-Black city (Dillard 2007). Detroit has also been a central hub of the gospel music industry and the inaugural home of the Gospel Music Workshop (Pollard 2008; Harold 2017). Even though *America's Black Journal* is a secular public affairs program, it too has consistently sought the council of Detroit's spiritual leaders to address social and political crises. To better understand the dynamics of Black media culture in Detroit and the local religious programs designed for residents, I follow the lead of *America's Black Journal* and look to the Black church for spiritual, economic, and political answers.

This chapter thus examines the emergence of local Black religious television in Detroit and considers ways Detroit preachers have sermonized for Black spiritual and economic uplift directives. I draw on the local WGPR-TV programs *March of Faith* (ca. 1979–present), offering viewers recorded services from the New St. Paul Tabernacle, and *Inspiration Time* (1975–78), a talk show featuring live gospel music performances, to analyze the aesthetic, economic, and ideological possibilities of locally oriented Black religious television.[1] I argue that these gospel programs serve as a nexus of sociopolitical discourse, cultural performance, and community formation in Black Detroit. Due to the ephemerality of local TV, few program tapes are extant. Thus, I mix scholarly methods, combining media scholarship, oral histories, and local press discourse to better elucidate the form and function of Black televangelism for the

Detroit market. In doing so, I strive to illuminate the complex role that religious television plays in local, civic life.

TELEVANGELISM IN BLACK AND WHITE

Religious broadcasts have been mainstays for local TV programmers primarily because they are cheap to produce, come with built-in viewership, and easily meet the FCC guideline that local stations offer content that serves public interests. However, religious broadcasting has evolved alongside trends in American culture and telecommunications policies. In the forties and fifties, broadcasters interpreted the FCC "public interest" clause as requiring "sustaining-time" programs, which meant that stations had to fund a certain amount of programs to best serve their respective publics (Federal Communications Commission 1946). Churches interested in television had to build relationships with local stations and adhere to their content guidelines. At this time, local and national broadcasters aimed to avoid any messaging that could alienate viewers.[2] Stations favored (white) "reputable and mainline religious groups" (Horsfield 2015, 3) that presented generalized, predominantly (white) Christian religious values and avoided discussion of controversial social issues, including race (Bruce 2019, 41). In 1960, the FCC eliminated the distinction between sustaining-time and paid-time programming, meaning both forms of local content production would satisfy the FCC's public interest requirement and stations could profit from their public service content (Frederick 2015, 25). By the decade's end, most religious programs financed their own productions, buying airtime from local stations. The delicate approaches to theological address diminished.

In the era of paid-time programming, television became an "institution of American evangelicalism" (Ward 2015). According to Mimi White (1992, 112), the most visible religious programs after the 1960s "featured evangelical Protestantism with a fundamentalist or Pentecostal emphasis. In this sense, the conservative religious doctrine purveyed by the programs embraces a popular, conservative religious subculture." Evangelicals like Billy Graham, Oral Roberts, Jerry Falwell, and Pat Robertson embraced mass media as an "electronic church," a potential way to convert large swaths of viewers to their ministries, reinforce their traditional social values about gender and sexuality, and expound right-wing political agendas. Quentin Schultze (2003) sees this "electronic church" as a distinctive form of religious broadcasting in which charismatic leaders promote entrepreneurial values, "experiential theologies," and faith in technology. They rely on the "prosperity gospel," which purports that God rewards faithful and generous devotees with health and wealth. Televangelists have faced fierce critiques for using congregants to fund their opulent lifestyles, marketing their published guides to business growth and spiritual healing to viewers as theology. The prosperity gospel, and sex scandals of figures like Jim Bakker and Jimmy Swaggart, may have tarnished the reputation of televangelism in American culture. However, televangelists continually shape modern television, using the medium to fuel debates about morality and promote policies to uphold their values.

However, the conservative, paternalistic evangelists iconic to the "electronic church" are not representative of all religious broadcasters and actively obscure the contributions of Black televangelists in TV history. As Jonathan Walton has argued, the dominant positioning of white televangelism as normative operates as a "crude historical and theoretical reductionism" (2009, 26). Despite an archival lacuna about Black broadcasting, scholars of Black religion have documented ways Black preachers have long used telecommunications technologies to amplify their spiritual teachings. Lerone Martin argues that the phonographic recording and distribution of Black sermons in the early twentieth century transformed "Black Christianity into a mass-produced commodity" and helped create the first generation of "commercial celebrity preachers" (2014, 5). Robert Marovich has shown how Pentecostal Holiness preachers in Chicago used radio to expand their ministries in the 1920s, producing shows like the *All-Colored Hour* and *Evening Light Broadcast* for WSBC (2015). William Barlow's (1999) history of Black radio frequently references religious broadcasters, who appealed spiritually and politically to Black listeners in cities and towns throughout the nation.

Indeed, Black churches have facilitated crucial social exchanges and political dialogues and developed economic opportunities (training programs, educational initiatives, and financial guidance) for Black community members. According to Sherman Jackson (2005, 33), "The central and most enduring feature of Black Religion is its sustained and radical opposition to racial oppression. At bottom, Black Religion is an instrument of holy protest against white supremacy and its material and psychological effects." Henry Louis Gates Jr. (2021, 3) has likewise argued that since the transatlantic slave trade "the Black Church [has] offered a reprieve from the racist world, a place for African Americans to come together in community to advance their aspirations and to sing out, pray out, and shout out their frustrations." Moderate Black intellectual and spiritual leaders have followed in the footsteps of figures like Booker T. Washington to advocate for Black capitalism as a key tactic to achieve Black advancement in American life (Marable 2000). Thus, Black televangelism typically includes an emphasis on economic self-help akin to the prosperity gospel, though these are also concepts long championed by Black churches to steer Black uplift.

Black televangelism is in conversation with both the aesthetic, theological, and corporate values of dominant televangelism and the liberation politics of the Black church. As histories of local broadcasting abound with narratives of employment discrimination and racist exclusions, Black creators have seldom had the same access to broadcasting technologies as white producers. The ones that do succeed typically are able to maintain a following based on their combined charismatic presence and entrepreneurial prowess. The same FCC policies that fostered the rise of the white "electronic church" also created openings for entrepreneurial Black preachers to buy airtime. The Black preachers who have become televisual icons are also savvy salespeople, often courting scrutiny for the way they represent Black culture. For example, Reverend Ike was both scorned and revered for what Marla Frederick (2015) calls his dandified preaching of the prosperity gospel from the 1970s to the 1990s. Twenty-first-century Black prosperity preachers like T. D. Jakes and Creflo Dollar have likewise drawn the attention of ethicist scholars like Frederick and Walton, who approach televangelism as an ideological apparatus that informs Black perceptions of gender, sexuality, racial justice, equity, and, of course, the racialized economics of class.

However, Black religious broadcasts that are less sensational and address a municipal parish are mostly absent from television history. According to Walton (2009, 3), "In contrast to white evangelist pastors who oversee media empires apart from a local congregation, the major producers of religious broadcasting in the African American community emerge from and remain rooted in the parish context." Accordingly, a focus on local Black religious programming reveals the connection between TV preachers, their congregations, and their emplacement in local sociopolitical formations. The faith leaders in Detroit I discuss offered spiritual guidance on the small screen while using their local prominence to promote social, political, and economic services that they felt would best support their congregants—and Black Detroit at large.

BROADCASTING BLACK RELIGION IN A RACIALLY DIVIDED CITY

Black televangelism in Detroit has been responsive to both the spiritual needs of parishioners and the socioeconomic constraints of living in a systemically racist city. Although Detroit was the fourth largest city in the United States and a major center of manufacturing at midcentury, suburbanization and the decentralization of the automotive industry began to diminish Detroit's employment opportunities beginning in the 1940s (Sugrue 1996). Discriminatory housing protocols relegated Detroit's significant Black population to areas with inadequate schools and poor housing conditions. Meanwhile, post–World War II freeway development to facilitate suburban expansion strategically demolished Detroit's core Black business and residential neighborhoods (Thomas 2013). While Black Detroiters did not have enough political or economic power to halt the spatial destruction of Black city space nor discrimination in public institutions, activists consistently fought to dismantle the local machinations of white supremacy. Black community members turned to local media—Black presses, radio stations, and later television programs—to expand Black business enterprise, foster Black cultural expression, and disseminate Black liberation discourse (Smith 1999; Shaw 2009; Sullivan 2022).

Despite barriers to inclusion in dominant civic life, Detroiters built a vibrant Black arts scene and created Black business opportunities for middle-class residents with income to invest. By the sixties, Detroit was home to the globally renowned Motown Records and two of the nation's very few Black-owned and -operated commercial radio stations, both of which programmed a mix of popular music, religious programming, and Black news fare. However, it was much more challenging for Black community members to find any place on local television in Detroit, as all local station management, employees, and on-air talent were almost exclusively white. One notable exception was Prophet Jones, a self-proclaimed faith healer and seer known for flamboyant religious spectacles that aired on local radio CKLW-FM starting in the 1930s and later WXYZ-TV Detroit on Sundays at midnight in 1955—the first Black Detroiter to host his own show. His reputation was eviscerated a few months after his show debuted when he was arrested for soliciting sex from an undercover vice officer. Tim Retzloff (2002) argues that the public fascination with Jones can be largely attributed to the queer subtext of his religious performance and that his morality arrest was part of a clear effort to diminish his growing power in the city. While an anomaly in 1950s white-dominated television, Jones demonstrates both the magnetic appeal of televangelists as local celebrities and the reactionary response of white city infrastructure threatened by Black social influence.

The white hegemonic control of local television emerged as a clear symbol of Detroit's violently enforced color line in the late sixties. On July 23, 1967, Detroit police raided a Black veteran's homecoming party, violently arresting all attendees. Black protests spread throughout the city, culminating in five days of chaos, called a riot by the white establishment and the Great Rebellion by Black residents and radical allies (Fine 2007). In the wake of Rebellion, Detroit became a focal point in national conversations about structural racism, social inequity, and police brutality. To quell concerns about the lack of Black inclusion in civic life, Detroit stations began integrating Black talent into existing broadcasts and airing locally produced programs specifically for the Black community.[3] While Black entrepreneurs and activists were unable to totally offset racist urban policies and white economic disinvestment in Detroit, these efforts increased Black access to media channels. By the mid-1970s Detroit had become the largest U.S. city with a majority-Black population and the first city in the continental United States with a Black-owned and operated television station, WGPR-TV: Where God's Presence Radiates.

WGPR was developed by William Banks, a prominent labor attorney, respected political advocate, and ordained minister with the Detroit Baptist Seminary (Gregory 1999). He founded the Free and Accepted Modern Masons, a nonprofit Black Christian fraternal organization dedicated to the moral and financial uplift of Black citizens. As I've discussed elsewhere (Sullivan 2019), WGPR's original programming roster was hampered by financial limitations. The TV station broadcast a mix of cheap syndicated fare and original Black news and talk-entertainment programs. When the station could not finance more original programs they turned to church. As marketing director George White states, "Well, let's face it, Dr. Banks is not only a lawyer, but also a minister. And we believe in the right of everyman to petition God in his own manner. But we probably would not have had as much religious programming on this station if it were not for economic reasons. All of that religion is paid religion. That's the route that many of the smaller UHF stations are taking" (Johnson 1979, 59).

Soon, WGPR-TV filled their Sunday roster with a mix of original and syndicated religious fare. It aired the local *Faith for Miracles*, sermons from Hicks Temple, and *The Spirit of Detroit*.⁴ WGPR-TV also included syndicated church broadcasts from other local stations and included (white) national televangelist programs like the *PTL Club* as a cost-saving mechanism to attract diverse viewers and reserve their limited funds for original Black programs. Notably, the station syndicated the variety show *Gospel Time TV* (1962–65), which Gayle Wald (2007) asserts was the nation's first series to use all-Black talent and staff. To correspond with the national program, WGPR created their own *Gospel Time*, hosted by local Rev. Robert Grant, to showcase Black churches performing the city's most praiseworthy hits. Considered together, the Black religious programs on WGPR-TV emphasized Black religiosity while dramatically expanding Black visibility on local television and offering Black residents the agency to produce their own paid-time programs.

Despite WGPR's mission to design thoughtful and engaging content for Black viewers, shows faced cancellation if not financially viable to the struggling station. To better understand how local Black televangelism sustained a place on the airwaves, I turn to two distinct WGPR shows that boosted the visibility of the Black church on the local airwaves.

MARCH OF FAITH

One long-running program that helped WGPR cut costs and project local Black culture onto the small screen was *March of Faith*. The show relies upon a multicamera recording setup to film church services led by Bishop P. A. (Phillip Aquilla) Brooks at New St. Paul Tabernacle of the Church of God in Christ denomination (or COGIC). It offers viewers thirty-minute episodes that intersperse gospel performances with sermons that connect to scripture. An episode or service often culminates in a riveting choral performance as (formerly elder) Brooks approaches the congregation to reach any worshippers in need of salvation. Brooks's sermons take on a musical tenor that shifts seamlessly into gospel performance; they are fiery and up-tempo, inviting a congregational call-and-response structure—a core tenet of both Black gospel and African folk music. The enthusiastic, interactive nature of the service is mirrored by the telecast's aesthetics. The cameras typically frame Brooks in alternating medium shots to emphasize the conviction of his preaching and long shots to capture his physical dynamism as he moves away from his lectern to engage congregants. As Brooks speaks or sings the words of God, the camera also cuts to wide shots of the full congregation and reverse shots of parishioners embracing his message, raising their hands in prayer, singing along, or nodding their heads in faithful agreement.[5] As such, *March of Faith* offers viewers a spiritual experience akin to attending a service at New St. Paul Tabernacle.

The sermons and gospel performances in *March of Faith* are reflective of broader COGIC theologies and practices. As with other Black Pentecostal-Holiness churches, COGIC doctrine calls for personal piety through sanctification (e.g., baptism), recognizes glossolalia (speaking in tongues) as evidence of the Holy Spirit's presence, and emphasizes evangelist missionary work to reach souls through salvation before the end of days (C. White 2012). While COGIC adheres to traditional evangelical values related to gender and sexuality, preachers have liberally supported civil rights politics and focused their missions on outreach in impoverished Black urban centers. Spirited gospel performance is also a central feature of COGIC services, making the denomination a wellspring in gospel music history. *March of Faith* reflects the dominant COGIC social and spiritual traditions by mixing evangelical theology, Black advocacy, and gospel performance. The series introduces viewers to key components of COGIC worship—charismatic preaching, a communal spiritual experience, and musical entertainment—which is a proven recipe for televangelist success.

Bishop Brooks first developed *March of Faith* for radio, akin to many local religious programs. He moved to Detroit from Chicago as a gospel musician in 1949 at the invitation of the Greater Love Tabernacle, which touted one of the many gospel choirs that performed on local radio. Brooks felt called to ministry in 1951 and soon started his own COGIC pastorage a few years later in an old bank building. However, Brooks used his gospel and radio experience to expand his ministry. *March of Faith* aired Sunday mornings in the 1960s on CKLW-FM and later WMUZ-FM. Radio publicity helped the congregation grow substantially; it was soon able to relocate and expand their community services. As such, the development of WGPR-TV created an opportunity for Brooks to bring the COGIC faith to Detroiters and essentially crowd-fund more social services for his congregants.

Like contemporaneous televangelist series, *March of Faith* incorporates fundraising and tithing directly into the address of the telecast service. In this way, *March of Faith* is both a religious experience and a charitable enterprise for Black Detroit. *March of Faith* episodes are regularly interrupted by infographics that provide numbers for prayer hotlines and to instruct viewers to buy additional theological materials (books, audio, supplemental videos) from the New St. Paul catalog. Although these tactics are far from unique, I caveat that in contrast to mainstream televangelism's emphasis on individual wealth accumulation, Brooks's interest in commercial television aligns more with a local Black capitalist ethos. He used the congregation's fund-raising returns to expand Black social and business infrastructure for a Black city that struggles with white state disinvestment. He created a day school, nonprofit housing corporation, affordable senior housing complex, head start agency, and economic resource center to increase employment opportunities for local Black residents. He founded a Black community bank and mortgage company, helped establish the Charles H. Wright Museum of African American History, and was in a consortium of Black business leaders that tried to buy WGPR and keep it with local Black leadership when CBS purchased it in 1994 after the death of Banks (Edwards 1997; McFarlin 1994; *Michigan Chronicle* 1981).

Brooks, who passed away in 2020, credited his success to a mix of "aggressive evangelism" and "practical outreach." He held traditional patriarchal views, but in my research his sermons rarely engage controversial topics and instead emphasize how to survive challenges of modern life by keeping faith.[6] While offering spirituality as a path to self-improvement, he appears acutely aware that it takes more than prayer to fix the institutional and economic factors limiting Black advancement in the contemporary United States. The visibility of *March of Faith* coincided with Brooks's increasing position as a high-ranking COGIC leader and frequent power broker in the city. His outreach work led him to connect with U.S. political leaders including Bill Clinton, Barack Obama, and Jesse Jackson. He used his platform to support Black communities, working with Desmond Tutu and Nelson Mandela in South Africa and collecting funds for Black residents displaced by Hurricane Katrina. A trusted pillar of the Black community, he helped Detroit politicians strategize how best to improve the city, brokering meetings at his church office between Black Detroit mayors (e.g., Coleman Young and Dennis Archer) and white state politicians (e.g., Governor James Blanchard). Brooks had opportunities to extend his political and business acumen further but remained dedicated to helping underserved members of his parish. His political and social influence is not clear just by watching *March of Faith* on its own. However, viewing his live-streamed "homegoing celebration" (funeral), listening to the words of those close to him, and reading through numerous local accolades and tributes printed over his long career, it's difficult to disentangle his popular persona as a media figure, his spiritual role as a faith leader, and his intellectual prowess and business acumen as an advocate for Black Detroit.

According to Detroit journalist Bankole Thompson, "He was not a headline seeker; he was not a press conference bishop; he was not a limelight seeking minister, despite his tremendous influence and despite his tremendous impact, he was not chasing the cameras" ("Remembering the Late Bishop Brooks" 2020). I would add that he seemingly preferred to direct the cameras. He introduced national COGIC bishops to religious broadcasting, including Bishop Patterson, whose church services would be nationally syndicated. He produced documentaries on COGIC, hoping to raise the national platform of their theology and project images of Black Christian respectability to pious viewers. Brooks briefly had syndication on BET in 1992 before refocusing his attention on his local telecast (*Michigan Chronicle* 1992). Like hegemonic televangelists, he sold spiritual self-help and theological materials to viewers, yet avoided flagrant displays of personal wealth that would raise eyebrows of religious ethicists. His televisual persona was that of a tempered and compassionate paternal figure, though his carefully choreographed gospel chorales and charismatic sermonizing worked well to entertain already religiously observant viewers. Here, we can see how a small-scale, televised church service amplifies the platforms of local leaders to support Black communities while offering traditional Black COGIC services to Detroiters. Indeed, *March of Faith* reruns and new broadcasts continue to air on the Impact Network, a Detroit Black-owned and faith-based television network with distribution on a broad variety of cable, digital, and satellite companies.

INSPIRATION TIME

Counter to Brooks's telecast COGIC services, beloved deejay Martha Jean "The Queen" Steinberg's gospel variety program *Inspiration Time* is structured akin to a daytime women's chat show and relies upon the local celebrity of its host. Born Martha Jean Jones in 1930, she first worked as a nurse and model before taking weekend on-air radio shifts at WDIA in Memphis. She rose to prominence as Martha Jean "The Queen," a nickname given to her by another deejay, as the station didn't want to use her married name. A rare female presence in the male-dominated radio industry, her working-class roots, soft-spoken drawl, and daily shoutouts to the blue-collar workers of the city endeared her to Black listeners when she relocated to Detroit in 1964.

The Queen claims she felt called by God to use her media platform to inform, advertise, educate, entertain, and serve Detroit's Black community. At first, she did so in a secular way; during the 1967 Rebellion she stayed on air for forty-eight hours straight, updating home listeners of events in the streets and urging protesters to stop the violence. She later cohosted a radio and television call-in program, *Buzz the Fuzz*, with the Detroit police commissioner to address citizen concerns about both crime and police misconduct. She organized a strike of Black broadcast workers calling for equitable treatment and Black inclusion in management at WJLB-FM. However, she encountered a spiritual epiphany during a power outage at the WJLB-FM studio in 1972 that changed her radio persona ("The Black Church in Detroit" 2023). As the power returned, she spoke on air, "I was just touched by the Holy Spirit ... it was as if something, a different entity, came through my soul and told me my mission is to help bring Jesus Christ to the people" (Fournier 2021). She thereafter began shifting her popular R&B program *Inspiration Time* to gospel. Neither the station nor her listeners protested the genre shift; she maintained a dedicated following while adding more spiritual guidance to her talk segments. In 1972, Steinberg became an ordained minister, founded a church called the Home of Love, and served as pastor to her newly established interfaith Order of the Fisherman Ministry. She baptized a hundred of her community workers, a tradition that continued with new members each year in the Detroit River. The Queen required members, estimated around five hundred in 1982, to tithe 10 percent of their gross income to the Home of Love. According to a *Detroit Free Press* article, current or former members of her church were happy to give, though the mission asked for a lot. The Home of Love hosted numerous charitable fundraisers annually (Holmes 1982). While her accounts were not audited, sources indicate that she maintained her personal wealth through her radio and television gigs, while the funds raised through the House of Love sustained her mission and their charitable endeavors.

Detroit at this time did not lack for Black ministers, but the Queen felt there needed "to be an example set by a Black woman" (Holmes 1982). Her mission was particularly dedicated to supporting Black working mothers, using tithes to open a daycare and nursery in the building next to the church. While her politics were far from radical, her status as a divorced single mother marks her as distinctive from televangelist contemporaries. Her daytime chat show, or "service" as she called it, also courted a predominantly female viewership. The program mixed Christian wisdom for self-empowerment, interviews with local celebrities, audience interactions, and gospel performances. Speaking of her broadcasts to the *Michigan Chronicle*, the Queen notes, "In a big city like Detroit where many people work different shifts, there are lonely people who are afraid to go out their doors. I hope that through my program people will understand that we must reach out and love somebody else if we are going to survive in this world" (McCoy 1975). As the Queen's ministry was non-denominational, most of her spiritual messaging combined generalized biblical lessons—a staple of early televangelism—with her own signature calls for maternal love and neighborly compassion.

In the 1972 pilot for *Inspiration Time*, shot in studio at WGPR, she begins by warmly welcoming her small, majority female, audience. She then cuts to a live gospel performance with Billy Preston on the *Inspiration Time* stage before sitting down to talk to him about his relationship to Black rhythm and faith. Preston, who had a popular soul and R&B career before returning to his gospel roots, is merely one example of the prominent musical guests and radio contacts used to market the series to viewers. After another performance by Preston, she offers her inspirational tip for the day. In this episode, she discusses (in close-up) how the conditions facing Black Americans might realistically sow anger and hatred; but viewers must remember to choose universal love, tolerance, and multicultural understanding. In a later episode, she featured the Unity Baptist Church Choir before interviewing the first Black Detroit city councilwoman Erma Henderson about the neglected political concerns of Black women and her role as a representative of the Detroit Black female population. They also talk about racist redlining policies and housing discrimination before turning to the power of prayer. At the end of the episode, the house lights dim and the guests share a moment of prayer as a final gospel performance wraps up the show.

Inspiration Time also presents a structure not dissimilar to mainstream televangelist programs like the *PTL Club* or *700 Club*, cutting between the performance stage, the audience, and the Queen standing or seated in close framing, directly addressing the viewers at home with tips for a spiritually uplifted life. However, the Queen always added a heaping side of Black pride, politics, and solidarity to her offerings. Her show, which was funded by WGPR, lasted only a few seasons and did not ask for any viewer donations—which perhaps contributed to its comparatively shorter run. However, her radio shows continued to broadcast her spiritual guidance until she bought her own gospel radio station in the 1990s—another anomaly in local Detroit history—which continued to replay her spiritual "services" long after her death in 2000.

Ultimately, the Queen's local success can be attributed to her magnetic personality, soothing vocal monologues, and business savvy. While she herself was not a gospel performer, she was a local media mogul who programmed gospel radio and hosted gospel concerts. Mia Mask (2010) has discussed Oprah Winfrey as a celebrity who combined maternal charisma with a modern therapeutic ethos and business marketing like televangelists. While her programs are secular, Oprah was, and perhaps is, worshiped like a religious icon. The Queen, like Oprah, proffered her own model of success for Black women as one built through compassion, tenacity, hard work, and faith; she consistently positioned herself as someone who cared for the welfare of her community and found spiritual value in all people, even those struggling in an economically and socially unstable city. She also ended each program with the statement, "God loves you and I love you," which reflected her elevated status as a local "Queen" and her personal, emotive address to local audiences. This endeared her to local followers; although the Queen's reign did not extend as far beyond her roots in Memphis and her chosen home of Detroit, it too inspired a gendered cult-like adoration from daytime viewers who watched her show, listened to her radio station, and joined her (broadcast) ministry.

CONCLUSION

The nondenominational Steinberg and the Pentecostal Brooks fit many major descriptors of televangelism that inspire scholarly debate including charismatic preaching, celebrity status, entrepreneurial endeavors, and a focus on musical entertainment—they just operate on a minor scale. Their lack of overt controversies and positioning within a primarily local context have occluded them from public and scholarly discussions of televangelism. Their spiritual and economic practices may not be above scrutiny. However, reading obituaries, commentary on YouTube clips, and social media posts about these two local icons, it's clear that their spiritual lessons still resonate with local followers who continue to express how "blessed" they have been to learn from their examples. While the reach of local media celebrities—including preachers—is decidedly smaller than their national counterparts, the impact they have on the lives of their viewers runs as deep.

In a local context, preachers tailor their televisual address to the perceived spiritual needs of local congregants. As demonstrated by the *America's Black Journal* anecdote that opened this chapter, local churches continue to adapt technology to address the shifting challenges facing Black Detroiters. As Marla Frederick has argued, televangelism is as much about faith in Jesus as about the "social, political, and economic considerations of the people who make, distribute, and consume religious broadcasting" (2015, 10). The Queen and Bishop Brooks did not maintain a presence in Detroit solely because of their charismatic address or knowledge of gospel, but because their specific brand of spiritual guidance resonated with the subject positions of residents. Their television ministries coordinated with other forms of Black social and economic services for congregants. While theologically and aesthetically divergent, both shows aired on the Black-owned and -operated WGPR-TV to affordably fill programming voids, showcase "respectable" forms of Black cultural expression, and challenge pathologizing ideas of urban life presented by dominant media. To fully understand their legacies, we must not only watch their religious broadcasts but work to understand their place in the business of religion, Detroit culture, and Black American history. A close study of local Black televangelism in Detroit reveals religious broadcasting functions as a sustainable business model for the local TV industry and Black churches as well as an ideological force that aims to shepherd residents as they struggle for social justice, economic advancement, and spiritual enrichment in civic life.

NOTES

1. There are conflicting dates for the *March of Faith* debut. It was first mentioned in local TV listings in 1979. It aired on WGPR-TV until 1994, at which point it shifted to the local CBS affiliate, before being broadcast on local cable access stations.
2. While generally broadcasters sought to avoid controversy, Detroit's own Father Coughlin courted a great deal of national controversy for his conservative and antisemitic sermons during the 1930s and 1940s (Hangen 2002).
3. *America's Black Journal* first aired in 1968 under the title *CPT*. This trend was not unique to Detroit. In the late 1960s, Black public affairs programs emerged in cities with sizable Black communities across the United States. For more, see Heitner (2013), Wald (2015), and Tait (2003).

4. This information was gathered by talking to former WGPR-TV staff ("William V. Banks Broadcast Museum"), reading TV listings in the *Detroit Free Press* and the *Michigan Chronicle*, and reading Johnson (1979).
5. Unfortunately, I have not been able to watch tapes prior to the 1980s, though discourse about the episodes indicates they had a similar format and style. I have contacted surviving members of the Brooks family and hope to track down earlier recordings. An official archive for these materials does not exist.
6. COGIC has a gender-segregated episcopal hierarchy with men holding positions of power within the international organization and women running "women's ministries" at local congregations. Brooks's daughter, Faithe, has discussed how he initially was unsupportive of her decision to earn a doctorate in theology. However, he grew to embrace her ministry. She now hosts the *March of Faith* telecast.

REFERENCES

Barlow, William. 1999. *Voice Over: The Making of Black Radio*. Temple University Press.

"The Black Church in Detroit: Women in Ministry." 2023. *American Black Journal*, season 51, episode 13. https://www.pbs.org/video/the-black-church-in-detroit-women-in-ministry-f3i124/.

Bowler, Kate. 2018. *Blessed: A History of the American Prosperity Gospel*. Oxford University Press.

Bruce, Steve. 2019. *Pray TV: Televangelism in America*. Routledge.

Buckser, Andrew. 2008. "Sacred Airtime: American Church Structures and the Rise of Televangelism." *Human Organization* 48 (4): 370–76. https://doi.org/10.17730/humo.48.4.b791525316152711.

Dillard, Angela D. 2007. *Faith in the City: Preaching Radical Social Change in Detroit*. University of Michigan Press.

Edwards, Eddie K. 1997. "Bishop P. A. Brooks: A Man Who Looks Out of the Window." *Michigan Chronicle*, February 12.

Federal Communications Commission. 1946. "Public Service Responsibility of Broadcast Licensees." Federal Communications Commission.

Fine, Sidney. 2007. *Violence in the Model City: The Cavanagh Administration, Race Relations, and the Detroit Race Riot of 1967*. Michigan State University Press.

Fournier, Gregory A. 2021. *Detroit Time Capsule*. Wheatmark.

Frederick, Marla. 2015. *Colored Television: American Religion Gone Global*. Stanford University Press.

Gates, Henry Louis, Jr. 2021. *The Black Church: This Is Our Story, This Is Our Song*. Penguin.

Gregory, Sheila T. 1999. *A Legacy of Dreams: The Life and Contributions of Dr. William Venoid Banks*. University Press of America.

Hadden, Jeffrey K., and Anson Shupe. 1987. "Televangelism in America." *Social Compass* 34 (1): 61–75. https://doi.org/10.1177/003776868703400105.

Hangen, Tona J. 2002. *Redeeming the Dial: Radio, Religion, and Popular Culture in America*. University of North Carolina Press.

Harold, Claudrena. 2017. "'Lord, Let Me Be an Instrument': The Artistry and Cultural Politics of Reverend James Cleveland and the Gospel Music Workshop of America, 1963–1991." *Journal of Africana Religions* 5 (2): 157–80. https://doi.org/10.5325/jafrireli.5.2.0157.

Heitner, Devorah. 2013. *Black Power TV*. Duke University Press.

Holmes, Jennifer. 1982. "Martha Jean Rose to Queenhood All by Herself; Now She Helps Others, but People Ask if She's Outgrown the Throne." *Detroit Free Press*, January 10.

Horsfield, Peter. 2015. *From Jesus to the Internet: A History of Christianity and Media*. John Wiley.

Jackson, Sherman A. 2005. *Islam and the Blackamerican: Looking toward the Third Resurrection*. Oxford University Press.

Johnson, Mary H. 1979. "A Case History of the Evolution of WGPR-TV, Detroit: First Black Owned Television Station in the U.S., 1972–1979." Ph.D. diss., University of North Carolina at Chapel Hill.

Junior, Nyasha. 2016. "Marla Frederick on Race, Gender, Religious Broadcasting and Social Media." *Marginalia Review of Books* (blog), April 26. https://themarginaliareview.com/nyasha-junior-talks-marla-frederick-race-gender-social-media/.

Marable, Manning. 2000. *How Capitalism Underdeveloped Black America: Problems in Race, Political Economy, and Society*. Pluto Press.

Marovich, Robert M. 2015. *A City Called Heaven: Chicago and the Birth of Gospel Music*. University of Illinois Press.

Martin, Lerone A. 2014. *Preaching on Wax: The Phonograph and the Shaping of Modern African American Religion*. New York University Press.

———. 2018. "Religion, Race, and Popular Culture." In *The Oxford Handbook of Religion and Race in American History*, edited by Kathryn Gin Lum and Paul Harvey, 110–22. Oxford University Press.

Mask, Mia. 2010. *Divas on Screen: Black Women in American Film*. University of Illinois Press.

McCoy, Robbie L. 1975. "Martha Jean Expands Ministry to Television." *Michigan Chronicle*, November 15, sec. D.

McFarlin, Jim. 1994. "Local Ministers Will Ask CBS to Keep the Faith—and Their Programming." *Detroit Free Press*, October 22, sec. C.

Michigan Chronicle. 1981. "COGIC Hosts Musical Afro-American Museum." September 19, sec. C.

———. 1992. "March of Faith Joins BET." April 15.

Pollard, Deborah Smith. 2008. *When the Church Becomes Your Party: Contemporary Gospel Music*. Wayne State University Press.

"Remembering the Late Bishop Brooks." 2020. *REDLINE with Bankhole Thompson*.

Retzloff, Tim. 2002. "'SEER OR QUEER?': Postwar Fascination with Detroit's

Prophet Jones." *GLQ: A Journal of Lesbian and Gay Studies* 8 (3): 271–96. https://doi.org/10.1215/10642684-8-3-271.

Schultze, Quentin J. 2003. *Televangelism and American Culture: The Business of Popular Religion*. Wipf and Stock.

Shaw, Todd C. 2009. *Now Is the Time! Detroit Black Politics and Grassroots Activism*. Duke University Press.

Smith, Suzanne E. 1999. *Dancing in the Street: Motown and the Cultural Politics of Detroit*. Harvard University Press.

Steinberg, Martha. 1995. "Martha Jean 'the Queen' Steinberg Historical Interview." Black Radio: Telling It Like It Was, ca. 1920s–97, series 2 and 3. Interviews, 1988–96, box 6, Archives of African American Music and Culture, Indiana University.

Sugrue, Thomas J. 1996. *The Origins of the Urban Crisis: Race and Inequality in Postwar Detroit*. Princeton University Press.

Sullivan, Annie Laurie. 2018. "Between Rebellion and Ruin: Local Documentary, Civic Infrastructure, and the Manufacture of Black Futures in Detroit." Ph.D. diss., Northwestern University.

———. 2019. "WGPR-TV Detroit: Building Black Media Infrastructure in the Post-rebellion City." *Velvet Light Trap*, no. 83 (March): 32–45. https://doi.org/10.7560/VLT8304.

———. 2022. "Who Controls the Media: The Racial Politics of Local Television: Negotiating Public Interests and the Black Freedom Struggle." In *The Routledge Companion to Media and the City*, edited by Erica Stein, Germaine R. Halegoua, and Brendan Kredell, 317–28. Taylor & Francis.

Tait, Alice. 2003. "Ethic Voices: Ethnocentric Public Affairs Television Programming." In *Television: Critical Concepts in Media and Cultural Studies*, edited by Toby Miller, 32–38. Taylor & Francis.

Thomas, June Manning. 2013. *Redevelopment and Race: Planning a Finer City in Postwar Detroit*. Wayne State University Press.

Thomas, Pradip, and Philip Lee, eds. 2012. *Global and Local Televangelism*. Palgrave Macmillan.

Torres, Sasha. 1998. *Living Color: Race and Television in the United States*. Duke University Press.

Trulear, Harold Dean. 2016. "The Black Church and Public Policy: Retrospect and Prospect." In *The Black Church Studies Reader*, edited by Alton B. Pollard and Carol B. Duncan, 177–88. Springer.

Wald, Gayle. 2007. *Shout, Sister, Shout! The Untold Story of Rock-and-Roll Trailblazer Sister Rosetta Tharpe*. Beacon.

———. 2015. *It's Been Beautiful: Soul! and Black Power Television*. Duke University Press.

Walton, Jonathan L. 2009. *Watch This! The Ethics and Aesthetics of Black Televangelism*. New York University Press.

Ward, Brian. 2006. *Radio and the Struggle for Civil Rights in the South*. University Press of Florida.

Ward, Mark, Sr. 2015. *The Electronic Church in the Digital Age: Cultural Impacts of Evangelical Mass Media*. 2 vols. ABC-CLIO.

———. 2018. "Increase Your Faith: The Domestication of Black Televangelism." In *Media across the African Diaspora*, edited by O. Banjo Omotay, 18–34. Routledge.

White, Calvin. 2012. *The Rise to Respectability: Race, Religion, and the Church of God in Christ*. University of Arkansas Press.

White, Mimi. 1992. *Tele-Advising: Therapeutic Discourse in American Television*. University of North Carolina Press.

"William V. Banks Broadcast Museum." n.d. Accessed April 26, 2023. https://wgprtv62museum.org.

CHAPTER 7

JONATHAN MACDONALD

LEARNING THE
BASIC ISSUES OF MAN

MIDCENTURY HUMANISM, SOCIAL SCIENCE,
AND EDUCATIONAL TELEVISION

"Is Man good? Is Man evil? Is he a mixture of both?" the female narrator pauses, "the wondering will not end today. If Man's knowledge of himself fails to keep pace with his knowledge of the physical universe, the gift of intelligence that created human society can destroy it." So began the promotional film for the twelve-part television series *Basic Issues of Man* (1962). Created by the University of Georgia's Center for Continuing Education on behalf of National Educational Television (NET), the series advocated for liberal humanist study in the face of perceived social and political problems. If, as *Basic Issues* suggested, liberal arts education was a viable remedy to existential global nuclear threat, then there was no problem it could not solve. Yet the universalism of *Basic Issues* also silenced local concerns. Started as an extension program at a segregated university during the height of Jim Crow, the series elided the pressing racial tensions of the day, insisting, instead, on the importance of abstract liberal values. As the series began to broadcast nationally, the University of Georgia became embroiled in a lawsuit to admit Black students (Pratt 2005). The series disavowed local concerns in an effort to endorse broader, and supposedly more fundamental, aims. In so doing, *Basic Issues of Man* reminds us that locally produced television can just as readily silence concerns as amplify them.

Rather than speak to the national debate over desegregation, *Basic Issues* served the interests of its "local" producers: the university and its affiliates. It mobilized intellectual labor from faculty, financial resources from the Ford Foundation, and considerable filmmaking talent toward national ambitions. The program's silence on racial politics was typical of educational television in this period and may evidence a concern with being pigeonholed as a "southern" production. The climate at the University of Georgia prior to its 1961 court-mandated integration also likely played a role in its avoidance of race. According to historian Robert Cohen, UGA faculty avoided discussing integration "out of fear for their jobs." Soon after the campus was integrated, a student-led white supremacist riot brought unwanted national attention to the university (Cohen 1996, 630–31, 616–19). It is not surprising that *Basic Issues* avoided these local concerns, as it was produced with the aid of faculty who were hesitant to discuss race prior to national scandal.

Fusing popular conventions and avant-garde visual techniques, and hailing viewers as learners and members of a democratic public, *Basic Issues* strove to elevate educational television into a lively and engaging art. *Basic Issues* is emblematic of what scholar of midcentury media Anna McCarthy (2010) calls "governing by television" and belongs to a tradition of social-scientific human management through mass media. By introducing the viewing public to the basic tenets of a liberal studies curriculum, *Basic Issues* recast the ideological concerns of America's intellectual classes into a legible and entertaining format for general audiences. Program producers traded on well-worn tropes, including scripted debates about Cold War ideology, exoticized depictions of Indigenous people, and the valorization of individual agency against the social forces of so-called conformity. Although the series spoke in a language of universal humanism, as with most educational television from this period its presumed audience was white and male (the implied titular "Man"), a figure who already enjoyed full participation in American political and intellectual life.

At midcentury, television presented its viewers seemingly intractable social and political problems, such as nuclear annihilation and civil unrest. Many Americans became aware and critical of the complex social structures in which they participated, as suggested by the surprise popularity of sociological works such as David Riesman's *The Lonely Crowd* (1950) and William H. Whyte's *The Organization Man* (1956). Self-awareness of these problems produced what historian Howard Brick has called an "age of contradictions" in which intellectuals and laypersons sought answers to pressing epistemological and social questions (Brick 1998). In an effort to create effective educational television, *Basic Issues* channeled this *longing* into a *looking*: a *looking* at the television screen and at American society. Informed by decades of research on the educational potential of mass media, the program directed audience attention to a liberal Cold War humanist ideology and repackaged midcentury intellectual concerns as matters of "human nature." By transforming these concerns into subjects of popular inquiry, *Basic Issues* naturalized contemporary social issues and placed the liberal-democratic citizen within the narrative of human history. According to this logic, the citizenship enjoyed by white Americans in the postwar decade was a tautological end of history *and* a fragile construct that needed to be protected and nurtured by targeted ideological intervention.

EXPERTISE, SOCIAL SCIENCE, AND EDUCATIONAL MEDIA AT MIDCENTURY

The postwar United States witnessed the rise of a new kind of expertise in the form of social and behavioral scientists. Social experts of all kinds reached new levels of visibility and public trust. Within and between academic institutions, government bureaucracies, professional organizations, and private foundations, greater numbers of educated technocrats worked on social problems ranging from the complex and intractable to the quotidian and mundane. In the postwar decade, experts believed their specialized knowledge had to be turned to socially productive ends. A "politics-patronage-social science nexus" emerged and funded projects with the explicit goal of "social engineering," in part to demonstrate social scientific utility vis-à-vis the "hard sciences" (Solovey 2013, 5–9). Working under the assumption that social science needed to operate persuasively (as human subjects were primed to resist), efforts at "human engineering" in the social sciences vacillated between scientific rationality and "irrational" emotional appeals (Derksen 2017, 199–201).

At the heart of these expert social interventions lay a contradiction. Social experts were informed by optimistic and pessimistic assessments of society, and hence prescribed both "freedom" *and* "control" (Herman 1995, 11–12). Experts believed their work could inspire an informed citizenry to "redefine and enrich democracy, eliminate poverty, enhance popular participation in government, expand opportunities for self-fulfillment, put reason at the helm of public policy, and make flexibility and variation keys to a new order of social roles," through democratically driven reform (Brick 1998, xii). For these thinkers, citizenship was "a developmental journey," a subject status both indispensable and not guaranteed (McCarthy 2010, 21). The ideal Cold War citizen would exhibit what historian Jamie Cohen-Cole calls "the open mind," a psychologically inflected reprise of possessive individualism and autonomy complemented by postwar ideals of tolerance, flexibility, and the capacity to work in groups. As a normative "model of human nature," open-mindedness suffused American social science and naturalized liberal democracy. It also found a place for the "expert" within the political structure of democracy (Cohen-Cole 2014, 1–4).

During the first half of the twentieth century, the persuasive power of radio and film disturbed critics and mass communications researchers (Turner 2013, 15–38). Film, radio, and television were developed not only as tools for entertainment but also for research, military logistics, education, and state-building projects. Mass media were understood to exercise transformative power on the public (Orgeron, Orgeron, and Streible 2012, 15–66; Acland and Wasson 2011). More worryingly, these media were implicated in the destruction of "high culture" and the rise of European fascism, with Adolf Hitler's apparent "hypnotic" deployment of radio and film propaganda (Turner 2013, 24–38). American wartime films, particularly when they were entertaining, were understood to unite diverse publics by speaking across generational, geographical, educational, class, and racial lines. Following the war, television emerged as a venue for educational materials (Orgeron, Orgeron, and Streible 2012, 24). Early educational television echoed consensus politics and presented this outlook as rational and disinterested. The language of rational moderation was, in fact, "a language of conflict" that reframed existing social disparities as mere competing interests (McCarthy 2010, 1–4, 22). The language of political consensus thus hoped to produce what it purported to describe.

THE BASIC ISSUES OF THE *BASIC ISSUES OF MAN*

Basic Issues of Man was developed by the Georgia Center for Continuing Education and the College of Arts and Sciences at the University of Georgia in response to a "widespread interest" for a program in the liberal studies. According to the program manual, "liberal studies" existed "for understanding, for renewal, for enjoyment, for encouragement, and for clarification of the issues of life." UGA program planners sought external funding as the program's complexity and scope expanded (Mahler and Appy 1965, vii–ix).[1] The UGA team was awarded grant funds by the Ford Foundation's Fund for Adult Education (Wells 1960).[2] Together, they planned a "maxim[ally] flexible" program designed for "groups on campus, in the local community, or in the home" (Mahler and Appy 1965). Unusually, the home station for the program would be an educational television station based out of a university: WGTV at the University of Georgia. Gerard Appy, associate director within the Georgia Center and head of film and television operations at WGTV, framed their early educational television activities within UGA's land-grant mission to "extend the assets of the university and the university activities to people throughout the state" (quoted in Robertson 1993, 117). A narrative of modest local origins cast *Basic Issues* as an organic development of a liberal, forward-thinking, and interdisciplinary faculty, but the scope and content of the program reveal Cold War nationalist interests, and its evasion of American racial politics suggests a selective engagement with national concerns and imagined viewing audiences.

The Ford Foundation's mission statement called for mass media to be used in "the rapid and extensive education of adults about the world situation, the nature of the struggle in which we are engaged, and the heritage we are seeking to defend." Ford program officers worried "unenlightened" Americans would pose a danger to themselves and to the globe (Ford Foundation's 1949 "Gaither Report," as quoted in McCarthy 2010, 120). Subsidiary organizations took up this mission, including the aforementioned Fund for Adult Education and the National Educational Television network. WGTV began as a NET member and joined PBS after its formation in 1970, where it continues operations as a member station.

In the report of the fund's decade of activities, officials emphasized the experimental nature of *Basic Issues*. The program was "conducted in a community laboratory context" as a university-based program that "combined residential periods and television offerings in an integrated plan." The "experiment" appears to have run at UGA in the early 1960s ahead of a national launch. Published materials from the University of Georgia Press appeared some years later.[3] Initially, the team's efforts focused on the effectiveness of a course of study when considered in various combinations of locations and mediums: a reading list, a television (or film) series (with a correspondence course), a community discussion group, and a classroom lesson plan. Despite its idiosyncratic origin, the program was designed to be useful beyond this experimental window; episodes were purpose-designed for exhibition "elsewhere over television stations and on 16mm projectors" (Fund for Adult Education, Ford Foundation 1962, 55). By the mid-1960s the program circulated on NET-affiliated stations in distant Boston and Los Angeles.[4] The full program consisted of a boxed collection of six purpose-written volumes (and a program manual), twelve half-hour television programs (or film prints), and an extended reference bibliography. Designers imagined the program could be taught as a whole or in parts, by turning a single volume, its bibliography, and/or paired broadcasts into a single course (Mahler and Appy 1965, vii–ix).

Early press coverage emphasized television's experimental teaching potential in the home. Planners imagined viewers as "students [who] don't know they are students." The Georgia Center saw the family as a critical nexus of social intervention and planned outreach programs to bring both "man *and* wife" to campus for "intellectual weekends." After attending special events, participants could "keep up on television with their work." The organizers planned telephone conferences between program participants to bring this multimedia "symphony of communications" full circle (Wells 1960, emphasis added). In this configuration, educational television would modulate between local, in-person group contexts (like the classroom or community meeting) and the privacy of the home, uniting both under the banner of continuing education and democratic citizenship. *Basic Issues* was imagined to reach beyond the individual student: "his" spouse and other WGTV viewers were welcomed as learners and participants.

Press reports and the program manual do not indicate whether participation was available, or indeed of any interest, to Georgia's Black residents.[5] Prior to campus integration in 1961, the Center for Continuing Education's student body would have been entirely white, and given racial etiquette under Jim Crow, a broadcast would likely not have been read as an invitation for Black participants to visit campus. Black Georgians may have watched broadcasts, and it is conceivable, though unclear, that they utilized the semi-anonymity of the program's structure to access Georgia's segregated educational services.

While the financial, ideological, and broader intellectual origins of *Basic Issues* come from a national Cold War milieu, its subject matter and writerly origins lay in the professoriate of the University of Georgia. All of the twelve episodes in the program were inspired by materials and themes contained in the print volumes written by faculty. In at least one case, a faculty member took over primary script writing duties.[6] While none of the scholars associated with the endeavor appear to have been major names in their fields, their undertaking was a novel multimedia and interdisciplinary effort. Participating faculty represented the departments of Sociology, History, Political Science, English, Biology, and Philosophy. They were joined by Georgia Center staff Thomas W. Mahler (a credited consultant on every one of the television programs) and Gerard L. Appy (credited writer and producer for every program). Most episodes were directed by Hill Bermont.[7] Supported by the Ford Foundation, this cohort produced a program that invoked the universal aspirations of the university's humanist mission, emphasizing (inter)national intellectual concerns while disavowing local particularities.

The planning committee at the University of Georgia outlined seven "types" of "man" the liberal studies could cultivate: Knowledgeable Man, Scholarly Man, Cultivated Man, Leadership Man, Social Action Man, "Organization" Man, and Free Man. Each figure warranted at least a paragraph-length description, and with the exception of the "Organization" Man, all were favorable. While the first four of these "types" trade on the Enlightenment notion that the liberal arts cultivate the individual, the final three described the individual's role in a complex modern society. Without citing William H. Whyte's study of the same name, the manual invoked the "Organization" Man as a particularly dispiriting development, produced by "the pressures of urban population concentration and increasingly complex social organization." Such a man, the manual warned, "cheerfully subordinates himself to the purposes and activities of the family, the church, the business, the agency, [and] the community." No worthy liberal studies program, the manual argued, should produce "such a slave to society" (Mahler and Appy 1965, 1–8).

As scholar Mark Grief has argued, midcentury intellectual discourse was characterized by a concern over the status of "man" or "the human" (2015). *Basic Issues*, in this context, is one of many texts announcing a possessive and universal characteristic of "man." These texts deployed a popularized "fundamental anthropology" premised on a "continuous stream of introspection" in search of a "majoritarian, unmarked human subject." For Grief, this discourse is fundamentally "empty" and "maieutic": insistent and forceful questioning brings into being, in the questioned individual, answers that reward the beliefs of the questioner. Thus, the discourse of "man" contains within it a series of recursive, deeply ideological presuppositions that operated didactically (Grief 2015, 4–13).

The *Basic Issues* program planners sought to cultivate a "man" capable of exercising the democratic power of choice. Thus, the "Organization" Man was offered as a foil to the "chief value outcome" of the *Basic Issues* curriculum: the Free Man. The authors argued that a measure of conformity and adaptability were required for a functioning society. They were adamant, however, that a "free man can choose that to which he conforms." Freedom was understood as both the capacity to exercise choice when "[making] significant judgments [and] decisions" and the ability "to recognize, understand, and react to choice-making situations." The Free Man resolved the question as to "whether or not man is sufficiently rational to govern himself." The Free Man was a rational actor who could exercise informed choices, chiefly, the choice to be free. The program, the section continued, "is based on the proposition that there are fundamental and persistent issues which have faced mankind continuously, at least in Western civilization, and further that there is a relationship between these persistent issues and the crucial choices man makes in his day-to-day activities. Expressed in another way, the proposition states that man develops viewpoints and values, consciously or unconsciously, about basic issues and these concepts have relevance for the significant choices he makes in the daily round of life." The program would contextualize these "issues" within human history, presenting "alternate viewpoints" so that the participant might "perceive a wide range of significant intellectual and practical choices [and] . . . choose effectively" (Mahler and Appy 1965, 6–8).

By juxtaposing the enslaved "Organization" Man with the Free Man, the designers packaged ideal democratic personality in a racialized discourse while evacuating these terms of their historical specificity. Here, freedom and slavery did not denote legal and ontological conditions but were outcomes of education, social conditioning, and individual agency. Rather than relegate slavery to the premodern era, program planners figured slavery as a consequence of industrial modernity through the figure of the "Organization" Man. The Free Man, by comparison, was capable of choosing freedom but in desperate need of the guidance to do so. Although racial idioms were implicit in the program's mission, gendered language was clearly embedded in the text. The program's titular "Man" and his various iterations demonstrated an investment in reproducing white masculinized authority through worldly, humanistic learning and mastery of the terms of debate.

Despite its origins as a local, university-produced program, *Basic Issues* circulated widely in the mid-1960s. It was distributed to other NET stations and broadcasts were theoretically coordinated with study and discussion groups, as the program manual included instructions for discussion proctors (Mahler and Appy 1965, 42).[8] *Basic Issues* was featured in an advanced high school class and offered at a Governor's Honors Program retreat at Wesleyan College in Macon, Georgia (Dellinger 1963). Alongside winners from major networks ABC and NBC, the *Basic Issues* episode "There Be Dragons" was awarded at the twenty-eighth American Exhibition of Educational Radio and Television Programs in 1964 for "brilliant photography . . . [and] keen analysis of an issue in a manner that is both beautiful and stimulating" (Jones 1964). By the late 1960s, *Basic Issues of Man* would also be available as a series of educational films ("Study—Discussion Programs" 1969).

According to the program manual, *Basic Issues* deliberately avoided "educational film traditions" and did not offer "final answers" to the questions it raised (Mahler and Appy 1965, 22–23). As a late 1960s American Library Association report described the series, the programs "point up the persistence of the problems" of "certain aspect[s] of man" and "[demonstrate] that people do not agree about them or their solutions" ("Study—Discussion Programs" 1969). Or, as described in the program manual,

> The Fundamental purpose of each film is to say these things:
> (1) This is a problem.
> (2) It has been a problem for a long time.
> (3) All people do not agree about this problem or how to solve it.
> (4) This presentation should help you recognize the problem.
> (5) If you wish to make an intelligent personal decision, you should look into the problem further. (Mahler and Appy 1965, 23)

Likely as a sample for educational institutions, a fifteen-minute promotional film was produced that featured selections from the series (Georgia Center for Continuing Education / National Educational Television 1961b).

Rather than litigate how audiences received these programs, I suggest that their existence demonstrates how midcentury social experts imagined themselves, their role, and the publics they served. Those who hoped to educate others using television were seduced by the medium's soft-power potential and "educated" themselves first. Educational programming was created and directed by those who saw commercial television as "the cultural equivalent of a sewage pipe" (McCarthy 2010, 2) or "a vast wasteland," to quote FCC chair Newton Minnow (Orgeron, Orgeron, and Streible 2012, 62). Decidedly not products of popular culture, potentially ignored by audiences at their time of production, and largely forgotten since, the *Basic Issues* programs nonetheless deployed the generic conventions of popular programming to complete their ideological objectives. As the program manual states, "The film makers have purposefully presented acknowledged arguments emotionally and sometimes dramatically ... to provoke, to excite argument ... and discussion" (Mahler and Appy 1965, 24). In light of the program's overwhelming investment in fostering rational, free citizens, such "emotional appeals" were a means to an end.

Scholars of popular culture and television have critiqued discourses that cast consumptive practices as "pacifying" and "feminizing" (Modleski 1991, 29–34; Newman and Levine 2012, 150–52). Mass culture critique imagines the audience as a submissive receiver of ideology embedded in programs. The manual gestured to this supposed problem to justify the program's avant-garde flourishes: "In these films ... there is an occasional experiment ... to employ [camera and editing] subjectively, somewhat as a painter might approach a canvas. The attempt is not to shock or jolt the audience simply for the sake of novelty but rather to prevent the viewer from watching the program passively" (Mahler and Appy 1965, 24). Optimistic that citizens could be trained for democracy, the program addressed them as agents and makers of meaning, and if that failed, it "shock[ed]" their faculties into response. Even though the program's presumed audience was already understood as agential makers of meaning, *Basic Issues* would nonetheless carefully curate the possible meanings that were available for them to make.

BASIC ISSUES OF MAN AND IDEOLOGICAL EDUCATION

Narrative approach and directorial style varied considerably between episodes in *Basic Issues*. However, the series creators understood that entertainment was an essential component of televised education. To capture audience attention, maintain engagement, and better communicate ideological lessons, producers borrowed generic popular-cultural conventions. What follows is a comparison of three programs from the series: "The Nature of Man" (paired with sociologist Rollin Chambliss's book *The Nature of Man*), "Sometimes Harmonious, Sometimes Not" (paired with historian C. Jay Smith Jr.'s book *Man and Society*), and "A Political Animal" (paired with political scientist George Parthemos's book *Political Perspectives*). These programs are not necessarily representative of the series' ideological concerns or aesthetic strategies. However, they pose a question central to the *Basic Issues* project: What is "man's" nature, and what are the political implications of that nature?

The intended first episode of the series, and an allegory of human existential morality throughout history, "The Nature of Man" is set in an "old Mexic[an]" village (Chiapas) where the ruins of precolonial civilization coexist alongside modern industry (Mahler and Appy 1965, 24–25).[9] In the opening shot, a man dressed in "traditional" Indigenous clothes hikes through a desert. Rather than comment on the scenes, the unseen narrator draws out the moral and social dimensions of what are represented as universal elements of quotidian human life. Aside from diegetic musical performance and the illegible noise of crowds, and accompanied only by English-language narration, the program's Indigenous performers are completely silent. This choice lends an ethnographic element (what the program manual calls an "accent") to a scripted dramatic exploration of "the problems inherent in the study of the nature of man" (Mahler and Appy 1965, 25). Put another way, the episode relies on racial and cultural difference to depict indigeneity as a simultaneous object of "wondrous difference" and universal human relatability for an imagined white viewer (Griffiths 2002). In so doing, the program exemplifies certain trends in midcentury anthropology, framing it as a "colloquial science" for general audiences (Milam 2019).[10] Although sameness is the provenance of the narration, difference is what is *shown*. "Nature of Man" crafts a narrative of human civilization and social development in broad sketches. During its first half, the program compares the philosophical differences of theism with humanism, considers the problem of sin, and asks how mankind has sought refuge in redemptive religious narratives or bodily pleasures. The second half of the program weighs two propositions: that man is inherently evil and that man is inherently good. Arguments to both ends are made through a parable of an old man who is beaten by young gang members and then nurtured back to health by a family of good Samaritans (Georgia Center for Continuing Education / National Educational Television 1961d).[11] According to an interview with Bermont, some of the actresses seen in this portion of the film were sex workers recruited from a brothel; their participation was secured after they were told the film would be a religious allegory about Mary Magdalene (Bermont 2003).

"The Nature of Man" portrays itself as an ethnographic documentary of Mexican village life with "art film" flourishes intended "to exploit the photogenic qualities of the Mexican Indian" (Mahler and Appy 1965, 25). According to film scholar Fatimah Tobing Rony, the "authentic artificiality" of the "lyrical" ethnographic film reveals a supposedly "higher truth" than a purely documentary or "objective" approach (1996, 13–15). Viewers are left to ponder the tension between difference and similitude from the comfort of their home. Distance, however, does not confer separation: Western intellectual history—from ancient Greek philosophy, through Christianity, the Renaissance, Reformation, and Industrial Revolution—has clear ideological and material repercussions for these Indigenous villagers. Commenting on how these pressures shape village life, the narrator warns that "more science and mathematics" will not enable man to escape contemporary dilemmas. Instead, he proposes additional "vigorous study of the nature of man." By juxtaposing so-called primitive and modern, the program suggests that Western humanism transcends time and place. Western knowledge is touted as the engine of political and social decision-making, while the legacies of colonial violence are obfuscated. In the second half of the episode, in order to translate complex ideas into an accessible format for the audience, the program adopts the generic style of a drama, featuring recurring characters, a setting, and story but no dialogue.

By comparison, "Sometimes Harmonious, Sometimes Not" offers no sense of verisimilitude. As in "Nature of Man," the narrator is the only one who speaks. However, in "Sometimes Harmonious," the narrator is visible and at times implicated in the themes he explicates, with humorous fourth-wall-breaking gags. Addressing the camera directly from behind a wooden desk, the narrator introduces elements and themes that are performed as skits. This format was intended to "lightly satirize the traditional character of educational television" as typically presented by "'the man behind the desk' or 'the man in the gray flannel drape,'" indicating that producers anticipated audiences would appreciate parody of such tropes (Mahler and Appy 1965, 27). The first half of the program compares various "social forces," such as religion, violence, cultural values, popular will, and economics, whereas the second half considers whether society meets individual needs or whether individuals are asked to meet the needs of society. These themes are expressed through provocative avant-garde imagery, including a segment in which a nursery rhyme about free will is recited over a claustrophobic stage play in which mannequins come to life and commit homicide. Invoking the program's title, in the final act the narrator tells viewers, "Your social life is not all determined. Nor is it solely the result of your exercise of free will. There is constant interaction, *Sometimes Harmonious, Sometimes Not*" (Georgia Center for

Continuing Education / National Educational Television 1961c). This tension between conformity and choice reflects the program planner's concern with "social slave" of the Organization Man and his counterpart, the Free Man (Mahler and Appy 1965, 1–8).

"Sometimes Harmonious, Sometimes Not" also shifts genres mid-program. What begins as a staid "sponsored film" transforms into a surreal and experimental production. As the discussion of "social forces" comes to an end, the camera returns to the narrator seated behind his desk; symbols of these forces—disembodied arms wield, in succession, a cross, a book, a newspaper, a gun, and mechanical gear—enter his diegetic space, which, frowning and annoyed, he swats away. Such subversive humor is present from the outset: early, the narrator breathlessly describes how societies seek "to rule for economic benefits for education benefit for cultural benefit for protection for pleasure for health against poverty against ignorance," landing humorously on "against cruelty towards crustaceans," as the camera shows a man "crushed" underneath these forces. In its second half, the program embraces surrealist and allegorical elements. As the narrator makes an argument for social determinism, a group appears onstage, inside individual wooden boxes, and moves robotically to jaunty jazz music. Among these automatons are various social "types": a wealthy woman sipping tea, a stoic farmer swaying while chewing straw, and a businessman frantically pretending to steer an automobile. The speed at which they perform these activities ramps up as the accompanying jazz piano increases in tempo, growing discordant. "You must accommodate," booms the narrator. "You have no control." This provocation deliberately "shock[s]" viewers into considering a rebuttal.

"A Political Animal" takes a different approach. A brief introductory sequence shows a balding man walking through a corridor lined with political iconography. Disembodied voices hint at the ideologies represented by the symbols around him. A *fasces*, for example, is accompanied by the voiceover, "Nothing outside the state, above the state, against the state. Everything to the state, for the state, in the state." The man exits the corridor into a space framed by contrasting painted backdrops. Two men await him, one of whom explains that they are "*spokesmen* for opposing political points of view." As "a service" to those who seek political knowledge, the man claims, he and his colleague "are stationed here to conduct somewhat continual debate." "Like diplomats without portfolio," jokes the other. One figure represents democracy, the other totalitarianism;

Fig. 7.1. "Sometimes Harmonious, Sometimes Not": Socially determined "types" exist in the confines of their boxes. Georgia Center Film and Videotape Collection at the Walter J. Brown Media Archives and Peabody Awards Collection, the University of Georgia Libraries.

each makes the case for his respective form of government to the onlooker (and the audience). The program explains that different forms of government depend on varying conceptions of human life. These explanations are juxtaposed with stock footage of political rallies and speeches (featuring J. Edgar Hoover, Franklin Delano Roosevelt, Adolf Hitler, and Vladimir Lenin, among others), animated sequences, and scenes of work and daily life. Lest the didactic fantasy-cum-reality narrative of a divine struggle over the soul of the American citizen is lost on the viewer, the film concludes with the narrator warning, "You are part of a massive conflict. Weigh the basic principles carefully" (Georgia Center for Continuing Education / National Educational Television 1961a).

When *Basic Issues* dealt with real-world political alignments, as in "A Political Animal," it strayed away from the artistic and experimental flourishes offered in "The Nature of Man" and "Sometimes Harmonious." Debate and discussion programs, performed by media personalities, actors, or average citizens, were a standard format seen on 1950s television. "A Political Animal" evokes such programs, as the audience is meant to weigh arguments and reach their own conclusions. Drawing its examples from recent history (such as Nazi rallies, the failed 1956 Hungarian Revolution, and American presidential addresses), the episode offered little abstract imagery. Its chosen images demonstrated how politics shape human life. Political debate and choice are presented as binaries within the purview of the white male citizen. Framed by illustrations of crooked arches etched with symbols reminiscent of swastikas and hammer and sickle symbols, the representative of the totalitarian state as "master of its citizens" is depicted as smug, condescending, and blunt. By comparison, the representative of democracy is framed by images evocative of classical Greece and stands before a felled, but newly budding, olive tree stump.

Although these programs are framed as debates and the program manual repeatedly emphasizes that answers are not provided to the issues presented, at key moments the narrative implies that there *are* "correct" answers. By implicitly proposing solutions to the problems depicted, filmmakers offered bromides to well-worn American values and entrusted viewers to make the proper connections and identifications. In "Nature of Man," for example, the narrator claims that after the Renaissance, "the image of man became blurred with contradictions" between those who celebrated and those who condemned worldly pleasures. But there was "a middle position: *trust the judgment of the individual. Let each man seek and find his own personal goals,*" or, as the narrator articulates later, "*freedom is the basis for all human dignity.*" In one of that program's final sequences, the camera provides a bird's-eye view of a crowd of Indigenous men, each obscured under identical white sombreros. The camera cuts to the faces in the crowd, at which point the narrator announces that "[if] we believe each man is an individual," then it follows that "the social expression of that image of man is democracy . . . individual men, all of the same kind, but unlike each other." Here, distant and "exotic" Indigenous people illustrate American political liberalism's emphasis on the dignity of the individual. By comparison, in its final moments, "Sometimes Harmonious, Sometimes Not" combines visual gags with explicit exaltations of individual agency. After the narrator is buffeted by snow and heat, confronts a caveman and a chef, and then transforms into a Stalinesque dictator, he finally warns that only with knowledge "may [you] challenge the determinist social forces armed with the *potent weapon of free will.*" In

"A Political Animal," the metaphysical representative of democracy puts it more bluntly: "You were not born to be forced," he tells the visitor and the audience.

CONCLUSION

Didactic despite its self-proclaimed neutrality, *Basic Issues of Man* could not quite determine its relationship to its imagined audience. Dually addressing viewers, the program hailed them as rational subject-citizens, but also signposted "correct" interpretations that reflected the expert and popular consensus. By naming and addressing viewers as self-possessed individuals with the capacity for reason and decision-making, *Basic Issues* worked as a creative tool to fashion the liberal subject-citizen. By situating viewers within the grand tradition of humanistic learning ("the wondering will not end today," the narrator of "Nature of Man" announces), the series claimed that the American citizen (coded as male and white) had a significant role to play in the preservation of democracy. The self-possessed individual was conceived in a dialectic with the concept of the "social slave." Citizen-viewers were trained to consider competing binary ideologies, but not the ideological model that produced them. Viewers were allowed to weigh the benefits of different iterations of democratic government—such as laissez-faire capitalism and social democracy, as opposed to fascist-communist "totalitarianism"—but the insights of liberal humanist inquiry were beyond question. As the narrator of "Sometimes Harmonious, Sometimes Not" unironically warns, "[Man] must strive to exercise free will. . . . It can be done."

Although the creators of *Basic Issues of Man* set the terms for specific social and political debates and purported to offer some arguments for both sides, they did not do so equally, nor did they anticipate that individuals would choose outside of the program's own narrow, didactic goals. More to the point, by framing arguments in terms of "universal" issues, the program actively disavowed its own local specificity. Produced at the height of Jim Crow by University of Georgia staff with Ford Foundation support, these programs were created specifically to train American citizens in the social attitudes and beliefs imagined to be necessary for participation in a modern liberal democracy. Even as the program attempted to make this case while expanding its viewers' aesthetic horizons, their target audience already enjoyed the fruits of American society: they were invited, on "intellectual weekends," to walk the halls of the all-white University of Georgia (Wells 1960). For the program's producers, who were swayed by Cold War liberal ideology, vigorous consent had to be engineered for enlightened technocratic social guidance. In its efforts to connect Georgia's television viewers to a larger democratic tradition, *Basic Issues of Man* was one part of that process.

NOTES

1. The program manual I consulted has a copyright date of 1963 and reprint dates for both 1964 and 1965.
2. Adjusted for inflation, $160,000 would be approximately $1.5 million today. By the time *Basic Issues* aired, the Ford Foundation had taken over direct administration of NET from its subsidiary Fund for Adult Education.
3. The programs I viewed feature a 1962 production date. Production occurred over several years starting in 1959, before editing and wider distribution on NET.
4. According to ProQuest Historical Newspapers, *Basic Issues of Man* appeared on NET-member television stations around the country between 1963 and 1966. See "Today on TV: High Spots," *Boston Globe*, February 13, 1963, 25; "WETA ... Ch. 26," *Washington Post-Times Herald*, March 1, 1963, C6; "Thursday's TV Programs," *Los Angeles Times*, February 24, 1966, C10.
5. Whether WGTV broadcasts included context for the program or instructions for participation is at this point unclear.
6. In a 2003 oral history video interview, Hill Bermont (the director of the television broadcasts) recalls the challenges of working from scripts written by faculty members: "The man on the faculty [Rollin Chambliss], the faculty-person who wrote the booklet [*The Nature of Man*], I let him write the script. From then on, no more. He was very academic and the narration was wordy." See Bermont (2003).
7. WorldCat shows a 1961 copyright. See Catalog Entry on WorldCat for Georgia Center for Continuing Education, *Basic Issues of Man* (University of Georgia Press, 1961–63), http://www.worldcat.org/oclc/6283419; Director Hill Bermont (occasionally misnamed "Bill"), a Jewish refugee from Europe, was granted American citizenship in 1946. Bermont worked at WGTV from 1957 to 1983. He is credited for "planning and creative decisions" with "extensive experience as a professional theater, film, and television specialist." See Mahler and Appy (1965, back matter) and "Obituary: Hill Bermont," *Atlanta Journal-Constitution*, July 23, 2009, https://www.legacy.com/obituaries/atlanta/obituary.aspx?n=hill-bermont&pid=130180736.
8. Discussion groups were a novel form of social-scientific (and consumer) research and associated with training democratic personhood. See McCarthy (2010, 83–116).

9. The program manual states that the "major portion" was shot in Chiapas and "the cast of Mexican Indians" was "almost exclusively" from "the Chamula [sic] and Zinacanteco [sic] Tribes." Mahler and Appy (1965, 24–25).
10. The contemporaneous primary school curriculum, *Man: A Course of Study*, used ethnographic films of Netsilik life in an attempt to locate a universal human nature. See Milam (2013).
11. The program combines "actual" ethnographic film content and scripted drama, though as scholars of ethnographic film note, making such demarcations is challenging and may ultimately be beside the point.

REFERENCES

Acland, Charles R., and Haidee Wasson, eds. 2011. *Useful Cinema*. Duke University Press.

Bermont, Hill. 2003. Interview by Sandra Berman and Ruth Einstein, January 15. Esther and Herbert Taylor Oral History Collection, William Breman Jewish Heritage Museum. https://archivesspace.thebreman.org/repositories/2/archival_objects/28914.

Brick, Howard. 1998. *Age of Contradiction: American Thought and Culture in the 1960s*. Cornell University Press.

Cohen, Robert. 1996. "'Two, Four, Six, Eight, We Don't Want to Integrate': White Student Attitudes toward the University of Georgia's Desegregation." *Georgia Historical Quarterly* 80 (3): 616–45.

Cohen-Cole, Jamie. 2014. *The Open Mind: Cold War Politics and the Sciences of Human Nature*. University of Chicago Press.

Dellinger, Ione. 1963. "Exceptional Children: Gifted Youths Try Depth Learning." *Atlanta Constitution*, May 21.

Derksen, Maarten. 2017. *Histories of Human Engineering: Tact and Technology*. Cambridge University Press.

Fund for Adult Education, Ford Foundation. 1962. "A Ten Year Report of the Fund for Adult Education; 1951–1961." ERIC (Educational Resources Information Center, U.S. Department of Education).

Georgia Center for Continuing Education / National Educational Television, dir. 1961a. *A Political Animal*. Basic Issues of Man. https://bmac.libs.uga.edu/pawtucket2/index.php/Detail/objects/51252.

———, dir. 1961b. *Promotional Short Film, Basic Issues of Man*. Basic Issues of Man. https://bmac.libs.uga.edu/pawtucket2/index.php/Detail/objects/48771.

———, dir. 1961c. *Sometimes Harmonious, Sometimes Not*. Basic Issues of Man. https://bmac.libs.uga.edu/pawtucket2/index.php/Detail/objects/51256.

———, dir. 1961d. *The Nature of Man*. Basic Issues of Man. https://bmac.libs.uga.edu/index.php/Detail/objects/48781.

Grief, Mark. 2015. *The Age of the Crisis of Man: Thought and Fiction in America, 1933–1973*. Princeton University Press.

Griffiths, Alison. 2002. *Wondrous Difference: Cinema, Anthropology, and Turn-of-the-Century Visual Culture*. Columbia University Press.

Herman, Ellen. 1995. *The Romance of American Psychology: Political Culture in the Age of Experts*. University of California Press.

Jones, Paul. 1964. "Dragons Pay Off for Athens WGTV." *Atlanta Constitution*, June 2.

Mahler, Thomas W., and Gerard L. Appy. 1965. *Program Manual: For Use with Six Essays and Twelve Television Films, Basic Issues of Man, in the Adult Liberal Studies Program*. University of Georgia Press.

McCarthy, Anna. 2010. *The Citizen Machine: Governing by Television in 1950s America*. New Press.

Milam, Erika Lorraine. 2013. "Public Science of the Savage Mind: Contesting Cultural Anthropology in the Cold War Classroom." *Journal of the History of the Behavioral Sciences* 49 (3): 306–30.

———. 2019. *Creature of Cain: The Hunt for Human Nature in Cold War America*. Princeton University Press.

Modleski, Tania. 1991. "Femininity as Mas(s)Querade." In *Feminism without Women: Culture and Criticism in a "Postfeminist" Age*, edited by Colin MacCabe, 23–34. Routledge.

"National Educational Television." n.d. American Archive of Public Broadcasting. Accessed September 26, 2022. https://americanarchive.org/special_collections/net-catalog.

Newman, Michael Z., and Elana Levine. 2012. *Legitimating Television : Media Convergence and Cultural Status*. Taylor & Francis.

Orgeron, Devin, Marsha Orgeron, and Dan Streible, eds. 2012. *Learning with the Lights Off: Educational Film in the United States*. Oxford University Press.

Pratt, Robert A. 2005. *We Shall Not Be Moved: The Desegregation of the University of Georgia*. University of Georgia Press.

Robertson, Jim. 1993. *Televisionaries: In Their Own Words Public Television's Founders Tell How It All Began*. Tabby House Books.

Rony, Fatimah Tobing. 1996. *The Third Eye: Race, Cinema, and Ethnographic Spectacle*. Duke University Press.

Sammond, Nicholas. 2005. *Babes in Tomorrowland: Walt Disney and the Making of the American Child, 1930–1960*. Duke University Press.

Smoodin, Eric. 2004. *Regarding Frank Capra: Audience, Celebrity, and American Film Studies, 1930–1960*. Duke University Press.

Solovey, Mark. 2013. *Shaky Foundations: The Politics-Patronage-Social Science Nexus in Cold War America*. Rutgers University Press.

Spigel, Lynn. 1997. "The Suburban Home Companion: Television and the Neighbourhood Ideal in Post-War America." In *Feminist Television Criticism: A Reader*, edited by Charlotte Brunsdon, Julie D'Acci, and Lynn Spigel, 211–34. Oxford University Press.

"Study—Discussion Programs: A Guide for Their Selection and Use." 1969. American Library Association. https://eric.ed.gov/?q=Study-Discussion+Programs%3b+A+Guide+for+their+Selection+and+Use.&id=ED027478.

"Television in the Library of Congress: Moving Image Research Center." n.d. National Audio-Visual Conservation Center, Library of Congress. Accessed September 26, 2022. https://www.loc.gov/rr/mopic/tvcoll.html.

Turner, Fred. 2013. *The Democratic Surround: Multimedia and American Liberalism from World War II to the Psychedelic Sixties*. University of Chicago Press.

Wells, Frank. 1960. "Center Broadens Base of Georgia Education." *Atlanta Journal-Constitution*, December 25.

CHAPTER 8

CAROLINE N. BAYNE

WSB-TV, ATLANTA

BROADCASTING THE NEW OLD SOUTH

The October 6, 1948, "Television Edition" of the *Atlanta Constitution* spent its pages reckoning with the arrival of television transmission in Atlanta, Georgia. WSB-TV, whose call letters stand for "Welcome South, Brother," went on air September 29, 1948, the first station in the American South to do so. Its inaugural lineup of programming included a Baptist choir, puppet show, country western musical group, and local news coverage. Contributing writer for the *Constitution* Wellington Wright (1948, 32) claimed, "Yes, television is here.... It's coming to Atlanta in a big way. Because of its location, Atlanta will be one of the nation's major television cities. So get your TV set ready."

This statement foresaw the major role Georgia would play in the global film and television industries. Georgia, nicknamed the Hollywood of the South, currently ranks third in national film and television production, after only New York and California, and is the fifth largest site of global film and television production (Dockterman 2018). Two years after its founding, WSB-TV became an NBC affiliate, a thirty-one-year partnership that ended in the early 1980s when the station became an affiliate of ABC. In 1954, it became the first station in the South to broadcast a network program, *The Camel News Caravan* (NBC, 1949–56), in full color. While Georgia's contributions to the television industry today cannot be overstated, little has been written about its earliest, local programming. Known as both the "Voice of the South" as a radio station and the "Eyes of the South" upon its transition to television, WSB-TV developed into a local station with national scope and recognition, accumulating many firsts for the South in television production.

This article presents two converging and interdependent histories, that of WSB-TV's long-running locally produced daytime program *Today in Georgia* and that of a cultural geography of Atlanta told through the city's growth into a televisual center of the South. Atlanta's campaign of double vision throughout the mid-twentieth century—continuing to grow the city's reputation as a site of industry, culture, and technological innovation in the Sunbelt South, alongside its preservation of the region's traditions through perpetual commemoration of its past—is largely articulated through the history of WSB-TV. *Today in Georgia* aired on WSB-TV for twenty-six years, its longest running locally produced program and one of the few that survived network affiliation with NBC. The program kept Georgia and the South on the air at a time when the region was all but absent from network television programming. *Today in Georgia* and its host, Ruth Kent, brought the world to Georgia through segments on international travel and interviews with public figures and Hollywood celebrities while retaining a majority focus on southern culture, food, and politics. In addition to its programming, WSB-TV's White Columns studio, the antebellum-style mansion that housed the station from 1956 until its demolition in the late 1990s, and its relationship to the 1939 film *Gone with the Wind* reveal much about the city's attempts to move forward without renouncing the past.

WSB-TV, local programming, and White Columns coalesce in a triad of technology, television, and tradition that not only shows the trends of early, local television in an often-overlooked region but also reveals the affective regional memory, and obligation to that memory, that influenced WSB's operations and programming from its start. WSB-TV aired depictions of the Jim Crow South, its highly publicized battles over desegregation, and the governorship of staunch segregationist Lester Maddox. WSB's news programming broadcasted the city's navigation of the civil rights movement and integration, hoping to confirm its reputation as "the city too busy to hate," as named by Mayor William Hartsfield at midcentury. As the first television station in the South, WSB-TV's initiatives included growing the station as both a technological and cultural force, representing the South on the small screen and Atlanta as a site of progress in a region generally associated with stagnation and resistance to change. Alongside this, however, WSB participated in the city's persistent memorialization of the antebellum South amid industrial and cultural growth. WSB-TV's programming, designed to bring the world to

Georgians, held the tenuous balance of the station and the city of Atlanta as future oriented yet always looking to the past for inspiration.

WELCOME SOUTH, BROTHER: TELEVISION COMES TO ATLANTA

While there is no lack of southern place-based television airing today, a trend that began in the 1960s primarily seen on CBS,[1] the southern industry and the South on the small screen experienced a slow start compared to the rise of television across the nation. NBC's early plans for rolling out television infrastructure outward from New York City proposed "gradual interconnection from major cities across the United States to 'lesser' markets. In 1939, the original plan extended program service in New York and acquired broadcast facilities in 'key markets,' identified as Philadelphia, Chicago, Boston, Washington, Cleveland, and San Francisco" (Johnson 2008, 41). NBC showed vested economic interest in serving the Northeast with television infrastructure and programming, as the region was regarded as the industrial and cultural center of the nation. NBC's plan for televisual development as of 1945 served "essential" markets in high-density metropolitan areas, followed by "desirable" markets they hoped to capture, and last, and of least consideration, "possible" markets such as the South and the Mountain West (Johnson 2008, 42). In addition to the Northeast, long the center of industrial, technological, and cultural production, the Midwest significantly shaped early television history and content. Victoria Johnson (2008) describes early network television as a reflection of midwestern cultural values. As network television sought to air the least objectionable programming to secure high viewing numbers, the Midwest represented the least objectionable region in the nation at the time of television's arrival to homes, as such states were considered "ideological middle-ground" (11).

Geographical, technological, and ideological factors influenced content and accessibility of early television, and as such the availability of television to southern audiences was uneven. Phoebe Bronstein (2020, 221) writes, "In 1953, Georgia had three stations, Florida had two, and Mississippi had none. By 1955, Georgia had thirteen, Florida had fifteen, and Mississippi had four." However, these stations were usually concentrated in more industrialized cities, as seen in Georgia, where seven of the state's thirteen stations were in Atlanta and Savannah (221). An article in the *Constitution*'s "Television Edition" briefly describes the process by which smaller southern cities would eventually gain access to the necessary infrastructure: "With television stations sprouting up all over the nation, hookup facilities loom on the not-too-dim horizon. The ever-expanding rural electrification program, which has left only 31.9 percent of Georgia farms without electricity, seems to indicate that television will eventually reach a sizable segment of the rural population" (*Atlanta Constitution* 1948, 39). As described by Pete Daniel (2000, 8), "Rural change, urbanization, science, technology, racism, and popular culture were interlocking revolutionary components that swept through the South after World War II." Atlanta continued to benefit from federal spending and urban renewal projects set in motion at the start of the midcentury. Richard Bernard and Bradley Rice (1983) identify four contributing factors to the prosperous conditions of southern Sunbelt cities like Atlanta: World War II defense spending, increased federal funds to the region, relaxed business and work regulations, and an overall lifestyle culture emphasizing leisure and recreation. Other factors included the rise of interstate highway construction, tourism, and the amenities that followed such as malls, business centers, and subdivisions.

Atlanta's prominence as an increasingly industrialized southern city, and its relationship with NBC beginning in the 1920s, contributed to its development as the first city to bring television to the South. WSB's relationship with NBC began in 1927 as an affiliate radio station, one year after the network's founding. WSB radio, like other network affiliates, "had to agree to clear the best parts of their schedules for network transmissions" and grew in profitability "by turning more and more hours of their broadcast ... over to network programs" (Hilmes 2007, 17, 22). Consequently, affiliate contracts "mandated fewer opportunities for opting out in favor of local tastes and interests," a trend traceable from WSB radio to its prime-time television schedule beginning in 1950 (22). The control over the prime-time hours of television by networks relegated locally produced programming to fill the daytime hours. By the end of 1950, programming on WSB from seven o'clock in the evening to midnight, when the station went off air, consisted almost entirely of network fare.

The South's presence on national television was seen not in sitcoms or dramas but instead in the televised violence of the civil rights movement and desegregation efforts throughout the mid-twentieth century. As Steven Classen (2004, 11) describes, "During the fifties and sixties the popular media institutions of ... the South were sites of pitched warfare" and "segregationist politicians, business people, and civic leaders recognized broadcast stations" as tools in the fight to maintain the "status quo and a particular southern way of life" seen as under attack. WSB-TV broadcasted the integration of Atlanta public schools seven years after the *Brown v. Board* (1954) ruling and the subsequent violence in other southern cities like Little Rock, Arkansas. Rebecca Burns (2011) writes, "At the end of the day, unlike scenes in other Southern cities that resisted desegregation, Atlanta was peaceful." President John F. Kennedy praised city leadership and cited Atlanta a model for future integration efforts. These events are recounted in the 1998 television special titled "WSB-TV: 50 Years in Atlanta," narrated by Monica Kaufman, who joined as an anchor in 1975. Kaufman states, "The difference between Georgia and the Old South and Atlanta and the New South was even more apparent during school integration" and that everyone in Atlanta, leadership and media included, sought to ensure "that Atlanta's television stories would look different than those everyone had seen from Little Rock" (WSB-TV Videotape Collection 1998a).

However, the station's preoccupation with iconography and memory of the Old South creates an antagonism between antebellum nostalgia and the forward momentum of integration and civil rights efforts; this antagonism persists as a condition of southern life seen throughout the twentieth century into the present. Alongside their cover of integration, WSB developed numerous specials dedicated to *Gone with the Wind*, completed the construction of White Columns studio, and witnessed the revival of southern heritage throughout the midcentury. As Karen Cox (2011, 3) describes, "The conflict between 'backward-looking pastoralism' and the impulse toward modernity [seems] incompatible; however, popular culture helped to bring both ideas together in the marketplace, and frequently the antebellum South acted as the conduit. That is to say that pastoral images and themes of the Old South . . . were used to sell goods and entertainment to American consumers, all of which made possible by the modern urban-industrial world in which they lived." Television, alongside other technological and cultural advancements, provided opportunities to relive and revive the Old South in Atlanta through images of plantation homes, Confederate legacy, and a South purportedly less affected by rapid industrialization and modernization compared to the urban North.

Atlanta, though, grew into one of the most industrialized cities in the South, often raising questions about its southern character remaining intact. A volume published by the Work Projects Administration of Georgia in 1942 claims, "At first sight the tourist may see no tradition at all [in Atlanta]. All the bustle and clamor of this ever-changing city seem to take no account of the past, to make no terms with anything but modern ways and rapid production. This city of big stores, of smoking factories, of handsome modern residences, is truly a city of the modern South" (3). Atlanta's reputation as a city of the modern South often conflicted with its dedication to preserving its other and no less important reputation as a former Confederate stronghold, a city with a "spirit of dogged survival that brought recovery and increased power after the town had been burned by General Sherman's destroying forces" during the Civil War (7). This tension is largely articulated through segments on *Today in Georgia* as relevant for southern audiences and sensibilities while speaking beyond the boundaries of the state and the South to promote WSB-TV and Atlanta as modern enterprises level with those in more urban, industrialized, and culturally significant U.S. cities.

DAYTIME PROGRAMMING AND *TODAY IN GEORGIA* ON WSB-TV

Local television produces its own set of regionally specific characteristics independent of network oversight. The histories of regional television and local programming are told primarily through the daytime lineup, as it was least affected by network constraints. Daytime programming on WSB-TV made up the bulk of the station's original programming; homemaking programs appeared on the schedules of local stations across the country quickly after going on air. According to Marsha Cassidy (2005, 29), a survey conducted at Iowa State College "found that at least 72 of the country's 108 prefreeze television stations were producing homemaking programs, half of them running 30 minutes daily." By 1950, WSB offered a block of women's programming in the daytime hours beginning at eleven o'clock, which featured a combination of recipes, cooking demonstrations, and generalized domestic advice. Local women's programming, then, meant local women hosts; presiding over homemaking programs, women across the nation, many of whom were trained in home economics or worked in women's programming divisions on radio, appeared on television screens to offer friendly, practical domestic advice to women watching at home.

In its earliest years, from 1949 to 1953, WSB-TV produced several daytime programs for women audiences, including *Strictly for the Girls*, *Come into the Kitchen*, *Rich's in Your Home*, *Nancy Carter's TV Cook Book*, and early magazine-style program *At Home with Elsbeth*. On September 28,

1953, the *Constitution* ran an article announcing the premiere of two programs, *Today in Georgia* and *Wayside Inn*, that were specifically "designed to attract the attention of feminine viewers" (Jones 1953, 8). *Today in Georgia* was described as "[emulating], on a Georgia basis, the popular NBC-TV *Today* program," featuring weather, interviews, and news as well as household and children's segments, hosted by Don Elliot and Ruth Kent (8). *Wayside Inn* was a "departmentalized program, making possible the sale of a variety of commercial products," with a "how-to-do-it department," also hosted by Kent, to provide tips for "painting furniture, making draperies and on allied arts" (8). *Wayside Inn* featured appearances by prominent Georgians, with the occasional national celebrity, like film and television actress Wendy Barrie and model Pat Reilly, passing through for interviews.

Both *Wayside Inn* and *Today in Georgia* utilized the magazine-style format in their programs, a strategy promoted by NBC's vice president in charge of television programming Pat Weaver, beginning with *Today* in 1952 and later adopted by *Home* in 1954. The similarities between NBC's and WSB's daytime programming, particularly *Today in Georgia* emulating the *Today* show, highlight the tensions and dynamics between local and network daytime programs, their content, aesthetics, and aspirations for their target audiences, as well as the ability for local programming to reflect local trends. Marsha Cassidy and Mimi White (2002) speak to these dynamics in their comparative history of two prominent daytime programs and their respective hosts, NBC's *Home* with Arlene Francis and the local Cincinnati, Ohio, program *Fifty-Fifty Club*, hosted by Ruth Lyons. Networks and local stations sought to develop the voice, image, and advice provided by their respective "[femcees] . . . charming, witty, middle-aged [hostesses] who presided over daytime broadcasts aimed at women viewers" (31). Johnson (2008, 48) notes that while regional stations were tasked with defining specific standards of public good for their audiences, networks in locations such as the Northeast were thought of as "extra-local, as exemplified by programming exhibiting high production values, genre diversity, and audience breadth." As such, the FCC described urban markets as inherently diverse, while "rural communities [were] removed from cultural flow" (48). In this sense, only some U.S. regions possess regional identities (the South), while others represent the nation comprehensively (the Northeast). Consequently, women's programming hosts, too, faced this local versus extralocal comparison.

As the host of *Home*, Francis was tasked with bringing metropolitanism to those outside of New York, despite the target audience for the program being a middle American housewife. To this end, Francis's "television persona perpetuated an unresolvable split between NBC's commitment to the diffusion of 'enlightenment' and the imperatives of mass appeal," resulting in the program's cancellation after only three years (Cassidy and White 2002, 51). In contrast, Ruth Lyons's *Fifty-Fifty Club* ran from 1949 until her retirement in 1967, arguably due to her ability to resonate with audiences from a middle-class, middle American position.

Ruth Kent and *Today in Georgia*, I argue, worked to position Atlanta as both regionally southern *and* metropolitan, attempting to lessen the antagonism and incompatibility between the local/network binary and their ideological preoccupations. This, though, was delicate work. Atlanta, alongside other cities across the region, was unwilling to abandon its southernness despite its growth. White supremacist groups in neighboring Mississippi saw network television as "anti-South" and believed network intervention threatened the southern (i.e., segregated) way of life in the mid-twentieth century. Kent and *Today in Georgia*, then, were tasked with navigating this way of life seen as under threat while simultaneously advancing the reputation of WSB-TV as regionally specific and nationally regarded.

Today in Georgia retained its southern affiliation through its focus on the people, events, politics, food, and news of Georgia and remained an important part of WSB-TV's daytime lineup while other local programs were lost to affiliate obligations. Although Georgia was the primary focus, Kent also traveled to France and Haiti, interviewed Hollywood celebrities, and attended international conferences, adding to the exoticism and travel offered to audiences by early television, with hosts like Kent serving as their guides. Many of Kent's segments on *Today in Georgia* demonstrate her ability to move between and bring into harmony both southern charm and big city savvy, a main goal of WSB-TV. Kent joined the station in 1951 as the cooking and recipe advisor and host of *Come into the Kitchen* before moving into her twenty-three-year tenure as host of *Today in Georgia*. Kent's time at WSB and her status as the host of the station's flagship local program contribute to the history of the station and its attempts to balance local and extralocal obligations in the burgeoning television city of Atlanta.

Ruth Kent served as a tastemaker and trusted source in multiple roles at WSB. The intermediary work of hosts like Kent brought "visual entertainment and education" to Atlanta viewers, acting as both a window to the world and a portal to the past (Jones 1948, 30). Kent described the function of *Today in Georgia* as such: "If we have a primary function . . . it is to get a better understanding of anything and everything and everybody" (Curry 1964, 43). Additionally, she claimed, "I don't consider myself a personality—I'm merely an instrument between guest and viewer. The program is about any and everything—weighty subjects to philosophy, music to humor to frivolity. I try to have at least one thing a day to make the viewer think" (Alexander 1965, 15). Kent served not only as a community leader but as an intermediary between content and viewers, taking her audience along on educational and exotic endeavors. As Lynn Spigel (1992, 7) explains, television offers exploration and entertainment insofar as viewers can experience far-off locales from their living rooms, their television sets serving as "a window on the world." Television, with its "ability to merge private and public spaces . . . was the ideal companion" for postwar audiences, particularly those migrating to newly constructed (and segregated) suburbs (Spigel 2001, 33). The program's target audience of Georgia housewives meant that Kent, a housewife herself, often presented homemaking and cooking segments, but the program's scope increased to include other topics the longer it remained on air. In an advertisement for the show in a 1960 issue of *Broadcasting* magazine, *Today in Georgia* claimed to "[operate] on the pleasant idea that ladies are interested in all that goes on around them" (*Broadcasting* 1960b). An episode from December 1967 provides a useful survey of a typical episode wherein Kent teaches viewers about the arts, culture, and hobby scenes across the state, including the Atlanta figure-skating club, the Azealia chapter of the American Rhododendron Society, and a how-to segment on shopping for sophisticated, personal holiday gifts.

As the program grew in popularity, the extent of what would interest Georgia citizens included news and events beyond the home, state, and region. Beginning in 1960, Kent and *Today in Georgia*, having won the Radio TV Mirror Award for Best TV Women's Interest Show in the southern states, began to include features outside the borders of Georgia. In 1964, Kent traveled to Nassau for an international tea manufacturing convention "filming holiday souvenirs for her Georgia viewers" (Curry 1964, 43). The trip extended to include stops in India, Ceylon, and Indonesia, where Kent interviewed industry and manufacturer leaders while also climbing coconut trees and doing the limbo. In response to her trip, though, Kent claimed, "I still think there is so much in Georgia that we'd never run out of material. . . . Contrary to some opinions . . . some of the swingingest and most sophisticated people around are in small towns" (43).

In addition to international travel, Kent often interviewed celebrities and local Georgia officials on her program about topics ranging from childbirth to time management and film, including renowned domestic scientist and time management expert Lillian Gilbreth in 1963. In 1967, Kent hosted *Gone with the Wind* actress Olivia de Havilland on the program, inquiring about the film's long-lasting effect on audiences, particularly those in Georgia. Throughout the interview Kent refers to de Havilland by her character's name, Melanie. Kent and de Havilland reminisce about Melanie's happiness and poise as if reflecting on the life of a friend. Kent states, "Something that I don't think anybody's been able to explain, other than that it was a great novel to begin with, and the most superb cast attainable, is the fact that this has lasted, and probably will for long after we're dead and gone," with de Havilland agreeing that the film is "an eternal classic" (Walter J. Brown Media Archives and Peabody Awards Collection 1967). De Havilland's appearance on *Today in Georgia* coincided with an anniversary premiere of the film held in Atlanta. The 1967 premiere included, much like each earlier premieres, the Tara Ball, described by attendee Susan Lindsley as such:[2] "Tara's Theme filled the ballroom and the Grand March began. Mayor Hartsfield and Olivia de Havilland came in, under the raised swords of Confederate soldiers" (2011, 332). In addition to *Gone with the Wind*'s recurrent presence on WSB-TV in the form of interviews, behind-the-scenes specials, and, in 1976, the two-night television premiere of the film on NBC, the film contributed much to the station and the city's identity throughout the twentieth century.

The history of WSB-TV remains complex and contradictory as told through the antagonism between the forward momentum of the station and the city and their simultaneous attachment to icons and ideologies of the Old South. As Susan Courtney (2017) describes, the genre of the film southern was not interested in the burgeoning New South of the early to mid-twentieth century, but instead obsessively depicted the antebellum era. She notes that "the period's screen Souths ... appear contained, and are routinely marked by the logics of containment" (16). Comparatively, television in the South (and elsewhere) was seen as a source of transportation, providing opportunities for exploration to audiences. In his article for the *Constitution*'s "Television Edition," Wellington Wright (1948, 32) describes television, "like the other great American industries," as "capable of annihilating both time and space!" The affordances of televisual travel, though, did not always direct audiences to the future but, as seen in instances at WSB-TV, served as transportation back to the antebellum South.

GONE WITH THE WIND: WHITE COLUMNS AND SOUTHERN REVIVAL AT MIDCENTURY

The presence and effect of *Gone with the Wind* on Atlanta cannot be overstated. For decades after the film's initial premiere, the city continued to celebrate the relationship between the two through anniversaries, premieres, and televised events. In late 1950, Paul Jones of the *Constitution* writes, "Memories of the greatest movie premiere of all time will be recalled Friday night when WSB-TV commemorates the 11th anniversary premiere of 'Gone with the Wind' with the first showing of video of films made at the gala opening in 1939" (40). The film features as narrator Mayor Hartsfield, a key figure in bringing the film's opening to Atlanta, and includes footage of the premiere, including a parade, ball, and celebrity arrivals to the Loew's Grand Theater in December 1939. Hartsfield is shown taking star Clark Gable and wife Carole Lombard to various landmarks around the city, particularly those of Old South relevance, such as the Cyclorama and the site of the Battle of Peachtree Creek (James G. Kenan Research Center 1939).

Four years later, the film re-premiered in Atlanta for its fifteenth anniversary. *Constitution* writer Celestine Sibley uses the film's original premiere and its upcoming anniversary to describe changes in Georgia and the world at large, writing, "Children have been born and grown old enough to read the book and see the movie. A world war has been fought, the United Nations born, the atom bomb developed, the last Georgia Confederate veteran is dead. Sometimes it breaks your heart to think that things survive after the people who used them are dead but that kind of feeling will not sadden the festivities attending the opening of Gone with the Wind at Loew's Grand May 20. . . . Good work, a good book, a good performance, lives on to delight generations as yet unborn" (1954, 15). Despite such change, loss, and growth, *Gone with the Wind* persisted as part of Georgia's present at midcentury, serving as an anchor to the Old South during periods of sustained growth and advancement. Perhaps the greatest testament to the perseverance of the film and its Old South iconography in a city of rapid development is

White Columns, WSB-TV's state-of-the-art television studio, dressed in antebellum style.

A history of southern architecture and its embedded ideologies must begin with the largest looming sort—the plantation home, or Big House. *Washington Tribune* columnist Melvin B. Tolson ruminates on the Big House as seen in *Gone with the Wind*. He writes, "Every civilization has its symbols, its cornerstone, its label, its trademark . . . the symbol of the South is the Big House" (Farnsworth 1982, 221). The Big House, represented by the plantation home, Tara, in the film adaptation of *Gone with the Wind*, serves as the most enduring example, acting as a site of replication, tourism, and white southern fantasy. The Big House in *Gone with the Wind*, as well as all subsequent iterations seen in southern revival architecture and across big and small screens, possesses a "veneer of glamor" (222). This veneer, as Tolson describes, dilutes and eventually erases any memory of the racist violence of the Big House and the "human misery" on which it was built and sustained, instead leaving behind a sterilized memory of a falsified genteel South of hospitality and white columns (222).

Variations of the plantation-style Big House seen in residential and public architecture are distinct southern styles that differed from architectural trends in other parts of the nation. Residential spaces embraced modern conveniences inside yet replicated "classical imagery akin to antebellum landmarks" outside that served to promote the South "as offering the best of modern reform . . . combined with the stable social hierarchy modeled by the Old South" (Bishar 1993, 28). Older antebellum style homes were carefully restored and updated with modern conveniences while new revival style homes were built; these architectural trends extended to southern suburbs built to accommodate the upper middle classes, identified with "traditional domesticity, respectability, and continuity" (34). Leigh Burns and colleagues (2001) note that in midcentury Atlanta, the Federal Housing Administration (FHA) sought to promote "neighborhood character" in newly constructed suburbs, defined largely by segregationist practices that kept these spaces predominantly white. In 1947, the FHA described "mixed" neighborhoods as potentially "less desirable to present and prospective occupants" (Burns et al. 2001, 7). To this end, by 1960, "only 5.5% of the Atlanta population resided in integrated neighborhoods" (15).

The revival style architecture popular in Georgia gained prominence in the 1930s; these revival structures make up most of the state's antebellum-style homes, as the plantation home in the pre–Civil War South was not as ubiquitous as such an architectural revival might suggest. As Tara McPherson (2003, 44) notes, "Such mansions were not widely prevalent in the antebellum South" and in the years before the war, "fewer than 2,300 families out of a population of 8 million owned substantial numbers of slaves, thus constituting the planter aristocracy." Author of *Gone with the Wind* Margaret Mitchell and technical advisor for the film Susan Myrick contested Selznick Studio's preoccupation with featuring a grandiose Tara in the film, as they consistently noted it did not align with the architecture of the region. In several personal letters, Mitchell speaks to the incongruence between North Georgia in actuality and the version created for the film. In April 1939, she writes, "The movie people wanted to see old houses that were built before Sherman got here and I obligingly showed them. While they were polite, I am sure they were dreadfully disappointed. . . . I had tried to prepare them by reiterating that this section of North Georgia was new and crude compared with other sections of the South, and white columns were the exception rather than the rule" (Myrick and Harwell 1982, 8–9). A letter written in 1942 reveals her continued exasperation at the misattribution of Old South aesthetics: "Since my novel was published, I have been embarrassed on many occasions by finding myself included among writers who pictured the South as a land of white-columned mansions. . . . I took great pains to describe North Georgia as it was. But people believe what they like to believe and the mythical Old South has too strong a hold on their imaginations to be altered by a mere reading of a 1,037 page book" (Myrick and Harwell 1982, 18).

While revival architecture borrows from the aesthetics of the antebellum era, the role of the on-screen plantation house cannot be disregarded as an influence on such styles well into the twentieth century and as an affordance of screen technologies. The "claustrophobia of mansions" and narratives of "circularity, entrapment, and stagnation" (Courtney 2017, 84) describe the South on film in the early twentieth century; homes represent entire worlds in the screen South and are renewed as containing entire worlds and lifetimes in inspired revival architecture. As de Havilland's character, Melanie, in *Gone with the Wind* remarks, "I love it as more than a house; it's a whole world that wants only to be graceful and beautiful." The Tara façade built for *Gone with the Wind* influenced southern architecture and its encompassing

Fig. 8.1. WSB-TV staff in front of White Columns studio with the station's helicopter.

ideologies, which saw lasting influence from seemingly benevolent residential dwellings to the use of plantation homes by white supremacist groups like the Ku Klux Klan and the United Daughters of the Confederacy in twentieth-century Atlanta; such groups purchased and restored homes for use as offices of operation throughout the city.[3]

WSB-TV moved into White Columns in April 1956, and the studio's dedication ceremonies were shown on the station. According to the *Constitution*, "Speakers lauded the $1,500,000 facilities as a blending of the Old South with the progress of the New" (Furhman 1956, 1). Speakers and attendees included Atlanta mayor William Hartsfield and chairman of the board of NBC David Sarnoff, among others. Music from the *Gone with the Wind* score was played during the ceremonies as guests sat on the lawn and left with a special White Columns edition of Margaret Mitchell's novel. WSB-TV's Don Elliot described the building as a "symbol of the tradition, the progress, and the prosperity of the South" (8). Speeches delivered by television industry leaders including Sarnoff spoke to the virtues of White Columns as the best of the traditional and the modern. Press and trade publication coverage of the studio focused on the blend of the most innovative and advanced communication technologies housed within a neotraditional façade. Additionally, White Columns' homage to the Old South was not vague recollection but instead one of technicolor Hollywood, an Old South specifically realized in 1939's *Gone with the Wind*. As executive director of WSB television and radio J. Leonard Reinsch describes, "While here is a touch of the Old South, White Columns is as modern as tomorrow. Yet, in a way, one can almost imagine Scarlett O'Hara opening the front door and stepping out upon this porch—which is a good old Southern word" (8).

The instillation of White Columns studio, inside a modern telecommunications facility, likely the most sophisticated in the region at the time, "high upon a green and tree-crowned hill," materializes Atlanta's nostalgia/future antagonism largely facilitated through the technological affordances of WSB-TV (WSB-TV Videotape Collection 1998b). The studio "bypassed the current station trend toward contemporary design to choose classic Georgia architecture" including "eight lofty, fluted columns," that could "pass as a mansion for Scarlett O'Hara" (*Broadcasting* 1956, 64). Importantly, too, the facility was built on the site of the Wash Collier plantation, which in 1864 served as a defensive site against General Sherman's invading army toward the end of the Civil War. The burning and reconstruction of Atlanta in the years following the Civil War contributed to the city's history as spirited, progressive, and prosperous. While the exterior of the building harkened back to an antebellum definition of success, the interior reflected WSB-TV's vision for a modern Atlanta. The state-of-the-art studio also included mobile news units outfitted with "2-way short-wave, mobile telephones, [and] police radio" in addition to a helicopter being "on call" to capture breaking news events across the city and state (*Broadcasting* 1960a, 41).

In his dedication speech, David Sarnoff speaks to the relationship between WSB-TV and NBC as well as television's unique ability to collapse distance, bringing the world to Georgia and vice versa: "This means that today Atlanta is less than one second away from any part of the world in which we live. [WSB] carried NBC's signal into the heart of the South for the first time" (WSB-TV Videotape Collection 1990). Through its relationship with NBC and its own local programming, WSB's reputation as the "Eyes of the South" produced numerous firsts for the South on the small screen, seeking to advance the region in terms of technology and cultural output and to define Atlanta as a modern, industrial city throughout the twentieth century. Sarnoff continues, "[White Columns'] architecture, its furnishings, and its 16 acres of beautiful landscaping reflect the grace of the Old South. It's completely modern TV and radio installations reflect the economic advances of the New South . . . a reminder of a gracious and revered southern past and a promise of a prosperous, progressive future in harmony with the great developments of the nation's electronics and broadcast industries" (WSB-TV Videotape Collection 1990). WSB-TV possessed a dual function for the South at midcentury—to distinguish the region as a viable producer of culture and to keep reverent and alive its Old South past. These functions were carried out by WSB-TV's programming and operation strategies since its start in 1948.

CONCLUSION

As the station's longest running local program, *Today in Georgia* aided in the development of Georgia's identity on the small screen, drawing together its momentum as a southern Sunbelt city and its dedication to memorializing a white, fantasy past facilitated through Old South imagery like that popularized by *Gone with the Wind*. Additionally, White Columns provided a physical manifestation of the region's synchronized push to the future and pull to the past with one foot on the grassy hill and the other stepping into a news helicopter. With WSB-TV's programming, its facilities, and its role as an NBC affiliate, the station preserved the past within an increasingly modern city.

In June 1998, WSB moved from White Columns into a facility "designed for the new millennium" (WSB-TV 2018). White Columns studio was subsequently razed, although four columns from the original structure were preserved and now stand in the garden of the new station.

Programs like *Today in Georgia* and structures like White Columns provide insight into the regional specificity offered by local programming and stations that reflect the conditions of their location, conditions so often eclipsed in television histories that privilege the extralocal, seemingly less complex years of network dominance.

NOTES

1. See Sara Eskridge's *Rube Tube* (2018), Jack Kirby's *Media-Made Dixie* (1978), and Allison Graham's *Framing the South* (2001).
2. Susan Lindsley is the niece of Susan Myrick, friend of Margaret Mitchell, columnist for the *Macon Telegraph*, and technical advisor for 1939's *Gone with the Wind*.
3. Clement Moseley (1968, v) describes the resurrection of Ku Klux Klan activity in Georgia in the mid-1950s, spurred by the *Brown v. Board* ruling: "The modern KKK was founded in Georgia. This state has been the Imperial Headquarters for the order during most of its modern history."

REFERENCES

Alexander, Raymonde. 1965. "Broad Education Is a Must for TV, Advises Ruth Kent." *Atlanta Constitution*, March 23.

Atlanta Constitution. 1948. "Small Cities to Get TV Relay Systems." October 6.

Bernard, Richard M., and Bradley R. Rice. 1983. *Sunbelt Cities: Politics and Growth since World War II*. University of Texas Press.

Bishar, Catherine W. 1993. "Landmarks of Power: Building a Southern Past, 1865–1915." *Southern Cultures* 1 (1): 5–45.

Broadcasting. 1956. "White Columns: Broadcasting in Ante Bellum Showcase." April 9.

———. 1960a. "Front Line of the WSB-TV News Team." August 1.

———. 1960b. "WSB-TV's Today in Georgia... Best Women's Interest Program on TV in the South." March 28.

Bronstein, Phoebe. 2020. "Southern Projections: Black Television Hosts, Madison Avenue, and Nationalizing the South in 1950s Primetime." *Television & New Media* 23 (2): 219–34.

Burns, Leigh, Staci Catron-Sullivan, Jennifer Holcombe, Amie Spinks, Scott Thompson, Amy Waite, Matt Watts-Edwards, and Diana Welling. 2001. *Atlanta Housing 1944 to 1965: Case Studies in Historic Preservation*. Georgia State University.

Burns, Rebecca. 2011. "The Integration of Atlanta's Public Schools." *Atlanta Magazine*, August 1.

Cassidy, Marsha F. 2005. *What Women Watched: Daytime Television in the 1950s*. University of Texas Press.

Cassidy, Marsha F., and Mimi White. 2002. "Innovating Women's Television in Local and National Networks: Ruth Lyons and Arlene Francis." *Camera Obscura* 17 (3): 30–69.

Classen, Steven D. 2004. *Watching Jim Crow: The Struggles over Mississippi TV, 1955–1969*. Duke University Press.

Courtney, Susan. 2017. *Split Screen Nation: Moving Images of the American West and South*. Oxford University Press.

Cox, Karen. 2011. *Dreaming of Dixie: How the South Was Created in American Popular Culture*. University of North Carolina Press.

Curry, Dale. 1964. "WSB's Ruth Kent Wins Limbo Contest." *Atlanta Constitution*, November 30.

Daniel, Pete. 2000. *Lost Revolutions: The South in the 1950s*. University of North Carolina Press.

Dockterman, Eliana. 2018. "How Georgia Became the Hollywood of the South: TIME Goes behind the Scenes." *TIME*, July 26. https://time.com/longform/hollywood-in-georgia/.

Eskridge, Sara K. 2018. *Rube Tube: CBS and Rural Comedy in the Sixties*. University of Missouri Press.

Farnsworth, Robert M. 1982. *Caviar and Cabbage: Selected Columns by Melvin B. Tolson for the Washington Tribune, 1937–1944*. University of Missouri Press.

Furhman, Lee. 1956. "$1.5 Million New Home of WSB Is Dedicated." *Atlanta Constitution*, April 9.

Graham, Allison. 2001. *Framing the South: Hollywood, Television and Race during the Civil Rights Struggle*. Johns Hopkins University Press.

Hilmes, Michele. 2007. "NBC and the Network Idea: Defining the 'American System.'" In *NBC: America's Network*, edited by Michele Hilmes, 7–24. University of California Press.

James G. Kenan Research Center. 1939. "William Hartsfield Gone with the Wind Premiere Film." James G. Kenan Research Center, Atlanta History Center, Atlanta, Ga. https://album.atlantahistorycenter.com/digital/collection/WH/id/2.

Johnson, Victoria E. 2008. *Heartland TV: Prime Time Television and the Struggle for U.S. Identity*. New York University Press.

Jones, Paul. 1948. "Television—A New Window of Entertainment, Education." *Atlanta Constitution*, October 6.

———. 1950. "GWTW Premiere Scenes on TV Show." *Atlanta Constitution*, December 15.

———. 1953. "Two Local Shows in TV Debut Today." *Atlanta Constitution*, September 28.

Kirby, Jack. 1978. *Media-Made Dixie: The South in the American Imagination*. Louisiana State University Press.

Lindsley, Susan. 2011. *Susan Myrick of Gone with the Wind: An Autobiographical Biography*. ThomasMax.

McPherson, Tara. 2003. *Reconstructing Dixie: Race, Gender, and Nostalgia in the Imagined South*. Duke University Press.

Moseley, Clement C. 1968. "Invisible Empire: A History of the Ku Klux Klan in Twentieth Century Georgia, 1915–1965." Ph.D. diss., University of Georgia.

Myrick, Susan, and Richard Harwell. 1982. *White Columns in Hollywood: Reports from the Gone with the Wind Sets*. Mercer University Press.

Sibley, Celestine. 1954. "GWTW Is Coming Back." *Atlanta Constitution*, April 19.

Spigel, Lynn. 1992. "Installing the Television Set: Popular Discourses on Television and Domestic Space, 1948–1955." In *Private Screenings: Television and the Female Consumer*, edited by Lynn Spigel and Denise Mann, 3–38. University of Minnesota Press.

———. 2001. *Welcome to the Dreamhouse: Popular Media and Postwar Suburbs.* Duke University Press.

Walter J. Brown Media Archives and Peabody Awards Collection. 1967. "WSB-TV Newsfilm Reel #163." Walter J. Brown Media Archives and Peabody Awards Collection, University of Georgia Libraries, Athens. https://bmac.libs.uga.edu/Detail/objects/275053.

Workers of the Writers' Program for the Work Projects Administration in the State of Georgia. 1942. *Atlanta: A City of the Modern South.* Smith & Durrell.

Wright, Wellington. 1948. "$5-Billion Television Industry 'Visualized' within 5-Year Period: 500,000 New Jobs Predicted." *Atlanta Constitution*, October 6.

WSB-TV. 2018. "History of WSB-TV/Channel 2." September 18. https://www.wsbtv.com/station/site-information/history-wsb-tvchannel-2/241892439/.

WSB-TV Videotape Collection. 1990. "I. Allen, Hightower, Truman, White Columns, Opening." WSB-TV Video: WSB-TV History Subseries. Walter J. Brown Media Archives and Peabody Awards Collection, University of Georgia Libraries, Athens. https://bmac.libs.uga.edu/pawtucket2/index.php/Detail/objects/375585.

———. 1998a. "WSB-TV 50 Years in Atlanta." Walter J. Brown Media Archives and Peabody Awards Collection, University of Georgia Libraries, Athens. https://bmac.libs.uga.edu/pawtucket2/index.php/Detail/objects/375539.

———. 1998b. "Remembering White Columns Reunion." WSB-TV Video: WSB-TV History Subseries. Walter J. Brown Media Archives and Peabody Awards Collection, University of Georgia Libraries, Athens. https://bmac.libs.uga.edu/index.php/Detail/objects/375587.

CHAPTER 9

EVELYN KREUTZER

BUSTING BEETHOVEN

NAM JUNE PAIK'S ELECTRONIC OPERAS AT WGBH

On the evening of March 23, 1969, viewers of the local Boston-area TV station WGBH were introduced to performance and video artist Nam June Paik's "Participation TV." In between brief shots of a female nude dancer, bathed in electromagnetically created green and blue color patterns and dancing to xylophone lounge music, insertions of black screens appear and a male voice-over narrator announces, "This is participation TV. Please follow instruction." Then, Beethoven's *Moonlight Sonata* begins to play and magnetically manipulated close-up images of human hands, of the dancer, and of news footage alternate with colorful geometric shapes and abstract patterns. Over these flickering images and the music, another male voice, speaking softly and with a notable non-American accent, gives the following instructions: "Close your eyes ... open your eyes ... three-quarter close your eyes ... two-third open your eyes."

"Participation TV" is quintessential Nam June Paik: facetious, interactive, playful, colorful, fragmented, jumpy, experimental, and experiential. It is an invitation for a meditation exercise with the TV screen, set to one of the most well-known musical expressions of melancholy. Conceptually, it parallels some of Paik's more well-known museum installation pieces, such as *TV Buddha* and *TV Garden* (both 1974), which ask for similar dialogical engagements with television sets yet do so in the physical exhibition space rather than the domestic sphere. The context of participation TV's reception, however, evokes a TV-specific notion of intimacy. Broadcast as part of a video art anthology program on the public TV station WGBH-Boston, it set out to turn individual viewers in their private homes into a virtual community of participants of an experiment. Television's potential to create communities (first locally and nationally, then globally) was a primary (at times utopian) drive in Paik's televisual oeuvre. He was a (classical) musician by training, and his vision of television's potential to connect people from different places and backgrounds echoes long-established Romantic ideas about (classical) music as a universal language with unifying power. At the same time, he rejected the discursive structures that categorized both television and classical music according to cultural hierarchies and situated them on opposite ends of the "highbrow"/"lowbrow" scale.

Paik's experiments with electromagnetic video tools show an approach toward TV as a multisided, democratically accessible communication medium, which grew out of his background in music and performance art. He was born in Korea, grew up in Japan, started his career in Germany, and eventually settled in New York City, the hub of the Fluxus and Happening avant-garde and seat of his mentor John Cage and his longtime performance partner Moorman. Yet, while he is a well-known figure in art- and media-historical scholarship,[1] his groundbreaking work with video-synthesizing technologies and music on public broadcast TV has received less attention.

In his gradual shift from performance art to video installations and TV work, the remaining constant was his background and interest in music (Kreutzer 2020). Music inspired his interart approach and his conviction that works of art are never single-authored but emerge from the participation and exchange of everyone involved, including the audience. Similar to his collaborations with and critiques of cultural foundations and media institutions, Paik's relationship to classical music history and its industry was both admirative and critical. In his integration of classical music into video art and TV, and against the backdrop of his own experiences as a person of color in a predominantly white, conservative, and patriarchal music scene, Paik attempted to deconstruct the classical music traditions in which he was trained and simultaneously give them a platform as well. This sense of ambiguity—appealing to public TV's educational mission by exhibiting classical music while also subverting and parodying it—is at the core of Paik's contributions to the medium.

This chapter discusses Paik's involvement in two video art anthology broadcasts on WGBH-Boston, where he was artist-in-residence in the late sixties and early seventies: *The Medium Is the Medium* (1969) and *Video Variations* (1972). While WGBH's local production context and its integration into a national educational network (first NET, then PBS from 1970 onward) stands in contrast to the global scale of Paik's later satellite broadcasts, *Good Morning, Mr. Orwell* (1984), *Bye, Bye, Kipling* (1986), and *Wrap Around the World* (1988), all realized at WNET-13 in New York, they demonstrate the same antielitist deconstruction, targeting "highbrow" culture (specifically classical music culture) and poking fun at television's reputation as a "lowbrow" medium of distraction.

Both anthologies were fundamental to WGBH's culturally and politically progressive appeal, while still adhering to its original educational agenda. They speak to an era in American television in which calls for television as a strong, distinctly American cultural, educational, and community-building service on both local and national levels proliferated. Beginning with FCC chairman Newton Minow's famous "Vast Wasteland" speech in 1961, in which he urged commercial broadcasters to use the medium for high-quality educational programs and the public good (1964, 54), ideals of television as a new public sphere and force of democratization surfaced throughout the decade and stood in opposition to cultural skepticism attached to the medium's supposed dulling effect. Despite efforts to establish an educationally and culturally significant public broadcasting system (such as the Public Broadcasting Act of 1967 and the resulting installment of the Corporation for Public Broadcasting), public television, including WGBH, continuously relied on funding from foundations like Ford, Rockefeller, and Carnegie as well as the National Endowment for the Arts. These institutions would finance ambitious cultural projects, many of which mixed artistic experimentation with technological innovation and played with clashes of "highbrow" and "lowbrow" culture, at times by specifically drawing on local cultural and educational institutions. Yet, while these structures secured the channels' monetary independence from commercial interests, they also associated them with the educational and political agendas of the respective foundations, which did not always align with the countercultural, revolutionary agenda of the avant-garde(s).[2]

Paik was involved in a number of such initiatives in the sixties and seventies, including the New Television Workshop, the Artists-in-Television program, and the Music-Image Workshop at WGBH, as well as WNET's TV Lab. His contributions to *The Medium Is the Medium* and *Video Variations*, "Electronic Opera No. 1" (which included "Participation TV") and "No. 2," present unusual structural convergences between classical music culture and experimental television, juxtaposing rather stringent, contemplative listening conventions around European classical music pieces and traditions with fragmentary, at times psychedelic video aesthetics. In so doing, they gesture toward a critique of the cultural coding and institutional politics at the basis of both cultural realms: the elitist traditions and canon politics of classical music culture on the one hand, and the passive, commercialized consumption patterns associated with mainstream television on the other. While "Electronic Opera No. 1" asks the viewer to participate in a musical meditation with the TV image, "No. 2" offers a tongue-in-cheek dethroning of Beethoven as the overshadowing genius figure in music history.

PAIK'S RESIDENCE AT WGBH-TV

From 1968 until 1972, Paik joined WGBH in Boston as part of the Rockefeller Artists-in-Television program and subsequently the WGBH Project for New Television, which replaced it. Paik's work at WGBH heralded a key moment, both in his own artistic development and in the history of video art more generally. WGBH producers and directors like Fred Barzyk, David Atwood, and Olivia Tappan actively sought out experimental artists and performers from the East Coast art scene (including the Fluxus group), provided them with a budget, and fostered collaborations between video artists and engineers (Isgro 2019, 2–3). At WGBH, Paik created his first live-broadcast experiments with video art on television, including *Video Commune: Beatles Beginning to End*, a collaboration with experimental artist Jud Yalkut, during which Paik accidentally set the WGBH's chroma filter on fire (Betancourt 2013, 165). Paik found new strategies to sync the manipulated video images with music and ultimately achieved a major breakthrough in his technological approach to video, television, and music with the invention of the Paik/Abe synthesizer, which he developed with engineer Shuya Abe in 1970. The first systematic video processing machine, it came close to Paik's vision of a device with which one could play television like a musical instrument. The new synthesizer enabled more ambitious, dynamic imagery and closer synchronicity between imagery and sound. Like all technology with which he experimented at WGBH (and like the Sony Portapak, which had previously revolutionized video production's accessibility), the synthesizer was built with relatively inexpensive equipment and was open for use by other artists. As such, it abided by a democratic approach to artistic production, reception, and participation that runs through Paik's work. The innovation and implementation of the Paik-Abe Synthesizer in the WGBH studios continued the channel's line of work in video art and musicalized imagery.

The two broadcasts at the focus of this chapter come from this period of innovation, which notably occurred at a time when the creative centers of network TV had largely left the East Coast and migrated to LA (Spigel 2008, 110–43). *The Medium Is the Medium* (1969) and *Video Variations* (1972) were among the earliest and most pronounced exhibitions of video art on public TV. Both programs were enabled by major federal grants: *The Medium Is the Medium* partly grew out of a Ford Foundation grant, and *Video Variations* was co-commissioned by the Boston Symphony Orchestra (BSO), which in turn had received a grant from the National Endowment for the Arts. In the same period, WGBH also collaborated with another local cultural institution, the Boston Museum of Fine Arts, on TV programs like *Museum Open House* (which, like *Video Variations*, was also hosted by Russell Connor) and *Eye-to-Eye*. Programs like these demonstrate WGBH's attempts to bridge high-art institutions and figures with public television's potential as a platform for cultural education and critical discourse. As part of the wider NET/PBS network, WGBH's local connections to Boston's cultural and educational institutions sometimes also appeared on partner stations in other U.S. regions, predominantly other metropolitan areas, such as New York and San Francisco. Segments from *The Medium Is the Medium*, including Paik's, further appeared at New York's Howard Wise gallery a few months after the WGBH broadcasts. They were part of *TV as a Creative Medium*, one of the first seminal exhibitions on video art overall. WGBH thus contributed to exchanges between the art scenes of different American cities.

MEDIUM IS THE MEDIUM AND "ELECTRONIC OPERA NO. 1"

While video installation art had gradually established itself as a recognized artistic medium over the course of the sixties, specifically in the New York art scene, its integration into television programming lagged behind. *The Medium Is the Medium*'s producer and director Fred Barzyk assumed the audience would be relatively unfamiliar with the form and begins the program with a male narrator,[3] who in a rather didactic tone asks, "What happens when artists explore television as a personal medium of expression? . . . What happens when artists take control of television?" The narrator introduces video art in comparative references to established visual arts, such as by calling the new technology an "electronic palette," with which artists would "change and expand our vision of the medium." He further states that artists "see in television an immediate way of reaching a vast audience and creating a museum for millions." This notion challenges persistent assumptions about TV as an inherently nonartistic medium—a myth that remained pervasive throughout video art's institutional elevation in the seventies and eighties (Spigel 2008, 285–86). In line with this instructive mode of address, *The Medium Is the Medium* also introduces each of its six pieces with a few notes on the background of the respective artist (Aldo Tambellini, Thomas Tadlock, Allan Kaprow, James Seawright, Otto Piene, and Paik) as well as the tools and material used for it. The title of the anthology broadcast itself, of course, is a playful reference to Marshall McLuhan, who was at the peak of his celebrity at the time and who saw television as an emerging art form. While the program's allusion to McLuhan is less argumentative than born out of the popularity of his famous slogan "the medium is the message," one might see its engagement with classical music on television as a convergence of "old" (or conservative) and "new" art forms that in fact challenges McLuhan's famously provocative use of dichotomies in "Media Hot and Cool."

As the voice-over narration remarks, Paik's tools in "Electronic Opera No. 1," which closes the program, are "magnets and junk television sets," and his images show "three hippies, a dancing model, and national political figures." Paik's sound material, as mentioned above, includes several music pieces as well as his own voice-over narration, which notably both is accented and includes grammatical mistakes (the latter of which could have easily been corrected), perhaps to establish or even play with the role of the "foreigner" or "outsider" that many expected him to perform. The piece begins with the segment introduced at the beginning of this chapter—"Participation TV." In typical Paik fashion, the images of the nude dancer, projected upon and encircled by magnetized colored shapes, and the accompanying xylophone lounge music get inserted in the middle of the shot and musical measure, respectively, as if one had just switched the channel and zapped into the program. "Participation TV" cuts back and forth between the nude dancer, performing gestures and postures that evoke images of Greek sculptures, and unidentifiable, pulsating abstractions and psychedelic forms on a black background, reminiscent of the phosphene light patterns we experience when we close our eyes. When Paik asks his viewers to indeed close their eyes, the image switches to a shrill red background and glimmering patterns that remain on screen until Paik requests them to open their eyes again. A similar shift occurs a minute later when he demands them to "three-quarter close [their] eyes." The contrast in color begs the question for whom the images that appear on screen after his instruction are meant: those viewers who do not follow his request (in which case one could read it as a visual reward for disobedience)? For himself? In a Cagean tradition, they might not be meant for anyone in particular or to be seen at all. Paik was outspoken about his embracing of randomness and of the unpredictability of affect and audience responses, so in his vision such images would be part of the overall piece, just as much as any individual's reaction to them. Finally, this segment alludes to the act of listening to music with closed eyes, an ideal in the Romantic period and a practice in radio consumption, which evokes a heightened sense of concentration that stands in contrast to television's associations with cognitive distraction (Johnson 1995; Negus 2006).

This meditative quality of "Participation TV" is strongly tied to its use of Beethoven's famous *Moonlight Sonata* (precisely the Adagio sostenuto from his *Piano Sonata No. 14* in C sharp minor, "Quasi una fantasia," Op. 27, No. 2). The piece's steady rhythm (based in regular triplet formations) and its lamenting melody set the rhythmic, meditative, and entrancing tone for the flowing visual shapes. Rather than just setting the mood for a potentially transcending experience, this particular Beethoven piece is among the most famous works of classical music ever written and therefore evokes an expansive cultural legacy. Considering Paik's playfulness and wit, I reduce this move neither to a simple choice of background music that fits the rhythm and tone of the visual material nor to an overt critique of "middlebrow" sensibilities associated with a crowd-pleaser like the *Moonlight Sonata*. Rather, I see him moving in between those approaches in a tongue-in-cheek, meta-conscious way, making this sense of ambiguity the actual agenda of his work.

When Paik asks his viewers to open two-thirds of their eyes, he cuts back and forth between the fragmented, alienated footage of Richard Nixon and Attorney General John Mitchell with shots of the dancer's body, and human silhouettes and gestures. These appear in close-ups (one of television's aesthetic key characteristics) in such highly altered, colored images that it becomes difficult to make out the objects and subjects we see on screen, which enhances the images' and the music's sensual, meditative, trance-like flow. The soundtrack further cuts back and forth between Beethoven's music and Nixon's speech in textual fragments and in poor, grainy sound fidelity. Paik interrupts, mutes, and delays the *Moonlight Sonata* in moments of great affective and harmonic tension, depriving the viewers of the dynamics of tension and resolution that are especially poignant in a piece like this one, where the relentless rhythm pushes toward its inevitable climaxes quite forcefully. This segment offers another expression of Paik's "TV-zapping" aesthetic, seemingly switching back and forth between two TV channels, as if to imply a correlation between the flow of disconnected, interchangeable TV content(s) on the one hand and the random, jumping thought patterns of the human mind as assumed and embraced in Zen Buddhist meditation practices on the other.

Engulfed in synthesized images, the dancer performs expressive, classical-ballet-inspired dance moves. This performance alludes both to the history of ballet and classical dance as well as to the history of nude painting and antique sculptures. The visual references to a long history of obsession with the nude female body are set against (and yet integrated into) the new aesthetics of video art, suggesting both continuity and rupture with regard to its historical position and its gender politics. The virtual neglect of female video artists in both anthologies, while not surprising, speaks to a certain incongruity between the video art movement's supposedly revolutionary appeal and the patriarchal presentations into which it tends to fall. The female artists who were part of avant-garde groups like Fluxus at the time were fundamental to ensuring exhibition outlets for the work of male artists: Charlotte Moorman, for example, single-handedly organized the Annual Avant Garde Festival of New York for over a decade. Yet female artists were often reduced to being performers, specifically nude bodies, in the works of their male counterparts. Video artist and critic Martha Rosler (1990, 45) points at this imbalance and specifically ties it to the sanctification of Paik. Because of his monetary support by long-established, exclusive foundations like Rockefeller and his "museumification" (the old trope of avant-gardists "selling out" to their patrons), Paik appears as "the hero [who] stands up for masculine mastery and bows to patriarchy," and yet, as Rosler claims, centers a lot of his work on "the fetishization of a female body as an instrument that plays itself, and the complementary thread of homage to other famous male artist-magicians or seers (quintessentially, Cage)."[4] The six contributions to *The Medium Is the Medium* all come from male artists and the female dancers who appear in several of the videos get reduced to artistic "material"—such as when the narrator announces that Otto Piene "uses 800 feet of polyethylene tubing, 22 tanks of helium, search lights and one 95-pound girl in his light electronic ballet." It is very difficult to find out the names of the dancers who appear in the program because their names were not included in any written material by either the artists or WGBH.

Paik's confrontation of a political figure like Nixon with the intimate, arguably sexualized or even fetishized images of the dancer's body recalls older modernist, politically charged uses of juxtaposition. However, the general flow of images and sounds (despite Paik's uses of fragmentation) avoid an intellectualized act of distanciation. The meditative, participatory mode of address and the composition intermingle all elements of the segment (including its politics) into an aesthetics of intimacy, the quality so intrinsically linked with TV's ontology. "Television has attacked us for a lifetime," Paik said, "now we have to strike back" (quoted in Hölling 2007, 83). He eventually skips over a longer segment of Beethoven's music and, to the images of the silhouettes' kiss, jumps to the end of the piece, hinting at its final resolution, only to deprive it of just that by quickly lowering the pitch like the sound of a deflating balloon or (more accurately) a TV set that gets unplugged. The effect, of course, is anticlimactic, surprising, funny, and antithetical to Beethoven's mythically inflated image.

After Beethoven, Paik uses a piece from Wendy Carlos's famous *Switched-on Bach* album (*Brandenburg Concert* No. 3 in G major, BWV 1048, Adagio) while repeating similar abstract visual patterns as before and alternating between different angles of three human faces in a negative-film aesthetic. The musical choice draws meta-parallels with Paik's innovations at WGBH, given that the album was created with Carlos's elaborate, novel Moog synthesizer around the same time as Paik was working on a new video synthesizer. In its electronic reinterpretation of Bach's music, Carlos's album further presents a canonical cornerstone in classical music's contemporary popularization.

After a while, the repetitiveness provokes a brief voice-over dialogue between Paik and the other male narrator,[5] in which the latter laments that he is "getting awfully bored." "Thank God, it's the last one," Paik responds. The screen goes black, the music is cut off, and the narrator asks, "What do we do now?" Paik then suggests, "Well, let's start it again from the beginning," after which the beginning of "Participation TV" gets repeated, only to be cut off again after the line, "This is participation

TV; please follow instruction." In an authoritative tone, the narrator (over a black screen) demands the viewers to "turn off [their] television sets," subsequently ending "Electronic Opera No. 1" and *The Medium Is the Medium* as well.

Paik's call for participation in acts of listening to classical music, such as in "Participation TV," moved away from pervasive social and cultural ideals in classical music that elevated serious, contemplative modes of listening, essentialist notions of music's ennobling nature, and *Werktreue* ("fidelity to the musical work"; Hölling 2017, 49). Associated with the Wagnerian concept of a self-contained, complete, "total" work of art (*Gesamtkunstwerk*), as well as to the dictum of the musical score and compositional authorship, *Werktreue* elevates the supposed intentions of a work's creator above all interpretive freedom. According to this ideal, a performance is "authentic" if it executes the intentions of its creator (not the performer). This notion evokes a strong sense of historicism that is prevalent in Romantic and Wagnerian thought and that opposes the embracing of new media technologies that Cage and Paik exhibited (Kreutzer 2020, 147). As such, Theodor Adorno ([1941] 2002) rejected musical mass mediations for evoking fascistic tendencies and distracted listening practices, and he claimed that new mediated modes of music experience, such as radio programs, "atomized" and diminished the artistic integrity of musical works. In Cage's and Paik's approaches, historical authenticity was replaced by fidelity to a musical idea or affect, which included both the audience and electronic tools (Hölling 2017, 88).

Paik's contribution to *The Medium Is the Medium* distinctly provokes the spectator's participation against the ideals of *Werktreue*. While it simulates televisual liveness (despite being prerecorded), it also plays with stereotypes about television's passivity, redundancy, and attention economy, as well as classical music's association with boredom. Paik's playful complaint about his own boredom at the end of the program thus connects opposites of the implicit "highbrow"/"lowbrow" divide through adjacent prejudices about television's cultural status. Had John Cage alluded to boredom as an important creative and Zen-spiritualist experience in his *Silence* lectures (Cage 1961, 93), Paik created loop meditations on boredom through the TV image. He played with boredom in many other works as well, poking fun at and undercutting the "boring" conservatism of "highbrow" classical culture and the flat, commercial nature and interchangeability of mainstream "lowbrow" television alike.

VIDEO VARIATIONS AND "ELECTRONIC OPERA NO. 2"

Rather than offering general introductory insights into the aesthetic and electronic breadth of the new art form, *Video Variations* (broadcast three years after *The Medium Is the Medium*) follows a clear thematic trajectory, which was partly due to its production background. Featuring contributions by Tsai Wen-Ying, Constantine Manos, Stan Vanderbeek, Douglas Davis, Russell Connor, James Seawright, and Paik, it was a collaboration between WGBH and the Boston Symphony Orchestra (BSO)—an unusual and remarkable convergence of classical "high art" culture and experimental public TV programming.

At fifty-seven minutes, compared to just under thirty, and with eight as opposed to six contributing artists, *Video Variations*' scope is more expansive than that of its predecessor *The Medium Is the Medium*. Rather than offering general introductory insights into the aesthetic and electronic breadth of the new art form (as *The Medium Is the Medium* did), it also follows a clear formal(istic) trajectory, which was a result of its production background. The unusual collaboration of public TV programming and a prestigious musical institution like the BSO had some grounding in the BSO's historical position as a progressive orchestra with a sophisticated, "highbrow"-literate, yet also politically and culturally modern audience (Horowitz 2005, 64). At the beginning of *Video Variations*, anchor and contributing artist Russell Connor introduces it as a program focused on music rather than video: "There are many qualities that contribute to making a symphony orchestra a great symphony orchestra... perhaps the most fundamental one is an understanding of the tools with which music is made." He then picks up Paik's often repeated metaphor of a TV set as a musical instrument (with countless electronic "keys" as Paik claims; Yalkut 1968, 51): "it's therefore not surprising that the Boston Symphony Orchestra... has recognized that it has in a sense added a new electronic instrument to the orchestra, with a character and potential of its own... that can enhance and enliven the visual aspects of individual musical works at the same time that it reaches a vastly wider audience."

Connor, like Barzyk in *The Medium Is the Medium*, gestures toward a relationship of mutual influence between visual and acoustic media and proposes that visual and musical artists have always inspired each other. While *The Medium Is the Medium* puts the visual spectacle of video art at the forefront, *Video Variations* clearly positions TV as a medium that converges these arts, such as when Connor announces, "Now, literally for the first time in history, there is a medium—television of all things—that's responsible and flexible enough to give real promise to that mythical union of the arts which artists have long been seeking." His claim to the novelty of TV may have partly been a hyperbolic marketing idea, but can also be read as a confident declaration for television's artistic potential. By directing attention to TV as an electronic instrument, however, he attaches this novelty not (or not *just*) to TV but rather to video and video synthesizers like the one used and codeveloped by Paik. In this, Connor hints at a differentiation between the apparatus (the TV set) and the artistic tools that create its transmitted content—a differentiation that was long established for film, yet not always acknowledged with regard to television, a medium at the time still predominantly associated with entertainment flow rather than outlasting, stand-alone works of art.

In its mixing of conventional performance footage with experimental video elements, *Video Variations* anticipates some key features of the music video format almost ten years before MTV. The introduction by Connor, which directly addresses the audience, was already a TV staple. The fact that the program's opening credits are set to the sound of orchestra members tuning their instruments imposes a simulation of liveness that, like its episodic structure, is reminiscent of both classical music concerts and TV programming. The musical flow across the individual pieces further follows an aesthetic of convergence rather than contrast or conflict. With music ranging from Bach, Beethoven, and Haydn to Ravel, Wagner, and Schönberg, the program isolates the individual pieces from the rest of the works from which they stem (essentially turning them into the format of popular songs) and detaches them from their historical contexts, instead joining them with historically unrelated pieces in nonchronological order. This (prototypically postmodern) move was not a new phenomenon. Over thirty years earlier, Adorno ([1941] 2002, 265) had already voiced his outrage at radio for atomizing musical works in such a way and for assembling repertoires that would never appear in such seemingly random orders in respectable concert curations. *Video Variations* openly embraced this atomization, yet other than in *The Medium Is the Medium*, all artists leave the individual music pieces they use intact. Most likely, this restriction was imposed by either WGBH or the BSO, whose officials were interested in promoting its musical repertoire.

Paik also does not inter- or disrupt the piece (Beethoven's Piano

Concerto No. 4 in G, Op. 58, third movement). He lets it play out almost in its entirety, leaving out only the first appearance of the exposition and doing so in a way that the cutout is apparent only to someone deeply familiar with the piece. However, "Electronic Opera No. 2" does not shy away from deconstructing Beethoven's master status further. While Paik dethroned Beethoven figuratively, rather subtly and merely musically, in "Electronic Opera No. 1," the act becomes visually and narratively explicit in "No. 2" (Paik's contribution to *Video Variations*). Paik lets the vibrant, light tone of Beethoven's Rondo guide the visual accompaniment and aligns them rhythmically throughout. "Electronic Opera No. 2" opens with a set of dynamic, colorful animations of various abstract shapes and candles that rhythmically dance across the screen, soon gaining a firework-like quality that corresponds to the jubilant tone of the music. Out of the collage of colors, lights, and footage of the orchestra's performance, the composer's face emerges in the form of a miniature-sized copy of a well-known, grim-looking Beethoven bust.

Once Beethoven's face, clouded in green, red, and violet colors, takes up the center of the image, Paik plays with the image further: the bust not only switches its coloring and glimmers frenetically in the midst of the dynamic color formations, but also wobbles from left to right. Moreover, he uses superimposition to let Beethoven appear in many different faces, all hidden within a single one—a tongue-in-cheek hint at the many virtual faces of the mythically inflated genius figure. In the midst of lights and colors, Beethoven disappears and fragments of other faces appear, one of which gradually emerges fully from the synthesized imagery. According to the credits, it is WGBH associate producer Olivia Tappan, whose face briefly appears in unsynthesized form, in a dreamlike upward stare. It might be a stretch to read the contrast between Tappan's lively human face and Beethoven's petrified bust as an allegory of the "old" (outdated) and new (living or *happening*) art forms that the two figures represent—a reading that would certainly contradict the orchestra's interest in the production. However, one can positively point at the playful ambiguity that shines through these cultural provocations and dualisms. It should also be noted that Paik's technical possibilities increased with the invention of the Paik/Abe synthesizer, which he was still working on when he produced "Electronic Opera No. 1."

Paik starts inserting footage from the BSO's performance of the piece into the visual mix. Then, suddenly, a human fist emerges from the lower left corner of the frame and punches the Beethoven figure in the face, hitting it from left and right several times. This does not cause the bust to fall over, but pushes it back and forth, as if an actual person was flinching and bouncing off (and in the fast-paced movements, the shadow of Beethoven's nose makes it look as if Beethoven was opening his mouth in pain and outrage when he retreats). It is a funny and surprising moment, not just because of its slapstick and overt metaphorical allusion (to punch the great master off his pedestal), but also because the bust's little resistance reveals its lightweight material and small size—a humorous deconstruction of the heavyweight composer. All the while, the intermittent superimposition onto pianist Istomin's performance suggests another battleground: that between the traditional performer Istomin on the one hand and Paik's use of TV as the new "musical" instrument of the hour on the other, both fighting over Beethoven's legacy. The animated elements in the visual composition gain an increasingly fiery quality in shades of red and switch from larger objects to small-scale candle-like figures. Eventually, out of the chaos of animated shapes and performing musicians, a miniature toy piano appears at the center of the frame. The animated candle lights quickly transform into actual fire, and almost exactly when the final piano cadenza begins, the miniature piano is burning. "Electronic Opera No. 2" ends the final climax and resolution of the music piece and the complete dilapidation of the piano under the applause of the concert audience.

By mixing footage of the orchestra's performance with ironic, disparaging images of a (miniature) piano and Beethoven himself, Paik targets a cluster of cultural markers with legacies of class aspiration, bourgeois ideology, and musical deification. Piano Concerto No. 4 is and was a common item in piano concert repertoire and the *Moonlight Sonata* has been an absolute staple for piano students and amateurs throughout the twentieth and twenty-first centuries. Through his choice of music, Paik reaches for several different realms of music culture, including the middle-class aspirations attached to the piano—an instrument tied to bourgeois culture as well as femininity and domesticity.[6] One can assume that Paik saw a parallel or a continuity between the piano—the culturally charged piece of furniture of bourgeois domesticity in the nineteenth century when mass culture's association with femininity took off (Huyssen 1986, 46)—and the TV set, which performed a similar function in the middle of the twentieth century. Paik challenges "high-" and "lowbrow" as well as feminine and masculine associations on the basis of integrating classical music performances into the mass-cultural domestic realm of television and domesticity.

At the same time, ironically, this act might still be read as fitting into a patriarchal logic, in which he positions himself as the artist who towers over these dichotomies, including through voice-over instructions from male voices only. Again, one might certainly claim (as Rosler has) that his critical engagement with classical music's patriarchal, hierarchical focus on individual genius figures reveals a lack of self-reflection when it comes to the patriarchal and hierarchical politics of his own work and the art scene from which he emerged. While playfully emasculating the overpowering composer and conductor figure in his broadcasts, he engaged in performances of his own fame and artistic figure throughout his career. However, on a performance level, he usually did so in a tongue-in-cheek way and by playing with and caricaturing prejudices against his nonwhite identity and international position. On a conceptual level, the participatory philosophy of his work questions the distinctions between composer, performer, and viewer/listener altogether.

Both "Electronic Operas" allude to Paik's implementation of amateurish and/or improvisational elements in his video pieces. "Electronic Opera No. 1" includes (presumably purposefully) poor sound recording and mixing, including microphone popping sounds, and "Electronic Opera No. 2" opens with the sounds of instruments being tuned, associating the accompanying video work with a sense of immediacy, liveness, and artistic labor. In "No. 2," the Boston audience applauds the final downfall of the piano—an innovative, yet provocative gesture toward the orchestra that funded the program, but also a gesture toward connecting the local symphony audience with the local TV audiences of WGBH and its partners. As much as *Video Variations* was an unusually experimental and culturally progressive event, it was a balancing act for Paik to comply with the orchestra without betraying his own anti-institutional politics and whimsical rejection of music education. The program's attempt to bring classical music to a wider audience, and to do so with intermedia art, may have shared an ideological base with Paik's confrontations of the culturally, socioeconomically, and educationally rather exclusive demographic of symphony attendees. But "No. 2" still reveals Paik's skepticism toward the institutional authority of major orchestras and questions the canon politics of musical repertoires. Beethoven is arguably the most obvious example of these romanticizing, traditions and not surprisingly his work appears throughout Paik's oeuvre.[7] The composer's symphonic compositions have historically functioned as blank canvases onto which any and all political agendas may be projected. His ninth symphony is the most famous example: it has been used in Nazi propaganda, in Maoist events, and as the anthem of the European Union (also called the "Marseillaise of Mankind").[8] After World War II, Beethoven turned into an icon of mass culture, exemplified succinctly by Andy Warhol's image of the composer, which put him alongside Marilyn Monroe and Mao as icons of the twentieth century. According to Esteban Buch (2003, 7), this revealed "the banalization of the Beethoven mythos, a process that had, indeed, already bothered the Romantics even as they were creating it and that, with Nietzsche in particular, had succeeded in making the composer himself slightly suspect."

Even within *Video Variations*, the anachronistic legacy of Beethoven appears in several episodes. For example, Jackie Cassen (the only female artist in the collection and an occasional collaborator of Paik's) employs Beethoven's "Eroica" as background music for an overt leftist critique, which mixes electronically distorted news imagery and concert footage of the BSO under conductor Erich Leinsdorf, who—within this audiovisual mix—appears particularly authoritative and intimidating. The provocative positions apparent in Cassen and Paik's pieces also reveal traces of the artists' conflicts regarding the seemingly incongruous avant-garde anti-institutionalism of their backgrounds, the threat of hierarchical attachments and artistic limitations on public television, and yet the promise of exhibiting their works to a larger range of (local) audiences.

By interrupting the music in "Electronic Opera No. 1" and strongly juxtaposing it with visual destruction in "Electronic Opera No. 2," Paik plays with both musical and televisual notions of flow. Paik's common use of "zapping aesthetics" ties in with Raymond Williams's (1975) famous concept of TV (or media) flow, which refers to TV programs' open form and segmentation into blocks of programming. Rick Altman (1986) expands Williams's discussion with a focus on music, claiming that TV sound is the main element of continuity and the flow of the (possibly visually distracted) viewer/listener's experience. In the majority of his works, Paik purposefully subverts this sense of continuity of sound in a critical mode toward TV's reputation as a medium of mass distraction, and simultaneously embraces the shock factor of sudden, loud, contrasts in sound. Paik ([1970] 1986) himself used the term "flow" in his media-ecological writings, in which he envisioned communicational and informational flows and media networks to democratize media participation and replace physical traveling. Paik's distortions present individual disruptive acts upon the signal flow from broadcaster to receiver (as well as from musical performance to listener), which parallel the cultural "destruction" prevalent in the burning piano and the shaking Beethoven bust.

In the seventies and eighties, Paik's experiments with video feedback and anti-elitist deconstruction transitioned from local audiences (in the concrete spaces of his performance art first and regional TV audiences second) to producing multiregional and then global modes of participation. This development mimics a general cultural transition of video art's integration into cultural institutions and popular media cultures. Paik's productivity and success during his residency at WGBH was made possible by major grants received by WGBH and associate institutions. These systems of institutional support allowed him to pursue his artistic and technological innovations full-time. Before his regular and extensive engagements on public TV, Paik had been a struggling artist for many years. Knowing that his collaborator Charlotte Moorman struggled even more, he kept doing public performances with her for many years, even though it had been his wish to quit performance art and focus on further developing video and TV technology since the early sixties (Rothfuss 2014, 145). Except for his commissioned works at WGBH during the residency, securing funding for most of his TV projects proved difficult. In his extensive projects for WNET-13 he usually did not receive fixed grants and only partial funding from the channel, which meant that he had to act like a producer for most of his TV specials and find (often unconventional) funding sources. In many cases, he contributed portions of the budget from his private funds or asked his more affluent friends for contributions, effectively transferring money that came out of video art's increasing standing in the art establishment (such as exhibitions at major institutions like the Museum of Modern Art and the Whitney Museum) into still underfunded experimental television. Meanwhile, WGBH continued the New Television Workshop until 1993 and collaborated with more cultural institutions beyond the Boston area, such as at the Long Beach Museum of Art in 1976, and invited Paik to return for several individual productions during that time.

CONCLUSION

Paik's vision of participation turns every performer and audience member into cocreators. While it may still reproduce some of the political problems ingrained in the cultural hierarchies it sets out to deconstruct (such as the patriarchal traditions of classical music canons), it opens up a realm of cultural production from the active/passive dichotomy of Romantic music culture, the producer/receiver binary of modern capitalism, as well as the sender/receiver communication model associated with TV. On a structural level, his work for WGBH presents gestures of crossing between players and performative modalities of an anti-institutional avant-garde on the one hand, and established (media-)cultural genres, conventions, and institutions on the other. This ambiguity is at the core of both WGBH's role in the development of video art at the time and Paik's contributions to TV. His work challenged and subverted the conservatism and isolationism of classical music history and performance practices, but music still remained the main point of connection in his broadcasts. While eventually he would focus less on local connections and more on satellite television's capacity to bridge global networks, his contributions to *The Medium Is the Medium* and *Video Variations* provide strong insights into the ways in which both Paik and producers at WGBH envisioned television's potential "as a creative medium," as a medium of intimacy and immediacy, and as a point of connection between audiences across different physical and virtual spaces.

NOTES

1. For comprehensive studies on Paik, see Decker-Phillips (1988), Kim (2009), Lee (2010), and Hölling (2017).
2. For a longer history of these institutions' involvement in the "cultural cold war" at the time, see Saunders (1999).
3. Marina Isgro (2019) identifies the announcer as Ron Della Chiesa. In my own research, I have not been able to definitively confirm or deny this claim.
4. See also Kreutzer (2020, 145, 154–55).
5. According to Isgro, it is Barzyk's voice.
6. See the second chapter in Scott (2001) and Loesser (1954).
7. For more on the reception history of Beethoven both in Europe and in the United States, see Comini (2008) and Broyles (2011).
8. This phenomenon is also taken up in Slavoj Žižek's 2012 BBC documentary *The Pervert's Guide to Ideology* (dir. Sophie Fiennes).

REFERENCES

Adorno, Theodor. (1941) 2002. "The Radio Symphony." In *Essays on Music*, edited by Richard Leppert, translated by Susan H. Gillespie, 251–70. University of California Press.

Altman, Rick. 1986. "Television/Sound." In *Studies in Entertainment: Critical Approaches to Mass Culture*, edited by Tania Modleski, 39–54. Indiana University Press.

Betancourt, Michael. 2013. *The History of Motion Graphics: From Avant-Garde to Industry in the United States*. Wildside Press.

Broyles, Michael. 2011. *Beethoven in America*. Indiana University Press.

Buch, Esteban. 2003. *Beethoven's Ninth: A Political History*. Translated by Richard Miller. University of Chicago Press.

Cage, John. 1961. *Silence*. Wesleyan University Press.

Comini, Alessandra. 2008. *The Changing Image of Beethoven: A Study in Mythmaking*. Sunstone.

Decker-Phillips, Edith. 1988. *Paik Video*. Station Hill Press.

Hölling, Hannah. 2017. *Paik's Virtual Archive: Time, Change, and Materiality in Media Art*. University of California Press.

Horowitz, Joseph. 2005. *Classical Music in America: A History of Its Rise and Fall*. Norton.

Huyssen, Andreas. 1986. *After the Great Divide: Modernism, Mass Culture, Postmodernism*. Indiana University Press.

Isgro, Marina. 2019. "Video Commune: Nam June Paik at WGBH-TV, Boston." *Tate Papers* 32. https://www.tate.org.uk/research/tate-papers/32/video-commune-nam-june-paik.

Johnson, James. 1995. *Listening in Paris: A Cultural History*. University of California Press.

Kim, Eunji. 2009. *Nam June Paik: Videokunst in Museen*. Reimer Dietrich.

Kreutzer, Evelyn. 2020. "Mediating and Disrupting the Flow: Classical Music Conventions in the Performance and Video Art of Nam June Paik and Charlotte Moorman." *Music, Sound, and the Moving Image* 14 (2): 141–58.

Lee, Sook-Kyung. 2010. *Nam June Paik*. Hatje Cantz.

Loesser, Arthur. 1954. *Men, Women and Pianos: A Social History*. Dover.

McLuhan, Marshall. 1964. *Understanding Media: The Extensions of Man*. McGraw-Hill.

Minow, Newton N. 1964. "The Vast Wasteland." In *Equal Time: The Private Broadcaster and the Public Interest*, 45–69. Atheneum.

Negus, Keith. 2006. "Musicians on Television: Visible, Audible and Ignored." *Journal of the Royal Musical Association* 131 (2): 310–30.

Paik, Nam June. (1970) 1986. "Global Groove and the Video Common Market." In *Videa 'n' Videology*, edited by Philip Rosen. Everson Museum of Art.

Rosler, Martha. 1990. "Video: Shedding the Utopian Moment." In *Illuminating Video:*

An Essential Guide to Video Art, edited by Doug Hall and Sally Jo Fifer, 31–50. Aperture and Bay Area Video Coalition.

Rothfuss, Joan. 2014. *Topless Cellist: The Improbable Life of Charlotte Moorman*. MIT Press.

Saunders, Francis Ford. 1999. *Who Paid the Piper? The Cultural Cold War: The CIA and the World of Arts and Letters*. Granta.

Scott, Derek B. 2001. *The Singing Bourgeois: Songs of the Victorian Drawing Room and Parlour*. Routledge.

Spigel, Lynn. 2008. *TV by Design: Modern Art and the Rise of Network Television*. University of Chicago Press.

Williams, Raymond. 1975. *Television: Technology and Cultural Form*. Edited by Ederyn Williams. Preface by Roger Silverstone. Routledge.

Yalkut, Jud. 1968. "Art and Technology of Nam June Paik." *Arts Magazine*, April, 50–51.

CHAPTER 10

CHRISTINE BECKER

CREATIVE BEYOND THEIR YEARS

THE UNIQUE ALCHEMY OF *BEYOND OUR CONTROL*

> Imagine for a moment you're 17 again. You've grown up with television as your babysitter, your educator, your entertainer. But now much of what television is doing somehow fails to interest you. You're turning it off—simply because most of the time it's turning you off. And then someone asks, "What would *you* do if you were given a half-hour of television time to fill each week?" For 25 teenagers in South Bend, Indiana, that question is being asked. I'm one of those doing the asking—and we're expecting not only a good theoretical answer, but an actual half-hour program.
>
> —DAVE WILLIAMS (1971)

That actual half-hour program was *Beyond Our Control*, a sketch comedy series that aired on a commercial television station in northwestern Indiana for thirteen weekends in the first quarter of each year from 1968 through 1986. The series was a product of a nonprofit youth initiative called Junior Achievement, which aimed to teach high school students principles of economics and free enterprise. Under this mission and the guidance of creator Dave Williams and a handful of other adult advisers, South Bend–area students between the ages of fourteen and eighteen undertook nearly every job required to put a commercial TV series on the air, from writing scripts to operating studio cameras and switchers to selling commercial time. *Beyond Our Control* was billed as "A TV Show about TV," featuring parodies of local and network news, prime-time dramas, sitcoms and variety shows, daytime game shows and soap operas,

B movies and art cinema, and nature documentaries and commercials. As such, the series is a remarkable document of American televisual culture across two decades as well as a gauge of how predominantly white middle-class teenagers in the Midwest assessed the entertainment in which they were steeped.

Nineteen years is a very long stretch for any TV series to survive, let alone one made by teenagers with annual labor attrition enforced by high school graduation. A "good theoretical answer" is thus required to explain how the actual half-hour program worked for as long as it did, in the particular city in which it did, and in the format that it did even starting before its famous national counterparts like *Saturday Night Live* were conceived. That answer is neither simple nor singular, and it demands understanding of an intricate balance of multiple intertwined forces. *Beyond Our Control* was both a business operation and a creative pursuit, beholden to the demands of commercial television yet enabled by its local context to innovate within them. The production meshed together adult oversight and youthful energy, and the humor it featured could be both mature and juvenile. It saw high school social dynamics shaped by the demands of a professional production, accelerating a maturation process that was still rooted in aspects of adolescence. The participants were all from the same region, thus representing a monoculture, but in bringing together high schoolers from across a forty-mile range surrounding South Bend, there were elements of experiential diversity. The series also thrived on the combination of individual genius and collaboration as well as on the simultaneity of creative harmony and cliquey division.

Spanning this broad scope, *Beyond Our Control* provided a space for education and professionalization that the students likely couldn't have experienced in their own individual high schools, even in those with broadcasting programs. This wasn't small-scale, in-school production contained to closed-circuit television. This was professional-grade production, with corporate ad sales to boot, at a network affiliate television station broadcasting across a seventy-five-mile radius. The participants learned in their teenage years not only how to run cameras and switchers but also how to function in a fully professional community and navigate social relations and hierarchies of labor that reflected those in the mainstream entertainment industry, albeit sometimes for the worse in regard to class, gender, and race.

Most distinctively, *Beyond Our Control*'s participants obtained a cultural education in TV thanks to the parody format, which required participants to decode mainstream television as a communication and entertainment medium. Parody is not a genre readily aligned with a scholastic institution's aims, and it could even be deemed not just culturally suspect but subversive (Thompson 2011). However, parody arguably fosters even greater media literacy than genres common in secondary school production like news and sports coverage. As Ethan Thompson explores in *Parody and Taste in Postwar American Television Culture*, parody as a format requires thorough understanding of the materials it is mocking before they can be reconstructed: "Parody, because it always includes some earlier source material, provides evidence of reading practices. A parody is evidence of how at least one person made sense of some communication message or some cultural text" (2011, 8). In this case, *Beyond Our Control*'s contributors made sense of both the production practices and the content formulas of local and national news, commercials, sitcoms, and dramas, not simply to replicate new versions of that material for broadcast television but also to position them for universally recognizable mockery. In assessing how *Beyond Our Control* evolved into a pioneering, award-winning television program, this chapter uncovers how the show's production and parody methods functioned together as a scholarly enterprise, thereby offering an instructive lesson for television scholars about alternative forms of media literacy.

THE DEVELOPMENT STAGE OF *BEYOND OUR CONTROL*

Beyond Our Control (*BOC*) was a business before it was a TV show. Participants referred to themselves as part of "the company," and while that might sound like a label a group of performing artists might naturally use, *BOC* was actually a company in the business sense stemming from its sponsorship by the nonprofit youth initiative Junior Achievement (JA). JA's model in the 1960s involved having regional student groups form companies around a product they made for general sale, usually a practical good such as a bird feeder, coatrack, or candle. William Thomas Hamilton, general manager of the South Bend, Indiana, NBC affiliate WNDU, was a member of the JA board of directors and a strong believer in the ideal of broadcasting as a public service, so it was natural for the JA product made by the company under his purview to be a WNDU television show. Thus, the Junior Achievement Television Company or WJA-TV was born in 1960 (Dundon 2022).

While William Thomas Hamilton initiated the business infrastructure for what would become *BOC*, the creative force behind its emergence was Dave Williams, who was employed at WNDU as promotions director. In its early years, WJA-TV produced a set of quiz programs, but Williams was concerned the students weren't learning much about the television business if they merely stood in front of cameras answering trivia questions, and he also recognized that the students yearned to produce something more consequential than a quiz show. He (1974–75) explained that teenagers "had grown up with television as babysitter, instructor and constant companion. Somehow, the thought of doing yet another game show was not proving to be a strong attraction to a broadcasting career." The 1967 company members reportedly underwent a few weeks' discussion of what kind of series they wanted to do, and, Williams attested, "they decided on a program that would use television as a mirror of American culture" (qtd. in Bullock 1974) in the vein of the 1963–65 NBC David Frost–hosted series *That Was the Week That Was* ("*Beyond Our Control Memorybook*" 2001, 35), which was a satirical comedy-variety show that combined topical news spoofs, political sketches, and parody songs. Thus, WJA-TV begat *BOC*, the title evoking "the familiar broadcaster's admission of problems 'Due to circumstances beyond our control'" (Williams 1974–75). Notably, comparable sketch shows like *Saturday Night Live* (1975–present) and *Second City Television* (1976–84) were years away, *Monty Python's Flying Circus* didn't start airing in the United States until 1972, and *Laugh-In* (1968–73) premiered only in the same month that *BOC* did, so the series likely was a TV pioneer beyond just its youth participants.

Partly this genre switch was driven by Dave Williams's own interests, as he was an ardent fan of the emerging satirical comedy troupes Firesign Theater and Credibility Gap as well as TV innovators like Ernie Kovacs (Karaszewski et al. 2022). But the students themselves also brought minds saturated in popular culture. Seventies company member David Simkins (2022) described, "We were right in the middle as teenagers of that assault from movies and television and advertising, it was hitting our eyeballs every day." Together, Williams and company members consumed a steady diet of cultural influences past and present (Karaszewski et al. 2022). Importantly, though, they didn't aim to copy those works on *BOC*; instead, they strove to *parody* them and everything they were seeing on television. That would first require learning how such material was made.

PROFESSIONAL AND PERSONAL LESSONS IN TELEVISION PRODUCTION

Though the format change to "A TV Show about TV" happened virtually overnight, the students needed a broader education in production before they could make an effective parody of the real thing. The training of company members started with the technical elements of studio broadcasting and then carried over into the social components necessary for large-scale creative collaboration. Some of those components were uniquely framed by local and high school contexts, while others bore similarities to the professional entertainment industry, and in both circumstances adverse inequities inevitably shaped both the creative process and the final product.

One unique element was that *BOC* wasn't a product of just one high school; basically, any teenager who could find regular transportation to South Bend was welcome. Unlike other JA companies, though, *BOC* did not accept all volunteers, and participation was capped at around thirty students each season. An audition process was required, and depending on the company's makeup in any given year, only around one in four who tried out would get accepted (Patnaude 2022). Once new students were accepted into the company, an orientation and training process commenced. Technical positions were operated by WNDU staffers until the early seventies, but Dave Williams always intended for students to take over complete production of the show (Dundon 2022), and once that was achieved, older students would train the younger ones. Also assisting *BOC*'s operations as adult advisors were Joe Dundon, who worked in ad sales at WNDU and with *BOC* from 1968 to 1981, and Denny Laughlin, who was employed as WNDU's art director for forty-two years and served in that capacity for *BOC* from the early seventies to its end (Hughes 2000b, A10).

Production had to happen according to a regimented weekly schedule or the series wouldn't make it to air, one among many bedrock principles of the commercial television business that delivered both professional and social lessons. Meanwhile, this all took place while the students were attending high school. To help encourage students to stay afloat, the advisers devised a points system to keep track of participation, allowing for expulsion from the group if anyone was repeatedly lacking. While this was ostensibly about making sure the episodes got delivered on time, it also set forth a model for productive teenage behavior in a setting that mixed professional and social responsibilities. A company member could earn points for things like attending meetings, helping out with a location shoot, and bringing a needed prop, and one could lose points for absences, being disrespectful to a peer or advisor, and even "lying to your parents about being at a writer's meeting when you were not" ("Official Beyond Our Control Handbook" 1974). Williams kept a public record of points using a leaderboard, and he wrote a weekly newsletter mailed to company members' homes so their parents could track developments across the season and trust that their kids were in capable hands. In addition to detailing how ad sales and weekly production quotas were going, the newsletters would call out company members for absences or not pulling their weight in the studio.

The creative starting point for every episode was the writers' room, which for the first half of the show's life meant Dave Williams's living room. It was run just like how a writers' room in Hollywood would operate, according to David Simkins, who would later become an executive producer on network television dramas (Karaszewski et al. 2022). Williams would sit at a typewriter clacking away faster than anyone had ever seen, as teenagers, mostly boys, sat around him firing out ideas. Much like what we would now call a showrunner, Simkins (2022) explained, "Dave was kind of there to be the filter and the assembler of all these notions flying in and out.... He was my first experience with that old improv notion of, 'Yes, and,' where the kids would come to him with an idea, or he would come to the kids with a notion, and they would talk it out." Writers' meetings were open to any company member at the start of the season, but the "Official Beyond Our Control Handbook" (1974), written by Williams, warned, "You are welcome . . . but unlikely to feel so at first. Like all cliques, the writers committee is difficult to penetrate. Persevere.... Some people just aren't right to write. Art-by-committee is difficult at best, and you may not fit in." Writers' room fixture Larry Karaszewski also acknowledged that there was an arrogance within the writers' committee because they were deemed the funniest, and no one else could get started with their jobs until the writers finished theirs (Karaszewski et al. 2022). As a result, many company members, especially the girls, were too intimidated by the idea of the room to even show up. Some of the women reflecting back on the experience today insist this wasn't because Williams or anyone else discouraged them from participating; they said it was more so a product of the time and of high school culture (Werts 2022; Dudley 2022). However, this circumstance also strikingly resembles the patriarchal dominance of Hollywood's writers' rooms, offering a less sanguine indication of how the writers' room ran just like a professional version.

Notably, a handful of young women would take on positions of leadership within the company, including as writers. Diane Werts (2022) said she loved being in the writers' room, calling it "safe and fun," and another company member, Jenny Davis, insisted in an email following her 2022 interview, "From an adult feminist perspective, I never felt hindered, marginalized, or diminished by anyone in the company based on my sex or cultural norms at that time. There of course was flirting and there were romances in the company, but never once were the girls in the company expected to stand back or demur based on gender stereotypes. Everyone was always expected to pitch-in and bring your best." While there were only a handful of women in the writers' room in any given year, by the late 1970s they came to dominate in positions of technical leadership, such as production manager and director (Werts 2022). Research by DeeDee Halleck and Erin Hill could suggest explanations for this circumstance. In *Hand-Held Visions: The Impossible Possibilities of Community Media*, Halleck notes that public access television provided women readier access to positions of power than studios did (2002, 196), while Hill's *Never Done: A History of Women's Work in Media Production* (2016) argues that women in mid-twentieth-century Hollywood found easier routes to jobs that rewarded stereotypically feminine skills of organizational and emotional labor compared to the creative positions that men were deemed most apt for. In *BOC*'s version of this, young women may have gradually become more accepted as the conscientious technical director figure rather than the innovative writer.

While gender diversity on *BOC* increased over time, racial diversity did not. According to former company members, with additional confirmation from annual cast photos, there were never more than two or three Black company members in a season, and in many years there were none. (For reference, according to the St. Joseph County Public Library [1971], 14 percent of the South Bend community in 1970 was Black.) Yet, despite being the lone Black company member to participate in the 1976–77 season, Lewis Boyden (2022) said something similar to Jenny Davis's comment about being a woman in the male-heavy company: "No one ever treated me poorly or with any disdain or disrespect, they just treated me just like one of the family." Unfortunately, Boyden was able to participate in *BOC* only for one season because he needed to take public transportation to get to meetings, but the city's bus system was unreliable, so his frequent absences dropped him too far down on the points leaderboard to be asked back for another year. This would indicate that class status could be a factor in participation too. Here again we see a parallel between the local and the professional realms, wherein systemic inequalities curb diversity. Much like how Hollywood internships and early career assistant jobs are limited to those who come in with the affluence necessary to sustain themselves on low or no pay, *BOC*'s participatory diversity likely suffered from inequities in infrastructural services. That said, for those who were able to stay in the company while coming from high schools that didn't have the access to high-quality equipment, *BOC* gave them opportunities their schools likely could not (Szalewski 2022).

The *BOC* experience also fostered social dynamics that weren't typical for the confines of a single high school. Eighties company member Donnie Rogers (2022) explained that a lot of the company members were "people who were just happy to not be in the high school clique they grew up in." In that vein, numerous company members who speak of their experiences use the word "misfits" to describe themselves. Shawn Perry (2022) expressed this in terms of social pressures within his rural town: "For a teenage boy who was pretty much an oddball, and especially in farm country, you know it's like, 'Shawn, do you wanna play football?' 'No. I wanna shoot movies with my camera,' and they're like 'huh?' *BOC* was a saving grace for me. I was like, wow, there's other people who actually like the same thing I do." Nonetheless, these were still teenagers thrown together at the most fraught age for socialization, and cliques within *BOC* did develop, well beyond the writers' room "in-group" already discussed (Fye 2022; A. Rogers 2022). But at least for thirteen episodes a year, this gaggle of misfits united around one goal: to make fun of television.

THE TV SHOW ABOUT TV

TV Guide described *BOC* in 1973 as "a kind of 'Mad Magazine of the Air.'" In his history of postwar television parody, Ethan Thompson writes of the humor magazine *Mad* that it "became an indispensable weapon for youth audiences making sense of postwar popular culture, and in particular the commercialism and consumerism which so permeated and defined it" (2011, 10), and the same description could apply to *BOC*. Further, Thompson argues that *Mad*'s parodic style "taught an alternative language for making sense and finding pleasure in and through American popular culture" (2011, 75). Across its own seventy-five-mile reach, *BOC* did something similar but was couched in an even more explicit educational context, and the parody format channeled through broadcast production methods provided high school students with invaluable media literacy. There's a telling note in a February 1977 newsletter to students along those lines, wherein Dave Williams told the students they should go see the recently released film *Network* (1976): "The more you know about TV, the more you can appreciate this hilarious and outrageous attack on television . . . exaggerated just enough to be funnier than life, but not so much as to be totally unbelievable" ("*BOC* Newsletters" n.d.).

That quotation could have served as a mission statement alongside the *BOC*'s "A TV Show about TV" tagline, which David Simkins (2022) described as the "sort of envelope for the show, a beginning and an ending for looking at the kind of material we were going to lampoon or satirize. Commercials, movies, television shows, talk shows, whatever. And it gave us a framework, a track to run on, as opposed to sort of freestyling." A related visual motif in the show was "channel switching," a term that described how segments were bridged by a visual and audio representation of the static produced when a viewer clicked to a new channel on an old analog TV set. Company member Jim Poyser (2022) described the interstitial's utility for the show's pacing: "That channel-switching motif was the most brilliant move because it meant that a skit would never get boring, you could always cut out of it, and you could cut back to it if you wanted. But if you had like a little nugget that wasn't a full piece you could throw it in." Those little nuggets could be as throwaway as silly dancing or as central to the show's acerbic tone as a mock station voiceover teasing an upcoming "special tribute to the Inquisition, the Friars roast of Joan of Arc" ("Beyond Our Control Audio-Visual Material" n.d.).

Analysis of select episodes and sketches indicates that *BOC*'s humor could be quite caustic, particularly when the company turned its attention to the pretensions and hypocrisies of television. In this, the series serves as an example of Ethan Thompson's characterization that "parodic performance could work both as criticism and as successful commercial content" (2011, 2). *BOC* company members sold airtime to local businesses and in some cases even produced their ads, while in between those legitimate commercial segments a viewer would see fake ads and sketches that highlighted the incompatibility of broadcasting's public service aims with its commercial context. For instance, one undated segment presents a pseudo-serious talk show session on drug abuse featuring an angry teen who blames his father for his drug addiction, followed by a fake commercial for a sleeping aid called Semi-Coma, which "makes all your cares go bye-bye" ("Beyond Our Control Audio-Visual Material" n.d.).

BOC also made fun of the type of shows that filled WNDU's airwaves in prime time, frequently highlighting the banality of sitcom formulas in particular. A 1974 parody of *The Donna Reed Show*, scatologically retitled *The Donna Rea Show*, serves as an example of how the students could re-create a sitcom while lampooning its inanity. In addition to using an excessive laugh track, which resounds when nothing funny has been said and occasionally cuts off abruptly to draw attention to its artificiality, the segment features a preposterously affectionate household, as every family member kisses every other family member upon every entrance and exit. The episode's premise begins like any domestic sitcom might with a generational conflict between father and child, as son Bud wants to start a rock band over his dad's objection. From there, the absurdities multiply, as Bud sneaks in his friends and their large instruments right behind his oblivious father, they make a huge cacophony playing in his bedroom while Buds yells out to his parents that they're not doing anything, and then the first act climaxes with one friend electrocuting himself on an amplifier. After a commercial break, Donna tells her husband that Bud is keeping a dead body in his room, and he observes with mild dismay that it's not like Bud to keep secrets, again tying the ridiculous plot to a familiar sitcom trope of communication problems between parents and kids. Bud then calls his father into his room, apologizes for disobeying him, and offers "I guess all I can say is sorry" in regard to his dead friend, still lying on his bed. Father praises son for doing the right thing in admitting he was wrong and says they'll call the dead boy's family in the morning, certain that they'll understand because, after all, they have another son. Enter the rest of family for a group embrace, as Donna offers a stock platitude for closure: "I knew it would work out because, well, father knows best." From start to finish, the segment expertly draws on sitcom conventions in everything from plot construction to production design while lampooning the perfunctory moral lesson of a typical sitcom episode by taking it to a nonsensical extreme.

The superfluousness of live news conventions was also a frequent target. Larry Karaszewski (2022) identified this as a natural circumstance because the students were trained to use WNDU's own news equipment and were hyperaware of how that content was created. In that vein, *BOC* aired a remarkably prescient sketch a year prior to the 1981 assassination attempt on Ronald Reagan, part of a running series about a presidential candidate named Ronald Clark. Taking to its natural extreme the strategy of politicians insisting they were outsiders and not politicians at all, Clark declares he is not running for president and that no one should vote for him, which just makes his followers rally around him all the more. The segments culminate in an assassination attempt on Clark, only he is the self-perpetrator. Breathless news anchors break down the shooting footage in slow-motion detail, much like *Saturday Night Live* would depict the following year with their Buckwheat parody of the Reagan assassination ("Beyond Our Control Audio-Visual Material" n.d.). Asked how *BOC* company members could anticipate such real-world *and* parody material, Karaszewski (2022) recalled that because of their combined viewing and production experience, they knew it was just what TV would have done, and they knew how to make fun of it: "It wasn't a parody of a specific event. Rather a reaction to the way news was beginning to get covered. Something terrible would happen and then they would go over it again and again, and then have a half hour news special after the late local news."

BOC's parodies could even touch upon aspects one might assume were beyond the knowledge of average sixteen-year-olds, as well as their legal age, including R-rated movies. A *Taxi Driver* send-up provides an example and also points toward the love-hate relationship the group had with television. The sketch's Travis Bickle figure is driven to kill by his adoration for classic sitcoms like *The Beverly Hillbillies* and *Gilligan's Island* and his contempt for recent comedies like *Laverne & Shirley*. He angrily tears up a copy of *TV Guide* and sets out to kill a network executive, whom we overhear ordering a spinoff for *Laverne & Shirley*'s Potsie before he's murdered. The kicker is a set of op-eds that thank the killer "for getting all the scum off television," which enabled the return of *The Beverly Hillbillies* ("Beyond Our Control Audio-Visual Material" n.d.). In many such sketches, *BOC* evinced equal parts of a love of commercial television and a savaging of everything its powers represented.

The series was considerably less sophisticated when it came to issues of identity representation and discrimination, however, as there were elements of sexism, racism, and homophobia evident across the series' run. In part, sexy female cheerleaders and Arab terrorist characters appeared because the students were parroting what they saw on American television every day. But unlike the explicit deconstruction of TV conventions described above, these depictions were presented as fodder for laughter in themselves rather than satire of the bigotry in which they were rooted. Company member Marc Wellin (2022) reflected upon looking back, "The really sad thing about it is the sexism and the racism that were inherent in our society [were] in what we did as well. That was the one thing I wish we could have spoken out against. Maybe there wasn't a funny way to do that back then, but we weren't aware enough." Besides their youth, that lack of awareness surely stemmed from the diversity deficiencies highlighted in the previous section, which would have been exacerbated by the "yes, and" model of comedy writing the series utilized. Amy E. Seham argues in her book *Whose Improv Is It Anyway? Beyond Second City* (2001) that the "yes, and" improv style is prone to the perpetuation of racial stereotypes because of their immediate recognizability to comedy partners and to the audience (102–3). She adds, "Because popular culture is the source of most improvisers' references, these stereotypes are repeated and revalidated by audience laughter and recognition" (103). *BOC* company members couldn't hear viewer laughter, but they could hear each other's responses. Company member Kevin Fye (2022), who as an adult would come out as gay, acknowledged that he willingly played "pansy" characters in *BOC* sketches because it achieved the desired goal: laughter from his peers. The patriarchal dominance of the writers' room also often resulted in young women being subordinate comedic foils in segments led by young men. The "yes, and" model operates based on successive consent, and as Seham explains, "Women, following the rules of agreement, frequently find themselves defined as girlfriends, wives and mothers, and far less often as central agents" (66). Students in any minority identity category would be expected to follow the same rules of agreement dictated by the majority.

One sketch about racism stands out as an exception to the show's identity myopia while still proving the rule. This 1969 spoof commercial for Cool Power laundry detergent features Mrs. Jeannie Redneck of Savannah, who praises the product for cleaning the Georgia red clay out of her husband's sheets and then shows off the proof: her husband in a Ku Klux Klan robe and hood. She exclaims, "No stains at all! Our town is all white, thanks to Cool Power!" ("Beyond Our Control Audio-Visual Material" n.d.). While this sketch evinces an obvious awareness of racism, it perpetuates the cultural assumption that such bigotry is a problem contained to the American South. Indiana has a prominent legacy of KKK activity, but because southern racism is a common trope in TV representation and the students weren't well equipped to call out racism within their own communities, this segment's critique was directed far from home.

Local television conventions were certainly far easier targets for the students to tackle. Company member Kate Doherty-Murphy explained, "I think a lot of [the sketches] were really crap, but then the bar was pretty low for locally produced television. I think we all understood that we were parodying something that was so close to a parody itself. We didn't have to take it that much further to make it a joke." In terms of the quality bar, with nearly five hours of original content each season and much of it produced under onerous time pressures, there was plenty of bad lumped in with the good. But while there were passing moments of flubbed lines, mistimed edits, and wobbly sets, the series does not look at all like an amateur operation. In fact, *BOC* was good enough to win an award in direct competition with professional productions, as it was named the winner in the television category at the 1977 Chicago International Film Festival based on a one-hour compilation episode (*"Beyond Our Control* Memorybook" 2001, 84). The students were anointed award-winning masters of their parodic craft.

CIRCUMSTANCES BEYOND THEIR CONTROL

While most TV shows are canceled due to declining ratings, a more complex range of forces brought about *BOC*'s end in 1986. Tragically, Dave Williams died unexpectedly in 1977, and while Joe Dundon, Denny Laughlin, and a returning cadre of alumni kept *BOC* operating in his absence, considerable production upheaval followed in the early 1980s (Dundon 2022). The series' original booster William Thomas Hamilton retired from WNDU in 1980, and in 1982 WNDU-TV moved into a brand-new facility and barred *BOC* from using the new studio. David Simkins (2022) speculated that once Williams died and publicity attention for the series faded: "The station at that point kind of went, 'Well. . . . It's really not serving us and it's a bit long in the tooth now and Dave's gone. And so let's slowly starve this thing.'" The company persevered for a few more years in other local spaces with old WNDU equipment but had to set up the studio space anew every time.

The cancellation order finally came down in 1986 as a combined result of JA and WNDU decisions. First, the national JA organization shifted away from their singular focus on sponsorship of high school student-run businesses and toward in-school presentations for all K–12 students (Francomano 1988, 69–76). This came home to roost in South Bend in 1986 when the regional chapter pulled its sponsorship of the WJA-TV company (Hughes 2000a, E3). That didn't have to result in the end of *BOC*, but Joe Dundon (n.d.) believed it was just the excuse WNDU needed to finally cancel the series, "a financial decision by management," as he put it. That financial decision surely proceeded partly from substantial structural changes in local television wrought by Reagan-era deregulation and consolidation in broadcasting. As individual station owners gave way to high-powered station groups and budgets tightened, the pressure to squeeze every penny out of commercial time slots increased and the ability of local affiliates to capitalize upon programming freedom and innovation in their non-network hours declined precipitously (Sterling and Kitross 2002, 610–11). In turn, the public service mission of local broadcasting that Hamilton had so championed dwindled. Bob Medich, a company member-turned-adviser whom many credit with keeping *BOC* afloat right after Dave Williams died, departed WNDU in dismay in 1987 and explained, "The 80s were the time when every bit of fun was like, zapped out of broadcasting. Because it just became—they didn't produce any TV shows, your whole focus became the local news. You might as well have been selling widgets" (qtd. in *"Beyond Our Control Memorybook"* 2001, 48).

JA's evolution embodied a similar sign of the economic and cultural times across the United States. In the 1960s, JA as a national organization sought to educate young people about free enterprise by empowering them to forge their own real-world business experiences; by the 1980s, the organization was driven by a top-down model for proselytizing. A history of JA written by a longtime executive noted the "dizzying pace" of JA growth in the late 1970s and contrasted that with the 1960s period: "The young people of the 1960s expressed in no less than violent terms their aversion to 'The Establishment,' business, government—almost anything their parents had succeeded in. The complete turnaround of the 1980s youth might have caught JA off guard" (Francomano 1988, 103). Perhaps not surprisingly, this echoes the changes some described in the type of student who participated in *BOC*. Said Steve Wyant, a company member in the 1970s who returned as an adviser in the 1980s, "Early on, it had a hippie, rebel kind of feel to it. By the time I was advising, they were preppy" (Karaszewski et al. 2022). Future study of *BOC* could explore how its evolution mirrored shifting comedy trends across its lifespan, such as George Carlin's shift from subversive iconoclast in the 1970s to more mild observational comic by the mid-1980s.

Joe Dundon (n.d.) lamented of WNDU's cancellation order, "I think that *BOC* was looked upon more as a liability, an irritant, than an asset. If only they could have seen in 1986 the larger vista of what *BOC* was really producing year-in and year-out in men and women, in creative entertainment, and in present and future goodwill and national publicity for WNDU-TV and South Bend. I know that many can see it now. Too late." Now in the 2020s, those executives would see company members who forged successful entertainment careers in Hollywood, while others have had decades-long careers in broadcasting and video production on the local level or thrived in adjacent pursuits, such as photography, novel writing, cultural criticism, and arts management. Even those with careers that had nothing to do with television would still point toward the heavy influence of *BOC* on the rest of their lives. Heidi Moser (2022) offered, "The individual creativity and teamwork developed in *Beyond Our Control* have colored and influenced every other thing I have done in my life. I didn't become famous; I'm satisfied with making my contributions in quieter and more subtle ways. *BOC* mattered not simply because it launched careers, but because it influenced creative minds."

This is a common description of the broader benefits of youth media production, as the experience helps young people to develop advanced social skills, understand the power of their own voices, and expand their sociocultural capital (Charmaraman 2013, 103–4). Relatedly, Diane Werts (2022) has said she wishes that there was a way to have a *BOC* in every town to help kids today, given its benefit during "that stage of vulnerability in your life, and your uncertainty and your development of your own sense of self, to have someone who can help you see things in yourself that you can't see, that you can build upon and that you can better understand yourself and where you fit in the world and what your possibilities are." There actually are still opportunities for such collaborative youth media production today, albeit more so in community media centers than commercial television stations. But this essay proves that it wasn't television production alone that was at the heart of *BOC*'s educational enterprise. It was an inestimable artistic, social, and cultural training ground for hundreds of teenagers because of the collaborative system that Dave Williams put into place, while the parody format further obliged the students to master television's wide variety of visual codes and content formulas as well as to recognize the medium's fallibilities and insufficiencies. The students weren't always capable of recognizing the latter in their own efforts, particularly when it came to issues of representation and equity. But that stands as an educational lesson for television studies scholars today, particularly in helping us to recognize the inequalities embedded in spaces like writers' rooms and in methods like "yes, and"–inspired comedy writing, including on the local level. Even accounting for these pitfalls, *BOC*'s story helps to highlight the essential creative vitality, social value, and educational power of locally produced television and of parody as a communication format. In this manner, "A TV Show about TV" said more about the medium and its potential than even Dave Williams ever envisioned it could.

REFERENCES

"Beyond Our Control Audio-Visual Material." n.d. Beyond Our Control Records, University of Notre Dame Archives, Notre Dame, Ind. http://archives.nd.edu/findaids/ead/xml/boc.xml.

"*Beyond Our Control* Memorybook." 2001. Beyond Our Control Records, University of Notre Dame Archives, Notre Dame, Ind. http://archives.nd.edu/findaids/ead/xml/boc.xml.

"*Beyond Our Control*: A Very Nice TV Show." n.d. Accessed May 26, 2022. https://www.beyondourcontrol.org/boc4/page81/page81.html.

"*BOC* Newsletters." n.d. Beyond Our Control Records, University of Notre Dame Archives, Notre Dame, Ind. http://archives.nd.edu/findaids/ead/xml/boc.xml.

Boyden, Lewis. 2022. Interview by author, Zoom, March 29.

Bullock, Betti. 1974. "Youngsters Produce Top-Rated Variety Television Show." *Michiana Magazine, South Bend Tribune*, August 25. https://www.beyondourcontrol.org/boc4/page29/page80/page80.html.

Charmaraman, Linda. 2013. "Congregating to Create for Social Change: Urban Youth Media Production and Sense of Community." *Learning, Media and Technology* 38 (1): 102–15.

Christian, Aymar Jean. 2019. "Expanding Production Value: The Culture and Scale of Television and New Media." *Critical Studies in Television* 14 (2): 255–67.

Davis, Jenny. 2022. Interview by author, telephone, March 16.

Doherty-Murphy, Kate. 2022. Interview by author, telephone, June 7.

Dudley, Christine. 2022. Interview by author, Zoom, March 10.

Dundon, Joe. 2022. Interview by author, telephone, March 22.

———. n.d. "Denny." https://www.beyondourcontrol.org/boc4/page1/page6/page6.html.

Francomano, Joe. 1988. "Junior Achievement: A History." https://archives.indianapolis.iu.edu/items/a4638391-c598-48f8-86ad-7496fe5256b8.

Frank, Phil. 2022. Interview by author, telephone, March 17.

Fye, Kevin. 2022. Interview by author, Notre Dame, Ind., March 25.

Halleck, DeeDee. 2002. *Hand-Held Visions: The Impossible Possibilities of Community Media*. Fordham University Press.

Hill, Erin. 2016. *Never Done: A History of Women's Work in Media Production*. Rutgers University Press.

Hughes, Andrew S. 2000a. "For 18 Years, 'Beyond Our Control' Was Hands-On Training Ground for Students." *South Bend Tribune*, October 8, E1, E3.

———. 2000b. "Rerun Set for Alumni of Teen TV Show." *South Bend Tribune*, April 8, A1, A10.

Karaszewski, Larry. 2022. Email to author, May 18.

Karaszewski, Larry, David Simkins, Dan Waters, Chris Webb, and Steve Wyant. 2022. Interview by author, Zoom, March 29.

Moser, Heidi. 2022. Email to author, April 12.

"The Official Beyond Our Control Handbook." 1974. Beyond Our Control Records, University of Notre Dame Archives, Notre Dame, Ind. http://archives.nd.edu/findaids/ead/xml/boc.xml.

Patnaude, Phil. 2022. Interview by author, Granger, Ind., April 1.

Perry, Shawn. 2022. Interview by author, Zoom, April 21.

Poyser, Jim. 2022. Interview by author, telephone, March 14.

Rogers, Andrea. 2022. Interview by author, South Bend, Ind., March 12.

Rogers, Donnie. 2022. Interview by author, South Bend, Ind., March 12.

Seham, Amy E. 2001. *Whose Improv Is It Anyway? Beyond Second City*. University Press of Mississippi.

Simkins, David. 2022. Interview by author, telephone, May 11.

Sterling, Christopher H., and John Michael Kitross. 2002. *Stay Tuned: A History of American Broadcasting*. 3rd ed. Lawrence Erlbaum.

St. Joseph County Public Library. 1971. "Indiana Population by Race, 1950–1970." https://michianamemory.sjcpl.org/digital/collection/p16827coll4/id/329.

Szalewski, Circus. 2022. Interview by author, Zoom, April 13.

Terry, Clifford. 1973. "One Vice President Resigned Because He Was Failing Algebra." *TV Guide*, June 9. https://www.beyondourcontrol.org/boc4/page29/page77/page77.html.

Thompson, Ethan. 2011. *Parody and Taste in Postwar American Television Culture*. Routledge.

Wellin, Marc. 2022. Interview by author, telephone, March 18.

Werts, Diane. 2022. Interview by author, Mishawaka, Ind., April 1.

Williams, Dave. 1971. "Beyond Our Control—a Junior Achievement Television Program." *Educational Television*, April, 11–14.

———. 1974–75. "Beyond Our Control." *Bolex Reporter* 24 (1). https://www.beyondourcontrol.org/boc4/page29/page95/page95.html.

PART III

AMPLIFYING COMMUNITY VOICES THROUGH LOCAL TELEVISION

CHAPTER 11

HELEN MORGAN PARMETT

PLACEMAKING AND COMMUNITY ACCESS MEDIA IN VERMONT

HISTORIES, ARCHIVES, AND ACTIVISM

In the run-up to Bernie Sanders's 2020 bid for the democratic presidential nomination, the national media discovered the archives of the 1980s public access television program *Bernie Speaks with the Community*. In the program, Bernie, then the socialist mayor of Burlington, Vermont, goes on location to talk to the people of Burlington. Chittenden County Television (CCTV), the local cable access channel that produced the show and holds its archives, had started digitizing the program in the mid-2000s and put in an effort to digitize more of the collection after Bernie announced his bid for the 2016 presidential election in recognition that his "celebrity" status would make the archive of interest to a wider public outside Vermont (Meghan O'Rourke, CCTV channel director, personal communication, March 8, 2022). *Politico* paid to digitize the remaining programming, which they called "a bizarre, charming and, at times, startling cable-access TV show," for their article on Bernie (Otterbein 2019). In so doing, a major new media news outlet turned what was otherwise a local and specific public access show into a national enigma. Responses were predictably comedic, holding it up as another example of the quirky oddities of memeable Bernie, Vermont, and public access TV—a trifecta of a political culture from what appeared to be a bygone era. But *Bernie Speaks* is also more than this. It embodies a specific local media culture and the social and cultural geography of Vermont; those specificities get lost when the program is extracted from that context.

This chapter elucidates this context by providing a cultural history of community access media (CAM) in Chittenden County, Vermont. I consider how CAM constitutes placemaking in Vermont and especially how it intervened in struggles over locality in symbolic, practical, and material terms in the 1980s and 1990s as CAM took shape. Drawing on archival research conducted at CCTV alongside interviews with community media activists and TV producers, I trace that history of CAM activism, demonstrating how Vermont's social and cultural geography, including the production of Vermont as a rural and pastoral place of escape in the American cultural imaginary and the "hippie influx" of the 1960s and 1970s, contributed to its site-specific community media culture. I show how those conditions gave rise to *Bernie Speaks*. I then turn to consider how this history comes to bear on Vermont CAM's present-day struggles to maintain relevance and financial sustainability. This chapter thus contributes to existing research on local media by demonstrating how CAM not only serves community but is bound up with the constitution of (and struggle over) community and the production of place and locality. Exploring the relationship between CAM and place, I articulate their site-specific, historical, and contemporary roles in the production of locality in the context of Vermont's rich history of CAM.

CAM AND PLACEMAKING

CAM is intertwined with place. Early CAM advocacy began in major cities, including New York, Chicago, and Boston, though significant activism for cable access, rarely explored in the scholarship, emerged in areas outside urban centers long underserved by legacy media, including Vermont. As Higgins (1999) notes, "U.S. public access was influenced by social and media activists, video artists, and the 'counterculture' of the late 1960s and early 1970s. These joined an unlikely coalition of groups from business, academic and government circles to promote cable television and public access" (624). CAM outlets are tasked with serving their local communities. That duty stems from their relationship to institutions and infrastructures of broadcasting and cable that define service responsibility in terms of geographical communities (Huntsberger 2020). But CAM does not only serve communities; CAM constitutes community and a sense of place. Community media centers are material places where those involved in media production make community through participation in production, and these practices and resulting content play a role in struggling over who and what a place represents and how it is practiced (Ali 2014; Dewey 2021). Notably, these outlets provide opportunities for marginalized peoples underrepresented in legacy media, including local media, to make media and be represented in ways that can foster agency and counter dominant modes of production and representation as they stake a claim to their inclusion in the local (e.g., Ali 2014; Herold 2021; Howell 2017; Howley 2005; King and Mele 1999; Linder 1999; Schooler 2018).

As Ali (2014) argues, these practices of struggling over the local speak to "the importance of place, bodies and practice" in CAM (72). As CAM scholarship on place demonstrates, CAM histories and cultures are both shared and site specific. CAM are shaped by broader social, cultural, and material geographies as well as media policy and infrastructures, but CAM are also tied to the local conditions in which those infrastructures are emplaced (Ali 2014; Dewey 2021; Howell 2017; McMurria 2017). Yet the majority of cable access research tends to the specific conditions of the nation's urban centers. Much cable access history risks being lost due to the antiquated technologies on which programs were recorded and the aging of people involved in their production (Herold 2021). A lack of investment and interest in more peripheral cable access outlets puts them at further risk, making it ever more pressing to preserve those histories. Thus, in the remainder of this chapter, I excavate some of that history in the context of Vermont, building on scholarship on CAM and place in addition to research that has considered public access activism in more rural areas of New England, including Davies's (2020) analysis of cable access advocacy efforts in Maine and King and Mele's (1999) research on Cape Cod Community Television. Although neither explore issues of place and placemaking explicitly, both gesture to how the more rural and peripheral geographies of these access outlets distinguished them from urban CAM, particularly in how they defined and constituted the local. In Maine, for example, Davies shows how CAM advocates drew on residents' sense of systemic economic disinvestment because of its rurality and their resultingly "fiercely independent" mindset to garner public support for CAM. Similarly, as I discuss below, it is the site-specific cultural, economic, and political forces as they are tied to Vermont's social and cultural geography and its role in the American cultural imaginary that helped to shape the history and practice of CAM in Chittenden County, Vermont.

PASTORALIZING VERMONT AND THE "HIPPIE INFLUX"

Vermont has a strong brand identity protected by the state legislature. The production of "Vermont" is rooted in a long history of efforts by state officials to "sell" Vermont to residents, tourists, and newcomers in the wake of the state's waning agricultural economy and declining population since the late 1800s (Rebek 1976). Visual media, especially photography and print magazines like *Vermont Life*, were central in constituting and selling the image of Vermont as a pastoral, pristine, and idyllic place seemingly untouched by the chaos, danger, and grime of modern, urban, industrial life (Rebek 1976; Harrison 2006). This representation of Vermont through a tourist gaze (Urry 2009) figured the state as a unique place to which one could escape. These representations are bound up with ideals of the rural as a place of "community," a fraught discourse that often idealizes a nostalgic romanticization of an essentialized communal identity counterposed to an Other from whom the community must be protected (Butchart 2010). As Vanderbeck (2006, 641) notes, despite discourses of Vermont's "progressivism" that position the state "as a place where 'race is of little significance,'" the production of Vermont as a pristine rural opposite of urban decay is inextricably linked to whiteness.

Representations of Vermont thus generally romanticize the pastoral in ways that evacuate the state's histories of political struggle and inequities, including racial and class struggles over migrant farmworkers rights within the languishing agricultural sector on which its pastoral image lies. So too the representation of Vermont as a rural place belies divisions within the state between its more rural and urban spaces, and especially the state's vast class divides, which are not easily mapped onto rural/urban but rather reflect the effects of migration into the state by so-called flatlanders or "out of staters," from areas of suburbanizing and urbanized New England and elsewhere, and the struggles over gentrification this migration has precipitated in both rural and urban Vermont. Those tensions were acutely felt during the first two years of the COVID-19 pandemic, as city dwellers, desperately looking for more space, bought up property in both rural and urban areas of Vermont, often sight unseen, after which real estate prices rose 38 percent (O'Connor 2021). Undoubtedly, Vermont was attractive to those fleeing the city because of its image as a pristine place of escape.

But this was not the first major influx of migrants drawn in by Vermont's representational taxonomy. In the late 1960s and 1970s,

Vermont experienced a 15 percent population increase as thousands of counterculture activists, or "hippies," migrated to Vermont, often fleeing urban and suburban areas as part of an ethic of getting "back to the land" (Calder and Gustin 2016). The counterculture movement was drawn to the state's pastoral representation in the cultural imaginary as well as to cheap land that could be bought from struggling farmers (Daley 2018). The influx of counterculture activists made an indelible mark on the state's culture, economy, and politics, shifting the consistently Republican state into one of the nation's most liberal strongholds.[1] Thus, Vermont's image as a rural, pastoral space is distinct from other representations of the rural in the American imaginary, such as the Midwest, which are often constructed as provincial and conservative. In contrast, Vermont's image is infused with a sensibility of progressive politics and hip cultural practices more often associated with the urban.

Bernie Sanders, elected as the first self-proclaimed socialist mayor of a U.S. city in 1981 when he won Burlington's election against the multigenerational conservative Vermonter George Paquette, was himself part of the "hippie influx." Seeing a promotional campaign for "cheap land" in Vermont in a subway in Brooklyn first sparked his interest in the state; he was "captivated by the photos of beautiful panoramas and iconic farmhouses" as an alternative to his cramped urban apartment (Daley 2018, 22). Drawn to the image of Vermont that appealed to so many others of his generation, Bernie has now become a part of that representational schema. But like the earlier photos that appear in issues of *Vermont Life*, the reality is more complicated.

CONSTITUTING THE LOCAL: CAM ACTIVISM IN BURLINGTON

It is in this context of Vermont's representation in the cultural imaginary, the hippie influx, and a shifting political landscape in Vermont that both Bernie Sanders and the state's community media activism emerged as central forces in the state. Vermont's and particularly Burlington's and the greater Chittenden County region's history of CAM activism was borne out of these site-specific—and historically specific—forces. CAM's interventions into that imaginary speak to its role in the symbolic, practical, and material struggles over place and Vermonter identity.

Early activism around access media in Vermont can be traced to Goddard College's Community Media Center, which organized advocates, producers, and citizen groups around community media. Goddard, a small liberal arts college outside Montpelier and inspired by the progressive educational philosophy of John Dewey, was heavily influenced by the countercultural influx into the state; its enrollment swelled with students and faculty "disillusioned with traditional structures and lifestyle" and drawn to its educational philosophy and location in pastoral Vermont ("About Goddard" n.d.). Goddard hosted the Alternative Media Conference in 1970, a gathering of over two thousand radio and music professionals along with activists and artists that aimed to forge "connections between people who were interested in civil rights, environmental, anti-war, 'anti-Establishment,' anti-Mainstream media" (Faber and Hochheimer 2016, 203). Faber and Hochheimer note the conference resulted from converging forces, including the antiwar and civil rights movements and their influence on media policy and the rise of underground/alternative media. But the conference was precipitated by local forces as well, including the countercultural influx into Vermont.

Though the Community Media Center disbanded in the late 1970s, alternative media activism remained ingrained in the state, including activism centered on public access. The state's first public access channel was established in 1982 in Brattleboro, a small town in southern Vermont that had a contract to record town council meetings (Davitian 1987). Shortly thereafter, access channels began popping up in other Vermont localities, including St. Johnsbury and Bellows Falls. In Chittenden County, which includes Burlington (the state's largest city), community media activism was part of the activist fervor taking hold amid Bernie's election to mayor, or what Lauren-Glenn Davitian, one of the state's early public access advocates and longtime executive director of CCTV, called the "Bernie zeitgeist" (personal communication, February 3, 2022). That zeitgeist both centered on Bernie and exceeded him, as it was linked to the longer history of countercultural movement in the state. Bernie was a part of what Davitian calls the "progressive miracle" taking place in Burlington, driven by the changing dynamics of the city in the wake of aging hippies who turned to wield their power in the political realm (Daley 2018).

Davitian, who along with Nat Ayers started CCTV, the first cable access channel in Chittenden County, worked in Bernie Sanders's office in the 1980s. She became interested in public access after studying social documentary abroad and learning about John Grierson's and George Stoney's Challenge for Change program, a Canadian alternative film and video project. Davitian connected with public access advocates in New York and Boston and was determined to start a public access channel in Burlington. She went to the local cable company asking for a camera. Initially oblivious, they showed her to a closet with some ancient equipment. "At that moment," Davitian claims, "I went from becoming a documentary filmmaker to an organizer because I realized that the only way to get my hands on the means of production and distribution was to organize" (personal communication, February 3, 2022). At this time, in 1984, Nat Ayers was doing video work for Bernie Sanders, filming him at fundraisers and around town, and a friend suggested they put the videos on TV. Ayers connected with Davitian, relating that she "wanted to start a channel in Burlington.... But I was the one who had the camera. So we started doing more and more together" (Marcel 2019). The two set out to start a public access channel in Burlington, putting up flyers around town and inviting residents to public forums to drum up support.

But creating a viable public access channel would require more than public support and community interest; they would have to take their case to the Public Service Board (PSB), responsible for regulating cable television service, to fight the cable company and ensure they were accorded the equipment, funding, and services the federal legislation required. They connected with Samuel Press, a local lawyer who agreed to represent them pro bono to the PSB because he believed in their mission (Samuel Press, personal communication, March 10, 2022). Together, he and Davitian worked to articulate an argument for how public access would serve the local, public interest in Chittenden County and to lobby community stakeholders, such as churches, schools, nonprofits, libraries, and other local media outlets to support the channel for how it could meet their own community-related needs. Davitian also forged into legislative advocacy. Bernie, then Burlington's mayor, asked her to serve on the Mayor's Task Force on Cable Television, which he had formed as part of his effort to start a municipal cable system in Burlington. On the Task Force, Davitian lobbied for city and state backing of public access TV.

A picture of how advocates saw the relationship between public access and the local emerges in the archival documents from the Task Force, CCTV's PSB filings, and documents and ephemera from early CCTV organizing efforts. Similar to other public access advocates, Burlington's advocates viewed public access as an "electronic soapbox" (Linder 1999), or a kind of public sphere for the community. For example, in a 1983 memo for the Task Force, Davitian argued, "Each and every citizen can use the medium of television to say or communicate what she or he wants to say," as public access enables "citizens in the community to produce programs directed at their neighbors and fellow citizens" (CCTV Collection). In a circa 1985 memo titled "What Is Public Access?," Davitian analogized public access to the "hometown newspaper," arguing, "Just as local newspapers supply communities with information of particular interest to their citizens, public access television provides programming unique to the individuals within the service area," but in a noncommercial format (CCTV Collection).

While this discourse of localism and community was similar to broader public access advocacy efforts, Burlington advocates also used rhetorical appeals and organizing strategies specific to the social and cultural geography of Vermont. Because of the state's rural geography, much early organizing emphasized the role public access could play in unifying the county's disparate and dispersed communities. Organizers articulated the appeal of local, public access TV as a response to Vermont's peripheral geography in relation to centers of television production and distribution. Burlington's access advocates emphasized how the state's peripheral location meant the people of Burlington and of Vermont, more generally, were rarely represented on TV or in other forms of national media. As Davitian argued in a circa 1983 "Report of the Task Force on Cable Television," "Many of our evenings are filled with situation comedies written in New York and made in California and broadcast throughout the country. Much of what we know about Burlington comes to us from daily local news broadcasts.... What becomes clear, as we consider television in general, and cable television in particular, is how much it shapes our lives, and how that shaping has gotten beyond our control" (CCTV Collection, 4). Whereas television "has often turned us away from our communities," Davitian argued, through public access, it "now has the capacity to build our communities" (5). Thus, public access was imagined not only as representing existing communities but also as helping to construct them. For Davitian and other access advocates, that constitution of community was made possible through watching local content as well as through producing it, which, she argued, transformed passive television viewers into active citizens (5). Hence, Burlington's access advocates argued that what made public access distinct from other kinds of media was that it was produced by community members themselves, "rather than professional broadcasters or a remote, corporate network" ("What Is Public Access?" 1985, CCTV Collection). Producing video, they argued, "demystifies the electronic media" by providing technical training on video production and visual media literacy, and by helping people see that "programming no longer has to originate far away, created by some anonymous and conglomerate producer with profit as motivation" (CCTV Collection).

This localism discourse responds to FCC broadcasting discourse, which prioritized localities gaining access to national networks as a solution to what was perceived as their provinciality (Morgan Parmett 2016). Those policies constructed the local in relation (and in subordination) to the nation and its urban centers, as problems a national network connection could resolve. Burlington's advocates challenged this logic by arguing public access was a way for peripheral and rural localities to participate in their own production and redefine their relation to the national, and international, realm. As Davitian argued in her 1984 pre-filed testimony to the PSB, "Since 1972, the FCC has recognized that cable television serves more of a purpose than to draw distant signals to a local community. They view cable television as an opportunity to develop 'community information systems' and local programming . . . public access is made possible when the cable provider's implicit commitment to 'community service' is made explicit through a contractual agreement between the cable provider and the community served" (CCTV Collection).[2] Drawing on discourses produced by the FCC, Davitian and other access advocates worked to shape how that discourse defined and understood the local and the service responsibilities of cable companies.

While public access locality was geographically defined by the technological infrastructures and regulatory policies of broadcasting and cable, Burlington's public access advocates also tried to shape those material conditions. Public investment in facilitating cable infrastructure building was one of the reasons cable companies ultimately supported the idea of public access (Streeter 1996). Burlington's access advocates became involved with infrastructural advocacy to support connecting all parts of the county and tried to influence the nature of that connection. Toward these ends, they organized a conference and trade show in 1984, titled "Beyond Broadcast: Communications 1985," described as focusing on "the benefits and drawbacks of telephone, television, and computer services getting wired into Vermont, including issues of access and affordability, deregulation, the role of government policy, costs, and educational and economic goals" (CCTV Collection). The conference featured a public forum titled "Does Vermont Need the Information Age?" and panels such as "Burlington: The Wired City." In numerous archival documents, the infrastructural needs of Chittenden County were emphasized, demonstrating that Burlington's advocates understood that public access was constitutive of community not only in symbolic terms but materially as well. They understood public access advocacy could help connect localities to wider infrastructures of media and communication and that their advocacy could help shape those connections in political, economic, and cultural terms. However, as public access "service areas... conform to the areas served by cable companies" and depend on their infrastructure, "many rural Vermont towns have neither a cable company nor a PEG provider," and that uneven geography persists today in the state's broadband coverage (Bluhm and Loube 2021, 10). Thus, while access advocates in some ways worked to reconstitute the local through altering the spatial dynamics of television production, consumption, and infrastructures in Chittenden County, it has also been constrained by cable's cultural and material infrastructures and spatialities.

THE BIRTH OF *BERNIE SPEAKS*

After Davitian's testimony to the PSB in 1984, the cable company shifted their position on cable access and put out an article in the local newspaper stating they would provide public access in four Vermont communities: Burlington, Middlebury, Montpelier, and Rutland (Davitian, personal communication, February 3, 2022). By June there was still no equipment, but Davitian connected with local photographer and University of Vermont professor Dan Higgins along with Nat Ayer, and they began producing their own content. *Bernie Speaks* would be one of the channel's first programs.

Bernie Speaks arose from the confluence of public access activism taking shape in Burlington as it was caught up in a particular political conjuncture in Vermont. As Davitian notes, "The idea was for Bernie... to go ... and cover the things that were happening. Burlington, this progressive miracle that was concerned... with the wellbeing of low-income people, which no one had really concerned themselves with, or the quality of life and creating new progressive institutions... but also to think about international issues and how we were connected to the international realm" (Davitian, personal communication, February 3, 2022). While national media's discovery of *Bernie Speaks*, such as by *Politico* (Otterbein 2019), figures the show almost exclusively as a testament to Bernie's quirky, leftist/socialist politics, and his hostility to journalists, this coverage misses the important context, including the advocacy around public access, out of which the show emerged.

That context is evident from the first episode, which features an interview between Davitian and Bernie, wherein viewers are educated about public access and invited to participate in CAM production and advocacy ("Introduction to the Series" 1986). Seamlessly, Bernie discusses his desire to be an accessible mayor and to speak directly with the people, which is the heart of the show but also the heart of public access. And, indeed, the media remain a topic of discussion across numerous episodes. Although many of the episodes feature Bernie in his office speaking about a range of issues, dozens include Bernie going on location in the city to speak directly to the community or to situate viewers in the places at stake in the episode topic, such as at the Burlington Waterfront, the senior center, city parks, and the dump. A few episodes featured conferences, such as the "*Vanguard Press's* 10th Anniversary Media Bash" (1988), which celebrated the alternative news outlet's anniversary by inviting activists Abbie Hoffman and Dave Dellinger alongside Sanders to hold a forum critiquing corporate media (including local media). At the end of the episode, Davitian, as an audience member, speaks to conference-goers on behalf of alternative media and public access as a solution to the harms of corporate media and invites the audience to participate in and support CCTV. Another episode featured the Burlington Housing Summit ("Burlington's First Housing Summit" 1987), which brought together dispersed nonprofit groups working on the housing crisis, gentrification, and economic disparity. These episodes demonstrate Bernie was part of a broader conjuncture taking shape in Vermont, in large part influenced by the counterculture movement as hippies turned from living on the land to engaging in politics and helped to entrench progressive institutions in the city.

But perhaps the most compelling episodes, and certainly the most well trafficked, are those where Bernie talks to people on the proverbial street. In the most infamous episode, endlessly chided on social media and pilloried by Trevor Noah on *The Daily Show* for its seeming representation of the oddities of Bernie, Vermont, and 1980s culture, Bernie talks to people at the downtown mall, including a couple of "mall punks" ("Mayor Sanders Sets Up in the Burlington Square Mall" 1988). Although the goth-dressed teens espousing anarchist, anticapitalist politics to the city's frumpy, socialist mayor is certainly remarkable, what strikes me most about this episode is the place itself. Referring to this episode as "positively haunting," Grasso (2020) remarks, "The architecture of the mall can't help but evoke memories of similar shopping centers all across America in viewers of a certain age." But that haunting takes on a different tone when considering the history of *this* mall, which undoubtedly both Bernie and many viewers knew. The mall was the result of an urban renewal project in 1976, made possible by a 1963 project that razed the city's "Little Italy" neighborhood, displacing many from the working-class neighborhood in the name of beautification and removal of blight (Kelley 2016). As Bernie chats up locals in the mall about housing and economic insecurity in this and other locational episodes, *Bernie Speaks* challenged the rural imaginary that haunted Vermont's representation by drawing attention to how wealth, gentrification, and other seemingly "urban" problems (other episodes, for example, addressed drugs, crime, violence) were present in Vermont as well. The locational nature of the series participates in what Dan Higgins, drawing from John Berger, referred to in our interview as "recording" rather than "reporting." Higgins, who did video work for CCTV during this time, notes that recording, which was one of the key aims of their early public access work, "is like a family album where [the] picture, stays in your album, and people know the story and they... can fill it in" (personal communication, February 10, 2022). But once that story is extracted from the place, it transforms and becomes something different. This is precisely what happened with the "mall punks" and *Bernie Speaks* as it has been taken up by national media, discarding the contexts out of which they emerged.

These examples and other episodes from *Bernie Speaks* are an embodiment of the progressive politics that emerged out of the countercultural movement and the "hippie influx," including the movement for public access. Burlington's advocates were invested in discourses and practices of local public access that were explicitly linked up to social change, challenging dominant media, and holding cable companies accountable for serving the community. In so doing, cable access participated in struggles over the local and worked to reconstitute Vermonter identity and locality in Chittenden County not only through its content but also through practices of production, infrastructural interventions into cable's material geography, and advocacy efforts of access activists.

CONCLUSION: CAM PLACEMAKING BEYOND CABLE

Bernie Speaks is testament to the specific historical and cultural contexts of Vermont and Chittenden County's struggles over locality and CAM. However, while *Bernie Speaks* has made it into the national mediascape because of Bernie's relative celebrity, the vast archives of CCTV's other shows are unlikely to ever get the kind of recognition accorded to *Bernie Speaks*. Undoubtedly the marginality of many CAM producers and the consequentially related distaste for public access as "low-brow" culture unworthy of critical attention is likely to blame. Countless programs remain undigitized or even lost, and with them the broader histories of locality and the ways in which place is constituted and struggled over remain opaque.

That opacity is further exacerbated by the threats to CAM in the status quo. CAM receive the bulk of their funding through cable companies that set aside equipment, space, and funding for PEG programming in exchange for their license to operate in the community. In the wake of digitization, streaming, and cord-cutting, that funding is under threat, as cable companies claim their uncertain economic future means they can no longer afford to fund these outlets. Further, cable companies argue social media platforms like YouTube obviate the need for PEG, since anyone with a cell phone can now produce and distribute their own media content. While CAM centers have responded to these technological and cultural changes in various ways, including moving content online and emphasizing their role in production training and media literacy, their overarching claim to relevance is their connection to place—unlike these other outlets, CAM is made in and responds to the conditions of a specific social and geographical locality (Ali 2014; Dewey 2021).

Vermont has not been as hard hit by these shifting conditions as other localities, as the state's aging population and lack of access to broadband have forestalled dramatic cord-cutting (Jess Wilson, codirector of the Media Factory, personal communication, April 13, 2022). Still, the state's CAM centers understand they need to prepare for a future that is not dependent on the 5 percent franchise fee, and they have thus taken on multiple strategies to prepare, including diversifying revenue, operating like a more traditional nonprofit (including fundraising), merging to share costs, and emphasizing the role of the center in multimedia production skills and media literacy (Wilson, personal communication). But for Vermont access advocates, the overwhelming emphasis has been on viewing CAM in terms of the production of social change, and at the center of that view is legislative advocacy. Davitian argues, "Cable access TV is not the main thing we do. Connecting people with media as a tool for social change—that's what we do. And, so, it could be cable TV, or it could be the internet or . . . whatever is available at the time. Cause it's all going to change. But the main thing underneath, for me, is that unless the regulatory arena, the regulatory framework supports public benefits like PEG access or universal service . . . you have got to be working . . . in that realm too" (personal communication, February 3, 2022). Thus, Burlington's public access advocates continue to attend to media policy at national, state, and municipal levels. Due in large part to the early advocacy efforts of CAM activists, Vermont has some of the strongest CAM regulations in the nation (Bluhm and Loube 2021, 6–7). The regulatory climate in Vermont has made it possible for CAM to thrive in the state, with twenty-five access media organizations (AMOs) that produce on average over seventeen thousand hours of programming per year (8). And Vermonters are overwhelmingly supportive of CAM, with 72 percent reporting they've watched a public access channel and 52 percent reporting they think public access is "very important" and 31 percent "moderately important" (Vermont Department of Public Service 2018).

The state's largely rural geography has driven home the importance of CAM to Vermont legislators especially amid moments of crises, such as during the devastating effects of Hurricane Irene in 2011 and the COVID-19 pandemic in 2020, when they were some of the only sources of local information and connection for Vermonters. Amid the pandemic, the state commissioned a report on PEG access (Bluhm and Loube 2021) to provide solutions to the cable funding crisis, and the legislature utilized COVID-19 relief funds as short-term bridge funding through 2023. As Jess Wilson, codirector of Chittenden County's public access outlet the Media Factory, noted in our interview (April 13, 2022), though, bridge funding from the legislature is not sustainable, and so CAM advocates across the state continue to push for a longer term solution at state and federal levels while also seeking ways to diversify revenue. Arguably, the archiving of these older materials from programs like *Bernie Speaks* is one of those avenues for maintaining a revenue stream while also gaining new interest and new audiences.

As I've argued in this chapter, Vermont plays a unique role in the American cultural imaginary, one that is always already marked by a kind of nostalgic attachment and constituted through a tourist lens that often imagines it as a rural, pastoral landscape, frozen in the past of its agricultural glory. The archives I've considered here are themselves the results of that nostalgic attachment, as they were produced out of and in response to this unique context of nostalgic productions of Vermont as a pastoral place of escape. When they were produced, they intervened into and struggled over that image and practice of Vermont, troubling and reconstituting place in new ways. But as archives, they are also objects of that attachment as well, as their digitization and archiving make them newly available and subject to being taken up in ways that position them along this trajectory of a nostalgic imagination of Vermont.

Public access archives are especially interesting sites of nostalgia, as their often grainy, DIY aesthetic quality materially bears the time in which they were made and notes the time that has passed (Howell 2017). Because of this aesthetic quality, there is a danger to that nostalgia that risks public access archives being taken up as stylized commodities in ways that evacuate them of their histories of political struggle (Jameson 1992). But nostalgia is not only about time, a regressive longing for an imagined better past, or about the objects that signify that past. Nostalgia, in its original formulation, was tied to place, and a longing for home (Boym 2001). Local TV and CAM bear those marks of not only times but places past, such as Bernie in the mall that is currently a pit in the center of Burlington. Considering CAM in terms of placemaking and as an intervention in the struggle over locality, as I've done throughout this chapter, suggests these nostalgic attachments to place and their histories perhaps also open a potential for politicization. Nostalgic attachments to place via CAM can draw attention to urban and rural changes, gentrification, and disinvestment; struggles over who gets to lay claim to a place; and the roles media culture and ownership play in that struggle.

NOTES

1. As Daley (2018, 21) notes, although many other cities across the United States experienced a similar migration of counterculture activists, these are cities rather than states and are urban rather than rural; no other state was as impacted as Vermont. Most settled in Chittenden County, the state's most urban area (Calder and Gustin 2016). The county is diverse in scale, including a small urban center, suburbs, and vast areas of rural farmland. The "hippie influx" sparked tension in the state, precipitating continued cultural and class divides between multigenerational/native Vermonters and migrants, so-called flatlanders.

2. Here, I am distinguishing between peripheral and rural in that peripheral locations are near to urban centers (Burlington is approximately an hour and a half from Montreal and three hours from Boston), but they are peripheral to them and also have a more rural geography. Not all rural spaces are peripheral in this way, as some have no peripheral location to urban centers because they are so distant.

REFERENCES

"About Goddard." n.d. *Goddard College* (blog). Accessed April 20, 2022. https://www.goddard.edu/about-goddard/.

Ahmed, Sara. 2004. *The Cultural Politics of Emotion*. Edinburgh: Edinburgh University Press.

Ali, Christopher. 2014. "The Last PEG or Community Media 2.0? Negotiating Place and Placelessness at PhillyCAM." *Media, Culture & Society* 36 (1): 69–86. https://doi.org/10.1177/0163443713507815.

Berlant, Lauren, and Michael Warner. 1998. "Sex in Public." *Critical Inquiry* 24 (2): 547–66.

Bluhm, Peter, and Robert Loube. 2021. "Analysis of the Financial Viability for Public, Educational and Government Access Television in Vermont." Berkshire Telecommunications Consulting, Submitted to Vermont Agency of Commerce and Community Development. https://legislature.vermont.gov/assets/Legislative-Reports/Report-2021-02-07.docx.pdf.

Boym, Svetlana. 2001. *The Future of Nostalgia*. Basic Books.

"Burlington's First Housing Summit." 1987. *Bernie Speaks with the Community*, May 6. CCTV Center for Media and Democracy. https://www.cctv.org/watch-tv/programs/24-burlingtons-first-housing-summit.

Butchart, Garnet C. 2010. "The Exceptional Community: On Strangers, Foreigners, and Communication." *Communication, Culture & Critique* 3 (1): 21–25. https://doi.org/10.1111/j.1753-9137.2009.01055.x.

Calder, Jackie, and Amanda Gustin. 2016. "Counterculture in 1970s Vermont: The 1970s Brought an Influx of Young Newcomers with New Ideas to the Green Mountains." *Vermont History*, Winter, 94–102.

Caterino, Brian. 2020. *The Decline of Public Access and Neoliberal Media Regimes*. Palgrave Macmillan.

CCTV Collection. CCTV Center for Media and Democracy, Archival Collection, Burlington, Vt.

Daley, Yvonne. 2018. *Going Up the Country: When the Hippies, Dreamers, Freaks, and Radicals Moved to Vermont*. University Press of New England.

D'Auria, Peter. 2022. "Killing of Transgender Woman in Vermont Draws Condemnation, Grief." *VTDigger*, April 13. https://vtdigger.org/2022/04/13/killing-of-transgender-woman-in-vermont-draws-condemnation-grief/.

Davies, Lyell. 2020. "Civic Activism for Community Access Television in the US State of Maine." *Journal of Alternative & Community Media* 5 (2): 135–52. https://doi.org/10.1386/joacm_00080_1.

Davitian, Lauren-Glenn. 1987. "Building the Empire: Access as Community Animation." *Journal of Film and Video* 39 (3): 35–39. http://www.jstor.org/stable/20687781.

Dewey, Matthew. 2021. "Anyone Can Do YouTube, but Not Everyone Can Do Public Access: Urban Politics, Production Tools, and a Communications Infrastructure to Call Home." *Television & New Media* 22 (7): 779–98. https://doi.org/10.1177/1527476420928462.

Duffort, Lola. 2022. "Vermont GOP Officials Double Down on Anti-Trans Line of Attack." *VTDigger*, April 11. https://vtdigger.org/2022/04/11/vermont-gop-officials-double-down-on-anti-trans-line-of-attack/.

Faber, Liz W., and John L. Hochheimer. 2016. "Networking the Counterculture: The 1970 Alternative Media Conference at Goddard College." *Journal of Radio & Audio Media* 23 (2): 200–212. https://doi.org/10.1080/19376529.2016.1223960.

Grasso, Michael. 2020. "The Hauntological President: Citizen Media, Analog Memory, and Bernie Sanders." *We Are the Mutants* (blog), February 12. https://wearethemutants.com/2020/02/12/the-hauntological-president-citizen-media-analog-memory-and-bernie-sanders/.

Hanson, Alex. 2022. "At 150th Tunbridge World's Fair, Despite Change, Much Has Stayed the Same." *Valley News*, September 17. https://www.vnews.com/Tunbridge-Worlds-Fair-150th-anniversary-vt-48054686.

Harrison, Blake A. 2006. *The View from Vermont: Tourism and the Making of an American Rural Landscape*. University of Vermont Press.

Herold, Lauren. 2021. "Cable Comes Out: LGBTQ Community Television on New York Public Access Stations." Ph.D. diss., Northwestern University.

Higgins, John W. 1999. "Community Television and the Vision of Media Literacy, Social Action, and Empowerment." *Journal of Broadcasting & Electronic Media* 43 (4): 624–44. https://doi.org/10.1080/08838159909364513.

Howell, Charlotte E. 2017. "Symbolic Capital and the Production Discourse of *The American Music Show*: A Microhistory of Atlanta Cable Access." *Cinema Journal* 57 (1): 1–24. https://doi.org/10.1353/cj.2017.0053.

Howley, Kevin. 2005. "Manhattan Neighborhood Network: Community Access Television and the Public Sphere in the 1990s." *Historical Journal of Film, Radio and Television* 25 (1): 119–38. https://doi.org/10.1080/01439680500065402.

Huntsberger, Michael W. 2020. "Community Media in the United States: Fostering Pluralism and Inclusivity in Challenging Times." *Interactions: Studies in Communication & Culture* 11 (2): 191–205. https://doi.org/10.1386/iscc_00018_1.

"Introduction to the Series and City Issues." 1986. *Bernie Speaks with the Community*, December 3. CCTV Center for Media and Democracy. https://www.cctv.org/watch-tv/programs/1-introduction-series-and-city-issues.

Jameson, Fredric. 1992. *Postmodernism; or, The Cultural Logic of Late Capitalism*. Duke University Press.

Kelley, Kevin J. 2016. "Before Burlington's Proposed Mall Makeover, They Called It 'Urban Renewal.'" *Seven Days*, May 25. https://www.sevendaysvt.com/vermont/before-burlington-town-centers-proposed-makeover-they-called-it-urban-renewal/Content?oid=3377522.

King, Donna L., and Christopher Mele. 1999. "Making Public Access Television: Community Participation, Media Literacy and the Public Sphere." *Journal of Broadcasting & Electronic Media* 43 (4): 603–23. https://doi.org/10.1080/08838159909364512.

Kirste, Lynne. 2007. "Collective Effort: Archiving LGBT Moving Images." *Cinema Journal* 46 (3): 134–40.

Linder, Laura R. 1999. *Public Access Television: America's Electronic Soapbox*. Praeger.

Marcel, Joyce. 2019. "Lauren-Glenn Davitian: Free Speech Is Her Business." *Vermont Business Magazine*, July 21. https://vermontbiz.com/news/2019/july/21/lauren-glenn-davitian-free-speech-her-business.

"Mayor Sanders Sets Up in the Burlington Square Mall to Speak with Passers-By." 1988. *Bernie Speaks with the Community*, March 5. CCTV Center for Media and Democracy. https://www.cctv.org/watch-tv/programs/41-mayor-sanders-sets-burlington-square-mall-speak-passers.

McMurria, John. 2017. *Republic on the Wire Cable Television, Pluralism, and the Politics of New Technologies, 1948–1984*. Rutgers University Press.

Morgan Parmett, Helen. 2016. "KVOS in the Local, Public Interest: Early Broadcasting and the Constitution of the Local." *Journal of Radio & Audio Media* 23 (1): 95–108. https://doi.org/10.1080/19376529.2016.1155992.

Nakayama, Thomas K., and Charles E. Morris. 2015. "Worldmaking and Everyday Interventions." *QED: A Journal in GLBTQ Worldmaking* 2 (1): v–viii. https://doi.org/10.14321/qed.2.1.000v.

Niemeyer, Katharina, ed. 2014. *Media and Nostalgia: Yearning for the Past, Present and Future*. Palgrave Macmillan.

Ober, Lauren. 2010. "Faerie Tale: A Radical Faerie Sanctuary in Southern Vermont Practices a Different Kind of Camp." *Seven Days*, July 21. https://www.sevendaysvt.com/vermont/faerie-tale/Content?oid=2140912.

O'Connor, Kevin. 2021. "Covid-19 'Newcomers' Find Challenges in Moving to Vermont." *VTDigger*, May 16. https://vtdigger.org/2021/05/16/covid-19-newcomers-find-challenges-in-moving-to-vermont/.

Otterbein, Holly. 2019. "'Anyone Ever Seen Cocaine?' What We Found in the Archives of Bernie Sanders' Long-Lost TV Show." *Politico Magazine*, May 3. https://www.politico.com/magazine/story/2019/05/03/bernie-sanders-burlington-tv-show-video-2020-226761/.

Raphael, Rina. 2019. "Why Doesn't Anyone Want to Live in This Perfect Place?" *New York Times*, August 24. https://www.nytimes.com/2019/08/24/style/womyns-land-movement-lesbian-communities.html.

Rebek, Andrea. 1976. "The Selling of Vermont: From Agriculture to Tourism, 1860–1910." *Vermont History* 44 (1): 14–27.

"Rev. Yolanda—Bio." n.d. Accessed April 20, 2022. https://yolanda.net/bio.

"Ric Kadour, Periwinkle." 1998. *Cherie & Yolanda LIVE!* Media Factory. https://www.mediafactory.org/cherie-yolanda.

Schooler, Larry. 2018. "You're on the Air! How Government Access Television Enhances Public Engagement." *National Civic Review* 107 (1): 31–35. https://doi.org/10.1002/ncr.21358.

Streeter, Thomas. 1996. *Selling the Air: A Critique of the Policy of Commercial Broadcasting in the United States.* University of Chicago Press.

Urry, John. 2009. *The Tourist Gaze: Leisure and Travel in Contemporary Societies.* SAGE.

Vanderbeck, Robert M. 2006. "Vermont and the Imaginative Geographies of American Whiteness." *Annals of the Association of American Geographers* 96 (3): 641–59. https://doi.org/10.1111/j.1467-8306.2006.00710.x.

"Vanguard Press's 10th Anniversary Media Bash." 2011. *Bernie Speaks with the Community*, February 17. CCTV Center for Media and Democracy. https://www.cctv.org/watch-tv/programs/vanguard-presss-10th-anniversary-media-bash-hoffman-dellinger-and-sanders.

Vermont Department of Public Service. 2018. "2018 Vermont Telecommunications Plan." https://publicservice.vermont.gov/sites/dps/files/documents/2018%20Telecommunications%20Plan_0.pdf.

CHAPTER 12

DAPHNE GERSHON

MINORITY MEDIA FOR THE MAJORITY

THE SURVIVAL STRATEGIES OF THE MILWAUKEE GAY/LESBIAN CABLE NETWORK (1986–1994)

The affordances of the digital media landscape have provided queer creators with unprecedented opportunities to finance, produce, and distribute televisual content for and about their communities. Yet to fully comprehend the innovation the internet holds for LGBTQ television and the promise of streaming platforms such as REVRY (2016–present), Dekkoo (2015–present), TysonPlus (2014–present), and OTV | Open Television (2015–present), it is essential that we understand how these advancements relate to endeavors from decades prior, such as ones found in local, alternative, and independent television. Public access television, for example, has been a vital yet frequently overlooked part of LGBTQ media history and local media production (Herold 2021; Howell 2017; Howley 2009). To help shed light on the historic value of public access television for the gay community and other marginalized groups excluded from commercial national media, this chapter explores the operations of the groundbreaking Milwaukee Gay/Lesbian Cable Network (MGLCN), which aired from 1986 to 1994 on Milwaukee's public access cable channel 14. During its operations, the network produced numerous specials as well as three regular series, *Tri-Cable Tonight* (1987–89), *The New Tri-Cable Tonight* (1990–92), and *Yellow on Thursday* (1990). Active during the first decade of the AIDS crisis, the network enabled the local gay community to have control over its own media representation at a time when it was facing substantial hate, ignorance, and fear. As one of the very few organizations at the time to air exclusively gay content on television, MGLCN serves as an illuminating example of local noncommercial programming that contributes to our understanding of how minorities have utilized media to enter the local public sphere. Moreover, the network's strategies for survival provide important insights regarding the struggles queer creators continue to face as they attempt to produce content that is sustainable and financially viable while also sensitive to their community's needs. Drawing on archival research of the network's internal documents and a textual analysis of forty-eight episodes produced by the network, I argue that while MGLCN attempted to create content devoted to and created by the local gay community, its operations and programming were largely defined by its objective to garner the support and approval of straight midwesterners. The objective to broaden the network's appeal to non-gay viewers and organizations was expressed in MGLCN's three key strategies: (1) to broadcast quality rather than salacious content, (2) to present a positive and normative image of gay life, and (3) to create ties with other marginalized groups. These strategies, designed to advance the standing of the gay community and to ensure the network's survival, both contributed to and confined MGLCN's revolutionary potential, presenting a humanizing, multidimensional, politically conscious, and intersectional portrayal of the gay community that simultaneously silenced certain queer groups and subcultures, such as drag queens, transgender people, bisexuals, members of the leather/BDSM scene, sex workers, and political radicals.

By examining the network's objectives and constraints, this chapter deepens our understanding of the political and social potential of this form of community media and its limitations. Furthermore, it provides the opportunity to recover and expand the history of queer television beyond the confines of the entertainment hubs of New York City and Los Angeles. The story of MGLCN is largely shaped by the history of the state of Wisconsin and the resources of the city of Milwaukee, demonstrating how public access television, similar to many other forms of community media, is "intricately tied to the notion of place" (Ali 2012, 1122).

In 1986, members of the gay community in Milwaukee, proud to live in the first and only state to ban discrimination based on sexual orientation, were facing new threats to their rights and freedoms. The continued AIDS crisis led to mounting discrimination; both local and national media were either largely dismissive or hostile toward gay people and their struggles. Additionally, in November 1986, Governor Tony Earl, a longtime supporter of gay rights and the gay community, lost his seat to Tommy Thompson, known for his anti-gay platform and his call to abolish the Council on Lesbian and Gay Issues that Earl appointed during his time in office (InStep 1986). Thompson's declaration quickly led the members of the council, among them Mark Behar, who would later become one of the founding members of MGLCN, to resign in protest. Rather than cower, the community seemed to galvanize: local gay magazines and newspapers urged the community to come together and fight (InStep 1986). It is within this context that MGLCN was born. The network was headed by executive producers Mark Behar and Bryce Clark, with gay activist Mike Lisowski also serving a central role within the production management team (*CCF Newsletter* 1987). Throughout its run, fifty volunteers were active within the network, working as members of the production crew and/or as regular on-air guests and hosts (CCF n.d.).

In addition to the tireless work of regular volunteers, the network was founded and able to continue its operations largely due to two local organizations, the Cream City Foundation (CCF) and the Milwaukee Access Telecommunications Authority (MATA). CCF, which was Wisconsin's sole charitable organization for gay causes and initiatives, received considerable donations from a fundraising event during 1986 that were used to help launch the network's first and longest running program, *Tri-Cable Tonight*, a show that established the identity of MGLCN as a network. In the following three years, CCF continued to provide the majority of the funding for the network and helped to promote it (CCF n.d.; CCF Records 1982–2001). MATA, a 501(c)(3) nonprofit and independent public service corporation established in 1985, was equally essential to MGLCN's operations, providing valuable production training and access to equipment and facilities (CCF Records 1982–2001). With the help of these organizations, members of MGLCN were able to produce 106 episodes of specials and regular programming, all centered on gay issues and designed to provide a platform for local gay activists, organizations, and initiatives.

CCF and MATA not only made the network possible but also played a pivotal role in shaping its vision and survival strategies. Throughout this chapter, I demonstrate how the network aimed to gain legitimacy, secure its sustainability, increase funding, and advance the standing of the local gay community by aspiring to reach non-gay viewers. I show how this objective, exhibited through the network's three strategies detailed in the following sections, both contributed to and confined MGLCN's revolutionary potential, motivating the network to create groundbreaking programming that was informative, counter-stereotypical, and racially conscious, yet that simultaneously adhered to a homonormative respectability politics that created a hierarchy of visibility within the local LGBTQ community.

QUALITY CONTROL

The accomplishments of MGLCN were groundbreaking, not only since it produced television content created by and for the gay community but because it provided informative and political programming that showcased and encouraged civic engagement. Such an achievement has even eluded commercial cable networks aimed at gay people that emerged decades later, such as PrideVision (2001–4) and Logo TV (2005–present), whose business models have relied predominantly on depoliticized shows anchored in consumption, lifestyle, and interpersonal relationships (Freitas 2007).

MGLCN's substantive content exemplified its commitment to air "quality" programming, an approach that was designed to help ensure the network's longevity and survival. Given the network's limited funding, inexperienced crew, and sparse studio set, MGLCN was not known for its stylistic and technical standards. Rather than establishing its quality status through its production value, a common metric within media industries (Christian 2019), it solidified its quality through comprehensive coverage of gay issues. MGLCN seemed to primarily link notions of quality to serious, politically and socially conscious programming that also exemplified sexual respectability, veering from content that might be associated with indecency, vulgarity, and sexual explicitness. This strategy, which emphasized traditional news reporting, encouraged the production of valuable content, yet simultaneously prioritized a politics of respectability, which limited the range of gay life it could represent on screen.

Throughout its run, MGLCN aired special programming that featured a variety of political content, including footage of charity benefits and theater productions designed to raise AIDS awareness, forums addressing regional races and politicians' stances on gay issues, and meetings of gay organizations such as the Cream City Business Association, the Lambda Rights Network, and the National Association of Black and White Men Together.[1] To cover these events, the network also sent reporters to ask hard-hitting questions to their leaders and attendees. As co–executive producer Mark Behar commented in an interview to the

Advocate, "When the Surgeon General hosted a press conference on AIDS, our reporters asked pointed questions of interest to the gay community—in front of our city's timid press corps" (Walter 1988).

The network's interest in "quality" news was evident in its regular programming, most notably in *Tri-Cable Tonight*. One CCF press release read, "Far from being a 'talk-talk' show, the program within thirty minutes covers literally every important issue for the community in a sophisticated, urbane and often witty manner" (CCF Records 1982–2001). The magazine-style program, which featured six to seven segments in each episode, included in-studio news reporting, interviews, field segments, and discussion panels on numerous topics, such as hate crimes, influential court cases, relevant legislation, and momentous events (CCF n.d.; MGLCN Records 1987–94). It also provided practical information regarding local health services and resources, primarily about HIV, and legal advice tailored specifically to the gay community on topics such as parental rights and housing. It featured multiple segments relating to sports, art, and culture and a regular segment about gay history narrated by Terry Boughner, a former history professor and the editor of an LGBT newspaper in Milwaukee (MGLCN Records 1987–94).

The network attempted to raise its "national exposure and prestige" by entering in numerous competitions, which its members hoped would solidify and legitimize the network and help it to gain additional support (CCF Records 1982–2001). MGLCN received accolades both from gay groups, such as the Cream City Business Association and the Gay and Lesbian Press Association, and from non-gay media organizations, earning multiple local awards from MATA. Moreover, it won the Hometown USA Video Festival Award in 1989 for *Tri-Cable Tonight*, marking the first time a gay and lesbian cable TV show won the prestigious award (CCF n.d.). In part, MGLCN was lauded for acting as an accessible source of information for the general population, covering important topics about the gay community in a manner that did not presuppose an existing body of knowledge. In 1989, Time Warner's Channel 14 honored the MGLCN's production team with the Paulo Freire Award for their "continued success of teaching others about the gay and lesbian community" (MGLCN Records 1987–94). Thus, the ability of the network to be rewarded and to gain recognition as a network that produced quality programming was greatly influenced by the approval of straight audiences and the network's efforts to make its content accessible to said audiences.

The network's decision to maintain high standards for the content produced was meant to help keep the network on the air and to broaden its audience. A letter between the CCF and the network regarding *Tri-Cable Tonight* stated, "The Foundation and the Network have primarily their public images as assets. Therefore, it is agreed that program content will be in good taste so as not to hurt the public's perception of either organization" (CCF Records 1982–2001). CCF and MGLCN's concerns about public perceptions were deeply tied to desires to minimize potential outrage and critique from straight audiences, as evident by a CCF press release for *Tri-Cable Tonight*, which proclaimed "the quality is so high, it will be difficult for the 'straight' community to find it offensive" (CCF Records 1982–2001). While more controversial public access shows, such San Francisco's *Electric City*, which regularly featured drag queens and members of the leather community (Johnson and Keith 2014), faced homophobic attacks that involved the robbery of its equipment (MGLCN Records 1987–94), MGLCN believed that its quality could serve as a protective shield and help keep it on the air. A *CCF Newsletter* from 1988 states, "By qualifying as a regular series, Warner Cable is flatly saying that they aren't afraid to have Gay/Lesbian programming on the cable waves. And further that this series is of such high quality that it deserves a chance to find an audience by having regular times for showing the program."

Devoting resources to create "tasteful" programming was also meant to expand MGLCN's visibility and audience. The heads of the network used the caliber and tastefulness of their content to persuade other local stations to air the network's programming and assuage the possible reservations of these local programmers. For example, in a letter to Harold E. Potter, the general manager of the local Milwaukee television channel WVTV Super 18, Mark Behar makes the case for airing *Tri-Cable Tonight* by stressing that while "almost everything dealing with human sexuality is thought to be 'controversial,'" this particular program that offers a gay and lesbian perspective "is not obscene," and adds, "We have been told by many people—both heterosexual and Gay/Lesbian—including those skilled in television production, that we have an excellent quality cable program" (CCF Records 1982–2001). It is unclear whether this strategy was in fact helpful in expanding *Tri-Cable Tonight*'s distribution. According to the network's progress report, *Tri-Cable*'s respectable content hindered the series from being shown in some of the most popular gay establishments in the Milwaukee area, such as the M & M Club, whose clientele showed a lack of interest in the program since it was "not light enough" and "too informational" (CCF Records 1982–2001). While a lack of archival records about the reception to public access television makes it difficult to determine the wide range of audience responses to *Tri-Cable Tonight*, these internal documents represent the network's clear belief that "quality" and "tasteful" content would ensure the success of their programming.

Over the years, the network attempted to diversify its programming by producing more shows that centered on entertainment, creating the comedy show *Yellow on Thursday* (1990), which featured shorts, skits, parodies, and musical numbers. Unfortunately, due to a lack of volunteers and insufficient funding, the show ended after only six episodes, and the network's plans to develop other entertainment programming such as soap operas, gay situation comedies, and dance and singing shows did not come to fruition. To help sustain and broaden the network, MGLCN had hoped to garner other sources of funding in addition to the CCF (CCF Records 1982–2001). It appears such hopes did not materialize. As a result of a shortage in funds and the growing fatigue of existing talent, *Tri-Cable Tonight* was unable to sustain its ambitious format. The show switched to an in-studio discussion panel format, a simpler and lower-cost option, and tended to discuss only one topic for each episode.

While *Tri-Cable Tonight* was able to adapt and maintain its thoughtful programming through its panel discussions, its inclination toward quality programming that avoided the lewd and salacious, especially in the eyes of straight audiences, contributed to a desexualized portrayal of the gay community.[2] During the 1980s, across the country public access television tested the limits of offensive and controversial programming, including airing explicitly sexual content and gay pornography (Herold 2021, 236–37). MGLCN refrained from showing same-sex intimacy or graphic imagery, exemplifying instead a tendency toward sexual respectability. Even *New Tri-Cable*'s two-part episode on safe sex was very didactic and rather tame, despite its content warnings (MGLCN Records 1987–94). More playful segments, such as one on phone sex, did not feature any suggestive images and instead included cuts to popular movie scenes of people using the phone in a nonsexual context. Cohost Rick Poplawski, who delivered the segment, stressed the activity also had social rather than strictly sexual potential and added, "It's maybe not quite as hot as the tacky advertising suggests" (MGLCN Records 1987–94).[3]

According to Sender (2005), sexual decorum has been constructed as an essential marker of tastefulness and quality. This is especially true for gay media, given that images of same-sex intimacy have more commonly been labeled as offensive and in poor taste, regardless of their level of explicitness. Therefore, engaging in sexual respectability has been a common practice among gay media designed to reach broader markets and appeal to national mainstream advertisers (Sender 2005). Yet according to Wagner (2020), timidity toward sexual content seemed to be a common practice among gay media in Wisconsin in particular. Referring to local gay publications from the 1980s and early 1990s, Wagner states that while they pushed some sexual boundaries "in general their Midwestern values did not let them go that far" (200). This tendency hindered the ability to fully depict and discuss an important part of gay life and perpetuated a long-standing pattern of desexualized gay representation within commercial television (Becker 2006; Gross 2001; Sender 2005).

Furthermore, the network's prioritization of professionalism and respectability also prevented it from fully showcasing the rage and grief members of the gay community experienced as a result of the AIDS epidemic and the government's inaction. According to Gould (2009), emotions, feelings, and affects have played a fundamental role in political activism and AIDS activism in particular; however, *Tri-Cable Tonight* and *New Tri-Cable Tonight* typically refrained from emotional displays on camera, including during segments that were related to the AIDS crisis. Instead, these shows emphasized fact-based reporting, practical information on available resources, and reason-based arguments about HIV/AIDS. Even the few episodes that did center emotion-based language and questions, such as a *New Tri-Cable Tonight*'s episode dedicated to the NAMES Project AIDS Memorial Quilt, which featured four panelists and a host who had lost someone close to the disease, were still emotionally restrained, devoid of any heated debates and vocal or tearful outbursts. A notable exception to the network's approach concerned not the AIDS crisis but Jeffrey Dahmer's serial killings, which were particularly traumatic for Milwaukee's gay community since most of his victims included gay men and teen boys (of color) in the Milwaukee area (Barnard 2000). In a *New Tri-Cable Tonight* special ninety-minute live episode with telephone call-ins about local reaction to Dahmer's murders, host Michael Ross began the program by stating, "We're here to express our anger, shock, grief, fears, frustrations, blame, one at a time. You're free to scream, cry, speak whatever you like for this is a safe haven."

A POSITIVE LIGHT IN A TIME OF DARKNESS

Complementing the network's emphasis on "quality" programming, MGLCN was largely defined by the mission to feature a "positive" portrayal of the gay community, a point mentioned explicitly in Cream City newsletters and annual reports, ads in local newspapers, and the network's programming. When plans for Tri-Cable Tonight were announced, the CCF claimed that the show "will depict as many positive aspects of our life-style as possible within the time available" (*CCF Newsletter* 1987). From the network's internal documents and programming, it appears that MGLCN defined positive images as anti-stereotypical portrayals that would depict gay people as regular and personable human beings, showcase their talent, success, and contributions to society, and display the joyful lives they led. While this interpretation celebrated gay identity and communities, similarly to the network's push for quality, it was also oriented toward respectability and homonormativity, which hampered the network's ability to show the complexity, diversity, and reality of gay life in Milwaukee.

MGLCN highlighted the achievements and cultural contributions of gay people in the Midwest and the active community life of the gay people of Milwaukee by conducting interviews with local gay artists, comedians, musicians, poets, authors, and community activists and by featuring stories on various fundraisers, social events, and businesses associated with Milwaukee's gay community. Those behind the network viewed this kind of positive image as valuable since it countered long-standing representations from both local and national media that sensationalized and pathologized homosexuality, representations that had become only more prevalent and pernicious with the onset of the AIDS crisis. Bob Melig, CCF's development chairman, expressed the significance and urgency of promoting a positive depiction and the belief that the network could help accomplish this goal, stating in a press release for the network, "We can think of no more important Community Service the Foundation can support in order to depict Gay People in a positive light and to breakdown stereotypes, especially in the era when AIDS has the general Community thinking of us as ogres and monsters" (CCF Records 1982–2001). As a result, at a time when society had linked homosexuality to disease, death, deviance, and promiscuity (Becker 2006, 140) and mainstream media had reduced gay people to either victims or villains (Gross 2001), MGLCN presented a more multifaceted portrayal that engaged in what Richard Dyer calls "the politics of affirmation": "taking hitherto despised gay identities and embracing them as something positive" (2003, 216).

As indicated in MGLCN's internal documents and *Tri-Cable Tonight* episodes, the network's emphasis on a positive image was linked to the desire to "generate a sense of pride" in the community and to "offer hope and positive role models to those just coming out" (CCF Records 1982–2001). By showing that being openly gay could be a fulfilling and positive experience, members of the network hoped to combat the internalized homophobia, self-hate, and low self-esteem that plagued the gay community at the time and, as *Tri-Cable Tonight*'s sign-off states, to "keep those closet doors open."

As opposed to the positive portrayals of 1990s network prime-time television, which typically featured LGBTQ people within heterosexual worlds, disconnected and isolated from gay communities and social networks (Becker 2006, 180), MGLCN utilized and interpreted the concept of a positive gay image in ways that encouraged gay people to have a sense of pride, connection, and responsibility toward Milwaukee's gay community. For example, in the eighth episode of *Tri-Cable*, Ralph Navarro in his editorial segment commented that for gay individuals to embody and project a positive image, they must first "build community and contribute to its evolution in a positive manner" and added that true gay pride "is most fulfilled in a community of individuals nurturing and building each other" (MGLCN Records 1987–94). Navarro's appeal, clearly aimed at the gay community, showcases how the network promoted a positive gay image that was based not only on self-acceptance but also on the ability to advance the gay community and their activist efforts.

Tri-Cable's goal to feature "a positive reinforcement of the gay image to help break down stereotypes" was explicitly designed to reach both "closeted and straight communities" (CCF Records 1982–2001). This dual effort to also appeal to straight audiences shaped and circumscribed MGLCN's positive portrayals. The network's effort to garner the support of straight viewers led the network to conflate the notion of a positive image with a normative one. The network reflected the dominant strategy of gay media activism in the 1970s and many subsequent gay rights advocacy groups into the 1990s, such as GLAAD, whose call for "positive" depictions was oriented toward respectability and "homonormative gay politics," often replicating middle-class, heteronormative ideals rather than challenging them (Doyle 2016; Martin 2021). *Tri-Cable Tonight* typically showcased people who conformed to gender norms in their speech patterns, styles of dress, and mannerisms and rarely gave a platform to more fringe or controversial subgroups within the queer community, such as drag queens, transgender people, members of the leather/BDSM scene, sex workers, and others who might be deemed too offensive for straight audiences. Similar to other mainstreaming efforts of gay programming, the network's content primarily focused on stories that emphasized gay people's pursuit to be included within dominant social and state institutions, such as the military, organized politics, church, and conventional family structures, rather than to dismantle or reimagine them, and hardly gave coverage to activist groups that were considered radical and confrontational, such as ACT UP (Doyle 2016).

As Ward notes (2008), such "normative logics" are largely strategic, motivated by the need to procure capital and to navigate the demands of multiple groups and organizations. The network's homonormative image likely stemmed partly from the need to gain the support of the CCF and MATA. The CCF, which attempted to promote a positive image of gay people that appealed to the straight community in its various initiatives (CCF Annual Report 1989; *CCF Newsletter* 1986), was responsible for both the network's funding and its public image; "all ads, articles, posters, publicity of any type" had to be approved by the organization (CCF Records 1982–2001). The CCF had agreed with *Tri-Cable Tonight* that the program would place an emphasis on the positive aspects of gay/lesbian life and seemed pleased by the type of representation *Tri-Cable Tonight* was advancing. A note to the *Tri-Cable* staff read, "The program is going very well and we stand behind your efforts to build it into a bigger and better image of the Gay community" (CCF Records 1982–2001). The degree to which the CCF valued and prioritized a normative image that would gain approval from the straight community was made clear in a 1989 *CCF Newsletter* describing *Tri-Cable Tonight*'s anniversary program. In the piece, the PR chairman of the foundation commented, "The need to show we are just regular people who happen to be Gay/Lesbian is a message that must be gotten out and we at the Foundation are proud that Tri-Cable Tonight is able to meet that need" (*CCF Newsletter* 1989). The feature, titled "'Straight Community' Watches *Tri-Cable Tonight* 1st Anniversary Live Call-in Draws 'Straights' . . . 'Straights' Dominate Evening Calls," demonstrates that for CCF the need for a normative image was associated with the need to gain the support of straight viewers.[4]

The network also suggested that its positive and normal portrayal was essential in order to receive continued support from MATA, and members of the network believed MATA approved the renewal of their contract due to the network's ability to portray their community in "a favorable light" (CCF Records 1982–2001). It is clear that the network viewed MATA as a straight organization they had won over, remarking on MATA's actions, "I wonder if the gay/lesbian community likes the program effort as much as the straights do!!" The strategy to feature positive and respectable portrayals likely contributed to the sustainability of the network and countered the pattern of mainstream media, and news media in particular, to focus on the most unconventional, scandalous, and sensationalist aspects of gay community life (Doyle 2016). As explained in the script for *Tri-Cable Tonight*'s anniversary show, "There was a need to . . . portray us as we are—in most cases just like everyone else, rather than the biased ways that the mainstream media portrays some of the fringe element" (MGLCN Records Scripts 1987–94a). The dire need for such counter-programming became particularly apparent in 1991 following the Dahmer case, which prompted even more sensationalist and damaging media coverage that associated homosexuality with depravity. Local media in Wisconsin seemed to be particularly reckless: Channel 12 news aired a four part series titled *Flirting with Danger* in November 1991, which not only demonized the gay community but also broadcast a detailed map of the "Cruise Route" used by the gay men of Milwaukee, making members of the gay community vulnerable to homophobic, violent attacks (MGLCN Records 1987–94).

The network's strategy to feature predominantly homonormative portrayals also prevented MGLCN from displaying the full complexity and multiplicity of the gay community and from showcasing how AIDS prompted a renewed radicalism for many lesbians and gay men. As opposed to contemporaneous public access shows such as *Dyke TV*, whose stated purpose was "to incite, subvert, provoke and organize," the network neglected to harness the potential of public access television to act as a disruptive public force that offered a platform for radical and counterhegemonic media (Witchel 1994). In addition, this portrayal hindered the network from showcasing the more eccentric, avant-garde, inventive, creative, and campy forms of television that several other public access shows were experimenting with, such as *The American Music Show* in Atlanta, which helped launch drag queen RuPaul's career in the 1980s (Howell 2017). While limited in its representation, MGLCN was still able to acknowledge the cultural specificity and significance of gay identity and community and to shine a light on the political issues and struggles the local and national gay community faced in the 1980s and 1990s, unlike many other portrayals of gay people on commercial television.

THE POWER OF DIVERSITY

The final strategy that MGLCN adopted was to highlight the diverse nature of the gay community by providing representation of women and African Americans on screen. This strategy led to a more inclusive image of the gay community, which was rare at the time. Still, the network, by interpreting diversity in a way that would primarily resonate with straight minorities, did not fully explore people's intersectional struggles and the racism that existed within the local gay community. While those working behind the scenes were predominantly white men, the network was aware of the divisions and discrimination within the gay community and sought to heal those divisions, not only by creating a sense of unity but also by acknowledging and celebrating the community's diversity. The network's commitment toward this goal is expressed in its vision for *Tri-Cable Tonight*. A phrase repeated in internal documents, advertisements, and *Tri-Cable* episodes states, "*Tri-Cable Tonight* hopes to showcase the color, talent, and diversity of Milwaukee's gay and lesbian community" (CCF Records 1982–2001). While commercial and mainstream television has often excluded and ignored women and people of color in their representation of the gay community (Becker 2006; Martin 2021), MGLCN worked to subvert this harmful pattern, frequently including women and African Americans in its on-air panel discussions, interviews, and historical segments celebrating the contributions of important gay figures.

To achieve a balanced gender representation, *Tri-Cable Tonight* featured a regular female cohost, Juana Sabatino, and aired segments aimed specifically at women, such as ones about the Womyn's Art Fair, the Women's Alternative Health Center, and the launch of the book *Lesbian Ethics: Towards New Values* (1989). In addition, while the production team was overwhelmingly male, its members also seemed to possess a feminist consciousness: multiple scripts included the nonstandard spelling for the word "women" (womyn), which was used by some feminists in order to avoid ending the word with "men" (MGLCN Records Scripts 1987–94b). The network also exemplified its dedication to racial diversity, creating special programming that included shows such as *AIDS of a Different Color*, *James Baldwin in Retrospect*, and *The Other Gay America:*

David Fair Speaks about Economically Disadvantaged Gays; Joseph Beam Speaks about Being Black and Gay in America (CCF Records 1982–2001). Its regular programming raised awareness of support groups and networks for gay and lesbians of color and included features on Black civil rights, and *Tri-Cable Tonight* aired a regular segment by the Lesbians of color group (MGLCN Records 1987–94). Executive producer Mark Behar and regular host and producer Mike Lisowski, though both white, were also passionate about racial equality: they were active members of the local chapter of the Black and White Men Together organization.

Influenced by the belief that an emphasis on diversity would also broaden support for the network and the gay community at large, much of the network's reference to race centered on the parallels between racial and sexual minorities. In several programs, the hosts and guest commentators noted how the advancements made by Black community organizing show what is possible for the gay community and legitimize the gay community's own mobilizing efforts. This sentiment was also invoked in a letter Behar wrote to WVTV, in which he argues, "We have fascinating stories about a sexual minority attempting to define itself as a community. Impossible?! Several years ago society said the same thing about the Black Community!" (CCF Records 1982–2001). Within the network's regular programming there were repeated remarks about how racial and sexual minorities experience a shared sense of marginalization and exclusion from society. In a *New Tri Cable* episode, Bill Menunier comments, "You know for years working with various community groups . . . and trying to get them to understand that it's all the same battle, you know, when a Black person is discriminated against it's the same thing as when a gay person is discriminated against" (MGLCN Records 1987–94).

The emphasis on the parallels between Black and gay people and the calls for solidarity illustrate an attempt to build a wider coalition with non-gay audiences who might be willing to join the efforts of the gay community due to a shared struggle against oppression. This perspective was clearly expressed in *Tri-Cable Tonight* episode 7, in which Ralph Navarro, in his regular segment, commented that to "ensure broad acceptance and understanding" of the gay community's "agenda" it must also immediately network with other minority groups (MGLCN Records 1987–94). Consequently, while the network featured a few episodes dedicated to the challenges faced by gay minorities and made repeated references to the need to address the sexism and racism within the gay community, it interpreted diversity in a way that would primarily resonate with marginalized straight groups. As a result, the network did not fully explore and centralize the experiences and perspectives of those who are multiply marginalized. The network's inclination to approach diversity, and racial difference in particular, as a way to strengthen its advocacy efforts and the standing of the gay community reflect what Ward (2008, 6) terms the instrumentalization of diversity. In her book she shows how queer activists utilize difference as a strategy, harnessing diversity rhetoric to gain legitimacy, broader support, funding, and liberal capital. As Ward contends, while this instrumentalization led to the proliferation of important queer multi-issue projects, it has failed to disrupt the racial and class- and gender-based hierarchies embedded in queer cultures and helped to reinforce the continued centrality of normative, upper-middle-class values, logics, and culture in the queer movement.

CONCLUSION

The story of the Milwaukee Gay/Lesbian Cable Network is an illuminating example of how cable access television has enabled gay and other marginalized communities to have control over their own media representation and enter the public sphere. It also reveals the complex struggles and constraints that producers of noncommercial grassroots media face. In an effort to gain legitimacy, secure the network's sustainability, increase funding, and advance the standing of the local gay community, the network aimed to do more than strengthen ties among the gay community of Milwaukee, aspiring to reach non-gay viewers. As a result, the network's history mirrors the history of mainstreaming and the respectability strategies enacted by gay media advocacy groups that began in the 1970s. Similarly to other forms of respectability programming, MGLCN's emphasis on positive and normative portrayals led to the relative erasure of multiply-marginalized queer groups, subcultures, and narratives. While narrow in its representation, MGLCN also provided an essential form of counter-programming at a time when the gay community of Milwaukee was in a state of crisis. Additionally, the network's thoughtful coverage of political, social, legal, and medical issues, its focus on community, and its representation of gay women and African Americans were relatively groundbreaking for the era and remain quite lacking within current mainstream televisual portrayals of LGBTQ people. Unfortunately, the network was unable to harness its appeals to straight and mainstream populations in ways that led to substantial or enduring financial support:

it eventually ceased its operations in 1994. However, some of the network's members continued their work with public access television. Most notably, Michael Lisowski went on to create the call-in show *The Queer Program*, which he has hosted for over twenty years; his continued work in public access highlights the long-term impact that initiatives such as MGLCN can have on individual producers.

Throughout its run, MGLCN demonstrated determination, adaptability, and ingenuity, utilizing the limited resources at its disposal to accomplish a groundbreaking endeavor. The network operated for nearly a decade and produced 106 episodes of specials and regular programming, all centered on gay issues and designed to provide a platform for local gay activists, organizations, and initiatives. While noncommercial local media, especially media produced outside of the entertainment hubs of New York City and Los Angeles, are often overlooked in scholarship, they offer us a valuable history of LGBTQ television production. The story of MGLCN helps to expand our understanding of the achievements made by local communities to create spaces of inclusive representation for marginalized subjects through television address and the complex negotiations of identity and community that such efforts entail.

NOTES

1. Black and White Men Together was a nonprofit organization dedicated to overcoming racial barriers within the gay community that formed in May 1980 and had chapters in various places, including Milwaukee (Black and White Men Together—Milwaukee Records 1981–89).
2. MGLCN's sexual respectability was likely also shaped by its pledge in MATA's Statement of Compliance not to display obscene material (Cream City Foundation Records 1982–2001).
3. Rick Poplawski cohosted *Tri-Cable Tonight* with Joanna Sabatino for the show's first twelve episodes.
4. Local ACT UP activist Dan Fons accused CCF of having a "closeted mentality" that was "too concerned with getting the straight community to accept them and making sure straight people saw them as 'nice and upstanding'" (Milwaukee Gay/Lesbian Cable Network Records 1987–94).

REFERENCES

Ali, Christopher. 2012. "Media at the Margins: Policy and Practice in American, Canadian, and British Community Television." *International Journal of Communication* 6 (20): 1119–38.

Barnard, Ian. 2000. "The Racialization of Sexuality: The Queer Case of Jeffrey Dahmer." In *Thamyris Overcoming Boundaries: Ethnicity, Gender and Sexuality*, edited by Gert Hekma and Isabel Hoving, 67–97. Rodopi.

Becker, Ron. 2006. *Gay TV and Straight America*. Rutgers University Press.

Black and White Men Together—Milwaukee Records. 1981–89. Report for NA-BWMT Board for Convention, Mike Lisowski to Luther Carlisle, box 1, folder 11 (10/9/86), University of Wisconsin–Milwaukee Libraries, Archives Department.

CCF. n.d. "Milwaukee Gay/Lesbian Cable Network a.k.a. Tri-Cable Tonight." Accessed May 1, 2022. http://www.mkelgbthist.org/organiz/act_pol/ccf /tricable.htm.

CCF Annual Report. 1989. "Annual Report." December 31. http://www.mkelgbthist .org/organiz/act_pol/ccf/newsltr/ccf-annual-89.pdf.

CCF Newsletter. 1986. "CCF UPDATE." November. http://www.mkelgbthist.org /organiz/act_pol/ccf/newsltr/ccf-news-86nov.pdf.

———. 1987. "CCF UPDATE." July. http://www.mkelgbthist.org/organiz/act_pol /ccf/newsltr/ccf-news-87jul.pdf.

———. 1988. "CCF UPDATE." April. http://www.mkelgbthist.org/organiz/act _pol/ccf/newsltr/ccf-news-88apr.pdf.

———. 1989. "CCF UPDATE." January–February. http://www.mkelgbthist.org /organiz/act_pol/ccf/newsltr/ccf-news-89jan.pdf.

Christian, Aymar Jean. 2019. "Expanding Production Value: The Culture and Scale of Television and New Media." *Critical Studies in Television* 14 (2): 255–67.

Cream City Foundation Records. 1982–2001. Box 2, folder 7, University of Wisconsin–Milwaukee Libraries, Archives Department.

Doyle, Vincent A. 2016. *Making Out in the Mainstream: GLAAD and the Politics of Respectability*. McGill-Queen's University Press.

Dyer, Richard. 2003. *Now You See It: Studies in Lesbian and Gay Film*. Routledge.

Freitas, Anthony. 2007. "Gay Programming, Gay Publics: Public and Private Tensions in Lesbian and Gay Cable Channels." In *Cable Visions: Television beyond Broadcasting*, edited by Sarah Banet-Weiser, Chris Cynthia, and Anthony Freitas, 215–33. New York University Press.

Gould, Deborah B. 2009. *Moving Politics: Emotion and ACT UP's Fight Against AIDS*. University of Chicago Press.

Gross, Larry. 2001. *Up from Invisibility: Lesbians, Gay Men, and the Media in America*. Columbia University Press.

Herold, Lauren. 2021. "Cable Comes Out: LGBTQ Community Television on New York Public Access Stations." Ph.D. diss., Northwestern University.

Howell, Charlotte E. 2017. "Symbolic Capital and the Production Discourse of the American Music Show: A Microhistory of Atlanta Cable Access." *Cinema Journal* 57 (1): 1–24.

Howley, Kevin, ed. 2009. *Understanding Community Media*. SAGE.

InStep. 1986. "Letters." December. Accessed May 1, 2022. http://www.mkelgbthist.org/media/print/instep/issues-vo1-05/is-ex-vo3e/isvo3-23-p12.jpg.

Johnson, Phylis A., and Michael C. Keith. 2014. *Queer Airwaves: The Story of Gay and Lesbian Broadcasting.* Routledge.

Martin, Alfred L., Jr. 2021. *The Generic Closet: Black Gayness and the Black-Cast Sitcom.* Indiana University Press.

Milwaukee Gay/Lesbian Cable Network Records. 1987–94. University of Wisconsin–Milwaukee Libraries, Archives Department.

Milwaukee Gay/Lesbian Cable Network Records Scripts. 1987–94a. Subseries: B. Scripts, 1987–89 episode 13 (box 1, folder 12). University of Wisconsin–Milwaukee Libraries, Archives Department.

———. 1987–94b. Subseries: B. Scripts, 1987–89 episode 13 (box 1, folder 12), episode 16 (box 1, folder 15), episode 19 (box 1, folder 18), episode 26 (box 1, folder 25). University of Wisconsin–Milwaukee Libraries, Archives Department.

Sender, Katherine. 2005. *Business, Not Politics: The Making of the Gay Market.* Columbia University Press.

Wagner, R. Richard. 2020. *Coming Out, Moving Forward.* Wisconsin Historical Society Press.

Walter, Kate. 1988. "Out on the Airwaves." *The Advocate*, May 10.

Ward, Jane. 2008. *Respectably Queer: Diversity Culture in LGBT Activist Organizations.* Vanderbilt University Press.

Witchel, Alex. 1994. "Vox Pop Video: A Public Access TV Guide." *New York Times*, October 16. https://www.nytimes.com/1994/10/30/nyregion/vox-pop-video-a-public-access-tv-guide.html.

CHAPTER 13

MARY BELTRÁN

THE FIRST WAVE OF LATINA/O TV

EARLY CHICANA/O AND
PUERTO RICAN PROGRAMMING

While in the United States we now think of "Latino television" in relation to series viewed nationally and globally such as *Jane the Virgin* (2014–19), *One Day at a Time* (2017–20), and *Gentefied* (2020–21), the first English-language and bilingual television programs with a specific focus on Latina/o perspectives and audiences were local.[1] These series, including public affairs series *¡Ahora!* (1969–70), *Fiesta* (1969–71), *Realidades* (1971–77), and *Periódico* (1969–71) and the family drama *Canción de la Raza* (1967–68), aimed to serve, document the lives of, and inspire the Latina/o residents of their local communities. They were produced at public television stations in Los Angeles, New York City, and a few smaller cities nationwide and at the local affiliate stations of the commercial networks in Los Angeles. Created by Chicana/o (activist-minded Mexican American), Puerto Rican, and other Latina/o creative professionals as well as by white media professionals at local stations hoping to expand their audience base, this programming focused on issues and perspectives not previously seen on U.S. television and offered a number of Latina/os entrée into careers in television and film production. As the first U.S. television forums created for Latina/o Americans, they provide important windows to U.S. and television history in the late 1960s and early 1970s.

As I discuss in *Latino TV: A History* (Beltrán 2022), building on Chon Noriega's robust historical research in *Shot in America: Television, The State, and the Rise of Chicano Cinema* (2000), the programs produced for local Latina/o audiences in this era sprang from a wide variety of interests and initiatives. As Noriega notes, several of these series reflected and were instruments of civil rights activism on the part of Chicana/os and Latina/os interested in using television to support their communities and activist efforts (Noriega 2000). In contrast, some of these programs were launched by non-Latina/o television station professionals. From my study of these programs and the records that exist of their productions, it appears that these professionals wanted to serve their Latina/o viewers but typically began with little knowledge of what that meant or of how to partner with Latina/o community members in producing and promoting these programs (Beltrán 2022; Scott and Allen 1969; Marshall et al. 1974).

These series also were a reflection of the social values and media policies of the time period. In 1967, as many young Americans were becoming interested in activism and fighting social inequities, the federal government's Kerner Commission was investigating the inequities that had led to violent protests earlier that year on the part of African Americans in several U.S. cities. That same year, President Lyndon B. Johnson signed the Public Broadcasting Act into law.[2] It established a national system of public radio and television broadcasting and the Corporation for Public Broadcasting (CPB), a private, nonprofit organization that would serve as its steward. When announcing the new law, President Johnson cited the need for public broadcasting because of television's "immense—even revolutionary—power to change, to change our lives." He declared that with the law he wished to "rededicate a part of the airwaves, which belong to all the people . . . for the enlightenment of all the people" (Johnson 1967). Johnson also supported Federal Communications Commission (FCC) policies of this era that allowed community members to challenge the license renewals of radio and television stations that neglected to serve them. While these developments were largely curtailed by the end of the 1970s, in this brief period they resulted in a social and local media environment conducive to the production of local television programs that prioritized their Black and Brown communities.

The launching of African American– and Latina/o-focused television programs in these years also was made possible through outside funding. The Ford Foundation, a private charitable foundation that since the 1930s had funded a wide variety of initiatives and research studies that aimed to support public welfare and combat social inequities (Magat 2012), provided the seed money for many of these productions and linked studies that examined the media interests and needs of the local Latina/o communities they aimed to serve. In previous decades, the foundation had supported the development of educational television and the development of National Educational Television (NET), a network of stations that was the precursor of the Public Broadcasting System. In the late 1960s, it began to fund stations' grant proposals to develop new programs targeting their local African American or Latina/o (specifically Mexican American or Puerto Rican) community, as I describe in further detail in this chapter. The impact of the foundation on the birth of local Latina/o television programming cannot be overstated.

How did these shows' producers envision what Mexican American, Puerto Rican, and other Latina/o viewers might want to see and benefit from seeing, and what were these television series ultimately like? What was the production process like for this first wave of Latina/o programming? How popular were these local series with their target audiences, and what was their long-term impact? To explore these questions, I take up a combination of research methods, including archival research, textual analysis of relevant series episodes that have been preserved, discourse analysis of mainstream news coverage about these series, and interviews with several of the producers and actors who were part of the production teams or, in the case of the one scripted series, who were cast in one of the programs. To do so, I draw on research conducted for a previous study (Beltrán 2022), with an in-depth focus on a few case studies, *Canción de la Raza* (Song of the people) (1968–69), *¡Ahora!* (Right now!) (1969–70), *Fiesta* (1969–71), and *Realidades* (Realities, or Truths) (1971–74, 1975–77), as I describe in more detail below.

One challenge that arose in relation to this study is that there are few actual copies of series episodes that have survived—or at least that are accessible to researchers in the present day. I learned in my interviews with producers of these series that in these years of public television stations operated on minute budgets and with little sense of the historical significance of their programming, to the degree that station staff quickly recorded over videotaped episodes, veritably "erasing" them with new programming. Thus, much of this programming, beyond a small handful of episodes, was not preserved. For this reason, I had to seek out and find extratextual traces of series episodes whenever possible. This included study of promotional texts (which were minimal, given the shoestring budgets and small reach of these programs), descriptions of episodes by television critics, articles and books published by the series producers or researchers who worked with them, and mentions in Ford Foundation documents.

In the following sections I provide an overview of the local Latina/o programming that was launched in these years, with a focus on my four case studies in the three local markets where they were produced and viewed. The four series I explore in more depth include *Canción de la Raza* and *¡Ahora!* in Los Angeles, where public television station KCET produced these and other Latina/o-focused series and where the commercial network affiliate stations also were convinced to host Chicana/o-centric programming; *Fiesta*, produced at KUAT in Tucson, Arizona, as an example of a program produced in a smaller city; and finally *Realidades*, produced by activism-oriented creative professionals in the New York City metropolitan area, where its public television station WNET also launched subsequent nonfiction and narrative programs with a focus on Puerto Ricans and other Latina/os living in the region. *Realidades* also later became the first nationally broadcast Latina/o series, airing on PBS stations in different cities across the United States from 1975 to 1977. These series illustrated the rich possibilities of television programming with a focus on the interests and needs of local and national Latina/o communities as well as the untapped potential of putting television production and programming decisions in the hands of Latina/o creative professionals.

A FAMILY DRAMA FOR THE CHICANA/O COMMUNITY: *CANCIÓN DE LA RAZA*

Los Angeles was the home of the greatest number of Latina/o-focused local series in the late sixties and early seventies. This was likely linked to the city's large Mexican American and broader Latina/o population in these years, its importance as a central node of Chicana/o activism, its large and active public television station KCET, and its location in the hub of the national television industry. The Latina/o-oriented series that were produced and broadcast in Los Angeles in these years included *Canción de la Raza* (1968–69), *¡Ahora!* and *Acción Chicano* (1972–74), all produced by and aired on KCET; *Unidos* (1970–71) and *Reflecciones* (1972–73), produced and broadcast at ABC affiliate station KABC; the unfortunately named *The Siesta Is Over* (1972–73) (later renamed *Bienvenidos*) at KNXT, the CBS affiliate; and *Impacto* (1970–74), which was broadcast by the NBC affiliate station KNBC.

The first of these programs, KCET's *Canción de la Raza*, is the only scripted narrative series among the local programs that foregrounded Latinidad in these years. It was a bilingual family drama that aired each weekday, once in the afternoon and with a repeat episode in the evening, similar to the scheduling structure of a Spanish-language telenovela. *Canción de la Raza*, targeting the Mexican American audience in Greater Los Angeles during years when some of those viewers identified with the activist efforts of the Chicana/o movement for greater equity for Mexican Americans, can be thought of in part as an experiment taken up by KCET and the Ford Foundation. Given the sizeable Latina/o and predominantly Mexican American community in the region, it can be surmised that the proposed series was considered a way to ascertain the possibilities for tapping into the Chicana/o market with KCET programming. With respect to the Ford Foundation collaborating with KCET as the program's funder, it fit with the foundation's focus on community "uplift" and the eradication of structural barriers that particular cultural communities might experience. Notably, it was proposed by white station employees, led by Dr. Richard S. Scott, KCET's head of human affairs and a medical doctor (Scott and Allen 1969). He, station vice president Charles R. Allen, and the other station staff involved were interested in partnering with residents of the sizable Mexican American community in the development and production of a community program (Scott and Allen 1969). Ultimately, over one hundred Latina/o community members were purportedly hired to serve in a wide variety of roles for the program, including a small handful of positions as writers and directors (Scott and Allen 1969). This was especially remarkable because in these years and soon after, the employees of public television stations across the nation were almost completely white, as a study commissioned by the CPB found in 1978 (Task Force on Minorities in Public Broadcasting 1978).

The grant proposal submitted by Scott, Allen, and other KCET staff to the Ford Foundation to fund *Canción de la Raza* claimed that it would serve and be created in part by local Latina/o residents. What they did not anticipate were the difficulties of forging cultural and professional bridges between the white production team members and their Chicana/o counterparts as they worked to develop, produce, and promote the series (Scott and Allen 1969). The story behind the scenes was complicated, as the Chicana/o team members often had not had prior jobs in English-language media production, and the white crew members had little awareness of Chicana/o culture and the trust they would need to earn from their new colleagues. Given that most of the cast had no acting experience, a few seasoned Latino actors, Francisco Ortega, Natividad Vacío, and Victor Millan, were hired to lead the others in several weeks of acting rehearsals; these actors also directed some of the episodes. Two Latino writers, Richard Duran and Abel Franco, were hired as well. Even so, in my conversation with actor Richard Yniguez, who got his first television role on the series as one of the family's sons, I learned that the new actors were not always treated with the most respect by the production heads (Yniguez 2018).

Canción de La Raza follows the Ramos family, two parents with three teenage and two young adult children, who are questioning the inequities faced by Mexican Americans in Los Angeles. Unfortunately, out of the sixty-five episodes produced and broadcast, only the first episode has been preserved to be viewed by researchers. It begins during the aftermath of two of the teen children facing police brutality, after taking part in walkouts at their East Los Angeles high school to protest the inadequate conditions and inferior education they were receiving. It also includes allusions to teen drug use, a growing generation gap as younger Mexican Americans began to identify as Chicana/os and as activists, at times to their elders' consternation, and to the ways in which family members helped each other and maintained their cultural pride. Given that the other episodes no longer exist or have been lost, it's not possible to fully ascertain the many other subjects that were addressed in the family drama over the two years that it aired on KCET. Even so, the episode illustrates that the series boldly addressed many intense and at times controversial social and political issues that Chicana/o individuals and families were wrestling with in this period.

As the producers of *Canción de la Raza* realized their limitations regarding outreach to their desired audience, they hired Eduardo Moreno, who had been head of programming for KALI, a local Spanish-language radio station (Scott and Allen 1969). He became the production team's bridge to the Chicana/o regional community that they aimed to serve. Moreno began by conducting meetings with local community organizations and key individuals regarding the program and how it would be appealing and useful to community members (Scott and Allen 1969). Researchers, led by Harold Mendelsohn, a social psychologist from the University of Denver, also surveyed a random selection of residents from the local Mexican American community before the series began airing and after the last episodes appeared (Scott and Allen 1969). Interviewers asked residents, among other questions, which social issues that they felt should be addressed in a Mexican American family drama. The production team also installed several phone lines and set them up with bilingual staffers to respond to audience comments and questions during and after broadcasts. While these efforts aimed to ensure that community members could be pointed to relevant community resources, this communication offered the show's writers a chance to be responsive to feedback from their audience. The busy phone lines became the basis for a linked talk show, *Linea Abierta* (Open line), which brought on representatives from local organizations and other community advocates to further discuss the issues depicted in *Canción de la Raza* to which callers had responded. One of *Linea Abierta*'s goals was to help local residents connect with social service organizations and other resources that could assist them with challenges that they faced.

Notably, there was a dearth of scholarship on Latina/o audiences prior to the premiere of *Canción de la Raza*. To determine whether the production team had met its goals for the series, further surveys were conducted to learn who had tuned in, whether viewers felt it was a high-quality production, and what they felt they had learned from it. Based on this research, KCET and the Ford Foundation considered it a success. Encouraged, the foundation funded its airing in other cities in California and later at other public television stations that served large Latina/o populations. However, it did not do as well in other regions around the country. Based on what the Ford Foundation funded in the years that immediately followed, the tepid response *Canción de la Raza* received outside of California was likely taken as evidence of the impossibility of successfully appealing to Latina/os throughout the country with national television programming. This appears, however, to have reinforced the Ford Foundation's existing interest in supporting local television programming for marginalized communities. The foundation created the New Television Program fund in 1969 and invited grant proposals for local programs targeting African American, Mexican American, or Puerto Rican audiences.[3] The call for proposals resulted in their funding of dozens of series targeting African Americans and a smaller number of shows targeting Chicana/o or Puerto Rican communities (Heitner 2009).[4]

While the show was canceled in 1969, the lessons learned in the production and exhibition of *Canción de la Raza* influenced subsequent projects targeting Latina/o viewers at KCET and elsewhere as well as influencing the funding patterns of the Ford Foundation in relation to television targeting Latina/o viewers. Local and regional, rather than national, audiences became the focus. The foundation's initiation of the New Television Program fund highlights how it had come to view local rather than national television as an optimal forum for supporting individuals and communities in these years. The nascent system of public television, with its focus on and common roots in education, was clearly viewed as the ideal medium for programming with the goal of empowerment in these years. The New Television Program also gave the Ford Foundation opportunities to fund programming at the stations considered important to the National Educational Television network, which soon became the backbone of PBS.

TARGETING THE CHICANA/O COMMUNITY: *¡AHORA!*

The next series produced for a primarily Chicana/o audience at KCET was the public affairs program *¡Ahora!* (1969–70). It became a model for the politically minded Chicana/o news series later produced at other public television stations and at affiliate stations of commercial networks. It comes as no surprise that Los Angeles was the home for multiple Chicana/o news programs in these years. The region became one of a handful of epicenters of the Chicana/o Movement, as the first generation of Chicana/o college students had also started their college education. Antiwar activism responding to the Vietnam War and other social movements also brought these young people together. Having also been the first generation to grow up on television, many were interested in using television and film as tools to support their communities and to further their activist and creative goals.

As a part of these trends, the producers of *¡Ahora!* had high hopes for their series. They aimed to document this revolutionary, Chicana/o activism-oriented work as it happened, taking their video cameras to demonstrations and other community actions, in the hope of exposing their viewers to new insights and raising their consciousness about inequities and discrimination in need of remedy. They also aimed to educate their viewers about Mexican American history and political issues and to showcase the talent and achievements of artists, writers, and other creative professionals in the community. As Jesús Treviño, who was a coproducer of the series, noted in an interview with me, "This was a first. This was the first time anyone had bothered to document the lives of Latinos.... It did signal what could happen. The television was handed over to Latinos to talk about Latino issues" (Treviño 2016).

¡Ahora! was structured in a magazine format. Episode segments typically began with the host providing an overview of the topic in the studio,

subsequently cutting to interviews with community members, to footage shot on location in the city, or to archival footage that expanded on the topic. For example, in the first of a three-episode series called "The Image," Treviño, the episode's writer, coproducer, and host, shared some of the history of Mexican and Chicana/o representation in Hollywood films and the negative impact of these images on Chicana/os. Still photos of actors and actresses active in Hollywood since its inception were projected behind him as he spoke at a lectern on a small soundstage. He had gathered the photos and what scholarship he could find on the subject himself (Treviño 2016), which wasn't easy, as both film studies and Chicana/o and Latina/o studies were not yet established academic disciplines. As such, the episode and *¡Ahora!* as a whole were breaking new ground on topics of interest to the Chicana/o community. In other episodes, *¡Ahora!* focused on subjects that included local politics, organizations serving Mexican Americans in the Los Angeles region, and Chicana/o activism (including live footage of the high school "blowouts" and other protests). Community leaders and social service providers were brought into the studio to converse with the hosts on topics on which they had expertise, while musicians and poets performed for a live audience in their studio in many episodes.

Treviño, twenty-three years old when he was hired, got his first production job at *¡Ahora!* He later went on to produce another series at KCET, *Acción Chicano* (1972–74). As he noted in interviews with me, both series aimed to provide news coverage and discussion of the important history and issues of the day for Chicana/os and also to educate others in Los Angeles about their concerns (Treviño 2016). They did so with bare-bones budgets. As he and José Luis Ruíz, a producer of two other LA-based series, *Unidos* and *Acción Chicano*, joked in a joint interview, they had to figure out how to make do always with no more than "two chairs and a camera" as their budgeted props and stage dressing (Ruíz and Treviño 2018).

As Noriega has documented, despite these minimal budgets, the producers of *¡Ahora!* and other LA-based public affairs series chose to save some of their show's production funds to finance the production of documentary film shorts on issues of concern to Chicana/os. These were the first Chicana/o films, which they later aired on their local television programs. What is now known as the first wave of Chicana/o filmmaking was thus directly linked to many of these local series. The films that aired on *¡Ahora!*, *Acción Chicano*, *Impacto*, and other local Los Angeles–based shows included *Requiem 29* (David Garcia, 1971), about the Chicano Moratorium protest in East Los Angeles in 1970; *Yo Soy Chicano* (Jesús Treviño, 1972), about Chicano history, identity, and pride; *The Unwanted* (José Luis Ruíz, 1974), which shed light on the traumas experienced by undocumented Mexican immigrants; and *Garment Workers* (Sylvia Morales, 1975), on the harsh conditions experienced by Chicanas working in garment factories.

Additionally, the producers of the Chicana/o series subsequently networked and collaborated with their counterparts in Los Angeles and other cities as well. José Luis Ruíz, then working as a producer at KCET, played an instrumental role in organizing the formation of the Latino Consortium, which linked producers at twenty-nine stations in 1975 and was the precursor to the Latino Media Coalition (Ruíz 2018). Among other collaborative initiatives, show producers began to stretch their funds by sharing some of their taped episodes with each other. The process of delivering or shipping videotapes to other stations, known then as "bicycling" episodes, had become common by that time. *Acción Chicano* and *Realidades* were among the programs known to trade copies of episodes and air them for their respective audiences, presuming an interest on the part of their viewers across Latina/o national origin groups (Noriega 2000). This sharing of content and conversations among television professionals in different cities provided a foundation for subsequent pan-Latina/o media production for a pan-Latina/o and U.S. national audience, the target audience of the first feature films by Latina/o directors, such as *El Norte* (Gregory Nava, 1983) and *Born in East L.A.* (Cheech Marin, 1987), and of Latina/o television programming in later decades. However, the focus on the specific concerns of Mexican Americans in Southern California, which drove the production of *¡Ahora!* and other LA-based series, would often be lost with these later changes.

LATINA/O PROGRAMMING BEYOND THE COASTAL REGIONS: *FIESTA*

While *¡Ahora!*, *Realidades*, and other local Latina/o programs were being produced and broadcast on the two coasts, other local series funded by a Ford Foundation New Television grant were produced and broadcast in other parts of the country and took a decidedly less political approach. These included *Fiesta* (1969–71), produced at KUAT in Tucson, Arizona, and *Periódico* (1969–71) produced at KLRN in San Antonio, Texas. Like *Canción de la Raza*, these programs were initiated by television station personnel who happened to be white. They also addressed social issues that Mexican American residents faced in their communities. Likely related to their lack of Latina/o producers, however, they put more emphasis on arts and entertainment as opposed to politics and activism. Given public television stations' dearth of employees of color in these years, it makes sense that a grant proposal for a local Latina/o public affairs show would necessarily be initiated by non-Latina/os. Unsurprisingly, both of the above grant proposals indicated their productions would develop a collaborative planning process with Latina/o residents and hire community members to the production team (Marshall et al. 1974; Duane 1969). They also included a research component, which may have played a large role in convincing the Ford Foundation to fund them. Given this, it appears that the foundation was interested in funding programming that could document its function of community "uplift," evidence for the benefits of public television more broadly. These studies were designed and carried out by professors from nearby universities. They led bilingual research teams that conducted surveys with members of the local Latina/o community in the preproduction stage and after the series was broadcast, asking respondents what social and community issues they thought should be addressed, whether they watched and connected with the program, and their reactions to the content.

In the case of *Fiesta*, planning and preproduction began with KUAT program manager Wes Marshall, who was also a professor in radio-television at the University of Arizona in Tucson. The rest of the team included his UAT colleague E. B. Eiselein, a media anthropologist, who led the program's research team; John Thomas Duncan, who became the show's director and coproducer; and Hector Gradillas, who had previously worked on another study linked to radio-television at the university. Gradillas was influential in the design of the series: he suggested the show's unique set, meant to look like a backyard party, and thus what he deemed a culturally specific and intimate setting, and recommended many of the Latina/o professionals who were hired to serve as hosts of the show. Raúl Gamez Bogarín, a local media professional, presumably on Spanish-language productions, was also soon hired to coproduce and host the series. Even with Gradillas and Bogarín among the leadership of the production team, there were some differences that had to be bridged in helping the KUAT staff and Latina/o production team and cast members who had previously worked only on Spanish-language productions, to integrate as a cohesive cast and crew. Marshall and colleagues note that the production team had to find ways to build trust and bridge their cultural mindsets, including different notions of professionalism and of strictness about adhering to the production schedule, to come to trust and work well together (Marshall et al. 1974).

As I describe *Fiesta* elsewhere, the show's emphasis on arts and culture and occasionally on local news relevant to Mexican Americans proved to be popular with audiences in Tucson (Beltrán 2022). The series typically was entertainment-focused, including performances by Mexican American and Mexican musicians and bands as well as by theatrical and dance groups. In addition, segments on topics such as bilingual education, Mexican American holidays such as Las Posadas, and the experiences of students at local colleges were occasionally included in the episodes.

The show drew in a large audience of Mexican Americans in the region, 60 percent of their projected potential viewers (Marshall et al. 1974). Those who watched the series reported that it instilled feelings of cultural pride and that it at times encouraged them to take action as well. Given this response, the production team declared the series a success (Marshall et al. 1974). Marshall and his cowriters added in their summary of producing the show and its reception that the series would have been even more successful had they known beforehand what they learned about the local Mexican American community during the production. Regardless, when the Ford Foundation did not offer new funding for *Fiesta*, KUAT apparently did not attempt to renew it. These repeated dynamics across multiple television stations highlight the precarity of programming centering Latina/o audiences and concerns without a champion at the station or local community advocates fighting to keep a particular program on the air.

BY AND FOR NUYORICANS AND OTHER LATINA/OS IN NYC: *REALIDADES*

Meanwhile, across the country in New York City, *Realidades*, which aired from 1971 to 1974 and from 1975 to 1977, had a unique origin story. The producers, led by Humberto Cintrón, had been among a group of largely Puerto Rican activism-minded community members who staged a protest against public television station WNET in 1971 for choosing not to air the film version of a controversial Puerto Rican play, *La Carreta*. It eventually became a days-long sit-in that brought all broadcasting to a halt. To appease the protesters, the station management ultimately offered to fund and air a Puerto Rican–focused public affairs series, later named *Realidades* (Bell 2012).

The eventual production team, a large group of Puerto Rican and other creative professionals chosen by Cintrón, produced nineteen episodes (stretching a budget set for fifteen) in their first season. Similar to *¡Ahora!*, *Realidades* aimed to educate, entertain, and politicize local Latina/os, in this case Nuyoricans and other Latina/os living in the New York City region. Each episode, typically under the oversight of a pair of producers, explored a topic relevant to the community in depth. While many episodes focused on Puerto Ricans in the arts, such as poets Pedro Pietri and Julia de Burgos, the producers also dedicated episodes to timely social and political topics such as veterans' benefits, the treatment of Puerto Rican children in city schools, and mestizaje (racially mixed heritage) as a complex issue for Puerto Ricans and other Latina/os. Titles such as "Commonwealth," "Una Nación Bilingue" (A bilingual nation), and "Su Voto es Poderoso" (Your vote is powerful) hint at the various episodes' subject matter. At least one of their episodes was nominated for an Emmy, which speaks to their emphasis on production aesthetics and complex and well-researched subject matter.

Linked to *Realidades* and its impact was the fact that its station, WNET, offered bilingual workshops for community members. Some were taught by Puerto Rican filmmaker and scholar Lillian Jiménez and other Puerto Rican creative professionals. A number of community members with no production experience availed themselves of this training and eventually worked on *Realidades* or Latina/o-oriented programs in other cities. An attorney and community activist, Julio Rodriguez, also offered trainings on how to challenge local television stations' licenses in order to make them more responsive to their ethnic communities; the training became so well-known and popular that people traveled from other parts of the country to take it (*Realidades Revisited* 2019).

As noted earlier, conversations and collaborations soon began to spring up among some of the producers of Latina/o programs in different parts of the country by the first years of the 1970s. Local Chicana/o and Latina/o organizing was becoming national in focus, as activists and advocates aimed to have a more powerful voice and improve representation at national levels. Among other goals, local series producers came together to strategize for funding for a national series. *Acción Chicano* and *Realidades*, linking the Latina/o audiences in Los Angeles and New

York City through broadcasting each other's episodes, in particular were central to these discussions.

Linked to and culminating from this work, *Realidades* became the first local Latina/o television program for which the CPB provided funding to be broadcast on PBS stations across the country, from 1975 to 1977. I learned in my interviews that this development was agreed upon (after some initial disagreement and debate) by producers of Chicana/o series in other cities. As José Luis Ruíz described it, they chose to support *Realidades*' transition to a national series across PBS stations with the agreement and expectation that a Chicana/o-oriented series would next get the same treatment (Ruíz 2018). However, the funds to support a Latina/o television series had become much harder to come by, as Ford Foundation funds dwindled and many Latina/o producers of public affairs shows became more interested in film production as a new and important way to enrich their communities and break down barriers in Hollywood.

By the time greater collaboration and local shows were beginning to be imagined as national, the window of opportunity was closing. The New Television grant funding ended in the mid-1970s. While local Latina/o focused programs would occasionally be produced and broadcast especially at public television stations after this time, the concerted push to foster local Latina/o programming had ended.

CONCLUSIONS

In a time period in which Latina/os still were usually erased from the worlds of broadcast television, programs like *Canción de la Raza*, *¡Ahora!*, *Fiesta*, and *Realidades* made an important difference. This programming underscored the humanity, talent, and *ganas* (desire and determination) of Latina/os in their local communities in the late 1960s and early 1970s. Latina/os were included and featured for the first time, as complex subjects of program episodes, as creative professionals in a variety of roles, and as viewers deserving of attention and respect. A number of the Latina/o professionals who worked on one or more of these series also went on to continued careers as producers, writers, actors, and directors in television and film, careers that might very well never have come about otherwise.[5]

A linked takeaway from studying these disparate series is that their productions involved acts of learning and building relationships across previous cultural borders. While scholars have rightly linked some of the early Latina/o television programs to Chicana/o and Nuyorican activist-oriented media producers, many of these shows were in fact produced by white public television professionals motivated by the wish to serve their Latina/o community and explore the potential of public television. Most indicated that they had little or no awareness of what this would entail or the cultural significance of producing the first Latina/o television program in their region (Marshall et al. 1974; Scott and Allen 1969). While their efforts often didn't extend to sustaining the programming more than a year or two, they made important interventions by bringing Latina/o residents in as employees and participants at local stations.

The Ford Foundation's finding (which now comes across as common sense) that Latina/o audiences across the country had radically diverse viewing interests, in relation to not just their national origin groups but also their differing regional communities and histories, is one that is still important and timely for television producers and programmers today. Local television for Latina/o audiences still makes sense and could smartly be part of television programming strategies in 2023.

Latino Public Broadcasting (LPB), the entity that now supports the funding and broadcast of independently produced media projects by Latina/o makers through collaboration with the CPB, does so with an eye to programming that will air on NPR stations. While the programs are still aired locally in this regard, the vision is one of national television. Independent media producers also tend to privilege the goal of national and global exhibition of their work. This likely is with the idea that this means broader exposure, visibility, and thus opportunities for subsequent funding for future projects. Such a model of television also encourages learning across Latina/o national origin groups and pan-Latina/o identities. However, the local series of the sixties and seventies demonstrate the equal importance of *specificity and depth* in producing programming that is *meaningful* to a local community and its residents. Even while national television programming about and targeting U.S. Latina/os has been a progressive development, the power and potential of local programming by and for Latina/os communities continues to this day and should not be overlooked.

NOTES

1. I use "Latina/o" throughout this essay to refer to women, men, and gender-nonbinary people of Latin American descent in the United States. This term is utilized instead of "Latinx" to ensure greater accessibility outside of academia.

2. The National Advisory Commission on Civil Disorders, better known now as the Kerner Commission, was constituted in July 1967 by President Johnson to assess the catalysts of violent protests that had taken place a few months prior in many Black urban neighborhoods. The informal moniker for the commission came from the chair of the commission, Otto Kerner Jr., the governor of Illinois at the time. The commission released its report in 1968, after seven months of investigation.
3. While African American communities had been the sole focus of the Kerner Commission's 1968 report, which described disparities in relation to social conditions and social supports, the Ford Foundation appears to have seen Chicana/o and Puerto Rican communities as facing similar challenges.
4. In these years they were the two largest Latina/o groups, with Mexican Americans tallied as 60 percent and Puerto Ricans as 13.8 percent of all U.S. Latina/os in the 1970s. Cuban Americans and Cubans, at 5.5 percent, constituted a distant third (Feinberg 1982).
5. These individuals include but are not limited to television and film director, writer, and producer Jesús Treviño, actor and director Richard Yniguez, and producer and writer Susan Racho.

REFERENCES

Bell, Christopher. 2012. *East Harlem Remembered: Oral Histories of Community and Diversity*. McFarland.

Beltrán, Mary. 2022. *Latino TV: A History*. New York University Press.

Duane, Frank. 1969. *Broadcasting and Social Action: A Handbook for Station Executives*. National Association of Educational Broadcasters.

Engelman, Ralph. 1996. *Public Radio and Television in America: A Political History*. SAGE.

Feinberg, Lawrence. 1982. "Mexican-American Population Surged 93 Pct. in 1970s." *Washington Post*, September 17. https://www.washingtonpost.com.

Ford Foundation. Last modified 2022. "About Ford." https://www.fordfoundation.org.

Heitner, Devorah. 2009. "List of Black-Produced Shows Nationwide, from 1968 On." *Thirteen: Media with Impact*, February 27. https://www.thirteen.org.

Johnson, Lyndon B. 1967. "Remarks upon Signing the Public Broadcasting Act of 1967." In *Public Papers of the Presidents: Lyndon B. Johnson 1967: Book II*. LBJ Presidential Library. www.lbjlibrary.org.

Magat, Richard. 2012. *The Ford Foundation at Work: Philanthropic Choices, Methods and Styles*. Springer.

Marshall, Wes, E. G. Eiselein, John Thomas Duncan, and Raúl Gamez Bogarín. 1974. *Fiesta: Minority Television Programming*. Tucson: University of Arizona Press.

National Advisory Committee on Civil Disorders United States. 1967. *Kerner Commission Report on the Causes, Events and Aftermaths of the Civil Disorders of 1967*. Office of Justice.

Noriega, Chon. 2000. *Shot in America: Television, the State, and the Rise of Chicano Cinema*. University of Minnesota Press.

Realidades Revisited Panel Discussion, Part 1. 2019. "Taller Boricua/Puerto Rican Workshop, New York City." July 6. https://youtube.com/watch?v=OGuDcZ2q6gw.

Rosenfield, Patricia, and Rachel Wimpee. 2015. *The Ford Foundation: Themes, 1936–2001*. Rockefeller Archive Center.

Ruíz, José Luis. 2018. Interview by author, Los Angeles, April 11.

Ruíz, José Luis, and Jesús Treviño. 2018. Interview by author, Los Angeles, February 8.

Scott, Richard S., and Charles R. Allen. 1969. "Cancion de la Raza: An ETV Soap Opera." *Television Quarterly* 8 (4): 24–38.

Task Force on Minorities in Public Broadcasting. 1978. "Formula for Change: The Report of the Task Force on Minorities in Public Broadcasting." Corporation for Public Broadcasting, November.

Treviño, Jesús. 2016. Interview by author, Austin, Tex., November 3.

Yniguez, Richard. 2018. Interview by author, Studio City, Calif., April 10.

CHAPTER 14

AYMAR JEAN CHRISTIAN

CHICAGO RENAISSANCE REDUX

BLACK CULTURAL PRODUCTION AND
THE SOCIAL PRACTICE ART OF TELEVISION

As of 2022, Chicago television was ten years into a growth period propelled by Dick Wolf, who created four different interconnected network series about the city: *Chicago Fire* (NBC, 2012–), *Chicago PD* (NBC, 2014–), *Chicago Med* (NBC, 2015–), and *Chicago Justice* (NBC, 2017). Much like *Law & Order*, the procedural mega-franchise *One Chicago* was designed to last for years and years. *Justice* lasted only one season, but by 2022 the other three were still releasing new episodes with a combined total of twenty-six seasons and over five hundred episodes. Wolf was attracted to Chicago because it was "real," not Hollywood: "This is America.... If you set this show in Los Angeles, people would say, 'Oh come on.' But this is about the heart of the country. It's real," Wolf said (Braxton 2013). *One Chicago* benefitted from a yearslong public/private effort to woo Hollywood productions to the city. Wolf's assembly-line style of production, the formulaic nature of which has never endeared him to critics, was just what the city needed to build it into a production hub (Phillips 2012).

Big money collided in the 2010s to brand Chicago as an authentic city ripe for corporate exploitation, yet this runs counter to Chicago's historically small-scale and community-based legacy in the arts. Before its TV upsurge, the city's rising film director was independent producer Joe Swanberg. Known as one of the originators of the "mumblecore" genre, Swanberg made his name creating cheap, intimate, realist, quickly produced features filmed in homes and on digital cameras (Christian 2011). By 2011, right before *One Chicago* premiered, Swanberg was on the cusp of increasing his budgets after releasing *Uncle Kent*, one of his last films in the mumblecore genre. By then, Swanberg had perfected his realist style, shooting the feature in six days: "I'm getting faster . . . which is ironic because I plan more," he said (Borrelli 2011). Still, Swanberg was adamant about staying in Chicago and not moving to New York or Los Angeles: "Those places are competitive environments, and that's become less exciting to me."

I arrived in Chicago in 2012 amid this tension between the coming wave of big-budget TV productions and Chicago's legacy of small-scale, community-based, and—most importantly and invisibly—Black-led artistry. I had little sense then of how important both would be to the development of what I call "social practice television" in Chicago. Indeed, when we look at Chicago's history, the rise of corporate art production on the scale of Cinespace and *One Chicago* is an anomaly. Cultural production in Chicago historically skews closer to community-based and collective work that is best done when resources are scarce, avoiding the competition for resources that pits artists against each other, as in New York or LA. The city's innovations have been led largely by Black, Brown, queer, and working-class people, and perhaps that is why its contributions to artistic innovation are largely undervalued and understudied. In general, scholarship on the production and exhibition practices of historically marginalized people is relatively scarce.

What is "social practice television," and how can we understand Chicago as an innovator of the form? "Social practice" is a term most often used in the art world. In the next section, I unpack how this art form has emerged over the twentieth century outside of television. Then, I apply it to film, television, and radio using Chicago's historical contributions as a case study. Because television is a normative medium largely supported by institutions that use narrative formulas and hierarchical production practices to maintain consistent revenues, it is easy to see why television's social practice history remains relegated to the margins of TV scholarship. Social practice art, in general, "thrives out in the world and in non-art-related and non-institutional spaces that foster a messier sort of intersection between art and life, places less marked by normative power" (Smith 2014, 1). This essay is my attempt to suture the disjuncture between art versus television, community-based versus institutionalized production, through the primary lens of Black Chicago's contribution to social practice.

Black people, and other communities excluded from corporate media, practice media making differently out of necessity, just as Chicago has innovated across media forms because it has access to fewer resources than New York or Los Angeles. In Hollywood or Broadway, people come together to advance their careers in a local system set up to build national and global capital. In Chicago's Black communities, more often artists come together because they have only each other. This way of making media is community-based because people form deep relationships—accountability to each other—as part of a solidarity project, a necessary means of surviving and thriving, often without much promise of prominence or capital outside their community.

In the final section, I ask whether this legacy lives on in the digital era. In 2015 I experimented with social practice digital media by launching OTV | Open Television in collaboration with a team of Black trans, nonbinary, and women-identified artists, including Elijah McKinnon, who started as head of marketing and would eventually become its first executive director and cofounder. That we collectively created a platform for independent and community-based artists to make small, short-form television series extended Chicago's legacy of social practice to the digital era. OTV benefitted indirectly both from the rise of big productions, which kept crew members in the city working so they could discount services in the indie market, and from the presence of vibrant artist communities in theater, literature/poetry, dance, performance, and music, all of which embodied the city's legacy of collaboratively making art by and for artists and communities. While some of OTV's programs might individually bear some similarity to corporate fare, the platform's programming slate skews much more closely to community-based storytelling developed through a social practice orientation than those of Netflix, Disney, or other large corporate platforms. We see a greater proportion of communities who have been excluded from these systems for generations, in idiosyncratic short-form storytelling formats, in genres we are rarely allowed to lead, because we banded together to create television in our own, hyperlocal image.

Chicago's social practice tradition has received some scholarly attention in almost all art forms except film and television. This chapter fills that gap by exploring its history across art forms—all of which can contribute to film/TV—and using OTV as a case study for how this tradition lives on in TV's networked era.

CHICAGO AND THE SOCIAL PRACTICE TRADITION

"Social practice" art forms have many names. Claire Bishop's exhaustive history identifies terms such as "socially engaged art, community-based art, experimental communities, dialogic art, littoral art, interventionist art, participatory art, collaborative art, contextual art" as social practices. What connects these terms is "a definition of participation in which people constitute the central artistic medium and material, in the vein of theatre and performance" (2012, 1, 2). Focusing on *people as the medium* reorients our understanding of television away from the message, or the *product*, to the *process and politics* of making. Stephanie Smith, introducing the University of Chicago's book series on Chicago social practice history, agrees: "Socially engaged art practice prioritizes relationships, process and action" (Smith 2014, 1). Reviewing the symposium that coincided with the launch of Mary Jane Jacob and Kate Zeller's book series, Corinna Kirsch succinctly describes Chicago's social practice: "Long-term, local initiatives by artists are preferred to fly-by-night projects; one's life must be ethically rooted in the work; and the city's activist history has helped spur social-practice today" (2014). Because social practice rejects hierarchies in favor of collective action, making it particularly powerful for Black and other marginalized people, it has a fraught relationship with institutions and may be why documentation of Chicago's contribution to social practice art remains scattered.

Theater and performance, as Bishop persuasively argues, are unique in how they uplift people in the process of production, and Coya Paz, director of Free Street Theatre, argues that Chicago's contribution to theater is "ensemble made": "Performance processes that center on collective action, authored not by one but by many, by everyone in the room. . . . There are no writers, no actors, no directors—just a room full of creators." Ensemble-made theater responds to its environment, or "what works best *this* time, with *these* particular people" (2019, ix, x). Paz traces the roots of ensemble-made theater to Jane Addams, founder of the famed social service organization Hull House (1889–), drawing a direct line from Hull House to the foundation of Second City (1959–), arguably the most famous improvisational (improv) theater in the country and a pipeline to NBC's *Saturday Night Live* (1975–present). Yet Second City's national brand recognition eclipses the incredible diversity of Chicago's theater and performance scene. In addition to the famed ensemble-led Steppenwolf Theatre (1974–), Paz highlights contributions from Latina/

Latinx organizations Teatro Luna (2000–) and Teatro Vista (1990–) and Black and Black feminist groups like Honey Pot Performance (2000–), which I discuss later. While these Black and Brown companies emerged around the turn of the twenty-first century, Harvey Young and Queen Meccasia Zabriskie's (2014) history of Black theater in Chicago identifies its roots in the first decade of the twentieth century.

Midcentury Chicago saw an explosion of arts and culture led by the city's Black community. Perhaps it is because some of Chicago's greatest contributions in art making have been led by working-class Black people that its legacy is so little known (Hine and McCluskey 2012). During the Chicago Black Renaissance in the 1930s and 1940s, arguably as large, enduring, and influential as the better-known Harlem Renaissance, "the city became the center of an exchange between African American activists and artists and organizers within American leftist communities" (Young and Zabriskie 2014, 16). More working-class than its New York counterpart, Chicago's arts scene was intimately connected to politics, particularly communist politics, as evidenced by the oft-cited, if complex, legacy of Richard Wright's participation in the Communist Party (Mullen 1999).

Much less has been written about Chicago's legacy of social practice in television, but some scholarship indicates the city was a hub for early innovation in the form. Drawing on the work of Michael Patrick Ely and Robert Allen, Christopher Anderson and Michael Curtin identify Chicago as critical to the development of both the sitcom and soap opera (1999). Chad Raphael and Joel Sternberg write persuasively that before television's mass adoption throughout the 1950s, Chicago developed its own "school" of television, "a searching for television forms where no forms had existed" (Sternberg 1999, 229). The Chicago School of Television was defined by values key to social practice, including "liveness, spontaneity, informality, intimacy, and experimentation," and "distinguished itself through its collaborative and improvisational mode of production [and] its embeddedness in the local culture of Chicago" (Raphael 1999, 253). The Chicago School of Television's program innovations were most prominently seen in live variety shows that embraced the real-life stories of their cast members as writers. This collapsing of hierarchies is emblematic of social practice, where "the division of labor and hierarchy of creative roles was less pronounced than in New York or Los Angeles" stemming from "relative scarcity of resources" (255). In Raphael's analysis of Studs Terkel's *Stud's Place*, he shows how the variety series relied on local knowledge to represent "a semi-utopian vision of Chicago culture as a unique space in which popular and elite culture, working class and intellectual" (257). But Sternberg writes that even before its program innovations Chicago experimented in management, sales, engineering, and production (1999, 240).

The emergence of radio and television brought new opportunities for representing the Black community's collective struggle and innovation. Richard Durham has been underrecognized for his innovations in both media that span decades. In radio, Durham created *Destination Freedom* (1948), a show for the NBC affiliate WMAQ known for politically frank and educational stories that elevated the roles of Black women in the struggle for freedom: "*Destination Freedom* produced a body of intellectual work that stands apart from all other attempts to bring Black history and culture to a radio audience. The strident, undisguised messages in Durham's scripts would not have been acceptable on a national broadcast" (Savage 1999, 269). Yet Durham would not stop in radio: he went on to create the first Black soap opera in U.S. television history, filmed and set in Chicago, called *Bird of an Iron Feather* (1969), for public TV station WTTW. Funded by the Ford Foundation, which also funded other Black public affairs programs nationally (though few of them scripted as *Bird*), *Bird of an Iron Feather* unflinchingly dramatized the lives of working-class Black Americans in ways that would read as radical even by the standards of contemporary television. Many episodes have been lost to history, but the few digitized and uploaded to YouTube demonstrate how the series tackled issues of racial discrimination in ways that would have been unthinkable on commercial TV (Williams 2015). Durham drew from family and community stories for the series because at the same time he was editing a weekly TV news program, *Muhammed Speaks*, for the Chicago-based Nation of Islam. Leveraging community activism, the show fought to have a mostly Black crew (Television Academy 2011; Williams 2015), which included people like a young Pemon Rami, who would go on to produce independent Black films and theater for decades. *Bird of an Iron Feather* was part of a national movement that Devorah Heitner calls "Black power TV" (2013), characterized by the emergence of Black public affairs programming in cities across the country starting in 1968. Chicago had several programs produced by and for the Black community including *Our People* (WTTW, 1968–72), *A Black's View of the News* (WCIU, 1968–81), *For Black Only* (WLS, 1968–79), and *Common Ground* (WBBM, 1972–?). As evidenced by the titles, and suggested by

Heitner, Chicago's programs explicitly focused on Black community empowerment in branding and focus.

Indeed, the host of *A Black's View of the News*, Don Cornelius, would go on to create *Soul Train*, which started in Chicago on WVON. *Soul Train* is best known for representing community and was famously sponsored by Chicago-based Black media giant Johnson Publishing of *Ebony* and *Jet* magazine fame (Contreras 2021). In his history of the program, Christopher Lehman (2008) writes that the program innovated the live music TV show by bringing in young Black dancers from its surrounding community and focusing on community-developed dance moves, representing what young people were authentically wearing unlike larger programs like *American Bandstand*. *Soul Train* thus leveraged a hyperlocal production process to set a new standard to fusing music with television.

Building on Leon Forrest's assertion of Black Chicago as a "people in process, even in metamorphosis," Adam Green describes "black life in Chicago as [a] vital and unresolved process." From the Chicago Negro Exposition (one of the earliest and largest celebrations of Black people's contributions to American culture) to Black music (particularly blues, R&B, and rock and roll) and the Black press (*Chicago Defender* and Johnson Publishing, in particular), the "black modern posture" toward media institutions proposed "new perspectives on relations with institutions and conventions of society, as well as new ideas of self and community." Chicago's community orientation foregrounded a distinct form of Black nationalism before the idea took on national prominence: "'Culture' and 'community' were categories that took on meaning through the symbiotic interrelation of Black Chicago with wider worlds. They were not terms that could be subsumed or contained within its local boundaries," Green argues (2007, 2, 6, 9–10). We can see in Black Chicago the intimate connection between collective power and the production of culture.

We have undersold the role of Chicago, and particularly Black Chicago, in integrating social practice across art and media forms, advancing the idea of a community as an experimental political project combining individual innovations with collective ambitions. This orientation toward community-based innovation and progress remains in Chicago in the twenty-first century. I experienced its continued relevance in my own practice as I worked with communities in the city to develop independent television in the internet era.

OTV AS CHICAGO SOCIAL PRACTICE TELEVISION

We can see the social practice art of television in the indie, small-scale productions developed and distributed by myself and Black and Brown Chicago through OTV | Open Television. From 2015 to 2020, during the period of Chicago TV's great rise, my team and I opened the door to any artist in the city who identified with intersectionality, a Black feminist mode of analysis exploring multiple communities historically marginalized because of their race, ethnicity, gender, sexuality, religion, disability, nationality, or citizenship status. To contrast with the Hollywood system, where executives say no more often than yes to series pitches, we supported as many artists as we could. Because of our low budget, artists did nearly all of the work, but we said yes to whatever we could help with, including a nonexclusive fee for distribution ranging from five hundred to two thousand dollars and free consultation and support with financing, screenwriting, production, exhibition, and marketing. But the real value we brought was connecting artists to each other and the wider community. Screening projects locally helped forge organic connections among artists, workers, and community leaders necessary to produce complex film/TV works. It was how we recruited and supported a diverse, though largely Black, community of Chicago artists interested in producing indie TV during the latter 2010s.

Of the sixty-three pilots, series, short films, and video art works we distributed from 2015 to 2020, nearly two-thirds—or forty—could be said to indicate a social practice orientation to television development and production.[1] I categorized works as social practice based on embodying one of five characteristics, including whether the project (1) had multiple creators, (2) featured an ensemble cast, (3) featured two lead characters from different cultural backgrounds who share equal weight in the narrative, (4) featured community-based organizations prominently in the narrative, and (5) showcased cross-disciplinary collaboration as central to the narrative. The other third I categorize as solo works, in that they focus on one person's story or were largely created by one person who held multiple credits (creator, writer, director). Most of the sixty-three works featured Black creators (66 percent), and 83 percent were created by people of color (Black or Brown, e.g., Latinx or South Asian) creators. That our body of work is largely Black is indicative of a continued Chicago Renaissance, at least in media, but perhaps in other fields as well because film/TV is an interdisciplinary practice.[2]

These sections identify a variety of parameters that constitute social practice TV, but I am not arguing that these are exclusive to the indie/local space and completely lacking on corporate television, just that we can see them more prominently outside Hollywood, especially when it concerns stories by and about historically marginalized communities who are underrepresented or locally specific and thus seen as less profitable to corporate television. Moreover, my work with the creators revealed the use of social practice in the production of all of these series because producing indie TV in a city like Chicago, far from global media hubs, necessarily requires collective action in a gift economy, or community members lending support or labor beyond its value in economic capital. By characterizing OTV series by their social practice orientation in production or representation, I identify key characteristics of social practice television and highlight Chicago's contribution to the form.

Cocreated Works—Decentering the Solo Author

In 2014, I began planning the very first OTV projects, each collectively imagined by a team of creators. One of those projects, *Futurewomen*, featured the work of the aforementioned performance collective Honey Pot Performance (HPP), whom Coya Paz identifies as a key practitioner of ensemble made art. That year, HPP was devising their show *Ma(s)king Her*, an Afrofuturist dance theater work inviting community members to cocreate the characters and story of Black journeywomen across time and space. Paz writes that "finding ways of welcoming in the community is key to Honey Pot's practice," where member Felicia Holman says "every HPP show, every HPP public humanities program, every HPP project or event starts from the consideration of improving quality of life for our communities" (Paz 2019, 91). I started filming the *Ma(s)king Her* development process in 2014 and throughout 2015 to peel back the curtain on their community-based process. In workshops hosted on the South Side of Chicago, HPP asked about the experiences, dreams, fantasies, and fears of their collaborators and community, most of whom were Black women, and developed four diverse characters, all played by the collective, based on their responses. Each character spanned historical eras—from the Haitian Revolution to the 1919 Chicago riots—and space—from Earth to unknown worlds. What we see in *Futurewomen* is an expansion of Black womanhood that goes far beyond corporate TV representations to show how Black women collectively create whole worlds as containers for healing and discovery.

Overall, nineteen OTV projects had multiple creators, writers, or directors—sixty-five people total, meaning the average project had three key collaborators, a strong indication of a collective ethos. A few projects had large teams of creators, including *Velvet*, a three-episode series about Black female friendship, which had seven creators, and *Hair Story* (2018), a pilot of an experimental series about a Black co-op, which had thirteen writers and two directors. Much more common were projects that had two creators sharing writing, directing, and producing duties, amounting to nearly half of the projects with multiple creators. These creative teams worked collaboratively not only to share the labor and hold each other accountable but also to reflect the complexity and interdependency of identity.

Intersectional Friendship— Caring across Difference, Challenging Monocultural Storytelling

Indeed, I was struck by what appeared to be the emergence of a specific genre of storytelling in Chicago: the intersectional friendship series, where two people of different cultural backgrounds come together to support each other and share equal dominance over the narrative. Overall, thirteen series explicitly split the narrative between two or more central characters who hail from different cultural backgrounds, excluding projects with ensemble casts with more than two central characters. Several of these series represent Black and Brown (South Asian) solidarity and connections, something virtually unexplored in Hollywood, including Sam Bailey and Fatimah Asghar's *Brown Girls* (2017), Priya Mohanty's *FOBia* (2019), Nikkita Duke and Aalisha Sheth's *United States of Aliens* (2020), Karan Sunil's *Code-Switched* (2018–21), and Vincent Martell's *Damaged Goods* (2020–22). Other series showed Black-white interracial friendship, including Daniel Kyri and Bea Cordelia's *the T* (2018) and Kyra Jones and Juli Del Prete's *The Right Swipe* (2019), and Black-Latinx friendship, such as Michelle Zacarias's *THOTless* (2020). Still other shows focused on friendships of characters who have the same race but claim different genders, sexualities, or body types, including Zak Payne's *Kissing Walls* (2018–19), Shervin Bain and Victoria Lee's *Low Strung* (2019–), and Rachel Relman's *Kings and Queens* (2019).

These series expand narrative possibilities by taking seriously each character's journey while also showing where different struggles intersect. This is substantially different from Hollywood's "buddy comedies," where typically two characters of different identities are put on an explicit mission that drives the narrative, often focusing on policing crime (e.g., *Rush Hour*, *Naked Gun*). Instead, the framework of intersectional friendship specifies the ways systemic oppression impacts people differently. For example, in *United States of Aliens*, Duke and Sheth's characters, Rishita and Uduak, are Chicago-based immigrants from Nigeria and India, respectively. They face issues common to many immigrants, like accessing health care or fearing deportation, but also face specific challenges. In an opening scene on a video call with family back home, Uduak's long-distance sexual play with her partner is interrupted by their country's poor internet infrastructure; in a parallel scene, Rishita ends her call with her dad early when he starts talking about marriage after she mentions going on one date with a new guy. Sheth said she and Duke explicitly collaborated to bring out these themes of the similarities and differences in cross-cultural immigrant experiences: "We don't see multicultural friendships on-screen. It's always like two Brown girls or two white girls. Why? Because we live in a world where people of all backgrounds, of all races, of all ethnicities are trying to survive things together. . . . It's almost like the support system that they're creating while surviving individual experiences." We can see the importance and value of intersectionality as a framework for guiding collaboration and dispersing ownership over the narrative.

Ensemble Works—Decentering the Singular Narrative

Works that focus on two or more characters offer even more possibilities for representing communities on-screen. At the local level, creators can show diverse groups of people who are largely excluded from the ensemble genres on corporate television. Adding more characters increases production budgets because of having to pay more actors and spend more time in production capturing sound and choreographing scenes. Even though all OTV works had production budgets under $100,000 (less than 10 percent of the average single episode of mainstream television), a strong plurality, twenty-one projects, featured ensemble casts. I categorize these projects by three broad approaches: (1) love across difference, (2) difference within sameness, and (3) true anthology/decentered stories. Stories about love across difference show different types of people as part of an overall diverse community trying to support each other or band together. Sam Bailey's *You're So Talented* (2015–16) focuses on three friends—two Black women and one white man—and their broader diverse creative community who are all struggling for recognition. Projects that explore difference within sameness focus on an ensemble who share one identity and use the narrative to draw out differences within that community. Amid the lack of Latinx and queer community representation (especially outside the private family), Ricardo Gamboa's *Brujos* (2017–19) accomplishes this by representing three Latinx leads who have different orientations to class and family as well as different superpowers they use to rally queer people of color against the descendants of colonizers. Unlike the near complete lack of series about Black queer women's community, M. Shelly Conner's *Quare Life* (2018) focuses on four Black queer women who are variously butch and femme, nerdy and cool, coming together to support one member of the group after a breakup. Karan Sunil's *Code-Switched* explores a friend group comprising South Asian, Korean, and Black people, but spends most narrative time showing how different types of South Asian people—Hindu, Muslim, Indian, Pakistani—navigate the romantic and professional growing pains emblematic of the quarter-life crisis. Sunil created the show to disrupt the singular narrative of South Asians in Hollywood (*Master of None*, *Ramy*): "I think the media tends to make immigrants look like a homogenous group. There are so many different types of immigrants, forms of immigration, and many stories in front of us, in people we see everyday, that are yet to be told" (Khalil 2020). Knowing that his personal experience was specific, he engaged dozens of people and spent countless hours participating in Chicago's art scene before filming: "The process was long, fun, and interesting. Besides my own story of being a straight Indian Hindu-raised guy, there are a lot of stories that I don't know around me. So I spoke to focus groups of South Asian millennials between eighteen and twenty-five in Chicago and Seattle about their experiences. I handpicked the cast, who are mostly comedians, stand-ups and improvisers. I scouted comedy shows in Chicago for months, everything from paid tickets, to open mics at Mexican restaurants and sports bars. I wanted to find five people that embody the character's roles in some way" (Khalil 2020). Here we see how important it was for Sunil to include multiple voices and artists even as he was representing a community with which he identified, embodying Chicago's social practice values.

Community as a Character

Some OTV projects focus the narrative on hyperlocal communities as a character. These include some of the aforementioned anthology series, such as Christian Mejia's *Born and Raised*, which showcases his historically Latinx home neighborhood of Logan Square through the lens of three different character-based stories that elucidate a range of perspectives on gentrification. In Arnetta Randall's *Hook-Ups*, Black characters across a spectrum of gender and sexuality experience variously awkward and life-changing sexual situations; each character is connected to a character in the previous episode, painting a beautiful and hilarious portrait of how local Black communities are connected by our different sexual proclivities.

In other series, the community is the sole focal point of the narrative. We see this best in Sohib Boundaoui's *Arabica* (2020), in part inspired by his sister Assia Boundaoui's award-winning documentary *The Feeling of Being Watched*, which explores the real-life story of the FBI's surveillance of a Muslim and Palestinian community outside Chicago in the 1990s. Sohib's narrative series feels like a documentary. Using handheld cameras, real locations in Bridgeview, and largely untrained actors, he acts as a filmmaker trying to uncover the mystery of unmarked vans appearing throughout the neighborhood. The community expresses a wide range of reactions to his interest, from complete dismissal to burgeoning curiosity. Yet the story spends as much time on more mundane narratives of life in Bridgeview, from the customers at the local store who are skeptical of white patrons to the kids who forget to pick up their siblings from school. When asked why he made the story, Sohib started immediately by describing the neighborhood and the circumstances of his upbringing as a Muslim millennial: "I started off in film exploring my friends' perspective, what they thought being in the community.... [I'd] write scenarios that could easily have happened in that community. I feel like it was a space that wasn't explored, and by having so many connections in the community and being able to rally so much support... it was inevitable that these stories were going to be told and it would be a shame if someone outside the community came in and told our stories" (personal interview 2020). Sohib mentions community several times, signaling the neighborhood as the linchpin for all his storytelling, not just *Arabica*. Still it is in *Arabica* where we see his love for the richness and fullness of Bridgeview. *Arabica* reframes the community away from their misrepresentation by the government as criminals to a complex array of people who all share Muslim identity but also embody varying perspectives on what it means to live in the context of surveillance.

Several other OTV projects feature community organizations or issues prominently in the narrative. We filmed *Hair Story* at the Breathing Room, a Black-run co-op and venue for healing and activism in Chicago's

Back of the Yards, and the narrative reflects the pleasures and challenges of organizing as Black queer and woman-identified people. *Brujos* filmed as many scenes as possible in Chicago's predominantly Mexican American neighborhood of Pilsen, featuring local spots characters might actually patronize. Kayla Ginsburg and Ruby Western's *Afternoon Snatch* (2017), which explores the genre of the break-up comedy through a queer and gender-expansive lens, centers multiple episodes on Chicago-based organizations well-known as critical nodes in the community at that time, including Salonathon, a weekly "performance-based open mic" that ran for six years in Ukrainian Village, and About Face Theater, the city's LGBTQ+ theater that ran a well-known youth program. We see in OTV's programs how community emerges as a character through very specific local neighborhoods, organizations, and contexts that do not seek to stand in for anything other than a unique experience.

Collaboration as a Character

Finally, we see the idea of collaboration as a character in a few OTV works. These stories feature artist collectives working collaboratively to make new works and imagine new worlds. The core driver of the plot and the emotional arc of the story revolves around the shifting dynamics of different people making something together. Certainly *Futurewomen* fits into this rubric, but so do other dance-focused series such as *Darling Shear* (2018) and *The Furies* (2017). *Darling Shear* is centered on one character, Chicago-based Black trans choreographer and dancer Darling Shear, who is widely known and celebrated in queer, performance, and dance spaces throughout the city. Still, the actual narrative of the show is focused on her developing her biggest show to date for Links Hall, a space well known for collectively generated and experimental performance, in collaboration with dancers she hired. A critical part of the narrative involves Darling working with dancers to reinterpret dance sequences from classical Hollywood films; as a Black trans woman, Darling's embodiment of that work, even when scenes were implicitly racist, reconfigures its meaning, even though her dancers do not share all her identifications. We see how people with different identities grapple with the politics of identification in nuanced, embodied, and divergent ways, in ways we rarely see in dance documentaries.

My own work for the platform, inspired by the interdisciplinary arts space I matriculated in Chicago, asks how Black people can collaborate across gender expression and sexual politics. My first experimental pilot,

Nupita Obama Creates Vogua (2015), features three gender-nonconforming artists of color—Erik Lamar "Mister" Wallace, Kiam Junio, and Saya Naomi—caught in an uneven love triangle and forced to live together. They diffuse the tensions by creating a last-minute, improvised performance that married their three creative and self-care practices: yoga, vogue, and drag. The process of production mirrored the narrative, as I collaborated with three artists with expertise in those forms, who created this art form called "vogua" (vogue + yoga) in the days leading up to filming. In the sequel, *Hair Story*, the two Black characters who were frenemies in *Nupita Obama* have become friends; Gia (Naomi) and Curtis (Wallace) support each other as Gia tries to run a Black co-op filled with artists who all have different living styles. Again, the process of production mirrored the series as the twelve-person writers' room cocreated the story by contributing characters from their own series, making *Hair Story* a true collaboration of different art projects and narratives.

CHICAGO RENAISSANCE REDUX

OTV is far from the only example of the renaissance of social practice making in the new millennium. In our story you read about the Black feminist collective HPP, which for over twenty years has created new works based on collective, community-based processes for writing. In the field of journalism, there is *The Triibe*, a digital news organization for Black millennials on Chicago's South and West Sides; using Black feminist practices of care, *The Triibe* provided a platform for activists and community leaders, alongside traditionally trained journalists, to report on news affecting their communities (Peterson-Salahuddin 2022). In the art world and photography, there is Zakkiyyah Najeebah and L'Soft's Concerned Black Image Makers, continuing the legacy of OBAC and AfriCOBRA, and the work of Theaster Gates, known globally as a leader in a small group of artists innovating in social practice (McGraw 2012). In TV and audio, activist-created AirGo Radio has chronicled hundreds of local activists and community leaders, and even short-lived projects like Pilot TV spawned queer worlds. In social dance, whose roots in Chicago house music were outside the scope of this chapter, parties like Chances Dances and Slo Mo center care and community-based economics to create social dance space for people of all genders (Adeyemi 2019; Myint 2015; Salkind 2018). In performance, Salonathon spent six years hosting a weekly open mic, drawing artists across genders, sexualities, and races for avant-garde performance blurring the lines between artists and audiences.

It would be overly simplistic to say that the dynamics of storytelling and production we see in Chicago across media are completely absent in more corporate, national or mainstream media contexts. Instead, what is remarkable about Chicago's artistic production is the consistency with which creators privilege the social and communal, the improvisational and decentralized ways of making and expressing that are often more difficult to achieve in global media hubs. Indeed, if we look across this volume and in other contexts outside the United States, we will likely find a lot of similarities in how stories are produced and told outside of power centers. Amid scarce resources and absent institutional norms, artists and organizers find fertile ground for social practice. With OTV I was surprised how the vast majority of programs we developed cultivated this orientation to storytelling. It is not that Hollywood lacks ensemble TV shows or stories that focus on communities, but I would argue few if any corporate TV network original programming slates, in total, represent the diversity and complexity of community in the ways we see on OTV or have seen in Chicago historically. What's more, the hierarchies of production necessary to produce at the level and speed of Hollywood mean that even when the stories themselves resonate with some social practice values, the context of production rarely does. Through Chicago, we see how vibrant, if a little messier, our nation's stories could be if we distributed resources more equitably across all our localities.

NOTES

1. Nearly all projects were short form, with full series under sixty minutes and most episodes between five and fifteen minutes.
2. Indeed, many of the writers, actors, and directors had experience in theater, comedy, and live lit/poetry, forms Chicago is better known for nationally.

REFERENCES

Acham, Christine. 2018. "Subverting the System: The Politics and Production of *The Spook Who Sat by the Door*." In *Race and the Revolutionary Impulse in The Spook Who Sat by the Door*, edited by Michael T. Martin, David C. Wall, and Marilyn Yaquinto, 121–33. Indiana University Press.

Adeyemi, Kemi. 2019. "The Practice of Slowness: Black Queer Women and the Right to the City." *GLQ: A Journal of Lesbian and Gay Studies* 25 (4): 545–67.

Anderson, Christopher, and Michael Curtin. 1999. "Mapping the Ethereal City: Chicago Television, the FCC, and the Politics of Place." *Quarterly Review of Film & Video* 16 (3–4): 289–305.

Bishop, Claire. 2012. *Artificial Hells: Participatory Art and the Politics of Spectatorship*. Verso.

Borrelli, Christopher. 2011. "Mumblecore Grows Up." *Chicago Tribune*, May 4.

Braxton, Greg. 2013. "Slow Burn, but 'Fire' Ignites Strong Following." *Chicago Tribune*, April 24.

Chase, John, and Jeff Coen. 2011. "Taxpayers May Back This Coming Attraction." *Chicago Tribune*, October 9.

Christian, A. J. 2011. "Joe Swanberg, Intimacy, and the Digital Aesthetic." *Cinema Journal* 50 (4): 117–35.

Contreras, Ayana. 2021. *Energy Never Dies: Afro-optimism and Creativity in Chicago*. University of Illinois Press.

Field, Allyson N. 2016. "The Ambitions of William Foster: Entrepreneurial Filmmaking at the Limits of Uplift Cinema." In *Early Race Filmmaking in America*, edited by Barbara Lupack, 53–71. Routledge.

Green, Adam. 2007. *Selling the Race: Culture, Community and Black Chicago, 1940–1955*. University of Chicago Press.

Hallstoos, Brian. 2007. "Pageant and Passion: William Saunders Jones and Early Black Sacred Drama in Chicago." *Journal of American Drama and Theatre* 19 (2): 77–97.

Hardy, Debra. 2018. "And Thus We Shall Survive: The Perseverance of the South Side Community Art Center as a Counter-narrative, 1938–1959." In *The Palgrave Handbook of Race and the Arts in Education*, edited by A. M. Kraehe et al., 119–36. Palgrave.

Heitner, Devorah. 2013. *Black Power TV*. Duke University Press.

Hine, Darlene Clark, and John McCluskey Jr., eds. 2012. *The Black Chicago Renaissance*. University of Illinois Press.

Jones Hogu, Barbara. 2012. "Inaugurating AfriCOBRA: History, Philosophy and Aesthetics." *Nka: Journal of Contemporary African Art* 30: 90–97.

Khalil, Diane Bou. 2020. "'Code-Switched' Director Karan Sunil on His New South Asian Sitcom." *Borderless*, November 13.

Kirsch, Corinna. 2014. "What Is Social Practice Anyway? A Look at Chicago's 'A Lived Practice.'" *Art F City*, November 17.

Lehman, Christopher P. 2008. *A Critical History of* Soul Train *on Television*. McFarland.

Lems, Kristin. 2020. "Louder Than a Bomb: Poetry Slams and Community Activism Create a Powerful Brew." *Interface*, April.

Lewis, George. 2008. *A Power Stronger Than Itself: The AACM and American Experimental Music*. University of Chicago Press.

McGraw, Hesse. 2012. "Theaster Gates: Radical Reform with Everyday Tools." *Afterall* 30:86–99.

Metz, Nina. 2011. "Illinois Hopes Cinespace Helps Build on Big 2010." *Chicago Tribune*, May 11.
Mullen, Bill. 1999. *Popular Fronts: Chicago and African-American Cultural Politics, 1935–46*. University of Illinois Press.
Myint, Aay-Preston, ed. 2015. *Platforms: Ten Years of Chances Dances*. Gallery 400.
Novak, Tim, and Robert Herguth. 2021. "Studio Head Who Helped Bring Down Teamsters Boss Tied to Illegal Gambling Ring." *Chicago Sun-Times*, November 19.
Paz, Coya. 2019. *Ensemble-Made Chicago: A Guide to Devised Theater*. Northwestern University Press.
Peterson-Salahuddin, Chelsea. 2022. "Black Feminism in Popular Culture: Exploring Representations of Black Feminism in News and Entertainment." Ph.D. diss., Northwestern University.
Phillips, Michael. 2012. "Coaxing Film from a Former Steel Plant." *Chicago Tribune*, September 2.
Raphael, Chad. 1999. "Utopia Out of Place: *Stud's Place*, Popular Front Culture and the Blacklist in Chicago Television." *Quarterly Review of Film & Video* 16 (3–4): 253–70.
Salkind, Micah. 2018. *Do You Remember House? Chicago's Queer of Color Undergrounds*. Oxford University Press.
Savage, Barbara. 1999. *Broadcasting Freedom: Radio, War, and the Politics of Race, 1938–1948*. University of North Carolina Press.
Smith, Stephanie, ed. 2014. *Institutions and Imaginaries*. University of Chicago Press.
Sternberg, Joel. 1999. "Chicago Television: A History." *Quarterly Review of Film & Video* 16 (3–4): 229–52.
Stewart, Jacqueline. 2005. *Migrating to the Movies: Cinema and Black Urban Modernity*. University of California Press.
Television Academy. 2011. "Newton Minow Interview Part 6 of 6—emmytvlegends.org." March 9. https://interviews.televisionacademy.com/shows/bird-iron-feather.
Werner, Craig. 1993. "Leon Forrest, the AACM and the Legacy of the Chicago Renaissance." *Black Scholar* 22 (3–4): 10–23.
Williams, Sonya. 2015. *Word Warrior: Richard Durham, Radio, and Freedom*. University of Illinois Press.
Young, Harvey, and Queen Meccasia Zabriskie. 2014. *Black Theater Is Black Life: An Oral History of Chicago Theater and Dance, 1970–2010*. Northwestern University Press.
Zorach, Rebecca. 2019. *Art for People's Sake: Artists and Community in Black Chicago, 1965–1975*. Duke University Press.

CHAPTER 15

ANTOINE HAYWOOD

TELLING OUR STORIES

A REFLECTION ON REALIZING THE PROMISE OF PUBLIC ACCESS TV IN PHILADELPHIA

Before the COVID-19 pandemic, Fridays at PhillyCAM used to be a whole vibe. In the late afternoon, young people hung out upstairs in the community room, chatting about pop-culture trends and new ideas for upcoming video projects. Around the corner from them, in the WPPM radio studio, DJ Affirmation bopped along to the live broadcast of his funky jazz playlist. Whenever I heard muffled laughter and syncopated beats resonating through my office walls, I knew it was time to wander around and enjoy their company.

The transition from afternoon to evening activities was usually marked by the arrival of Chef Ali Hackett and his snazzily dressed guests, ready to record another episode of *Salt . . . Pepper N Memories* down in the first-floor television studio. My colleague Ariel Taylor, who managed our youth media program, once described this lively Friday atmosphere at PhillyCAM as Black church-like. I agreed. It was as if the young people were upstairs in Sunday school, waiting to join their elders down in the main sanctuary and fellowship hall. I used to imagine DJ Affirmation as a cool deacon, marching the youth choir down for the evening praise and worship service.

Chef Ali and his studio audience guests carried a dignified elegance that reminded me of my parents: hardworking African Americans born after the Second World War and into an era of state-sanctioned racial segregation, civil rights movement protests, and all-day Sunday church services. The *Salt . . . Pepper N Memories* crew would come to PhillyCAM ready to eat, laugh, and twirl their blues away. Their witty banter and 1960s R&B dance moves reminded me of home and the Black community bonding I experienced growing up. Vibrant Fridays at PhillyCAM made me proud of our community culture. Those days proved that PhillyCAM had become a multiethnic, multigenerational community media center (CMC) where Black people thrived. Realizing this potential of a public access center was a primary reason why I worked in the field for fifteen years.

Despite the pandemic's chilling effects, local producers have returned to PhillyCAM to produce studio programs, check out equipment, and participate in social events. This is a testament to PhillyCAM's resilient culture, which was born from a deep history of activism and the need for public access for local communication infrastructure. It's hard to believe that PhillyCAM, a community resource that has achieved so much in its first decade, almost didn't exist.

The following sections of this chapter provide a brief historical reflection on how and why the local government took so long to make good on its promise to grant concessions for Philadelphia's public access media system. Thanks to allies inside City Hall and three waves of grassroots coalitional activism starting in the 1980s, Philadelphia has a robust CMC with an exceptional track record of supporting historically marginalized communities. These communities converge at PhillyCAM to learn new communication skills, build social capital, tell authentic stories, and give back to society.

To shed light on the experiences of media makers who gather at PhillyCAM, this chapter also includes excerpts from five interviews conducted for a community media oral history project titled Telling Our Stories. In 2021, a small group of PhillyCAM members and I launched this project to initiate an archive of first-person narratives that convey why CMCs, buoyed by local access television infrastructure, remain relevant and valuable in the digital age.

PHILADELPHIA'S LONG FIGHT FOR PUBLIC ACCESS TV

When Philadelphia Community Access Media (PhillyCAM) started cablecasting on October 23, 2009, it put Philadelphia on the map as the most recent major U.S. city to get public access television. I was hired in 2010 to develop PhillyCAM's membership and outreach program, which was initially daunting, considering I did not grow up in Philadelphia. Although I had extensive experience working in community media, there was much to learn about Philadelphia culture and what delayed the development of public access television in a city filled with so much communication history. I had to learn why PhillyCAM was such a significant achievement for the activists, who spent nearly thirty years pressing the city to establish its public access television channels.

Before coming to Philadelphia, my career began at Atlanta's public access television operation, People TV. Unlike Philadelphia, Atlanta's public access channels started in the 1980s, when many local communities figured out how to operate local access channels and production facilities without government and commercial interference (Simama 2009; Linder 1999). In the 1970s, the Federal Communications Commission (FCC) required cable companies operating in the top hundred markets to provide access channels, technical staff, and production facilities that communities could use for public, educational, and governmental (PEG) communication purposes. But after the 1984 Cable Act, these provisions became optional, which marked a new era during which communities lobbied local governments for access to public channels and funds for production facilities.

Philadelphia approved its first ordinance to develop a public access television corporation in 1983. The vision, shared by grassroots coalitions like the Concerned Citizens for Cable Communications and city council members like John C. Anderson, who championed the cause inside City Hall, was to develop an independent nonprofit corporation that programmed the public access channels, trained residents in television production, maintained an equipment inventory, and managed administrative duties. While Philadelphia's governmental and educational channels got up and running by the late 1980s, public access became a promise put on hold for far too long (McCollough and Coates 1999). Many assumed W. Wilson Goode, the city's first African American mayor, would implement the public access plan as per the 1983 ordinance (Cliff-Evans 1998). However, Goode's administration (1984–92) never made good on the outstanding commitment to public access. The issue was unresolved and passed on to succeeding administrations.

In the 1980s, it became customary for local governments to enter into franchise agreements with cable companies for ten or fifteen years. Philadelphia used this lucrative arrangement, authorized by the Cable Act, to levy a franchise fee upon cable companies in exchange for using public rights of way, such as utility poles and cabling thoroughfares. The Cable Act allowed governments to collect up to 5 percent of a cable company's gross income from television subscribers in a local jurisdiction.

During the eighties and nineties, many communities started using part of their franchise fee revenue to pay for public access television operations. But this was not the case in Philadelphia.

A second wave of activists organized in the 1990s as the Access Coalition: Citizens for Public Access in Philadelphia began tracking the development of public access in other parts of the country (Spolan 1990). They also educated the public on why Philadelphia's administration still needed to fulfill its public access promise (Cliff-Evans 1998). Although the city took no action on the issue during this period, the Access Coalition provided insights that future activists could build upon.

In 1997, local performing artists, media makers, and social justice activists formed the Philadelphia Community Access Coalition (PCAC). This third wave of activism launched a citywide public access campaign during Philadelphia's 1998 franchise negotiation period. PCAC's efforts were reinforced inside City Hall by council members like David Cohen, Michael Nutter, and Angel Ortiz (three leaders whom John C. Anderson influenced before his untimely death in 1983). Applying political pressure inside and outside City Hall proved successful in cities like Boston and Detroit (Kiuchi 2012). However, in Philadelphia, several roadblocks persisted and hampered progress in the early 2000s.

The city's administration ultimately feared controversial public access programming that caused costly legal headaches in so many other communities (Parker 2003). Furthermore, the city struggled to figure out how to fund a public access facility. Administrators were reluctant to use part of the city's cable revenue to pay for public access (Quinn 1998). To make a case for these concessions, PCAC utilized various rhetorical strategies, including sharing extensive testimonials during city council hearings, wearing cardboard TV heads while staging public demonstrations in front of City Hall and outside Comcast special events, meeting with city administrators, and hosting prayer vigils outside of mayor's office. On several occasions, PCAC's leaders considered calling it quits. Thanks to timely inspiration from the Alliance for Community Media members and the global Indymedia movement that sparked the development of a Philly-based Indy Media Center (IMC) in 1999, PCAC members were motivated to press on.

Refusing to give up, PCAC filed a federal lawsuit against the city in 2002. This strategic move catalyzed a series of meetings that gave rise to a funding solution. A decision was ultimately made to collect an additional PEG fee directly from Philadelphia cable subscribers. With the funding issue resolved, the City of Philadelphia and the Comcast Corporation amended their franchise agreement in 2007, which initiated the charter and funds for Philadelphia Public Access Corporation (d.b.a. PhillyCAM). A charter board of directors was formed, an executive director and programming director were hired, and by October 2009 the city's public access channels were up and running—another first in Philadelphia history.

TELLING OUR STORIES IN SATURATED MEDIA ECOLOGIES

Over the years, I have contemplated why I have been devoted to what community media practitioners have called the "promise of public access" (Blau 1992). Working as an administrator in local access television operations has many exhausting, idiosyncratic ups and downs (Goldberg 1990). Yet as many access media pioneers have eloquently argued over the years, public access is a worthy cause when it lives up to its promise as a transformative communication tool (Halleck 2002; Devine 2001; Blau 1992). Even in a digital age highly saturated with media and information ecosystems, CMCs buoyed by local PEG channels have remained essential hubs that enable communities to experience a sense of place and connectedness (Ali 2014; Haywood, Aufderheide, and Sánchez Santos 2021; Dewey 2021; Haywood 2024).

With mixed emotions, I transitioned out of my position at PhillyCAM to attend graduate school. Fortunately, I remained connected with PhillyCAM as a project volunteer and community-engaged researcher, documenting insights that convey the contemporary relevance and value of its local access television infrastructure. To demonstrate this relevance, the following excerpts come from an initial round of interviews conducted for the Telling Our Stories community media oral history project initiated in 2021. These firsthand accounts shed light on why local producers are attracted to utilizing PhillyCAM's resources in Philadelphia's saturated contemporary media landscape.

Beatrice Joyner (BJ), professional educator, photographer, and *In Search of Knowledge* television program producer

    ANTOINE HAYWOOD (AH): How did you start making media?
    BJ: I grew up watching Gordon Parks or seeing Gordon Parks in *Life* magazine as a child. And I fell in love with photography. And so I began taking pictures from a young age. I had gone to school for En-

glish in my undergrad, met a lot of famous Black writers and started snatching their pictures whenever I could. But it was when I went to an elementary school one day for a career day, and I asked the children a typical question: "What do you want to be when you grow up?" And one little boy got very excited. He said, "I want to be a drug dealer." And I thought about it, I said it, that's the only occupation that he knows. We as adults are at fault, and we have to show him there's another way to earn his living. So I decided to use the photos that I had been taking to show our children role models, other people who had succeeded, who had come often from the same neighborhoods, but had been successful. Just that they knew that they didn't have to have an illegal career in order to be successful.

AH: And so that tells me the why. And so you're talking about photography, but you also do video, correct?

BJ: I did video because I had been telling someone about the project. It's called *In Search of Knowledge*, and I was speaking to someone from SCORE and he said, "You need to go to PhillyCAM and interview people." And I'm like, PhillyCAM, what's PhillyCAM? I had no intention of being in video, though I love film, but it was because of that introduction to the possibility of adding another dimension to my project that I started doing video.

AH: And what's your program called?

BJ: *In Search of Knowledge*. And I call it *In Search of Knowledge*, because I actually went to see the people because of some knowledge that they had, either because they were world famous or I discovered them. Because a lot of individuals I've discovered just being out in the community, finding people and saying, "Oh, okay, I need to interview you for my project."

AH: Okay, great. And so let's hear about your program. What do you produce? I don't know, maybe programs. I know of one, but yeah, please share about what you create, the stories that resonate with you, that you seek out to tell. And then of course, the why.

BJ: The why I do it is because I didn't want our children going through the school-to-prison pipeline. I wanted to show them that there were alternatives to careers that they could have. And it didn't require, not all of them require college. Some of the individuals in my collection have high school diplomas all the way up to doctorates. But I wanted to show them that if they really were interested in something, they could create a career out of it. So I began using the photos and just doing PowerPoint presentations with kids to talk to them about that.

I moved onto, like I said, to the TV station, but there's workshops, there's exhibits that could be done. My first major presentation was at the American Library Association's National Conference. And what I did is I took photos of notable Blacks and just put them on a table and said, "Do you know who this is?" Because a lot of times we in the Black community know who these individuals are, but outside of that, people don't know. So I wanted to give exposure, and that's what I look for. I look for the people who are not as well known in order to show our children that there's all kinds of ways that they can earn a living.

AH: And tell me a little bit about what it means to be a community media maker. What is that experience like? How's it been?

BJ: It's been amazing. I mean, I came to PhillyCAM not knowing what to expect and found a community of people who were willing to support me. I mean, I've met people in the hallways who say, "Hey, if you need any help, just let me know." I've had other people who say, "I'll volunteer." I had no budget for those four years. And people were generous enough to participate because I think we all believe in the fact that our stories need to be told. And there's a wide variety of ways to tell those stories. And so I believe that by telling and sharing the stories of these individuals, I'm going to help children. I'm going to help somebody. I'm going to help somebody say, "You know what? Maybe I need to take another look at this. Or maybe I should change what I'm doing. Or maybe I'm more intelligent than I thought, simply because I didn't realize I understand what they're saying."

Julian Seward (JS), poet, community activist, and *My Bittersweet Philosophy* radio program producer

AH: And what is your show? What is your radio program, and what is it about?

JS: Absolutely. So my show is *My Bittersweet Philosophy*. That show came about in college. I was originally a secondary education history student. And then I took an elective. And like I said, people just always said something about [how] your voice would be nice on radio. And I knew that with being in a radio elective, I had a chance to be at a radio station. I love music. So I was like, this can go hand in hand. And I took one elective and the next semester I changed my major and we had to form a show. And I said I wanted to be something where I can be around creatives and just invite my friends who were creatives in the area, who did do music, who did do poetry, who did do whatever form of expression it was. In Trenton, New Jersey, there was a huge pocket of just creatives at that point in time. This is around 2009 to 2013–15. And I just wanted to create that space. So I created a show where I could live DJ and talk about my love of music for half of it, and then interview artists for the other half. And I just, through trial and error, just tried to figure out how to kind of finesse that and how to sculpt that. And it turned into a very popular show at that school. And then I met my future producer by the name of Vanessa and I met her down in Trenton. And I talked to her about what my aspirations were. She invited me to come down and then the rest is history.

I got a show on the air there. And it just, again, with the community of PhillyCAM and with the opportunities of networking with artists in the area, by seeing what true expression is with tools that you can have with a place like PhillyCAM, it just spawned from there. So I took the same concept that I have of my love of music and DJing and then my interviewing style and just ran with it. And that's what the show has been. It really stayed within that format and it's hard to stray away from it because it really just works very well.

AH: Can you talk about your relationship with the PhillyCAM community and what has that been like? And also from your perspective as a member of that community, what space does it hold in the community, in the greater Philadelphia area?

JS: PhillyCAM changed my life, to tell you the truth. I had never seen anything quite like it. Again, coming from where I came from, we're between New York, we're between Philadelphia, but at the same time, there's nothing there that quite had that access to create a space where real artists can do something from a passion perspective and really have it reach the masses. I think being a part of that community is still a very special thing to hold. I think over time it becomes less of, this is a platform for me to create my artistry. And it becomes more of, this is a place to really be an artist in whatever facet it is, in front of the camera, behind the camera, in front of the mic, behind the mic or just being in the space to just enjoy it.

Yeah. I think specifically for me just being so engrossed in the radio aspect, I really found a sense of confidence in different forms of art that [I] would not normally have, especially really DJing. I have to give it up to DJ Affirmation first and foremost. That is a true friend, a true brother of mine. He has a show called *50 Shades of Jazz* that was directly before mine. We would be back to back on Fridays. And also Derwood with the Selby Signature. Those two men really gave me the confidence to really just like you said, as a springboard branch off and say, "This is something you can actually do, not just within the confines of this station, but really elsewhere." So there are opportunities to live DJ at certain clubs that we did. I remember you were a part of that as well out there on South Street.

So it really, that created a sense of community. And then just also having the access to try new things. I definitely dabbled with the TV studio because it was just, the sort of radio studio was upstairs, the TV studio was downstairs, and it was just free range to come back and forth in between and in a figurative sense and in a literal sense. So it just gave access to really just dabbling in things that you're not quite, that you might have told yourself that this is not a part of what your programming is. That's why I was mentioning to the gentleman before about how I'm thinking about starting a visual aspect of my program just because it's there and it's able to be used.

So I think that all of the, and I don't want to give too many names because I don't want to leave anybody out, but just all of the producers who were just open and curious and inviting. That definitely, I think as an artist, that's something that curiosity is something that you have innately. And having the resources to express that, whether it's through literal tools, whether it's a camera, whether it's a mic, or whether it's through people, that as well is just as important. Having access to those resources makes a world of a difference.

AH: When you talk about representation, what does that mean for people of color specifically?

JS: Oh yeah, absolutely. It means everything because there are so many people who try to represent you, who are not actually you. You know what I mean? So many people who are. . . . So let's say the Black community, for example. Everyone loves our artistry. Everyone loves the culture that we put out. But it's so disrespected. There's so many untruths and it's so halfway told. And I remember a term that I kept hearing so often. I remember there was a skit on *Key & Peele* a while back about we are not a monolith talking about Black Republicans. I thought it was so funny. But there's so many different facets to our culture and so many different qualities to our culture that to place us in a box and to place us as only being the, what's perceived to be the fun aspects. You know what I mean? Removes our true identity at a time where it's most crucial that our identity is told honestly. You know what I mean? At a time when our identity should be recognized so that it's not watered down, so it's not forgotten. So the narrative isn't changed.

There's a lot of narratives that are being changed nowadays to try to fit a comfortable truth. And I feel like representation, again, FUBU policy, for us by us, is very, very much needed. That does not mean that we exclude. It just means that we provide the format of what our truth actually is. And it's crucial. It always has been crucial. It always will be crucial. And I feel like the uncomfortable truths need to be told regardless, because they're needed. That means the representation means everything in an honest way.

Leticia Roa Nixon (LRN), professional journalist, community activist, and *Atrévete* community news program producer

AH: And how did you start making media?
LRN: Well, since I was in Mexico City, I studied communications, though my major was in research. But I immediately start[ed] working for a newspaper that had a children's section, every Sunday. So since then I've been a news reporter.
AH: Okay. And what inspired you to become a reporter and to get into media making and storytelling?
LRN: Yes. Well, I did that because I like journalism, but once I moved to Philadelphia, that was a different story, which it was great to be writing for the community. Not for, but within the community. And that's when I started to be a community news reporter. And mainly because I felt that there were few newspapers in Spanish at that time, but there were more at that time than now. And I thought it would be important for Latinos to see their stories reflected in the newspaper.

AH: Okay. And so that's the why. And then, can you tell me about the organizations that you have been involved in as a media maker and a local storyteller?

LRN: Well, yes. Mainly there were all the newspapers, the community newspapers, starting with one founded by Puerto Ricans, which was very pro-community, pro–human rights, civil rights. The name was *Community Focus, El Focal Communal*, and it appeared. And I also wrote for [inaudible 00:04:24] paper for Sol Latino, for Impacto. And when there was an opportunity to be producing stories for TV, that's thanks to Laura Dutch and Gretchen Claus, executive director of PhillyCAM, that invited the Latinos to be part of PhillyCAM and start producing their stories.

AH: And what group is there, and I'm my understanding, and I'm speaking from my experience, the group that you work with at PhillyCAM.

LRN: Yes, it was named Atrévete. It was a brainstorming session. I recall that very clearly. Somebody said Atrévete, so I dare you. And it has been five years. We've been producing on a monthly basis, different segments, different parts of the program. And I belong really to Atrévete. But recently, I was invited also to participate in [PhillyCAM] Voices, which I think is great. You said, my main community's Latino, but my second community is African American. My teacher was African American. All my sisters are, spiritual sisters, are African American. So I feel very connected because we have a lot of similarities.

AH: And can you talk about this? What are some of those similarities?

LRN: Yes. I think that first of all, the third root of Mexico is the African root, there were the Indians, the Spaniards, and Africans. And they deleted the African Mexicans for centuries. It just has been like forty years ago that they declared that there was an Afro-Mexican community.

AH: What types of stories are you all, or what stories really resonate with you that you all are working on?

LRN: It starts always with our own culture, since I was doing this reporting for printed media. But, I like to cover mainly the struggles for immigration reform, that as you know, recently, the Senate parliamentarian said: the legalization of eleven million undocumented people doesn't fit in the reconciliation budget. So that means, they're out. That means they can be deported any minute. There's no guarantees. So one of the topics I cover regularly is that, human rights, also the [fight] against discrimination. Maybe you recall the stop and frisk.

AH: What is your perspective of the space or that PhillyCAM like holds, what it offers for the community?

LRN: Sometimes I said PhillyCAM is the best-kept secret in Philadelphia. It's amazing how many people don't know it exists. But every time I have an opportunity to say, PhillyCAM offers the opportunity to learn the techniques, the technology to become your own producer, to broadcast your program, your messages, and in a very inclusive environment. Because really there are some places that they're not for minorities, definitely. Now one example, is the *Philadelphia Inquirer*, just recently, they have minorities writing, but it's not always the case. So PhillyCAM really provides a minimal cost for a membership, or a minimal cost for workshops for you to really not only record, but to edit your own programs in TV and radio. And to me, that is the greatest contribution we have of PhillyCAM making available to all of us the means to produce our own programs.

Earl Weeks (EW), retired disabled Marine, active PhillyCAM volunteer crew member/producer, and American Civil and Revolutionary War reenactor

AH: Can you tell us about what you produce currently? Then even just where your idea... what inspired what you produce today?

EW: Okay. There's a few different things that I have produced. One is a play called *Five, Four, Three, Two, One, Beat Them All*, and it was a short film. It was done through the Five Shorts Project and it was done in a theater, so basically the idea was that a slave from the past talks to a rapper of today. I ended up writing it and since it was a short, it was only fifteen minutes long, but I'm also a Civil War reenactor, a Revolutionary War reenactor, so it's also about the Civil War, tells some stories of the Civil War. The original guys, especially the unit I represent, the United States Color Troops. That was one thing that I did.

Right now, I'm working on a couple people's shows, *The Encouraged*, that's by Helene Bloodsaw. It's a positive show where people come on and talk about. . . . They may be actors, musicians or even regular people, people in the neighborhood but it's all to encourage people to do things and help each other.

I was working on this show with Zarinah Lomax, *Talking the Walk*. It's a gospel organic show and people would come in and perform and things like that, but also later on, she started getting into covering some of the murders in Philadelphia. That's what she's working on now. Myself, I'm doing a lot of filming and my friend owns a garage and he does custom cars. He has this thing called the Underground, so I record that, take pictures for him and everything, so they have hydraulic contests where the cars bounce up and down and they try and see how high the front end of the car gets.

AH: What space does PhillyCAM hold in the community? It sounds like you're saying people connect there. Can you talk about from your perspective what is PhillyCAM in Philadelphia?

EW: I would say that PhillyCAM is something that's really powerful, but that's if you see it. For me, I talked about school and stuff before. I was at school because I had nothing else to do. I'm retired and I was just taking classes. I ended up there helping students but I really stopped being a student for me. . . . I manage students, like I help students, because I was into helping with the administration of the school.

I stopped doing that and came to PhillyCAM, because with PhillyCAM, I saw that I can make a whole bunch of programs and maybe have, who knows, three hundred, five hundred programs on TV, knowing that I did it and they actually played on TV, not that the world would know but I know. You know? For anybody, anybody could walk off the street, take the training and they could be a TV producer, radio producer, or both. You know? And put any type of show almost that they can conceive on TV. You know? It may get them somewhere else. Who knows?

AH: What does it mean to be a TV producer? What does that feel like to you?

EW: It feels really good to me and I'm laughing because I remember before telling my niece, "Yeah, I'm a TV producer at PhillyCAM." "Uncle, why don't we see your shows on TV?" "I'm taking all these classes right now."

But now right now, my mini documentary *Mad Films: A Legacy of Community Journalism* is on TV. Just last week, I was sitting there watching it with my girlfriend's grandson and it goes off and he's like, "Poppy, Poppy, let's watch your show. Let's watch your show." I was like that's perfect. You know? It just excites me that he would even want to watch it again, and that he knows because I'm telling everybody but who knows who's watching it but it's a fact. You know? I'm a TV producer. Nobody can take that from me. It's the truth. I'm not lying.

AH: Is there something that distinguishes what you do now, your process in producing with PhillyCAM that distinguishes maybe perhaps just producing a video and putting it up on YouTube?

EW: Yes. Thinking about it, I think, for me, to put stuff on YouTube, that's just putting it there. You know? I can't control people looking at it. I'm not trying to contact the world, "Hey, watch my video, watch my video." But with PhillyCAM, there's listings, people can look up the listings, they can look at it on demand. It's on two different well-known cable giants. I think that gives a little bit more authenticity to it. I don't see them as the same. I see PhillyCAM as a bigger stage.

Kristal Sotomayor (KS), independent filmmaker, Latinx film festival curator, and cofounder of ¡Presente! Media

AH: And you're a part of a collective of media makers. Can you talk about that a little bit? What is that collective?

KS: So I would say I start with ¡Presente! Media. So that is a Latinx collective made up of filmmakers and journalists who are pretty much interested in getting stories told about the community. And so I cofounded that with two other incredible local Latinx filmmakers. And we've really been working to collect the stories of the community in written form and also in videos that can be shared with community members about the pressing issues that are affecting us. Then I'm also part of SIFTmedia 215, which supports Black and Latinx women and nonbinary filmmakers in the city. And they've been really wonderful and creating resources and tools for local filmmakers of color. And I'm also part of the video consortium, Philly Collective. I'm one of the organizers. And so the video consortium is a global filmmaking collective that they have in cities all over the globe. And pretty much we've been only starting up for a few months, but it's been pretty much just meeting other filmmakers and really starting to build something.

AH: And are what you're producing through the collectors and/or your personal, is that work also airing on PhillyCAM? Have you all submitted?

KS: Well, I think some SIFTmedia things have shown at PhillyCAM, and I think, well through ¡Presente! Media there was this video that was made about Latino organizations being involved in Black Lives Matter protests. And that one, PhillyCAM shared it along with another group of their shorts as part of this. I don't quite remember. I put it on our social, but PhillyCAM did share it because all three of us are members.

AH: And what does it mean to be a community media maker? Someone who's immersed in the community and telling us stories? What is that life like?

KS: Well, I think trying to be a filmmaker that is interested in community media means trying your best to be transparent and open with a community that you want to document, and forming lasting relationships with people. So for me, that means going to different events, means going into people's homes, being invited to weddings, to quinceañeras, and just being there for people in different capacities throughout the many ways that your work involves. So I've worked with Juntos, for example, independently through my film. Then I've worked with them with the Latino Film Festival, showing films together, putting together this workshop for the Juntos youth. So there's been many ways that I've worked with them and that I hope to continue to work with them because we've fostered a really strong relationship, built on a lot of trust and a lot of transparency. I've had to stop filming when I was on location, and that's okay, I'll just delete it.

It's not a big deal. And then I just go home and I delete that file, because it may have had some sensitive information for a community member. So I think it's just being really open like that, and also being really open to your own learning and your own, possibly things that you might not do so well or might do better. So I've been really open with them, especially when I was filming that I'm a student. Footage, maybe didn't look so great because I had just recently started making films, and it's been a long process because I've been really working to make it look strong and make it look good.

And so we're doing some more filming now that I'm better at what I'm doing. But I would say it's transparency and openness and being willing to learn collaboratively.

AH: Okay. And can you talk a little bit about some of the impact, if we can use that word. Can you talk about that? What your film and the stories that you've been able to tell working with organizations like Juntos. What has that done?

KS: Well, I think because Latinos are so underrepresented in media that sometimes we don't realize how amazing we are and the things that we're doing. And so in making *Expanding Sanctuary*, no one knew it was going to win in the end. They ended up ending this contract that the city had. No one knew that that was going to be the outcome. We all hoped, and we really all tried our best to support this. But really, I think that these things just aren't archived. There are probably one article written by someone who isn't from the community that has one quote from a community member. But really no one sees what's happening behind the scenes and no one sees how it's directly affecting people. And so, I think that that's how my films and my work helps the community. It's because our stories go untold truthfully. And our impact that we end up making to the city and to the country as a whole pretty much goes ignored. And so in filming these things, it gives it importance and it gives it weight and it gives it historical memory that it wouldn't have had otherwise. So I think that's my contribution.

AH: Can you talk about the space that PhillyCAM holds in this community and what does it offer? Yeah, what does it offer for people in Philadelphia?

KS: Yeah. So PhillyCAM, I think, is a really wonderful resource for people who maybe always wanted to pick up a camera, but felt a little nervous to do so. I think the place that PhillyCAM has is that it offers pretty much everything, workshops for how to make your film, then where you can distribute it, which I think is key. You can show it on public television, and most people are always like, well, how do I get my film out there? Well, you can always go to PhillyCAM.

So I think it really offers from the very beginning, from inception to creation, to then distribution. Which I think a lot of people need, especially when they're starting. And I've even talked to other filmmakers and we've toured the space with a Puerto Rican filmmaker who was like, "We need this on the island." We need something like this because we need studio space and we need a place to show our own work, and we also need a place where we can get good equipment. And that's not really something that they had. So I think that's why it's so crucial in Philly. It's because it really allows you to start and finish.

AH: Do you have a dream for community media? Something like a vision that's inspiring you to the work that you do and the work that you do with your collectives?

KS: Yeah, I think for me, I want community media to be taken seriously in the larger film ecosystem, because it isn't. When people think of community media, they think of someone who has maybe never picked up a camera, which is probably true, but it doesn't mean that it's going to be a bad quality video, audio, and not a great story. I think there's so many misconceptions about that, when sometimes there's some of the most beautiful films you've ever seen, but they're not given a fair chance, truthfully, to compete in the larger ecosystem. So, I think people really need to stop thinking about it as an amateur making a film. Because, really, the heart and soul of it makes it so much better than some of the films you might see somewhere else on television or through a streamer. It's just like the dedication that you put into it is really seen in every frame of the story in a way that you can't really see in popular media, that I think people just dismiss it, and it's really unfair.

THE FUTURE OF ACCESS: A CONCLUDING THOUGHT

Reflecting on PhillyCAM's history, legacy, and accomplishments demonstrates its contribution to Philadelphia's community history and media ecology. PhillyCAM represents a new generation of local community-centered television stations keeping pace with digital streaming migrations and fulfilling civic information needs in their localities. Most CMCs across the United States have developed online streaming channels and social media sites to expand their reach. Many have expanded their services to include community radio, local news, and topic-driven civic engagement programs. While the future of cable is uncertain, neighborhood-level communication resources like PhillyCAM remain essential to filling local information gaps and fostering community well-being. More case studies are needed to explore the contemporary value of CMCs and how they can help address prevalent local news and digital literacy needs. There is significant potential to enhance civic well-being throughout the United States by maintaining and expanding revitalized CMC models that facilitate the gathering, bonding, and transformation of multiethnic, multigenerational groups, while authentically portraying stories that matter to their communities.

REFERENCES

Ali, Christopher. 2014. "The Last PEG or Community Media 2.0? Negotiating Place and Placelessness at PhillyCAM." *Media, Culture & Society* 36 (1): 69–86.

Blau, Andrew. 1992. "The Promise of Public Access." *The Independent* 15 (3): 22–26.

Cliff-Evans, Kristina. 1998. "Guest Opinion: Public Access Coalition Ready for Action—Yours!" *Germantown Courier*, January 7, 6.

Devine, Bob. 2001. "33 Years Later Why Access?" *Community Media Review* 24 (2): 37–39.

Dewey, Matthew. 2021. "Anyone Can Do YouTube, but Not Everyone Can Do Public Access: Urban Politics, Production Tools, and a Communications Infrastructure to Call Home." *Television & New Media* 22 (7): 779–98.

Goldberg, Kim. 1990. *The Barefoot Channel: Community Television as a Tool for Social Change*. New Star Books.

Halleck, DeeDee. 2002. *Hand-Held Visions: The Impossible Possibilities of Community Media*. Fordham University Press.

Haywood, Antoine L. 2024. "Focused [in] the Frame: A Study of African American Community Participation in Philadelphia Public Access Television." Ph.D. diss., University of Pennsylvania.

Haywood, Antoine, Patricia Aufderheide, and Mariana Sánchez Santos. 2021. "Community Media in a Pandemic: Facilitating Local Communication, Collective Resilience and Transitions to Virtual Public Life in the US." *Javnost—The Public* 28 (3): 256–72.

Kiuchi, Yuya. 2012. *Struggles for Equal Voice: The History of African American Media Democracy*. State University of New York Press.

Linder, Laura R. 1999. *Public Access Television: America's Electronic Soapbox*. Greenwood.

McCollough, George, and Inja Coates. 1999. "A Philadelphia Story." *Community Media Review* 22 (4): 9–11.

Parker, Akweli. 2003. "Phila. Reality TV Gets Its Shot; Decision Expected on Public Access." *Philadelphia Inquirer*, July 23, D01.

Quinn, Kathy. 1998. "Group Pushes Public Access." *Greater Philadelphia Democratic Left*, June/July, 4.

Simama, Jabari. 2009. *From Civil Rights to Cyber Rights: Broadband and Digital Equity in the Age of Obama*. Community Technology.

Spolan, Sue. 1990. "Access Mess." *Philadelphia City Paper*, August 17.

LORI KIDO LOPEZ

EPILOGUE

MOVING LOCAL TELEVISION FORWARD
IN THE DIGITAL ERA

In an era when it seems that all forms of media have been indelibly transformed by the shift to digital technologies, it is important to continue to theorize what remains at the core of each specific medium. The case of "local television" seems a particularly tricky medium for reconsidering in the digital age. Digital objects are not known for staying bound to any one geographic locality, as accessibility from anyone anywhere with an online connection is one of the defining attributes of the World Wide Web. And while television signals have always been electronically transmitted and received, they are also closely bound to the technologies of cable and satellite transmission that have long defined television as a broadcast medium. Nonetheless, digital transformations have also meant that in spite of technological shifts and conceptual incongruities about what constitutes television, the identity of the medium has generally remained persistent and robust even amid seismic redefinitions. We can see this strongly in the case of streaming television, which has completely transformed the way that televisual content is distributed and accessed even as a sense of "television-ness" remains. The same can be said of local television in the digital era. Even when content is primarily accessible through a mobile device or computer screen it can still feel like television, and even when content is widely accessible it can still retain a strong feeling of locality due to the community bonds of its audience members.

If this is the case, then what can we say has truly changed and remained the same about local television in the digital era? While the chapters throughout this collection have largely examined histories of local television, this epilogue gestures to the ways contemporary local television is continuing to evolve in our digital era. In particular, it focuses on community television and the opportunities that have arisen for marginalized voices when creators bypass broadcast institutions and use digital platforms to connect with local communities and beyond. By examining some examples that fit into the category of micro media, we can start to see some of the ways that local television may be moving even further from traditional television industries and infrastructures thanks to digital innovations. Rather than see this as a weakening of what local television can offer, this epilogue points to the opportunities for micro television to continue expanding the breadth and depth of community representation afforded in a digital environment.

DEFINING DIGITAL COMMUNITY TELEVISION

To understand how local television has been impacted by digital technologies, we can begin by considering some of the different ways that television has transformed in the digital age. While broadcast technologies such as terrestrial broadcast and then cable signals and satellite transmissions once defined the boundaries of what constituted the medium of television, it is now standard practice to use the term "television" for digitally transmitted content such as streaming services, web series, and other "on-demand" platforms. The reliable stream of programs released in discrete episodes has come to redefine television as something that can be accessed on a cell phone, laptop, or tablet. But this does not mean that all audiovisual content can be considered television? For instance, it seems clear that a short art film, a TikTok dance meme, a recording of a video game, or an instructional safety video is not what we would traditionally call "television." Amanda Lotz (2017) argues that television remains distinctly defined due to certain textual characteristics, industrial practices, audience behaviors, and cultural understandings. This is important to point out, given the many shifts in television technologies since its invention in the 1930s. As Lotz claims, what we know as television takes on recognizable televisual genres, is understood as television by audiences, and is produced through distinct industrial formations that govern and shape television.

These industrial norms and expectations around television have always been challenged by the existence of local television and particularly community television, which has its own production cultures and industrial norms. Scholars have helped to define the boundaries of community media by pointing to their independence from traditional media structures and their emphasis on fulfilling the needs and goals of their specific communities (Howley 2005; Rennie 2006). This marks community media as an alternative to commercial television and other forms of mainstream media that often have high barriers to entry, are primarily concerned with financial profits, and must grow their audience to a certain threshold in order to survive. Community media are often motivated by goals such as promoting democratic participation, increasing educational opportunities, building community relationships, and diversifying representation. In some cases community media can be politically motivated, focusing on empowering citizens to take media production into their own hands. In doing so, they assert autonomy from corporate media structures and help to democratize media practices. Local and community television are not synonymous terms; as this edited collection demonstrates, many local TV series do not fall under the umbrella of "community media" because they are not necessarily motivated by the above goals. I focus on community television in this epilogue to explore how diasporic ethnic communities use community media as a vital lifeline for connecting individuals who may be culturally or linguistically excluded from mainstream media in their current locale.

While the mission and ethos of community television may differ from mainstream commercial television, there are still important institutional structures that have always supported community television. Ellie Rennie (2007) has specifically cautioned against losing the specificity of community media's institutionality, arguing that community media "are professional and industry-like, with an emphasis on standards, training and ethical responsibility when it comes to information dissemination" (31). In addition to these qualities, these organizations are also institutionalized through their heavy reliance on state funding structures. Community television is produced out of television stations that are owned and operated by nonprofit organizations, municipalities, or cable operators that can designate certain channels as public access. In the United States, this kind of access is supported through state funding, as community television is understood to provide a public good through offering programming focused on civic engagement.

Yet one of the important impacts of the rise of digital tools for media production is that these forms of institutional and state-sponsored support for community media have been significantly threatened.

Community television has shifted form alongside evolving technologies, especially with the rise of new media tools that are less expensive and easier to operate. For instance, throughout the 1990s, improvements in consumer video equipment meant that community television stations could shift toward lighter, more affordable cameras. In more recent years, digital tools have led to further increases in access to media making, as any individual with a webcam and an internet connection now has the ability to create and distribute video content. Community television has struggled to compete for viewers against offerings available on digital platforms like YouTube, Facebook, TikTok, Twitter, and Instagram that are similarly participatory and accessible as well as specifically catered to niche interests. This has resulted in a decline in both funding and the regulatory structures that protect noncommercial television providers (Ó Baoill and Scifo 2022). As low- to no-cost digital tools for media participation proliferate, there is increased pressure on community broadcasters to justify state-sponsored resources and the policies that protect them, and their budgets have been reduced. These concerns about how the rise of digital video has threatened state support for community media emphasize the importance of sustainability in community television institutions.

Yet not all forms of digital community television are so closely connected to traditional media infrastructures and state apparatuses. Indeed, the category of community television is exceedingly broad, with a diverse range of outlets spanning a multitude of content. To understand some of these possibilities, we can look to digitally distributed forms of community television that exist outside of institutionalized television stations. In particular, this next section examines the impact of small staff size on local television outlets and how individual makers are creating video content that builds from the form and content of local television.

MICRO MEDIA VERSUS COMMUNITY MEDIA

One of the differences between community television and traditional professional television is the kind of staff who work behind the scenes to produce and distribute content. Even the most modestly produced forms of traditional television, such as nightly newscasts and weekly public affairs programs, are generally created by a team of dozens of media professionals who are paid as full-time laborers to participate in shaping some component of the show. Some of these roles include on-screen talent, camera operators, editors, producers and directors, writers, and a variety of engineers and technicians. While community television can be produced by individuals who take on these roles, they most commonly do so on a part-time volunteer basis or as part of an educational training process rather than as their chosen career. The involvement of a constantly revolving crew of citizens and amateurs is one of the celebrated features of community television production, as it contributes to civic goals such as increasing media literacy and production skills, improving access to broadcasting, and democratizing media-making processes. Community media are sometimes seen as synonymous with concepts like "citizens' media," "grassroots media," or even "radical media" due to their potential political emphasis on disrupting the power dynamics traditionally located within media gatekeepers and professional media institutions (Howley 2013). This is made possible through ensuring anyone who wants to participate is invited to do so and barriers to entry are lowered as much as possible.

Yet with the advent of digital media production tools, a large number of contributors are no longer necessary for the maintenance of all small-scale media outlets. Indeed, a single person with a toolkit of even the most basic digital camera, editing software, and internet connection—all of which can be found in a smartphone—can somewhat easily turn out professional-quality video content in a short amount of time. Because of this, it is important to look beyond the two categories of professional television production and community media production to also consider an additional category of micro media production. As I have outlined in previous research, micro media can be understood as small-scale forms of media production and distribution with only one or two staff working behind the scenes (Lopez 2021). In addition to their micro-sized labor force, micro media are also often limited in terms of funding, audience size, and the ability to produce profits. Some common examples of media outlets that frequently fall into the category of micro media are rural newspapers, blogs, podcasts, and YouTube channels. In each of these cases there is a wide array of labor taken on by the individual or individuals at the helm—they produce content, manage new technologies, promote their brand, and respond to audiences all on their own.

There are many ways that micro media share important traits with community media. For instance, both micro media and community media serve as an alternative to the commercial mandate of mainstream media, which exist as a massively scaled enterprise designed to produce financial profits and require sizeable audiences. In contrast, those who engage in both micro media and community media can avoid the work of soliciting corporations for ad buys and are not beholden to the constant pressure to increase market shares and audience sizes. Indeed, in both cases they wield significant (if not ultimate) control over production decisions and content. Moreover, the specificity of their particular niche audiences means that in many cases they are undertaking the important political work of increasing representation for minority communities whose perspectives are underrepresented in mainstream media.

But this does not mean that the mandates behind micro media and community media are naturally overlapping or exactly aligned. As mentioned earlier, community media are often premised on the desire to democratize media production and bring more producers into the world of media making, which is why there is often a focus on media education, mentoring, and training programs. If micro media are defined by their small size and scale, it is often very difficult for micro media entrepreneurs to have the capacity to engage in time-consuming endeavors such as professional training, mentorship, or even managing volunteers. Since micro media are helmed by only one or two individuals, the concept of a community of practitioners or community engaged in making media together is almost nonexistent. This does not mean that the idea of community is entirely divorced from micro media, as micro media outlets importantly produce communities of listeners, followers, and supporters, and they can certainly participate in creating niche publics that open up community dialogues and spaces for discourse. But if community media are connected to an ethic of welcoming everyday citizens into the fold as media producers and makers, this is not necessarily possible within micro media outlets. Rather, many forms of micro media exist as a way of bringing attention, fame, or prestige to the individual at the helm, and they can emulate mainstream media forms and genres that extend far beyond the usual expectations for community media.

3HMONGTV: LOCAL TELEVISION AS MICRO MEDIA

To understand what this means for local television, we can turn to some examples of micro media outlets that have used digital technologies to shape their televisual practices. 3HMONGTV is a news outlet based in Saint Paul, Minnesota, and owned by local producer Mitch Lee. It focuses on providing local news and information to its Hmong American audiences, with programs that are primarily in Hmong language and discuss

Fig. E.1. Screengrab from a video posted to a YouTube channel of news anchor Yau Muas hosting the 3HMONGTV news brief in a studio.

issues such as politics, education, health, business, and popular culture. While 3HMONGTV programs appear indistinguishable from professionally produced television, Lee is the only paid staff member who takes on numerous roles such as reporting, producing and directing, shooting, and editing. He has a small number of volunteers who come in to host occasional programs, but most days he works alone. We can clearly categorize this outlet as micro media due to the extremely small-sized staff. But what has enabled this kind of outlet to exist and even thrive is that their programs are available via online platforms such as YouTube, Facebook, and their own website.

Even though their programs are exclusively posted to social media, it still makes sense to call 3HMONGTV television. Not only is "TV" in the name, but the programs produced for 3HMONGTV fit into the standard norms of broadcast television in terms of form and content. Their core programming of regular news updates look exactly like typical network television news programs. A professionally dressed news anchor named Yau Muas sits at a desk against a high-tech blue background and looks straight into the camera as she introduces the day's topics (Lopez 2021, 1). A chyron running across the bottom of the screen gives additional information, while the open space over the anchor's left shoulder contains digital graphics or photographs. After a brief introduction from the anchor, the coverage jumps to clips, interviews, footage from the field, and edited packages. Outside of these news broadcasts, regular programs like *Hmong Talk* and *Thamkuv Show* (Talk to me show) feature casual interviews with special guests in a format similar to *The Today Show* on NBC. These interviews create opportunities for viewers to learn more from local politicians and government officials and Hmong American community leaders, business owners, scholars, artists, and everyday individuals with compelling stories to share.

While it seems clear that the programs created by Mitch Lee for 3HMONGTV resemble the classic televisual genre of the news broadcast in many ways, we still might question whether or not they follow the "industrial norms" of television. Some of the traditional practices around television include the arrangements between studios and networks to sell television content across markets, the governmental regulation of commercial programming, the distribution of television content via broadcast and cable channels, the linear flow of programs and advertisements established in a schedule, and the reliance on financial models that require selling advertisements and subscriptions (Lotz 2007). A show that is posted directly to YouTube bypasses all of these industrial norms. Yet for the past twenty years or so the disruptions of digital and streaming television have upended the expectation that everything we call "television" must align with these practices, as online content ranging from Netflix shows to Vimeo web series to videos on the short-lived mobile platform Quibi are all pushing the boundaries of televisuality. In choosing to assiduously align itself with the aesthetic conventions of traditional television news, 3HMONGTV serves to expand definitions of television while also reasserting classic televisual forms and expectations.

BRIDGING LOCAL MICRO TELEVISION AND MAINSTREAM TELEVISION

Like all kinds of local television, digital micro television outlets are important because of their focus on the hyperlocal stories and issues that matter most to their specific communities. As Christopher Ali (2012) points out, the situatedness of community media within a specific place is one of its defining characteristics. In the case of 3HMONGTV, this means calling attention to what is happening to Hmong Americans in the Twin Cities and includes focusing on efforts by Hmong American political candidates to run for office, health issues like the impact of COVID-19 in Hmong American populations, cultural events like local festivals and tournaments, and debates surrounding current events. The metropolitan areas surrounding Minneapolis and Saint Paul are home to over ninety thousand Hmong Americans, composing the largest community of Hmong Americans in the United States. Yet their population is still less than 2 percent of the entire state, which means that they do not figure prominently in mainstream news media, and Hmong Americans in Minnesota still struggle to find information about their own community. As a result, Hmong Americans have needed to develop their own media outlets and news ecology, and they have done so despite a tremendous lack of resources and financial support.

One of the moments that revealed the strength of the Hmong local news ecology in the Twin Cities was the rise of Hmong American gymnast Sunisa Lee, who seemed to pop onto the global stage out of nowhere when she won the all-around gold medal in the gymnastics competition at the 2020 Olympics in Tokyo. Yet she was already well known to her local Hmong American community in Saint Paul thanks to reportage from Hmong news outlets like 3HMONGTV. In 2019, Lee and her parents were featured in a forty-minute episode of the talk show *Xav Paub Xav Pom*, where they were interviewed by host Padee Yang. While the program looked like a professionally produced segment, it also benefited from the freedom accorded to an alternative outlet. For instance, the extended length allowed for a kind of depth and nuance that are extremely rare within the news media landscape, where most stories about an Olympic hopeful would be reduced to a handful of minutes tacked onto the end of a twenty-two-minute broadcast. The interview was also bilingual—the young gymnast spoke English and her parents spoke in Hmong—which meant that Hmong American audiences with different linguistic preferences could all engage with the content.

The positioning of *Xav Paub Xav Pom* as a born-digital program also brought specific benefits for its Hmong American audiences. As with all programs produced for 3HMONGTV, this episode was posted to their YouTube channel. While local television programs that are broadcast live often disappear forever into the ether, YouTube videos allow for deeper engagement over time. Viewers can return to videos that they want to rewatch or finish at a later date, and they can slow down clips—for instance, to watch Lee's acrobatics in slow motion. The fact that this video was hosted in the channel's easily accessible YouTube archive meant that when Lee made it to the Olympics in 2020, the episode could gain a new audience of Hmong American viewers who wanted to learn more about this young superstar from their own neighborhood. They could also connect with other viewers in response to the program by using the comments function, where they expressed pride and admiration but also debated issues like the importance of Hmong language among younger generations. With over three hundred thousand views and over eight hundred comments, the interview is one of 3HMONGTV's most popular videos. Most videos on their channel receive between three and ten thousand views and rarely receive more than a dozen comments.

The heightened attention on Lee following her Olympic victory served to evidence the professionalism and legitimacy of 3HMONGTV as micro television. The network received national attention when the ABC News program *Nightline* featured news anchor Padee Yang and her interview in an episode on August 4, 2021. In a seven-minute segment, ABC News reporter Ashan Singh interviews Padee Yang while she is sitting amid the cameras, lighting rigs, and green screen of the 3HMONGTV studio. The feature is ostensibly about Sunisa Lee and her athletic accomplishments, but Yang and her important role as a Hmong American news reporter are also heavily emphasized. Singh visits the Hmong Wasau Festival to observe Hmong cultural performances and explains, "These are the kinds of events and stories that 3HMONGTV anchor Padee Yang wants to share with the world." Yang then affirms that her program had called attention to Lee's story two years earlier, when the gymnast was only an Olympic hopeful, in an effort to inspire other youth to set higher goals for themselves. The *Nightline* segment provided a bridge between this hyperlocal media outlet and the larger national and global audience that should be paying attention to news about minority communities. The respectful treatment given to Yang also positioned 3HMONGTV as a legitimate and professional news outlet, as the segment does not indicate that its offerings are available only on YouTube or that Yang is a volunteer rather than paid staff.

SALAXLEY TV AND FULL CIRCLE TELEVISION: EXPANDING LOCAL TV

Hmong communities are not the only ones responding to digital opportunities by creating micro television outlets with the most minimal staff possible. Many other communities are similarly using platforms like Facebook and YouTube to distribute television shows and bypass the high costs, technological demands, and regulatory barriers of a more traditional television station. For instance, Somali Americans are another refugee community that has developed a wide array of micro television and other targeted media outlets for their specific community needs. This includes providing information that is in Somali language for those who are not comfortable consuming media in English as well as audiovisual media for those who cannot read Somali. All-digital distribution platforms also allow for the growth of a geographically dispersed audience, which is particularly important for diasporic communities such as Hmong and Somali communities.

Salaxley TV is a digital television outlet that Mohamed Ahmed founded in 2015 to serve Somali American communities near Seattle, Washington. During the onset of the COVID-19 pandemic, videos for Salaxley TV posted to YouTube and Facebook provided vital information about the local resources and financial assistance that were available for app-based drivers in Washington State (Lopez 2021, 2). This was an issue of particular importance to Ahmed, who is one of only two part-time employees who run Salaxley TV, because he also maintained a day job as an Uber driver. But as Daniela Gerson (2020) found in her investigation of Salaxley TV, the news outlet oscillates between serving the needs of its local Washington Somali community of around ten thousand and a broader diasporic audience all around the world. Ahmed himself had left his home in Somalia in 1991 and moved through Ethiopia and Kenya before arriving in the United States. Given the political instability and civil war that have ravaged Somalia since the 1990s, there are over 750,000 Somali refugees and asylum seekers residing all over the world. Online outlets like Salaxley TV can connect a diffuse diasporic populace, rather than being limited to a local broadcast that can serve only a geographically circumscribed community. While some of the local content about Seattle may be of less interest to a global diaspora, Ahmed uses the global communication application WhatsApp to solicit questions for all of his interview subjects and in this way is able to connect with viewers from across the diaspora.

This kind of oscillation between local audiences and a broader audience is also effective for micro television outlets focused on genres outside of news and current affairs programming. For instance, Full Circle Television is a studio based out of Milwaukee that produces the talk show

Fig. E.2. Screengrab from a video posted to a YouTube channel of Salaxley TV host Mohamed Ahmed interviewing two representatives from local rideshare advocacy organizations in a studio.

Relationship Goals. The show gives Black couples the chance to talk about their relationships, whether those relationships are romantic, platonic, or centered on coparenting. Full Circle Television is run by the husband and wife team Marcus and Kayla Lewis-Allen, who describe themselves as a "two-man self-taught production crew, we are the creators, producers, editors, directors and marketing team" (*Shoutout Atlanta* 2021). While Kayla originally had aspirations of producing the series for a major network, she and Marcus realized they could take their show straight to YouTube and still reach audiences who found the show meaningful—including both local Milwaukee audiences and beyond. Yet one of their strategies for building the show has been to cultivate local support through in-person events and celebrations. For instance, Kayla and Marcus host local game nights in Milwaukee that "center around Black culture . . . [and] try to make it feel like you're at home" (Stone 2022). These locally centered events help to build awareness of the show and its creators as well as to connect their brand with Black-owned businesses. They credit the Business Coworking Lounge in Milwaukee with giving them a space for filming and a number of local podcasts for allowing them to share information about themselves and the show to listeners.

This kind of local support for independent television networks distributed online extends Aymar Jean Christian's (2017) findings about web series as networked television representation to other kinds of micro media. Christian argues that digital distribution has allowed for "small-scale development processes [that] restructure the politics of representation in television and art, allowing us to see value where it has historically been hidden." In his own development of the OTV | Open Television platform that focuses on intersectional storytelling by queer people of color creators, he reveals the significance of local Chicago connections, communities, and networks in supporting specific kinds of digital stories. For instance, *Let Go and Let God* focuses on a queer Black woman who wanted to tell a story about the depression brought on by the termination of a pregnancy and her use of sensuality, spirituality, and dance to find her strength. Creator and star Rashida KhanBey is able to bring this specific vision to life through her short film that is distributed on OTV. Christian explains the importance of coordinating the premiere of programs like KhanBey's in Chicago, where they could integrate live artist performances and discussions about the issues that are raised. This generates interest and excitement from local audiences and allows creators to assess live and embodied audience reactions in the moment rather than waiting for quantitative digital data such as clicks and views. This all happens in advance of the shows being posted online, where they are then available to a wider audience that builds from the local engagement and interaction. These different examples of micro television—including 3HMONGTV, Salaxley TV, Full Circle Television, and OTV | Open Television—reveal the diversity and cultural specificity of content available when individuals take television production into their own hands. While digital tools and online platforms are what promote success in spite of limited resources and workforce constraints, we can also see the enduring significance of local communities throughout. As local television expands into new realms, there are still core values and commitments that connect to the long histories of local television that came before.

CONCLUSION

Due to their flexibility, accessibility, and relevance, digital versions of micro television are on the rise across many different forms, genres, and subject areas. As we have seen throughout this epilogue, digital micro television has provided a useful alternative to legacy forms of broadcast television while also remaining somewhat distinct from the traditions of community media. While community television has a long history of foregrounding values such as democratizing media production education and opening up professional television stations to every citizen, not all alternatives to mainstream television share these ethical principles and norms. Micro television can still serve important local community needs, but it can do so through the efforts and labor of only a small number of enterprising individuals. These television outlets move away from the educational mandates of community media, engaging the concept of community through audience interactions and needs but not necessarily through production practices. In exploring outlets like 3HMONGTV, Salaxley TV, Full Circle Television, and OTV, this chapter has pointed to different versions of micro television that expand our understanding of what local television can do and how it can be made.

It is also important to return to the concept of "community" in relation to digital media, even if "community media" may not be the most appropriate term for all micro media. While digital micro television outlets may be able to function without a dedicated support staff and participatory culture is not foregrounded as a key mandate, they still engage with and produce communities in important ways. The community of audience members and followers who tune in to watch, comment, like, and share videos serves the vital function of making video production worthwhile. On a more substantial note, there are also many ways that micro media producers can work together across outlets to strengthen their offerings, creating a broader community of practice. One example of how this can work is in *Sahan Journal*'s Citizen Lab. *Sahan Journal* is a small digital news outlet based in Minnesota that focuses on immigrant news. In 2021, they received a small grant from Google News Initiative's North America Innovation Challenge to support the creation of a joint newsroom that brings together three micro media outlets serving specific communities in the Twin Cities—La Raza Radio for Latinos, Somali TV Minnesota for Somali Americans, and 3HMONGTV for Hmong Americans (*Sahan Journal* 2021). For nonjournalistic content like web series, there are dozens of examples of online networks that bring together small-scale television producers; some examples include OTV, Black and Sexy TV, SLAY TV, Between Women TV, and Color Creative TV (Christian 2018). Each of these indie channels focuses on content made by and for intersectional communities who have been disenfranchised within mainstream media industries, including women, LGBTQ+ people, and people of color. While they face similar challenges as all micro media makers in terms of instability, funding struggles, and lack of visibility, they demonstrate another way for small-scale media producers to support one another and increase the potential for longevity and sustainability.

This investigation of local television in the digital arena also leaves many questions unanswered that demand future research. For instance, if micro television relies on corporate platforms like YouTube and Facebook rather than state-supported television stations, we will need to look more closely at what impact those platforms have. Using a platform studies approach, we can ask what kinds of options are available (or restricted) due to the design of the interface and each platform's specific technological affordances, how each platform does or does not allow for monetization, and what kind of ownership or control the user wields. We can investigate the resilience of digital archives for posted content as well as the possibilities for using metadata and search algorithms to help audiences locate specific content. We must also consider the many labor issues that accompany micro television outlets, as a small workplace can lead to shifts in norms around professional identity formations, skill development, and career sustainability. Indeed, working alone and without potential for financial reward can engender significant possibilities for weariness and burnout, which threatens the future of a micro media landscape. Finally, as with all digital content, we must stay attuned to concerns about the potential for unregulated outlets, especially those that are deeply trusted by niche audiences, to contribute to the spread of misinformation and disinformation.

Despite these challenges, the existence of micro media programming that so closely resembles broadcast television reveals a deep desire for communities to see themselves represented in local television—even if that means they must create their own outlet in order to do so. When taken with the findings put forward throughout this book, we can see how the offerings available through local television and community television of all kinds continue to be more important than ever to producers and audiences who have been typically underrepresented in and underserved by commercial programming. We must remain committed to exploring a diverse array of television archives and historical television formations as a way of informing understandings of contemporary digital media such as micro media. As digital tools for media production and distribution continue to proliferate and expand participation to new makers and audiences, we have the opportunity to demonstrate how television as a medium is shaped by local and national production alike.

REFERENCES

Ali, Christopher. 2012. "Media at the Margins: Policy and Practice in American, Canadian, and British Community Television." *International Journal of Communication* 6:1119–38.

Christian, Aymar Jean. 2017. "The Value of Representation: Toward a Critique of Networked Television Performance." *International Journal of Communication* 11:1552–74.

———. 2018. *Open TV: Innovation beyond Hollywood and the Rise of Web Television.* New York University Press.

Gerson, Daniela. 2020. "Salaxley TV: Providing Vital Information via Social Media Broadcasts in Somali." *Digital First Responders,* April 1. https://immigrantmediareport.journalism.cuny.edu/salaxley-tv/.

Howley, Kevin. 2005. *Community Media: People, Places, and Communication Technologies.* Cambridge University Press.

———. 2013. "Community Media Studies: An Overview." *Sociology Compass* 7 (10): 818–28.

Lopez, Lori Kido. 2021. *Micro Media Industries: Hmong American Media Innovation in the Diaspora.* Rutgers University Press.

Lotz, Amanda D. 2007. *The Television Will Be Revolutionized.* New York University Press.

———. 2017. *Portals: A Treatise on Internet-Distributed Television.* Ann Arbor: University of Michigan Press.

Ó Baoill, Andrew, and Salvatore Scifo. 2022. "Fragility and Empowerment: Community Television in the Digital Era." *International Journal of Communication* 16:566–84.

Rennie, Ellie. 2006. *Community Media: A Global Introduction.* Rowman & Littlefield.

———. 2007. "Community Media in the Prosumer Era." *3CMedia* 3:25–32.

———. 2013. "Community Media Production: Access, Institutions, and Ethics." In *The International Encyclopedia of Media Studies,* edited by Angharad N. Valdivia, 582–600. Blackwell.

Sahan Journal. 2021. "Sahan Journal Receives Google News Initiative Funding to Collaborate with Community News Organizations That Broadcast in Spanish, Hmong, and Somali." https://sahanjournal.com/inside-sahan-journal/google-news-initiative-sahan-journal-la-raza-radio-somali-tv-minnesota-3hmong-tv/.

Shoutout Atlanta. 2021. "Meet Marcus and Kayla Lewis-Allen | Creatives." May 6. https://shoutoutatlanta.com/meet-marcus-kayla-lewis-allen-creatives/.

Stone, Nyesha. 2022. "Milwaukee Native Turns Journaling into Digital Platform with Husband." *Carvd N Stone,* January 4. https://www.carvdnstone.com/cns-news/positive-news-milwaukee-native-turns-journaling-into-tv-channel-with-husband.

CONTRIBUTORS

CAROLINE N. BAYNE is Visiting Assistant Professor at Millsaps College in Jackson, Mississippi. Her work has been published in *Journal of Cinema and Media Studies* and is forthcoming in *International Journal of Cultural Studies*.

CHRISTINE BECKER is Associate Professor in the Department of Film, Television, and Theatre at the University of Notre Dame. Her book *It's the Pictures That Got Small: Hollywood Film Stars on 1950s Television* won a IAMHIST Michael Nelson Prize for a Work in Media and History.

MARY BELTRÁN is Professor of Radio-Television-Film and a faculty affiliate of Mexican American & Latina/o Studies and Women's, Gender and Sexuality Studies at the University of Texas at Austin. She is the author of *Latino TV: A History* and *Latina/o Stars in U.S. Eyes*, and coeditor of *Mixed Race Hollywood*.

ANA HOWE BUKOWSKI is a doctoral candidate in communication at the University of Southern California's Annenberg School. Their research has been published in academic journals including *Spectator*, *Celebrity Studies*, and the *International Journal of Communication* as well as popular outlets such as *Viscose* and *Canadian Art*.

AYMAR JEAN CHRISTIAN is the Margaret Walker Alexander Professor of Communication Studies and Director of the Media and Data Equity (MADE) Lab at Northwestern University. He is also a 2024–25 Visiting Scholar at Harvard University's Berkman Klein Center for Internet and Society.

DAPHNE GERSHON is a lecturer at Gonzaga University. Her research interests center around TV representations of gender, sex, and sexuality. She has published work in *Feminist Media Studies*, the *International Journal of Cultural Studies*, and the *Journal of Cinema and Media Studies*. She is also currently coediting an instructional book on textual analysis under contract with New York University Press.

ANTOINE HAYWOOD is Assistant Professor in the Journalism Department at the University of Florida's College of Journalism and Communications. Before earning a doctorate from the University of Pennsylvania's Annenberg School for Communication, he worked extensively as a community media practitioner in Atlanta and Philadelphia. With collaborative support from practitioner networks like the Alliance for Community Media and News Futures, his research focuses on local media environments, community-engaged journalism practices, civic communication systems, and community media history.

LAUREN HEROLD is an independent scholar whose research explores community media, television history, and feminist and LGBTQ cultural production. Her work has been published in *Jump Cut*, *Television & New Media*, *Velvet Light Trap*, *Communication, Culture & Critique*, and *New Review of Film and Television Studies*. She has a Ph.D. in screen cultures from Northwestern University.

DYFRIG JONES is Senior Lecturer in Film at Bangor University in Wales. He is a former member of the S4C Authority, the corporation that oversees the provision of Welsh-language public television, and is the former editor of *Barn*, the current affairs magazine.

EVELYN KREUTZER is a postdoctoral researcher and video essayist at the Università della Svizzera italiana where she codirects the SNSF-funded research group "The Video Essay: Memories, Ecologies, Bodies" (with Kevin B. Lee and Johannes Binotto). Her work has been published in journals like *NECSUS*, *Music, Sound, and the Moving Image*, *[in]Transition*, and *The Cine-Files*. Her videographic book *Televising Taste: Performing Classical Music on American Screens* is forthcoming.

LORI KIDO LOPEZ is Professor of Communication Arts and Associate Dean for Social Sciences in the College of Letters and Science at the University of Wisconsin–Madison. She is the author of *Asian American Media Activism: Fighting for Cultural Citizenship* and *Micro Media Industries: Hmong American Media Innovation in the Diaspora*.

JONATHAN MACDONALD is a Ph.D. candidate at Brown University in the Department of American Studies. His scholarly work examines the relationship between social science and educational media in the mid-twentieth century.

DANIEL MARCUS is Professor of Media Arts and Studies at Goucher College in Baltimore. He writes on media and politics, media history, and documentary and alternative media. He is the author of *Happy Days and Wonder Years: The Fifties and the Sixties in Contemporary Cultural Politics* and coeditor of *Contemporary Documentary*.

TAYLOR COLE MILLER is Assistant Professor of Media Studies at the University of Wisconsin–La Crosse and a media history content creator under the handle tvdoc. His research focuses on television histories, syndication, and queer media studies and can be found in journals like *Camera Obscura* and *Television & New Media* as well as numerous anthologies and popular press outlets. He is coeditor of the forthcoming collection *The Golden Girls: Essays from the Lanai*.

HELEN MORGAN PARMETT, Edwin W. Lawrence Forensic Professor of Speech, is Associate Professor in the Department of English and Film and TV Studies. Her research and teaching center on critical media studies, where she focuses especially on relationships among media, identity, and space/place. She is the author of *Down in Treme: Race, Place, and New Orleans on Television* and a forthcoming book on sports stadiums and media infrastructure in U.S. cities.

ANNIE LAURIE SULLIVAN is Assistant Professor in the Department of English, Creative Writing & Film at Oakland University. Her work examines ways race, cultural identity, and locality intersect with histories of media infrastructure. Her current book project traces the history of local Black radio, film, and television production alongside broader processes of urban development and social change in Detroit. She has a Ph.D. in screen cultures from Northwestern University.

SHAWN VANCOUR is Associate Professor of Information Studies and Film, Television, and Digital Media at the University of California, Los Angeles. His research explores the history and preservation of film, electronic, and digital media in the United States. He is author of *Making Radio: Early Radio Production and the Rise of Modern Sound Culture* as well as several dozen journal articles and essays for edited anthologies. He served as past director of the Radio Preservation Task Force for the Library of Congress's National Recording Preservation Board and currently codirects his school's Center for Preservation of Audiovisual Heritage.

INDEX

ABC, 330; Chicago School and, 30, 45; in Miami, 116; WOI-TV partnership and, 54, 56, 67; WSB-TV affiliation and, 172
Abe, Shuya, 194
Academy of Television Arts and Sciences, 80
Access Coalition, 306
Acción Chicano, 271, 276–77, 280
activism, media, 7, 8, 12, 14–15, 88, 115; Black, 134, 138–39, 289, 297, 299; in Chicago, 288, 290; Latinx, 269, 271–73, 276, 279–80, 282; LGBTQ, 252, 257–60, 265; in New England, 232–33, 235; in Philadelphia, 304–6, 309, 312; in Vermont, 235–37, 240–42, 244
Addams, Jane, 288
Adlmann, J. E., 99, 101, 107
Adorno, Theodor, 200, 202
advertising, 5, 9, 15, 56, 60, 83, 91, 219–20, 257, 328; for *The Baxters*, 74, 81–83; for *Today in Georgia*, 180; for *Tri-Cable Tonight*, 262
aesthetics, 1–2, 6
affiliate stations, 4, 9, 11, 35, 74, 79; deregulation and, 224; in Miami, 116, 119, 125; of NET, 156; serving Latinx audiences, 268, 271, 275; WNDU as, 213; WSB-TV as, 172, 175, 179, 187
Afrofuturism, 293
Afternoon Snatch, 298
Ahmed, Mohamed, 331, 332
¡Ahora!, 268, 270, 271, 275–77, 281
AIDS crisis, 250, 251, 253–54, 257–58, 261, 262
AirGo Radio, 299
Ali, Christopher, 2–3, 32, 232, 328
Allen, Charles R., 272
Allen, Robert, 289
Alliance for Community Media, 306

Alternative Media Conference, 236
Americable, 117–23
American Exhibition of Educational Radio and Television Programs, 160
American Library Association, 160
America's Black Journal, 133–34, 147
Anderson, Christopher, 5, 289
Anderson, John C., 205–6
anti-institutionalism, 205–6, 208
Antin, Eleanor, 106
Appy, Gerard, 156, 158
Arabica, 297
architecture, 40, 183–84, 186–87, 242
archives, 17–18, 245; digital, 335
Artists Post-Production Studio (APPS), 95, 101, 103–5, 108–9
artists' television: as place, 101–5; public sector, 98–101; as social infrastructure and, 105–9
Artists-in-Television, 193, 194
Arts Forum (Long Beach), 99, 101, 107
Asghar, Fatimah, 294
Asian Americans, 326–30
At Home with Elsbeth, 177
Atlanta, 176–77, 183, 186–87; cultural geography of, 173; early TV in, 174–75. *See also* WSB-TV (Atlanta)
Atlanta Constitution, 172, 174–75, 178, 181–82, 185
Atrévete, 312
AT&T, 112–13, 114
Atwood, David, 194
audiences: of artworks, 95–96, 100–108; of Chicago School TV, 31–32, 34, 42–43, 47; cultivation of, 54, 56–57, 60–61, 77;

audiences (*continued*)
  direct address to, 36–37, 44, 47, 163, 199–200, 202; dispersed, 39; of educational TV, 54, 56, 58–61, 64, 65, 153; engagement, 46, 199–200, 333; historical, 18; in-studio, 72–73, 81–82, 84–88; as learners, 153; of local programming, 18, 68; participation of, 145; responses of, 77, 80, 274; surveys of, 273–74, 278; viewing habits, 36, 76
Avant Garde Festival of New York, 198
avant-garde, 153, 161, 163, 192–93, 198, 206, 208, 261, 300
Ayers, Nat, 237, 240

Back to You, 102
Bailey, Sam, 294, 295
Bain, Shervin, 294
Baker, John, 104
Bakker, Jim, 136
Baldessari, John, 94
Banks, William, 139, 142
Barlow, William, 136
Barrie, Wendy, 178
Barzyk, Fred, 194, 195, 201, 208n5
Basic Issues of Man: address to viewers, 167–68; analysis of, 161–67; circulation of, 159–60; creation of, 152, 155–59; ideology of, 152–53, 167–68; press coverage of, 157; types of "man" in, 158–59
Baxters, The: audience response to, 85–87; content of, 81–84, 88; criticism of, 89; as DIY television, 90; ephemerality of, 74, 82; as failure, 74–75, 91; as local and national coproduction, 75–76, 80–81; as participatory TV, 72–73
Beethoven, Ludwig van, 202–4; *Moonlight Sonata*, 191, 197–98, 204
Behar, Mark, 252, 253–54, 255, 263
behavioral sciences, 154
Bell Telephone, 58
Benglis, Lynda, 106
Benton, William, 66
Bermont, Hill, 158, 162, 168n7
Bernie Speaks, 231, 240–43
BET, 143
Beyond Our Control: cancellation, 223–25; as cultural education, 212–13, 215–18; development of, 213–14; diversity in, 216–18; homophobia in, 221–22; origins, 211–12;

parody and, 212–15, 218–22, 226; writers' room for, 216–18, 222, 226
Bienvenidos, 271
Big House, 183–87
Bird of an Iron Feather, 290
Bishop, Claire, 288
Black churches, 136–37
Black liberation, 12, 13, 134, 138
Black Lives Matter protests, 317
Black people, 6, 115, 117, 119–20; Afro-Mexican, 313; as broadcast workers, 144, 290; civil rights and, 263; community organizing and, 263; as creators, 286–87, 289–90, 292, 297–99, 311–13; in Detroit, 138–39, 143, 147; female, 145–46, 293, 294, 295–96, 298–99, 316, 333; in Georgia, 157; in Philadelphia, 304; religious traditions of, 134, 136–37, 141; representation of, 262–63, 311–12; as students, 152; as TV hosts, 133, 140–46, 331–33; as TV station owners, 139
—programming for, 14, 20, 22, 139–40, 269, 290–91; *America's Black Journal*, 133–34, 147; *Inspiration Time*, 134, 143–46. See also *March of Faith*; Open Television
Black power TV, 290
Black religious television, 134, 137–47
Black's View of the News, A, 290–91
Bloodsaw, Helene, 314–15
blue skies discourse, 15–16
Bogarín, Raúl Gamez, 278
boredom, 199–200
Born and Raised, 296–97
Boston, 20, 80–81, 90, 99, 157, 232, 306; public access TV in, 232, 236. See also WCVB-TV; WGBH
Boston Broadcasters, Inc. (BBI), 77, 80, 89
Boston Symphony Orchestra (BSO), 195, 201–3, 206
Boughner, Terry, 254
Boundaoui, Assia, 297
Boundaoui, Sohib, 297
Boyden, Lewis, 217–18
Brattleboro, Vt., 236
Brick, Howard, 153
broadcast workers: Black people as, 144, 290; teenagers as, 215; training, 215
Broadcasting (magazine), 180
Bronstein, Phoebe, 174
Brooks, P. A. (bishop), 140–43

Brown Girls, 294
Brujos, 296, 298
Buch, Esteban, 206
Burden, Chris, 102
Burlington, Vt., 231, 235; in *Bernie Speaks*, 240–41, 245; CAM activism in, 235–40
Business Coworking Lounge, 332
Buzz the Fuzz, 144
Bye, Bye, Kipling, 193

cable (television), 5; community access to, 16, 231, 238–39, 240, 242, 264, 305–6; corruption and, 118–20; development in Miami, 115–21; franchising phase of, 126; funding crisis, 244; history of, 14, 98, 113–14, 124–26, 233; infrastructure, 239–40, 242; museum collaborations with, 95, 97–98, 100–101, 103, 105–10; public, educational, and government (PEG) rule for, 15–16, 244, 303, 305; regulation of, 14–16, 114–15, 237. *See also* Chittenden County Television; Milwaukee Gay/Lesbian Cable Network; Philadelphia Community Access Media
Cable Center, 126
Cable Communications Policy Act of 1984, 15, 114, 305
Cablesystems, 117, 120
Cage, John, 192, 197–98, 200
CalArts, 99
California Video (exhibition), 94, 97–98, 110
Canción de la Raza, 268, 270–75, 281
Capital Communications Company, 68
capitalism, 35, 137, 167, 208
Carlos, Wendy, 199
Carnegie Commission on Educational Television, 13
Carnegie Corporation, 57
Carollo, Joe, 121
Cassen, Jackie, 206
Cassidy, Marsha, 177–78
CBS: advice to advertisers, 60; Chicago School and, 30; depictions of South on, 174; experimental cinematography on, 45; in Miami, 116, 125; purchase of WGPR, 142; radio, 43; WOI TV partnership and, 54, 56, 67
censorship, 16, 57, 78–79, 88
Challenge for Change, 236
Chambliss, Rollin, 161

Charles H. Wright Museum of African American History, 142
Chavoya, C. Ondine, 97
Chicago, 5–6, 60, 88, 136, 141, 174, 333; Black nationalism in, 291; Black Renaissance in, 289; Community Access Media in, 232. *See also* Chicago School
Chicago Renaissance TV, 292, 299
Chicago School (of television): aesthetics of, 29, 33, 37–40, 43–45, 289; defined, 29–30; localism and, 31–34, 46–48; performance practices, 36–37; reviews of, 40, 43, 45; spatial practice and, 35–39; sponsorship of, 40–41
Chicana/o people: as activists, 271–72, 275–76, 280–81; as creators, 272, 276–79, 281; programming for, 271–77; representation of, 276. *See also* Latinx people
children: programming for, 3, 10, 29, 59, 92n1, 178; representation of, 273, 280
Chittenden County Television (CCTV), 231–32, 236–40, 241–43
Christianity, 133–34
Church of God in Christ (COGIC), 141–43, 148n6
Cincinnati, 90, 178
Cintrón, Humberto, 279–80
citizenship, 20, 154, 157
civil rights, 12–13, 20, 134, 141, 173, 175–76, 236, 263, 269
CKLW-FM (Detroit), 138, 141
Clark, Brice, 252
class, 212, 218, 234, 245n1, 286, 296; hierarchies, 264; mobility, 12, 204; organizing around, 234; racialized economies of, 137
Class A stations, 5
Classen, Steven, 12, 175–76
classical music, 192
Claus, Gretchen, 313
Cleveland, Ohio, 174
Clinton, Bill, 142
CNN, 112, 123
cocreated television, 293–94
Code-Switched, 294, 296
Cohen, Robert, 153
Cohen-Cole, Jamie, 154–55
Cold War ideology, 153–54, 156, 168
College Art Association (CAA), 106
Come into the Kitchen, 177, 179
Common Ground, 290

community media, 15, 21–22, 96, 100, 217, 225, 319; advocacy for, 232, 235–40; aesthetics of, 245; defined, 7, 322–23; digital, 322–24; funding for, 244; micro, 324–30; place-making and, 232–33; in rural areas, 233. *See also* Chittenden County Television; Milwaukee Gay/Lesbian Cable Network; Philadelphia Community Access Media
community media centers, 8, 225, 232, 235–36, 304
Concerned Black Image Makers, 299
Concerned Citizens for Cable Communications (Philadelphia), 305
Conner, M. Shelley, 296
Connor, Russell, 201
consolidation, media, 16–17, 112, 114, 123, 224
content-based programming, 2
cooking shows, 10, 177, 179, 180
Coolidge, Bill, 86
Cordelia, Bea, 294
Cornelius, Don, 291
Corporation for Public Broadcasting (CPB), 13, 193, 269, 272, 281–82
counterculture, 116, 232, 235, 241–42, 245n1
Courtney, Susan, 181
COVID-19, 133, 234, 244, 329, 331
Cox, Karen, 176
Coy, Wayne, 66
Cream City Foundation (CCF), 252, 254–56, 258, 260, 265n4
credits, 32, 36, 202, 203
critical regionalism, 32–33
Crosby, John, 40, 43, 45
cultural geography, 231
Curtin, Michael, 5–6, 32, 289

Dahmer, Jeffrey, 257, 261
Damaged Goods, 294
dance, 287, 291, 303, 322, 333; Afrofuturist, 293; ballet, 198; programs, 11, 256, 298; social, 299–300
Darling, Lowell, 105, 106
Darling Shear, 298
David Ross Show, The, 106
Davis, Douglas, 201
Davis, Jenny, 217
Davitian, Lauren-Glenn, 236–41, 244
daytime programming, 177–82

de Havilland, Olivia, 181, 184
decentralization, 99, 300
Del Prete, Juli, 294
democracy, 16, 153, 154, 157–61, 166–68, 323–24
deregulation, 16, 91, 114, 224, 239
desegregation, 152, 173, 175–76
Destination Freedom, 290
Detroit: Black arts scene in, 138; Black religious TV in, 134, 137–47
Dewey, Matthew, 103
diasporic communities, 323, 331
digital era, 17, 287, 304, 307, 321–22
digital tools, 335
digitization, 21, 231, 243, 245, 290
Discovery Inc., 112–13
diversity, 117, 217, 222, 262–64, 288, 300, 333
DJ Affirmation, 303, 311
Doctrine of Cooperation, 57, 60
Doherty-Murphy, Kate, 223
Dollar, Creflo, 137
Dressing Up, 106
Duane, Hildegarde, 105–6
Duke, Nikkita, 294
DuMont, 54, 56, 67, 76
Duncan, John Thomas, 278
Dundon, Joe, 215, 223, 225
Duran, Richard, 273
Durham, Richard, 290
Dutch, Laura, 313

Earl, Tony, 251
East Is Red, 106
educational broadcasting, 9, 54–58, 68; noncommercial status of, 66; proponents of, 59–60, 62
educational television (ETV), 13, 15, 19–20, 153–57, 160–65, 269–70; for classrooms, 61; Federal Communications Commission and, 65–66; financial viability of, 56; funding of, 61–64, 67; marginalization of, 56, 60; programming, 63–65; after Television Freeze, 66
Edwards, Steve, 84–87
Eighth Decade Consortium, 90
Eiselein, E. B., 278
Elder, C. R., 67
"Electronic Opera No. 1," 193–94, 196–98, 200, 203, 205–6

"Electronic Opera No. 2," 193–94, 203–6
Elliot, Don, 178, 185
Ely, Michael Patrick, 289
Encouraged, The, 314–15
ensemble made theater, 288
"Eroica," 206
ethnography, 162–63
Expanding Sanctuary, 318
experiential education, 212–13
experimental TV, 20, 157, 193, 195–96, 207

Facebook, 324, 327, 331, 335
Fairness Doctrine of 1949, 12
Faith for Miracles, 139–40
Falwell, Jerry, 135
Federal Communications Act of 1934, 9, 16
Federal Communications Commission (FCC), 6, 9; cable regulation and, 14–16, 98, 114, 239, 305; Chicago TV investigation, 32; educational broadcasting and, 65–66; fairness doctrine, 12; license allocation and, 30, 55, 57, 65–67, 269; localism and, 73, 76–78, 82, 88–90, 239; public interest and, 77–78, 135; on urban versus rural markets, 178
Federal Radio Commission (FRC), 8–9, 77–78
Feeling of Being Watched, The, 297
Ferre, Maurice, 117–18
Ferris, Charles D., 77
Fiesta, 268, 270, 271, 277–79, 281
50 Shades of Jazz, 311
Fifty-Fifty Club, 178–79
Financial Interest and Syndication Rules (Fin-Syn), 16, 79
Five, Four, Three, Two, One, Beat Them All, 314
Fletcher, C. Scott, 62
Florida, 116, 119, 125, 174
flow, 2, 106, 198, 202, 206–7, 328
Fluxus, 192, 194, 198
FOBia, 294
For Black Only, 290
Ford Foundation: funding of *Basic Issues of Man*, 152, 155, 158, 167, 168n2; funding of *Bird of an Iron Feather*, 290; funding of Latinx TV, 269, 270, 272, 274–75, 277–79, 281–82; funding of *The Medium Is the Medium*, 195; funding of WGBH, 193; funding of WOI-TV, 61–65, 67–68; mission of, 156
Fort Wayne, Ind., 80, 81
Fort Worth, 89
Fox, Terry, 105–6
FOX News, 112
Francis, Arlene, 178–79
Franco, Abel, 273
Frantz, David Evans, 97
Frederick, Marla, 147
Free and Accepted Modern Masons, 139
free speech advocacy, 9
Free Street Theatre, 288
freedom, 159
Friley, Charles, 55–56, 59, 66
Full Circle Television, 331–32
Fund for Adult Education, 62–65, 67 155–56, 168n2
fund-raising, 142
Furies, The, 298
Futurewomen, 293, 298
Fye, Kevin, 222

Gable, Clark, 182
Gamboa, Ricardo, 296
Garment Workers, 277
Garroway, Dave, 29–33, 36–41, 43–48
Garroway at Large, 29, 32, 37–39, 41–45
Gates, Henry Louis, Jr., 136
Georgia, 187; architecture in, 183–84; early TV in, 174–75; as "Hollywood of the South," 172
Georgia Center for Continuing Education (University of Georgia), 152, 155–58
Gerson, Daniela, 331
Gibson, Theodore, 119, 121, 126
Gilbreth, Lillian, 181
Gillette, Anita, 82
Ginsburg, Kayla, 298
Goddard College, 235–36
Gone with the Wind, 173, 176, 181–87
Good Morning, Mr. Orwell, 193
Goode, W. Wilson, 305
Goodman, David, 68
Gospel Music Workshop, 133
gospel programs, 134, 140–46
Gospel Time TV, 140
governing by television, 153
Gradillas, Hector, 278

Graham, Billy, 135
Grant, Robert, 140
Great Rebellion (Detroit), 139, 144
Greater Love Tabernacle, 141
Green, Adam, 291
Grief, Mark, 158
guerrilla television, 99

Hackett, Ali, 303
Hair Story, 294, 297, 299
Halleck, DeeDee, 15, 217
Hamilton, William Thomas, 213–14, 223, 224
Hartsfield, William, 173, 181, 182, 185
Hayes, Joy Elizabeth, 68
HBO, 112, 116, 123
Heitner, Devorah, 290–91
Henderson, Stephen, 133
Hennock, Frieda, 66, 69n1
Herbuveaux, Jules, 33, 40–41
Hermanowski, Charles, 117, 119, 120, 126
Hicks Temple, 140
Higgins, Dan, 240, 242
Hill, Erin, 217
history from below, 4
Hmong Americans, 326–30
Hmong Talk, 328
Hodges, Johnny, 44–45
Hollywood, 43, 78, 89–90, 173, 186
Holman, Felicia, 293
Home, 178
Home of Love (church), 144
homemaking programming, 10, 177
homonormativity, 253, 258–61
Honey Pot Performance (HPP), 289, 293, 299
Hook-Ups, 297
Howard Wise (gallery), 195
Huffman, Kathy Rae, 99, 100, 105–7
Hull, Richard, 54, 55, 57–68
Hull House, 288
human management, 153
humanism, 20, 152–54, 158–59, 162–63, 167
Hutchins, Robert, 62, 65

immigrants: as creators, 295; programming for, 14, 334; representation of, 277, 296
immigration reform, 313–14
Impact Network, 143
improvisation, 40, 47, 108, 205, 216, 222, 288–89, 296, 299, 300
In Search of Knowledge, 308–9

inclusive programming, 13–14, 262, 265
independent stations, 4, 9, 30, 76, 79, 116
indigenous people, 5, 153, 162–63, 166
Indy Media Center (IMC), 306
inequities, 215, 218, 234, 269, 273, 275
infrastructural ethic, 98, 103, 109
infrastructure, 96–97, 103, 104–9, 174, 213–14, 233
innovation, televisual, 10–11, 43, 47, 89, 193, 195, 199, 207, 224, 250, 286, 289–91
intermedia art, 205
intersectionality, 251, 262, 292, 294–95, 333, 334
intimacy, televisual, 3, 20, 88, 106, 191, 199, 208, 289
Iowa, 19, 54, 56–57, 64–65, 67, 69
Iowa State College (ISC), 55–62, 65–68

Jackson, Jesse, 142
Jackson, Sherman, 136
Jacksonville, Fla., 80
Jakes, T. D., 137
Jessup, Hubert, 75, 80–81, 88
Jesús Treviño, 275–76
Jim Crow, 152, 157, 167, 173
Jiménez, Lillian, 280
Johnson, Lyndon B., 269
Johnson, Victoria, 174, 178
Joint Committee on Educational Television (JCET), 62, 65–66
Jones, Kyra, 294
Jones, Paul, 182
Jones, Prophet, 138–39
Joyner, Beatrice, 307–9
Junior Achievement (JA), 213–14, 223–24
Junior Achievement Television Company (WJA-TV), 213–14, 224
Juntos, 317–18

KABC (Los Angeles), 271
Kant, Immanuel, 39
Kaprow, Allan, 94, 196
Karaszewski, Larry, 216, 220–21
Kaufman, Monica, 176
KCET (Los Angeles), 271–77
Keith, Larry, 81
Kent, Ruth, 173, 178–81
Kerner Commission, 269, 283n2–3
KhanBey, Rashida, 333
Kings and Queens, 294

Kirby, Peter, 104
Kirkpatrick, Bill, 115
Kirsch, Corinna, 288
Kissing Walls, 294
Kiuchi, Yuya, 115, 306
KLRN (San Antonio, Tex.), 277
KNBC (Los Angeles), 271
Knight, Dick, 117, 119
knowable community, 5–6
KNXT (Los Angeles), 271
Kovacs, Ernie, 45, 214
KTLA (Los Angeles), 82
KUAT (Tucson, Ariz.), 271, 277–79
Kubota, Shigeko, 94
Kyri, Daniel, 294

Lacy, Suzanne, 94
Larkin, Brian, 101
Latino Consortium, 277
Latino Film Festival (Philadelphia), 317
Latino Media Coalition, 277
Latino Public Broadcasting (LPB), 282
Latinx people, 14, 282n1, 289, 294, 296–97, 312–19; as creators, 268, 272, 275–77, 278, 280, 288–89, 292, 313, 317; programming for, 268–82, 312–13; representation of, 276, 280
Laughlin, Denny, 223
Laverne & Shirley, 90, 221
Lear, Norman, 72–75; aesthetics of, 88–89; in Boston, 80; as hitmaker, 79; on local TV, 72–73, 88
Lee, Mitch, 326–28
Lee, Sunisa, 329–30
Lee, Victoria, 294
Lefebvre, Henri, 34–36, 39–40, 42–43, 47–48
Lehman, Christopher, 291
Leinsdorf, Erich, 206
Let Go and Let God, 333
Lewis, Louis, 60
Lewis-Allen, Kayla, 332–33
Lewis-Allen, Marcus, 332–33
LGBTQIA+ people, 14, 286; as creators, 251, 298–99; programming for, 296, 298 (*see also* Milwaukee Gay/Lesbian Cable Network); representation of, 296
liberal studies, 152–53, 155
Liberthal, Gary, 89
Linea Abierta, 274
Lisowski, Mike, 252, 263, 265

liveness, televisual, 200, 202, 205, 289
local television: budgets for, 4; defined, 2–7; development of, 8–17; FCC regulations on, 8–10, 12–17, 73, 76–78, 82, 88–90, 239; future of, 22. *See also* micro media
localism, televisual, 4, 15, 31–34, 46, 74, 76, 238–39, 243
local/network binary, 179
Lomax, Zarinah, 315
Lombard, Carole, 182
Lonely Crowd, The, 153
Long Beach, Calif., 98, 99
Long Beach Cable, 107, 109
Long Beach Museum of Art (LBMA): televisual interest at, 101–8; Video Annex, 104, 109; video program at, 94, 99–101
Los Angeles, 107–8, 268, 271–73; as center for video art, 94; Chicana/o news programs in, 275–77; Latinx audiences in, 280; screenings of *The Baxters* in, 73, 80–82, 84
Lotz, Amanda, 322
Low Strung, 294
low-power stations, 5, 9
L'Soft, 299
Lyons, Ruth, 178–79

Mad Films, 315–16
Maddox, Lester, 173
Mahler, Thomas W., 158
Maine, 233
Malone, John, 112–13, 117–18, 123, 126
Man and Society, 161
Mandela, Nelson, 142
Manos, Constantine, 201
March of Faith, 134, 140–43, 147n1, 148n6
marginalized people, 233
Marovich, Robert, 136
Marsan, Bruce, 75, 80
Marshall, John, 62
Marshall, Wes, 278
Martell, Vincent, 294
Martin, Lerone, 136
Mary Hartman, Mary Hartman, 79
Ma(s)king Her, 293
mass culture critique, 161
mass media research, 155
materiality, 4, 19, 96, 105, 110, 232–33, 239, 242
Mayer, Vicki, 115
Mayor's Task Force on Cable Television (Burlington, Vt.), 237

McCafferty, Jay D., 99
McCarthy, Anna, 153
McCarthy, Paul, 102, 106
McClanahan, Rue, 81–83
McKinnon, Elijah, 287
McLuhan, Marshall, 196
media literacy, 21, 213, 219, 238, 243, 325
medical programming, 11, 264
Medich, Bob, 224
Medium Is the Medium, The, 195–200, 207
Mejia, Christian, 296–97
Melig, Bob, 258
Mendelsohn, Harold, 273
Menunier, Bill, 263
Mexican Americans. See Chicana/o people
Miami, 89; development of cable in, 117–23; Spanish-language TV in, 116
Miami Herald, 119, 122, 124–25
Miami News, 119–22, 124–25
Miami Telecommunications (MT), 117–18
Miami Tele-Communications, Inc. v. City of Miami, 122
micro media, 322, 324, 333–35; versus community media, 325–26; defined, 325; local television as, 326–28, 330–33; mainstream television and, 328–30
microhistories, 4, 20, 97
Midwest (region), 36, 174, 212, 235, 257–58
Midwest Video Corp. v. FCC, 114
Millan, Victor, 272
Miller, Arthur R., 90
Miller's Court, 90
Mills, Ted, 33, 37, 40–41, 43
Milwaukee, Wis., 21, 250–51, 254–55, 257–64, 331–32
Milwaukee Access Telecommunications Authority (MATA), 252, 254, 260–61, 265n2
Milwaukee Gay/Lesbian Cable Network (MGLCN), 250–53, 264–65; diversity and, 262–64; mainstream appeal, 251; positive programming on, 258–62; quality programming on, 253–57
Minneapolis, Minn., 90, 329
Minnesota, 63, 326, 329, 334
Minow, Newton, 160, 193
Mississippi, 12, 174, 179
Mitchell, John, 197
Mitchell, Margaret, 184
Mogul, Susan, 94, 105–6
Mohanty, Priya, 294

Moonlight Sonata (Beethoven), 191, 197–98, 204
Moorman, Charlotte, 192, 198, 207
Moreno, Eduardo, 273
Moser, Heidi, 225
Motown Records, 138
MSNBC, 112
Muhammed Speaks, 290
Mullhall, Robert, 68
Murray, Susan, 11
museums, 95, 103, 109–10. See also Long Beach Museum of Art
music, 145, 146, 180, 185, 200, 309; on *Basic Issues of Man*, 162, 164; classical, 191–94, 200, 205, 208; on *Garroway at Large*, 29, 39, 41, 43, 44; gospel, 134, 140–41; on Latinx TV, 276, 279; on Open Television, 287, 291, 299; theme, 84; on *Yellow on Thursday*, 256. See also Paik, Nam June
Music-Image Workshop, 193
My Bittersweet Philosophy, 309–10
Myrick, Susan, 184

Najeebah, Zakkiyyah, 299
Nancy Carter's TV Cook Book, 177
Nation of Islam, 290
National Advisory Council on Radio in Education (NACRE), 57, 60
National Association of Broadcasters (NAB), 78
National Association of Educational Broadcasters (NAEB), 54, 55, 62
National Association of Television Programming Executives (NATPE), 77, 80, 90
National Center for Experiments in Television (NCET), 99
National Educational Television (NET), 152, 156, 159–60, 193, 195, 270, 275
National Endowment for the Arts (NEA), 104, 193, 195
nationalism, 156
"Nature of Man, The" (*Basic Issues of Man* episode), 161–62, 166, 167
Nature of Man, The (Chambliss), 161
Nauman, Bruce, 94
Navarro, Ralph, 259, 263
NBC: backing of NACRE, 57–58; Chicago School and, 29–30, 32, 35–36, 39, 45–46; daytime programming on, 178–79; infrastructure roll-out and, 174–75; in Miami,

116; WOI-TV partnership, 54, 56, 67; WSB-TV affiliation, 172, 175, 186–87
NBC v. United States, 78
New England, 233–34
New St. Paul Tabernacle, 134, 140–41
New Television Program fund, 274–75, 277
New Television Workshop, 99, 193, 207
New Tri-Cable Tonight, The, 250, 257
New York City, 174, 179, 192, 232, 251, 265; Latinx programming in, 268, 271, 279–81
news, televisual, 10–13, 173, 186, 253–54, 290, 312–14; parody of, 213; Salaxley TV, 330–34; 3HMONGTV, 326–30, 334; *Tri-Cable Tonight*, 250, 252, 254–63
newspapers, 122, 125
Nightline, 330
1996 Telecommunications Act, 16
Nixon, Leticia Roa, 312–14
Nixon, Richard, 197, 199
noncommercial television, 264–65, 324; public access TV as, 250; public interest and, 238; WOI-TV as, 56–58, 65–66, 69, 78
Noriega, Chon, 268, 276
nostalgia, 3, 176, 186, 234, 245
nudity, 102, 191, 196, 198
Nupita Obama Creates Vogua, 298–99

Obama, Barak, 142
Olympics, 329–30
Open Channels (grant program), 109
Open Television (OTV), 250, 287, 292, 333–34; cocreated works on, 293–94; collaboration as character on, 298–99; community as character on, 296–98; ensemble works on, 295–96; intersectional friendships on, 294–95
operational aesthetic, 37–39
Organization Man, The, 153, 158
Ortega, Francisco, 272
Our People, 290

paid-time programming, 135
Paik, Nam June, 20, 100, 106; *The Medium Is the Medium* and, 195–200, 207; as musician, 192; "Participation TV," 191, 193, 196–97, 199–200; residency at WGBH-TV, 194–95, 199, 201, 207; video art of, 192–94; *Video Variations* and, 201–8; work at WNET-13, 193
Paik/Abe synthesizer, 194–95, 203

Paper Tiger Television, 15
Park Street Under, 90
parody, 21, 29, 163, 192, 256; in *Beyond Our Control*, 212–15, 218–21, 226; Chicago school and, 41, 45–47
Parsons, Patrick, 115
"Participation TV," 191, 193, 196–97, 199–200
patriarchal logic, 205, 208
Patterson, Bishop, 143
Paulu, Burton, 63
Payne, Zak, 294
Paz, Coya, 288, 293
Pei, I. M., 99, 107
People for the American Way, 88
Periódico, 268, 277
Perry, Shawn, 218
Peters, John Durham, 96
Philadelphia, 22, 174. *See also* Philadelphia Community Access Media
Philadelphia Community Access Coalition (PCAC), 306–7
Philadelphia Community Access Media (PhillyCAM), 303–4; future of, 319–20; history of, 305–7; interviews with creators, 307–19
Philadelphia Inquirer, 314
Philly Collective, 316
Piene, Otto, 196, 199
place-based programming, 2–3, 251
plantation home, 183–87
platform studies, 335
police brutality, 116, 139, 273
"Political Animal, A," 161, 164–67
political culture, 231
Political Perspectives, 161
politics of place, 2–3
Poplawski, Rick, 256
Portapak camera, 94, 103, 194
postmodernism, 202
Poyser, Jim, 219
precarity, 4, 16, 279
¡Presente! Media, 316–19
preservation, 17–18, 270
Press, Samuel, 237
Prime Time Access Rule (PTAR), 16, 79, 91
Project for New Television, 194
prosperity gospel, 136–37
PTL Club, 140
public, educational, and government (PEG) rule, 15–16, 244, 303, 305

public access television, 14–16, 237–40, 304–7, 323; art programming on, 96, 104–5, 108, 110; funding for, 270; LGBTQ, 250; women and, 217. *See also* community media

public affairs programming, 10, 13–14, 21, 73, 78–80, 324; Black, 113, 147n3, 290; Latinx, 14, 268, 275–81

Public Broadcasting Act of 1967, 13, 193, 269

Public Broadcasting System (PBS), 15, 116, 156, 193, 195, 271, 273, 281

public interest requirement, 8–10, 12–13, 77–78, 135, 237; quantified, 79

"Public Service Responsibilities of Broadcasters" (FCC), 9

public television: artistic work in, 99, 206; budgets for, 270; educational, 195, 275; Latinx programming on, 275, 281–82; local, 13; racial dynamics of, 272, 278; roots of, 62

Puerto Rican people: as activists, 279; as creators, 268, 279–80, 313, 318; programming for, 270–71, 274, 280. *See also* Latinx people

Quare Life, 296
quiz shows, 78, 214

race, 12–14; televangelism and, 135
racism, 138–39, 153, 159, 183, 264; in *Beyond our Control*, 221–22; disavowal of, 20, 153, 156, 262
radio: Adorno on, 202; aesthetics of, 43–44; in Atlanta, 172, 175; in Chicago, 30, 290, 299; in Detroit, 138; educational, 55–60; in Miami, 125; music and, 197; in Philadelphia, 309–12; regulation of, 8–9; Spanish-language, 273; used by Black churches, 136, 138, 141, 143–46
Radio Act of 1927, 8–9, 78
Raindance Corporation, 99
Raleigh, N.C., 86, 90
Rami, Pemon, 290
Randall, Arnetta, 297
Range, Athalie, 118
Ransom Sherman Show, 32, 38–39, 41
rape, 72, 81, 83–86
Raphael, Chad, 289–90
ratings, 18, 36, 75, 89, 91, 223
Reagan, Ronald, 91, 221, 224
Realidades, 268, 270, 271, 277, 279–81
reception, 18, 255–56; spaces of, 36–37
recording versus reporting, 242

Reflecciones, 271
reform, television, 9, 10, 12, 114, 154
regulation, 8–10, 12–17, 73, 76–78, 82, 88–90, 239
Reilly, Pat, 178
Relationship Goals, 332
Reliable Sources, 112
religious broadcasting, 10; history of, 133–34. *See also* televangelism
Relman, Rachel, 294
Rennie, Ellie, 323
representations of space, 39–42
Requiem 29, 277
Rich's in Your Home, 177
Right Swipe, The, 294
right-wing politics, 135–36
Roberts, Oral, 135
Robertson, Pat, 135
Rockefeller Foundation, 62, 99, 104, 110n2, 193, 194, 198
Rodriguez, Julio, 280
Rogers, Donnie, 218
Rosler, Martha, 102, 198
Ross, David, 94–97, 99–106, 109–10
Ross, Michael, 257
Ross, Steve, 117–19
Ruíz, José Luis, 276–77, 281

Sabatino, Juana, 262
Sahan Journal, 334
Saint Paul, Minn., 236–37, 329
Salaxley TV, 330–34
Salt . . . Pepper N Memories, 303
San Antonio, Tex., 277
San Francisco, 98–99, 174, 195, 255
Sanders, Bernie, 21, 231–32, 235–37
sandwiching (programming strategy), 60–61
Santa Barbara Cable, 107
Sarnoff, David, 185–87
Saturday Night Live, 212, 214, 221, 288
Sauce (McCarthy), 192
Scannell, Paddy, 39
Schultze, Quentin, 135–36
Scott, Richard S., 272
Seattle, 90, 296, 331
Seawright, James, 196, 201
Second City, 214, 288
Segalove, Ilene, 94, 102, 106
segregation, 152
Seham, Amy E., 222

Semiotics of the Kitchen, 102
Seward, Julian, 309–12
sexism: in *Beyond Our Control*, 221–22; video art and, 198–99; in writers' rooms, 216–17
sexual assault, 72, 81, 83–86
sexual content, 256–57
Sherman, Ransom, 29–33, 36–41, 43, 45–48
Sheth, Aalisha, 294
Sibley, Celestine, 182
Siesta Is Over, The, 271
SIFTmedia, 316–17
Simkins, David, 214, 216, 219, 223
Singh, Ashan, 330
sitcoms, 77, 80, 88, 90–91, 289; parody of, 211, 213, 220–21
Six Star Nielson Cablevision (SSN), 118
SKC-TV (Flathead Indian Reservation), 5
sketch comedy, 21, 221. See also *Beyond Our Control*
Slaughter on Tenth Avenue (jazz ballet), 44
soap operas, 10, 79, 80, 211, 256, 271–75, 289, 290
social engineering, 154
social geography, 231
social practice art, 286, 288–91
social practice television, 22, 286–87, 292–99
social sciences, 154
Somali Americans, 331–33
"Sometimes Harmonious," 161, 163–64, *165*, 166, 167
Sotomayo, Kristal, 316–19
Soul Train, 291
South, the (U.S. region), 10, 20, 172–73, 178; aesthetics of, 182–84; early TV in, 172–75; Old versus New, 181, 183, 185, 187, 222; representation of, 173–74, 176
South Asian people, 292, 294, 296–97
South Bend, Ind., 211–13, 217, 224–25
Southern Revival, 182–87
Southland Video Anthology (exhibitions), 94–95, 101–3
spaces of representation, 42–46
Spanish-language TV, 14, 116, 272
spatial codes, 39, 42
spatial practice, 35–39
Spigel, Lynn, 10, 12, 33, 180
Spirit of Detroit, The, 140
sports programming, 5, 10, 254
Station Representatives Association (SRA), 91
Steinberg, Martha Jean, 143–46

Stelter, Brian, 112
Steppenwolf Theatre, 288
Sternberg, Joel, 289–90
streaming, 112, 243, 250, 319, 321–22, 328
Streeter, Thomas, 15–16
Strictly for the Girls, 177
Stud's Place, 45, 289
Sturgeon, John, 105–6
Sunil, Karan, 294, 296
Swaggart, Jimmy, 136
Swanberg, Joe, 285–86
Switched-on Bach (album), 199
syndication, 11, 19, 73–77, 88; defined, 76

T, the, 294
Tadlock, Thomas, 196
Tambellini, Aldo, 196
Tappan, Olivia, 194, 203
Tara Ball, 181
T.A.T. Communications, 77–80, 89, 91
Taylor, Ariel, 303
TCI (cable provider), 112, 120–21, 123, 127; franchising conflicts and, 118; success of, 114, 117
Teatro Luna, 289
Teatro Vista, 289
teenagers, 80, 212, 214, 216, 218, 225
televangelism, 133; Black preachers and, 136–37, 140; female preachers and, 143–46; history of, 134–36
television: defined, 321; in digital era, 321–22; early days of, 174; local, 1–2
Television Code, 78, 88
Television Freeze, 10, 55, 57, 65–68
Television Laboratory, 99
Terkel, Studs, 45, 289–90
Thamkuv Show, 328
That Was the Week That Was, 214
"There Be Dragons," 160
Theta Cable, 105–7
Theta Public Access (Los Angeles), 105
Thompson, Bankole, 143
Thompson, Ethan, 213, 218–19
Thompson, Tommy, 251–52
THOTless, 294
3HMONGTV, 326–30, 334
Time Warner, 112, 254
Today in Georgia, 20, 173, 177–82, 187
Today show, 30, 46, 178, 328
Tolson, Melvin B., 183

Toronto, 91
Torres, Sasha, 12
Triibe, The, 299
Trump, Donald, 112
Tsai Wen-Ying, 201
Tucson, Ariz., 271, 277–79
Tutu, Desmond, 142
TV as a Creative Medium (exhibition), 195
TV Buddha, 191
TV Garden, 191
TV Lab, 193
Twin Cities, 329, 334
Tyro, Frank H., 5
Tyson, Levering, 60

UC Irvine, 99
UC San Diego, 99
UCLA, 99
Unidos, 271, 276
United States of Aliens, 294–95
universalism, 56, 152
University of Georgia, 152–53, 155, 168

Vanderbeek, Stan, 201
Vario, Natividad, 272
Varnelis, Kazys, 107
Velvet, 294
Vermont, 21, 234–36; Chittenden County Television (CCTV), 231–32, 236–40, 241–43
video art, 94–95, 101–3, 109; funding for, 207; sexism and, 198–99
Video Art (cable program), 105–9
Video Commune, 194
video revolution, 98–99
Video Variations, 201–8
videotape, 17, 90, 94, 104–5, 107, 270, 277
Viola, Bill, 105, 106, 108
Vision Cable, 118, 120

Walton, Jonathan, 136
Warhol, Andy, 206
Warner Bros. Entertainment, 112
WarnerMedia, 112
Wash Collier plantation, 186
Washington (state), 331–33
Washington, D.C., 90, 125, 174
Wayside Inn, 178
WBKB-Chicago, 30, 36
WCVB-TV (Boston), 72, 75, 80, 90–91

WDIA (Memphis), 143
Weaver, Pat, 46, 178
Weeks, Earl, 314–16
Wegman, William, 102, 106
Wellin, Marc, 222
Werktreue, 200
Werts, Diane, 217, 225
Western, Ruby, 298
WGBH (Boston), 20, 99, 191–95, 199; New Television Workshop at, 207; Paik's residency at, 194–95, 199, 201, 207
WGPR-TV (Detroit), 134, 139–41, 145, 147
WGTV (University of Georgia), 156
WhatsApp, 331
White, George, 139
White, Mimi, 135, 178
White Columns (TV studio), 183–87
Whole Town's Talking, The, 63–65
Wide Wide World, 30, 46
Williams, Charles, Rev., 133
Williams, Dave, 211, 214–16, 219, 223, 225–26
Williams, Mark, 10
Williams, Raymond, 5, 206
Wilson, Jess, 244
Wilson, Pamela, 18
Winfrey, Oprah, 146
Wisconsin, 115, 251–52, 257, 261
WJLB-FM (Detroit), 144
WKRC-TV (Cincinnati), 90
WMUZ-FM (Detroit), 141
WNBQ-Chicago, 29, 30, 35, 38–39, 41, 43
WNDU (South Bend, Ind.), 213–14, 215, 220, 223–25
WNET-13 (New York), 99, 193, 207, 271, 279–80
WOI-TV (Iowa): early days of, 58–65; founding of, 54–58; after Television Freeze, 65–69
Wolf, Dick, 285
Wolfson Archives, 125
Wolters, Larry, 43
women: audience members, 86; Black, 145–46, 293, 294, 295–96, 298–99, 316, 333; in comedy sketches, 222; creators, 287, 316, 334; programming for, 143, 177–79, 182, 262; representation of, 262, 264, 290, 293, 295–96; technical directors, 217; ; TV writers, 216–17
—TV show hosts, 177–78, 262; Ruth Kent, 173, 178–81; Martha Jean Steinberg, 143–46

working-class people, 22, 143, 242, 286, 289, 290
World Wide Web, 321
WPIX (New York), 89
WRAL-TV (Raleigh), 81, 86
Wrap Around the World (Paik), 193
Wright, Richard, 289
Wright, Wellington, 172, 181
writers' rooms, 216–18, 222, 226, 299
WSB radio, 175
WSB-TV (Atlanta): daytime programming on, 177–82; *Gone with the Wind* and, 182–87; news programming, 173; origins, 172–77; White Columns studio of, 173, 176, 182–87
"WSB-TV: 50 Years in Atlanta," 176
WTTW (Chicago), 290
WTVJ (Miami), 125
WXYZ-TV (Detroit), 138
Wyant, Steve, 224

Xav Paub Xav Pom, 329

Yalkut, Jud, 194
Yang, Padee, 329–30
Yau Muas, 327–28
Yellow on Thursday, 250, 256
Yniguez, Richard, 273
Yo Soy Chicano, 277
Young, Harvey, 289
You're So Talented, 295
youth media, 225. See also *Beyond Our Control*
YouTube, 146, 243, 290, 316; as micro media platform, 324, 325, 327–32, 335

Zabriskie, Queen Meccasia, 289
Zacarias, Michelle, 294

THE PEABODY SERIES IN MEDIA HISTORY

Television History, the Peabody Archive, and Cultural Memory
EDITED BY Ethan Thompson, Jeffrey P. Jones, and Lucas Hatlen

The Archivability of Television: Essays on Preservation and Perseverance
EDITED BY Lauren Bratslavsky and Elizabeth Peterson

Local TV: Histories, Communities, and Aesthetics
EDITED BY Lauren Herold and Annie Laurie Sullivan

www.ingramcontent.com/pod-product-compliance
Lightning Source LLC
Chambersburg PA
CBHW030519230426
43665CB00010B/676